THE
Expositor's Bible Commentary

with The New International Version

JOHN

THE
Expositor's Bible Commentary

with The New International Version

JOHN

Merrill C. Tenney

ZondervanPublishingHouse
Grand Rapids, Michigan

A Division of HarperCollins*Publishers*

General Editor:

FRANK E. GAEBELEIN

Former Headmaster, Stony Brook School
Former Coeditor, *Christianity Today*

Associate Editors:

J. D. DOUGLAS

Editor, *The New International
Dictionary of the Christian Church*

RICHARD P. POLCYN

John
Copyright © 1995 by Merrill C. Tenney

Requests for information should be addressed to:
Zondervan Publishing House
Grand Rapids, Michigan 49530

Library of Congress Cataloging-in-Publication Data

The expositor's Bible commentary : with the New International Version of the Holy Bible /
Frank E. Gaebelein, general editor of series.
p. cm.
Includes bibliographical references and index.
Contents: v. 1–2. Matthew / D. A. Carson — Mark / Walter W. Wessel — Luke / Walter
L. Liefeld — John / Merrill C. Tenney — Acts / Richard N. Longenecker — Romans /
Everett F. Harrison — 1 and 2 Corinthians / W. Harold Mare and Murray J. Harris —
Galatians and Ephesians / James Montgomery Boice and A. Skevington Wood
ISBN: 0-310-50011-7 (softcover)
1. Bible N.T.—Commentaries. I. Gaebelein, Frank Ely, 1899–1983.
BS2341.2.E96 1995
220.7-dc 00   94-47450
                                                                                      CIP

Printed in the United States of America

95 96 97 98 99 00 / ❖ DH/ 10 9 8 7 6 5 4 3 2 1

CONTENTS

PREFACE

The title of this work defines its purpose. Written primarily by expositors for expositors, it aims to provide preachers, teachers, and students of the Bible with a new and comprehensive commentary on the books of the Old and New Testaments. Its stance is that of a scholarly evangelicalism committed to the divine inspiration, complete trustworthiness, and full authority of the Bible. Its seventy-eight contributors come from the United States, Canada, England, Scotland, Australia, New Zealand, and Switzerland, and from various religious groups, including Anglican, Baptist, Brethren, Free, Independent, Methodist, Nazarene, Presbyterian, and Reformed churches. Most of them teach at colleges, universities, or theological seminaries.

No book has been more closely studied over a longer period of time than the Bible. From the Midrashic commentaries going back to the period of Ezra, through parts of the Dead Sea Scrolls and the Patristic literature, and on to the present, the Scriptures have been expounded. Indeed, there have been times when, as in the Reformation and on occasions since then, exposition has been at the cutting edge of Christian advance. Luther was a powerful exegete, and Calvin is still called "the prince of expositors."

Their successors have been many. And now, when the outburst of new translations and their unparalleled circulation have expanded the readership of the Bible, the need for exposition takes on fresh urgency.

Not that God's Word can ever become captive to its expositors. Among all other books, it stands first in its combination of perspicuity and profundity. Though a child can be made "wise for salvation" by believing its witness to Christ, the greatest mind cannot plumb the depths of its truth (2 Tim. 3:15; Rom. 11:33). As Gregory the Great said, "Holy Scripture is a stream of running water, where alike the elephant may swim, and the lamb walk." So, because of the inexhaustible nature of Scripture, the task of opening up its meaning is still a perennial obligation of biblical scholarship.

How that task is done inevitably reflects the outlook of those engaged in it. Every biblical scholar has presuppositions. To this neither the editors of these volumes nor the contributors to them are exceptions. They share a common commitment to the supernatural Christianity set forth in the inspired Word. Their purpose is not to supplant the many valuable commentaries that have preceded this work and from which both the editors and contributors have learned. It is rather to draw on the resources of contemporary evangelical scholarship in producing a new reference work for understanding the Scriptures.

A commentary that will continue to be useful through the years should handle contemporary trends in biblical studies in such a way as to avoid becoming outdated when critical fashions change. Biblical criticism is not in itself inadmissible, as some have mistakenly thought. When scholars investigate the authorship, date, literary characteristics, and purpose of a biblical document, they are practicing biblical criticism. So also when, in order to ascertain as nearly as possible the original form of the text, they deal with variant readings, scribal errors, emendations, and other phenomena in the manuscripts. To do these things is essential to responsible exegesis and exposition. And always there is the need to distinguish hypothesis from fact, conjecture from truth.

The chief principle of interpretation followed in this commentary is the grammatico-historical one—namely, that the primary aim of the exegete is to make clear the meaning of the text at the time and in the circumstances of its writing. This endeavor to understand what in the first instance the inspired writers actually said must not be confused with an inflexible literalism. Scripture makes lavish use of symbols and figures of speech; great portions of it are poetical. Yet when it speaks in this way, it speaks no less truly than it does in its historical and doctrinal portions. To understand its message requires attention to matters of grammar and syntax, word meanings, idioms, and literary forms—all in relation to the historical and cultural setting of the text.

The contributors to this work necessarily reflect varying convictions. In certain controversial matters the policy is that of clear statement of the contributors' own views followed by fair presentation of other ones. The treatment of eschatology, though it reflects differences of interpretation, is consistent with a general premillennial position. (Not all contributors, however, are premillennial.) But prophecy is more than prediction, and so this commentary gives due recognition to the major lode of godly social concern in the prophetic writings.

THE EXPOSITOR'S BIBLE COMMENTARY is presented as a scholarly work, though not primarily one of technical criticism. In its main portion, the Exposition, and in Volume 1 (General and Special Articles), all Semitic and Greek words are transliterated and the English equivalents given. As for the Notes, here Semitic and Greek characters are used but always with transliterations and English meanings, so that this portion of the commentary will be as accessible as possible to readers unacquainted with the original languages.

It is the conviction of the general editor, shared by his colleagues in the Zondervan editorial department, that in writing about the Bible, lucidity is not incompatible with scholarship. They are therefore endeavoring to make this a clear and understandable work.

The translation used in it is the New International Version (North American Edition). To the International Bible Society thanks are due for permission to use this most recent of the major Bible translations. The editors and publisher have chosen it because of the clarity and beauty of its style and its faithfulness to the original texts.

To the associate editor, Dr. J. D. Douglas, and to the contributing editors—Dr. Walter C. Kaiser, Jr. and Dr. Bruce K. Waltke for the Old Testament, and Dr. James Montgomery Boice and Dr. Merrill C. Tenney for the New Testament—the general editor expresses his gratitude for their unfailing cooperation and their generosity in advising him out of their expert scholarship. And to the many other contributors he is indebted for their invaluable part in this work. Finally, he owes a special debt of gratitude to Dr. Robert K. DeVries, executive vice-president of the Zondervan Publishing House; Rev. Gerard Terpstra, manuscript editor; and Miss Elizabeth Brown, secretary to Dr. DeVries, for their continual assistance and encouragement.

Whatever else it is—the greatest and most beautiful of books, the primary source of law and morality, the fountain of wisdom, and the infallible guide to life—the Bible is above all the inspired witness to Jesus Christ. May this work fulfill its function of expounding the Scriptures with grace and clarity, so that its users may find that both Old and New Testaments do indeed lead to our Lord Jesus Christ, who alone could say, "I have come that they may have life, and have it to the full" (John 10:10).

FRANK E. GAEBELEIN

ABBREVIATIONS

A. General Abbreviations

A	Codex Alexandrinus
Akkad.	Akkadian
ℵ	Codex Sinaiticus
Ap. Lit.	Apocalyptic Literature
Apoc.	Apocrypha
Aq.	Aquila's Greek Translation of the Old Testament
Arab.	Arabic
Aram.	Aramaic
b	Babylonian Gemara
B	Codex Vaticanus
C	Codex Ephraemi Syri
c.	*circa*, about
cf.	*confer*, compare
ch., chs.	chapter, chapters
cod., codd.	codex, codices
contra	in contrast to
D	Codex Bezae
DSS	Dead Sea Scrolls (see E.)
ed., edd.	edited, edition, editor; editions
e.g.	*exempli gratia*, for example
Egyp.	Egyptian
et al.	*et alii*, and others
EV	English Versions of the Bible
fem.	feminine
ff.	following (verses, pages, etc.)
fl.	flourished
ft.	foot, feet
gen.	genitive
Gr.	Greek
Heb.	Hebrew
Hitt.	Hittite
ibid.	*ibidem*, in the same place
id.	*idem*, the same
i.e.	*id est*, that is
impf.	imperfect
infra.	below
in loc.	*in loco*, in the place cited
j	Jerusalem or Palestinian Gemara
Lat.	Latin
LL.	Late Latin
LXX	Septuagint
M	Mishnah
masc.	masculine
mg.	margin
Mid	Midrash
MS(S)	manuscript(s)
MT	Masoretic text
n.	note
n.d.	no date
Nestle	Nestle (ed.) *Novum Testamentum Graece*
no.	number
NT	New Testament
obs.	obsolete
OL	Old Latin
OS	Old Syriac
OT	Old Testament
p., pp.	page, pages
par.	paragraph
Pers.	Persian
Pesh.	Peshitta
Phoen.	Phoenician
pl.	plural
Pseudep.	Pseudepigrapha
Q	Quelle ("Sayings" source in the Gospels)
qt.	quoted by
q.v.	*quod vide*, which see
R	Rabbah
rev.	revised, reviser, revision
Rom.	Roman
RVm	Revised Version margin
Samar.	Samaritan recension
SCM	Student Christian Movement Press
Sem.	Semitic
sing.	singular
SPCK	Society for the Promotion of Christian Knowledge
Sumer.	Sumerian
s.v.	*sub verbo*, under the word
Syr.	Syriac
Symm.	Symmachus
T	Talmud
Targ.	Targum
Theod.	Theodotion
TR	Textus Receptus
tr.	translation, translator, translated
UBS	Tha United Bible Societies' Greek Text
Ugar.	Ugaritic
u.s.	*ut supra*, as above
v., vv.	verse, verses
viz.	*videlicet*, namely
vol.	volume
vs.	versus
Vul.	Vulgate
WH	Westcott and Hort, *The New Testament in Greek*

B. Abbreviations for Modern Translations and Paraphrases

AmT	Smith and Goodspeed, *The Complete Bible, An American Translation*	Mof	J. Moffatt, *A New Translation of the Bible*
ASV	American Standard Version, American Revised Version (1901)	NAB	The New American Bible
		NASB	New American Standard Bible
		NEB	The New English Bible
		NIV	The New International Version
Beck	Beck, *The New Testament in the Language of Today*	Ph	J. B. Phillips *The New Testament in Modern English*
BV	Berkeley Version (The Modern Language Bible)	RSV	Revised Standard Version
		RV	Revised Version — 1881–1885
JB	The Jerusalem Bible	TCNT	Twentieth Century New Testament
JPS	*Jewish Publication Society Version of the Old Testament*	TEV	Today's English Version
KJV	King James Version	Wey	*Weymouth's New Testament in Modern Speech*
Knox	R.G. Knox, *The Holy Bible: A Translation from the Latin Vulgate in the Light of the Hebrew and Greek Original*	Wms	C. B. Williams, *The New Testament: A Translation in the Language of the People*
LB	The Living Bible		

C. Abbreviations for Periodicals and Reference Works

AASOR	*Annual of the American Schools of Oriental Research*	BASOR	*Bulletin of the American Schools of Oriental Research*
AB	*Anchor Bible*	BC	Foakes-Jackson and Lake: *The Beginnings of Christianity*
AIs	de Vaux: *Ancient Israel*		
AJA	*American Journal of Archaeology*	BDB	Brown, Driver, and Briggs: *Hebrew-English Lexicon of the Old Testament*
AJSL	*American Journal of Semitic Languages and Literatures*	BDF	Blass, Debrunner, and Funk: *A Greek Grammar of the New Testament and Other Early Christian Literature*
AJT	*American Journal of Theology*		
Alf	Alford: *Greek Testament Commentary*	BDT	Harrison: *Baker's Dictionary of Theology*
ANEA	*Ancient Near Eastern Archaeology*	Beng.	Bengel's *Gnomon*
ANET	Pritchard: *Ancient Near Eastern Texts*	BETS	*Bulletin of the Evangelical Theological Society*
ANF	Roberts and Donaldson: *The Ante-Nicene Fathers*	BH	*Biblia Hebraica*
		BHS	*Biblia Hebraica Stuttgartensia*
ANT	M. R. James: *The Apocryphal New Testament*	BJRL	*Bulletin of the John Rylands Library*
A-S	Abbot-Smith: *Manual Greek Lexicon of the New Testament*	BS	*Bibliotheca Sacra*
		BT	*Babylonian Talmud*
AThR	*Anglican Theological Review*	BTh	*Biblical Theology*
BA	*Biblical Archaeologist*	BW	*Biblical World*
BAG	Bauer, Arndt, and Gingrich: *Greek-English Lexicon of the New Testament*	CAH	*Cambridge Ancient History*
		CanJTh	*Canadian Journal of Theology*
		CBQ	*Catholic Biblical Quarterly*
BAGD	Bauer, Arndt, Gingrich, and Danker: *Greek-English Lexicon of the New Testament* 2nd edition	CBSC	*Cambridge Bible for Schools and Colleges*
		CE	*Catholic Encyclopedia*
		CGT	*Cambridge Greek Testament*

CHS	Lange: *Commentary on the Holy Scriptures*	IDB	*The Interpreter's Dictionary of the Bible*
ChT	*Christianity Today*	IEJ	*Israel Exploration Journal*
DDB	*Davis' Dictionary of the Bible*	Int	*Interpretation*
Deiss BS	Deissmann: *Bible Studies*	INT	E. Harrison: *Introduction to the New Testament*
Deiss LAE	Deissmann: *Light From the Ancient East*	IOT	R. K. Harrison: *Introduction to the Old Testament*
DNTT	*Dictionary of New Testament Theology*	ISBE	*The International Standard Bible Encyclopedia*
EBC	*The Expositor's Bible Commentary*	ITQ	*Irish Theological Quarterly*
EBi	*Encyclopaedia Biblica*	JAAR	*Journal of American Academy of Religion*
EBr	*Encyclopaedia Britannica*		
EDB	*Encyclopedic Dictionary of the Bible*	JAOS	*Journal of American Oriental Society*
EGT	Nicoll: *Expositor's Greek Testament*	JBL	*Journal of Biblical Literature*
EQ	*Evangelical Quarterly*	JE	*Jewish Encyclopedia*
ET	*Evangelische Theologie*	JETS	*Journal of Evangelical Theological Society*
ExB	*The Expositor's Bible*		
Exp	*The Expositor*	JFB	Jamieson, Fausset, and Brown: *Commentary on the Old and New Testament*
ExpT	*The Expository Times*		
FLAP	Finegan: *Light From the Ancient Past*		
GKC	Gesenius, Kautzsch, Cowley, *Hebrew Grammar*, 2nd Eng. ed.	JNES	*Journal of Near Eastern Studies*
		Jos. Antiq.	Josephus: *The Antiquities of the Jews*
GR	*Gordon Review*	Jos. War	Josephus: *The Jewish War*
HBD	*Harper's Bible Dictionary*	JQR	*Jewish Quarterly Review*
HDAC	Hastings: *Dictionary of the Apostolic Church*	JR	*Journal of Religion*
		JSJ	*Journal for the Study of Judaism in the Persian, Hellenistic and Roman Periods*
HDB	Hastings: *Dictionary of the Bible*		
HDBrev.	Hastings: *Dictionary of the Bible*, one-vol. rev. by Grant and Rowley	JSOR	*Journal of the Society of Oriental Research*
		JSS	*Journal of Semitic Studies*
HDCG	Hastings: *Dictionary of Christ and the Gospels*	JT	*Jerusalem Talmud*
		JTS	*Journal of Theological Studies*
HERE	Hastings: *Encyclopedia of Religion and Ethics*	KAHL	Kenyon: *Archaeology in the Holy Land*
HGEOTP	Heidel: *The Gilgamesh Epic and Old Testament Parallels*	KB	Koehler-Baumgartner: *Lexicon in Veteris Testament Libros*
HJP	Schurer: *A History of the Jewish People in the Time of Christ*	KD	Keil and Delitzsch: *Commentary on the Old Testament*
		LSJ	Liddell, Scott, Jones: *Greek-English Lexicon*
HR	Hatch and Redpath: *Concordance to the Septuagint*	LTJM	Edersheim: *The Life and Times of Jesus the Messiah*
HTR	*Harvard Theological Review*	MM	Moulton and Milligan: *The Vocabulary of the Greek Testament*
HUCA	*Hebrew Union College Annual*		
IB	*The Interpreter's Bible*		
ICC	*International Critical Commentary*	MNT	Moffatt: *New Testament Commentary*

MST	McClintock and Strong: *Cyclopedia of Biblical, Theological, and Ecclesiastical Literature*	SJT	*Scottish Journal of Theology*
NBC	Davidson, Kevan, and Stibbs: *The New Bible Commentary*, 1st ed.	SOT	Girdlestone: *Synonyms of Old Testament*
NBCrev.	Guthrie and Motyer: *The New Bible Commentary*, rev. ed.	SOTI	Archer: *A Survey of Old Testament Introduction*
		ST	*Studia Theologica*
NBD	J. D. Douglas: *The New Bible Dictionary*	TCERK	Loetscher: *The Twentieth Century Encyclopedia of Religious Knowledge*
NCB	*New Century Bible*	TDNT	Kittel: *Theological Dictionary of the New Testament*
NCE	*New Catholic Encyclopedia*		
NIC	*New International Commentary*	TDOT	*Theological Dictionary of the Old Testament*
NIDCC	Douglas: *The New International Dictionary of the Christian Church*	THAT	*Theologisches Handbuch zum Alten Testament*
NovTest	*Novum Testamentum*	ThT	*Theology Today*
NSI	Cooke: *Handbook of North Semitic Inscriptions*	TNTC	*Tyndale New Testament Commentaries*
NTS	*New Testament Studies*	Trench	Trench: *Synonyms of the New Testament*
ODCC	*The Oxford Dictionary of the Christian Church*, rev. ed.	TWOT	*Theological Wordbook of the Old Testament*
Peake	Black and Rowley: *Peake's Commentary on the Bible*	UBD	*Unger's Bible Dictionary*
		UT	Gordon: *Ugaritic Textbook*
PEQ	*Palestine Exploration Quarterly*	VB	Allmen: *Vocabulary of the Bible*
PNF1	P. Schaff: *The Nicene and Post-Nicene Fathers* (1st series)	VetTest	*Vetus Testamentum*
		Vincent	Vincent: *Word-Pictures in the New Testament*
PNF2	P. Schaff and H. Wace: *The Nicene and Post-Nicene Fathers* (2nd series)	WBC	*Wycliffe Bible Commentary*
		WBE	*Wycliffe Bible Encyclopedia*
PTR	*Princeton Theological Review*	WC	*Westminster Commentaries*
RB	*Revue Biblique*	WesBC	*Wesleyan Bible Commentaries*
RHG	Robertson's *Grammar of the Greek New Testament in the Light of Historical Research*	WTJ	*Westminster Theological Journal*
		ZAW	*Zeitschrift für die alttestamentliche Wissenschaft*
RTWB	Richardson: *A Theological Wordbook of the Bible*	ZNW	*Zeitschrift für die neutestamentliche Wissenschaft*
SBK	Strack and Billerbeck: *Kommentar zum Neuen Testament aus Talmud und Midrash*	ZPBD	*The Zondervan Pictorial Bible Dictionary*
		ZPEB	*The Zondervan Pictorial Encyclopedia of the Bible*
SHERK	*The New Schaff-Herzog Encyclopedia of Religious Knowledge*	ZWT	*Zeitschrift für wissenschaftliche Theologie*

D. Abbreviations for Books of the Bible, the Apocrypha, and the Pseudepigrapha

OLD TESTAMENT

Gen	2 Chron	Dan
Exod	Ezra	Hos
Lev	Neh	Joel
Num	Esth	Amos
Deut	Job	Obad
Josh	Ps(Pss)	Jonah
Judg	Prov	Mic
Ruth	Eccl	Nah
1 Sam	S of Songs	Hab
2 Sam	Isa	Zeph
1 Kings	Jer	Hag
2 Kings	Lam	Zech
1 Chron	Ezek	Mal

NEW TESTAMENT

Matt	1 Tim
Mark	2 Tim
Luke	Titus
John	Philem
Acts	Heb
Rom	James
1 Cor	1 Peter
2 Cor	2 Peter
Gal	1 John
Eph	2 John
Phil	3 John
Col	Jude
1 Thess	Rev
2 Thess	

APOCRYPHA

1 Esd	1 Esdras
2 Esd	2 Esdras
Tobit	Tobit
Jud	Judith
Add Esth	Additions to Esther
Wisd Sol	Wisdom of Solomon
Ecclus	Ecclesiasticus (Wisdom of Jesus the Son of Sirach)
Baruch	Baruch
Ep Jer	Epistle of Jeremy
S Th Ch	Song of the Three Children (or Young Men)
Sus	Susanna
Bel	Bel and the Dragon
Pr Man	Prayer of Manasseh
1 Macc	1 Maccabees
2 Macc	2 Maccabees

PSEUDEPIGRAPHA

As Moses	Assumption of Moses
2 Baruch	Syriac Apocalypse of Baruch
3 Baruch	Greek Apocalypse of Baruch
1 Enoch	Ethiopic Book of Enoch
2 Enoch	Slavonic Book of Enoch
3 Enoch	Hebrew Book of Enoch
4 Ezra	4 Ezra
JA	Joseph and Asenath
Jub	Book of Jubilees
L Aristeas	Letter of Aristeas
Life AE	Life of Adam and Eve
Liv Proph	Lives of the Prophets
MA Isa	Martyrdom and Ascension of Isaiah
3 Macc	3 Maccabees
4 Macc	4 Maccabees
Odes Sol	Odes of Solomon
P Jer	Paralipomena of Jeremiah
Pirke Aboth	Pirke Aboth
Ps 151	Psalm 151
Pss Sol	Psalms of Solomon
Sib Oracles	Sibylline Oracles
Story Ah	Story of Ahikar
T Abram	Testament of Abraham
T Adam	Testament of Adam
T Benjamin	Testament of Benjamin
T Dan	Testament of Dan
T Gad	Testament of Gad
T Job	Testament of Job
T Jos	Testament of Joseph
T Levi	Testament of Levi
T Naph	Testament of Naphtali
T 12 Pat	Testaments of the Twelve Patriarchs
Zad Frag	Zadokite Fragments

E. Abbreviations of Names of Dead Sea Scrolls and Related Texts

CD	Cairo (Genizah text of the) Damascus (Document)	1QSa	Appendix A (Rule of the Congregation) to 1Qs
DSS	Dead Sea Scrolls	1QSb	Appendix B (Blessings) to 1QS
Hev	Nahal Hever texts	3Q15	Copper Scroll from Qumran Cave 3
Mas	Masada Texts		
Mird	Khirbet mird texts	4QExod a	Exodus Scroll, exemplar "a" from Qumran Cave 4
Mur	Wadi Murabba'at texts		
P	Pesher (commentary)	4QFlor	Florilegium (or Eschatological Midrashim) from Qumran Cave 4
Q	Qumran		
1Q, 2Q, etc.	Numbered caves of Qumran, yielding written material; followed by abbreviation of biblical or apocryphal book.	4Qmess ar	Aramaic "Messianic" text from Qumran Cave 4
QL	Qumran Literature	4QpNah	Pesher on portions of Nahum from Qumran Cave 4
1QapGen	Genesis Apocryphon of Qumran Cave 1	4QPrNab	Prayer of Nabonidus from Qumran Cave 4
1QH	*Hodayot* (Thanksgiving Hymns) from Qumran Cave 1	4QpPs37	Pesher on portions of Psalm 37 from Qumran Cave 4
1QIsa a,b	First or second copy of Isaiah from Qumran Cave 1	4QTest	Testimonia text from Qumran Cave 4
1QpHab	Pesher on Habakkuk from Qumran Cave 1	4QTLevi	Testament of Levi from Qumran Cave 4
1QM	*Milhamah* (War Scroll)	4QPhyl	Phylacteries from Qumran Cave 4
1QpMic	Pesher on portions of Micah from Qumran Cave 1	11QMelch	Melchizedek text from Qumran Cave 11
1QS	*Serek Hayyahad* (Rule of the Community, Manual of Discipline)	11QtgJob	Targum of Job from Qumran Cave 11

TRANSLITERATIONS

Hebrew

א = ʾ	ד = $\underline{d}$	י = y	ס = s	ר = r
ב = b	ה = h	כ = k	ע = ʿ	שׂ = ś
ב = $\underline{b}$	ו = w	ך כ = $\underline{k}$	פ = p	שׁ = š
ג = g	ז = z	ל = l	ף פ = $\underline{p}$	ת = t
ג = $\underline{g}$	ח = ḥ	ם מ = m	ץ צ = ṣ	ת = $\underline{t}$
ד = d	ט = ṭ	ן נ = n	ק = q	

(ה)ָ = â (h)	ָ = ā	ַ = a	ֲ = ^{a}
ֵה = ê	ֵ = ē	ֶ = e	ֱ = ^{e}
ִי = î	ֹ = ō	ִ = i	ְ = ^{e} (if vocal)
וֹ = ô		ֹ = o	ֳ = ^{o}
וּ = û		ֻ = u	

Aramaic

ʾ b g d h w z ḥ ṭ y k l m n s ʿ p ṣ q r ś š t

Arabic

ʾ b t ṯ ǧ ḥ ḫ d ḏ r z s š ṣ ḍ ṭ ẓ ʿ ġ f q k l m n h w y

Ugaritic

ʾ b g d ḏ h w z ḥ ḫ ṭ ẓ y k l m n s ṣ́ ʿ ġ ṗ ṣ q r š t ṯ

xv

Greek

α	—	a	π	—	p	αι	—	ai
β	—	b	ρ	—	r	αὐ	—	au
γ	—	g	σ,ς	—	s	ει	—	ei
δ	—	d	τ	—	t	εὐ	—	eu
ε	—	e	υ	—	y	ηὐ	—	ĕu
ζ	—	z	φ	—	ph	οι	—	oi
η	—	ē	χ	—	ch	οὐ	—	ou
θ	—	th	ψ	—	ps	υι	—	hui
ι	—	i	ω	—	ō			
κ	—	k				ῥ	—	rh
λ	—	l	γγ	—	ng	ʽ	—	h
μ	—	m	γκ	—	nk			
ν	—	n	γξ	—	nx	ᾳ	—	ā
ξ	—	x	γχ	—	nch	ῃ	—	ē
ο	—	o				ῳ	—	ō

THE GOSPEL OF JOHN

Merrill C. Tenney

THE GOSPEL OF JOHN

Introduction

1. Background

The Gospel of John was probably the last of the Gospels to be written and circulated; yet it is definitely a document belonging to the first century. Its action took place between A.D. 30 and 36, when Pontius Pilate was removed from office by the order of Tiberius Caesar. Although it contains fewer allusions to contemporary history than the Synoptics, John's Gospel depends on information that was parallel to theirs.

Much of Jerusalem was destroyed by the Roman suppression of the Jewish revolt of A.D. 66–70. Thus the detailed references in John to many of the ancient landmarks indicate that the author was acquainted with them and that he must have been in Jerusalem before A.D. 70. He mentions the five colonnades at the Pool of Bethesda (John 5:2), which recent excavation has revealed; the Colonnade of Solomon at the outer edge of the temple enclosure, where Jesus taught (10:23); the palace (praetorium) (18:28) and "The Stone Pavement" (19:13), where the hearing before Pilate was held; the place of execution called "Golgotha" (Heb. for "skull") (19:17); and the garden of Joseph where Jesus' body was buried (19:41).

Furthermore, the author was acquainted with Jewish religion. He mentions the Passover (2:13, 23: 4:45; 6:4; 11:55–56; 12:1, 12, 20; 13:1; 18:28, 39; 19:14), the Feast of Tabernacles (7:2, 8, 10–11, 14, 37), and the Feast of Dedication (10:22). He was familiar with Jewish customs such as weddings (2:1–10), Sabbath-keeping (5:9–10; 9:14–16; 19: 31), methods of burial (11:44; 19:40), and the methods of observing the feasts (7:37; 13:1–11). Insofar as these allusions to places and customs are paralleled by reference to other literature, they corroborate the setting of the action presented in the Gospel.

The writer of this Gospel knew the topography of Palestine. He refers correctly to the divisions of the land into Judea, Samaria, and Galilee. Details about cities and towns such as Nazareth (1:45–46), Cana (2:1), Capernaum (2:12), and Sychar (4:5) are all accurate.

This Gospel was probably written at a time when the church was composed of second- and third-generation Christians who needed more detailed instruction about Jesus and new defenses for the apologetic problems raised by apostasy within the church and by growing opposition from without. The understanding of the person of Christ that had depended on the testimony of his contemporaries was becoming a philosophical and theological problem. Doctrinal variations had begun to appear, and some of the assertions of the basic Christian truths had been challenged. A new presentation was necessary to meet the questions of the changing times. As the Gospel states, "These things are written that you may maintain your belief that Jesus is the Christ, the Son of God" (20:31).[1]

The Gospel of John is, therefore, more theological and in some respects more cosmopolitan than the Synoptics. It is not necessarily less Jewish. It has, however, a wider appeal to growing Christian experience and to an enlarging Gentile constituency than the others.

The question has been raised whether John's Gospel is a theological treatise rather than a historical narrative. Does it represent Jesus as he really was, or does it clothe the human figure with an imaginative dress of deity? Theological it certainly is, but so are the Synoptics; and the difference between them largely reflects the respective intended readership, not the person described. In all four Gospels Jesus is unique in his character, authority, and message. The Synoptics present him for a generation in process of being evangelized; John presents him as the Lord of the maturing and questioning believer.

This Gospel contains little information about general historical events. It does refer to the ministry of John the Baptist (1:19–37; 3:22–36; 4:1); Herod's rebuilding of the temple (2:20); the high priesthood of Annas and Caiaphas (18:13–14); and the person of Pontius Pilate (18:28–19:16, 38), prefect of Judea. The Roman domination of Palestine is implied but not featured. There is almost no direct allusion to current political affairs and no mention of the church by name. While the Gospel must have been written for the use of believers, virtually nothing is said about their organization. The author seems to be concerned less with time than with eternity.

2. Unity

The combination of intricacy and simplicity in the structure of the Gospel of John conveys the unavoidable impression that it is the product of one mind. Its consistency of structure, distinctive vocabulary, uniformity of style, and directness of purpose can best be explained by ascribing it to a single author. It may be conceded that it has some chronological gaps and literary peculiarities hard to explain. For example, the opening words of ch. 6, "Some time after this, Jesus crossed to the far shore of the Sea of Galilee," abruptly begin a new topic after narrating Jesus' argument with the Jews in Jerusalem. Also, his statement at the end of ch. 14, "Come now; let us leave" (v. 31), is followed by an extended discourse before he finally leaves for Gethsemane. Some scholars have explained these anomalies by attributing them to "sources" that were incorporated into

---

[1]For a discussion of this rendering of v. 31, see Note on 20:31.

the Gospel without regard for their interrelationship by a series of editors, the last of whom produced the final work.

Others have suggested that the apparent irregularities come from a primitive disarrangement of the original MS, which was then reorganized by an editor who did not know how to restore the sequence.[2] There is, however, no existing MS evidence of such dislocations; and attempts to reconstruct the initial order have proved fruitless.

Without denying that the author may have had numerous sources of information about Jesus' activities and teaching apart from his own experience, there is no good reason to assume that he used a scissors-and-paste method of composing this Gospel. Nor is it necessary to assume that he needed sources other than his own participation in the events of Jesus' life and his personal contacts with other participants. Neither is the theory of accidental dislocation inevitable. Some of the sharp transitions in the Gospel may show that the author assumed a knowledge on the part of his readers that would not be possible today, or that he was less interested in chronological sequence than in the consecutive impact of his presentation. He says plainly that his method is selective, but the episodes he chose are united by the single purpose of promoting belief.

The criterion of unity does not lie in literary smoothness so much as in the purpose of the work. Lightfoot states, "From beginning to end this Gospel is a compact whole" (p. 19). After observing the method the author has used to present his picture of Christ, Lightfoot adds, "The unity of this Gospel is not only a unity of structure, it is also a unity of themes" (p. 21). The different topics it deals with—such as the "signs," the "I Am's," the debates and personal interviews, and the discourses to the disciples—may not all appear in uniform sequence; nevertheless, there is complete unity in their teaching. All of them focus on the purpose expressed in the author's final note (20:30–31) and give the impression that they are just the sort of thing a friend of Jesus would remember about him.

3. Authorship

a. External Evidence

The earliest tradition of the church ascribes the fourth Gospel to John the son of Zebedee, one of the first of Jesus' disciples, and one who was closest to him. Irenaeus bishop of Lyons (fl. c. 180) stated plainly that "John, the disciple of the Lord, who also had leaned upon his breast, had himself published a Gospel during his residence in Ephesus in Asia" (*Against Heresies* 3.1). Irenaeus's testimony has been corroborated by other writers. Theophilus of Antioch (fl. c. 165) alluded to the Gospel (*To Autolycus* 2.22). Clement of Alexandria (fl. c. 220) quoted at considerable length from almost every chapter of John. Tertullian of Carthage, Clement's contemporary, used it freely in his works. Tatian (fl. c. 150) included it in his *Diatessaron*, or Harmony of the Four Gospels,

---

[2]Hoare, Bernard, and Moffat hold this or a similar view. The only instance where a positive textual variant may be found to support this hypothesis occurs in John 18, where the Sinaitic Syriac text changes the order of the verses to 13, 24, 14–15, 19–23, 16–18, 25–27; a somewhat similar arrangement appears in 225 and in a quotation by Cyril of Alexandria (c. 444). By far the oldest MSS and the vast majority of the extant witnesses do not support the variant. It seems that in the latter case the variant is due to a late alteration and that the hypothesis of accidental confusion of order in the original text, while not impossible, cannot be proved. See further discussion in section on Displacement of Text, p. 21.

which he produced about the third quarter of the second century. Eusebius, the church historian of the fourth century, attributed the Gospel to "John, the companion of Peter, James, and the other apostles" (*Historia Ecclesiastica* 3.34.5). Although Eusebius seemed uncertain concerning the authorship of the Apocalypse, he agreed with the other witnesses concerning the Gospel. The early Fathers did not hesitate to acknowledge the Johannine authorship of the Gospel, and from the time of Irenaeus there was almost unanimous agreement about this.

b. Internal Evidence

Internal evidence also testifies to the unity of this Gospel. The epilogue closes by focusing on "the disciple whom Jesus loved" as the witness and writer of the content of the Gospel (21:20–24). He was among those Jesus appeared to at the Sea of Tiberias (Galilee) after their night of unsuccessful fishing (21:7). This disciple was a particular friend of Peter and was one of the sons of Zebedee (John 21:2; cf. Matt 4:21; 10:2). The preceding chapters couple him with Peter in the events on the morning of the Resurrection (20:2–8) and also identify him as the one Jesus committed his mother to at the Crucifixion (19:25–27). It is possible that he is the one who is called "another disciple," the one who led Peter into the court of the high priest's palace at the trial of Jesus (18:15–16). He was present at the Last Supper, where he reclined next to Jesus and was questioned by Peter (13:23–24). Undoubtedly he belonged to the Twelve and was probably a member of the inner circle. Obviously he was not Peter nor one of those mentioned in the third person in the main body of the Gospel. Presumably he was John, for he was Peter's close associate after the Resurrection (Acts 3:1–11; 4:13–20; Gal 2:9). He would have been able to hear both Jesus' public and private discourses and would have been actively engaged in the development of the church from its inception.

The characteristics of the Gospel confirm the credibility of apostolic authorship. Westcott demonstrated from internal testimony that it must have been written by a Jew who was acquainted with Jewish opinions and learning and with the details of Jewish customs (1:ix–lix). The author's vocabulary and general style are Semitic; though the Gospel was written in Greek. The OT is frequently quoted, and the necessity of prophetic fulfillment is emphasized (John 13:18; 15:25).

Second, the author was a Palestinian Jew, not a member of the Diaspora. His knowledge of Palestinian topography was accurate. He distinguished between Bethany, the suburb of Jerusalem where Mary and Martha lived (11:1), and "Bethany on the other side of the Jordan," where John the Baptist preached (1:28). Some of the sites he alluded to, such as Aenon (3:23) and Ephraim (11:54), are not described elsewhere; but, obviously, they were actual places well known to him. His description of the features of Jerusalem, such as the pool by the "Sheep Gate" (5:2), the "pool of Siloam" (9:7), the "Stone Pavement" (Gr. *lithostrōton*, 19:13), and the varied references to the temple (2:14–16; 8:20; 10:23), show that he was familiar with the city before its destruction. (The devastation was so complete by the middle of the second century that the face of the city had changed entirely. The buildings had been razed, and the surface of the land had been buried under their rubble. Following the Second Revolt of 133–135, Hadrian built a new town, Aelia Capitolina.) Archaeological investigations have confirmed the accuracy of many of the author's allusions, though complete data are presently unattainable.

The genuineness of the fourth Gospel has been challenged on the basis of its language, which differs from the synoptic record of Jesus' discourses and also from that of the early Fathers. For example, the contrast of light and darkness that appears in the first chapter has frequently been regarded as evidence of a Hellenistic influence in the Gospel. Yet the discovery at Qumran of the Jewish writing *The War of the Sons of Light and the Sons of Darkness* shows that this contrast was current in Judaism during the intertestamental period and was not necessarily an importation from Hellenism.

A further deduction from the internal evidence of the Gospel is that the author personally witnessed the events he described, or else he must have had contemporary informants who were themselves eyewitnesses. He spoke easily and familiarly of the disciples and associates of Jesus (6:5–7; 12:21; 13:36; 14:5, 8, 22) and knew the background of those Jesus had only casual contact with, such as Nicodemus (3:1) or Annas (18:13). Small details appear frequently, such as the barley bread used at the feeding of the five thousand (6:9), the fragrance of the ointment Mary poured on Jesus (12:3), or the time at which Judas left the Last Supper (13:30). These are not the creation of literary imagination, but they are the natural touches that come from personal memory. As Westcott said, "The age of minute historical romance had not yet come when the Fourth Gospel was written, even if such a record could possibly be brought within the category" (1:xliv).

Not only must the writer have been an eyewitness, but he also was closely acquainted with the personal career of Jesus from beginning to end. The author was aware of the thinking of the disciples, and apparently he shared their interests and hopes. He reports the private discourses of Jesus at some length; and even though the criticism has been raised that they are given in the Johannine style rather than in the epigrammatic style quoted in the Synoptics, some quotations in the Synoptics show that Jesus occasionally used the same language when alluding to himself (Matt 10:24–27; 26:64). Even if the author reported Jesus' words in his own style, he cannot justly be charged with inaccuracy. Also, he shows knowledge of Jesus' inner consciousness that would have been possible only to a close associate (6:6, 61, 64; 13:1–3, 11; 18:4).

Although the author never names himself, it seems that his identity was well known to his contemporaries. Just why he or his colleagues who wrote the final colophon should have left the Gospel anonymous is not clear; though, as a matter of fact, none of the Gospels mentions the name of its author. If it were written during a period of persecution, the writer possibly would have preferred to remain unidentified, though some of the recipients must have known who produced it.

By process of elimination, it seems reasonably certain that this anonymous disciple and author must have been John the son of Zebedee. Peter did not write the fourth Gospel, for it mentions him frequently in the third person. James the son of Zebedee did not write it, for he was executed by Herod Agrippa I prior to A.D. 44 (Acts 12:2). The remaining possibility is John, who fits the requirements of its authorship quite well. Although tradition is not always reliable, in this case it corroborates the implications of the internal evidence. It also confirms the conclusion that this Gospel was written by one who knew Jesus personally, who had followed him throughout his career, and who had become one of the leaders in the movement that grew out of Jesus' life and teaching. We accept it as a genuine document of the first-century witness.

Objections to the Johannine authorship have been raised from time to time. It has been suggested that a fisherman like John would have been incapable of composing a Gospel of such profound meaning. To be sure, the enemies of Peter and John characterized them as "unschooled, ordinary men" (Acts 4:13), but that does not mean they were illiterate or stupid. It does mean they had not received the formal education in the Law that was the prerogative of biblical scholars of their day. They were not lacking in knowledge of the content of the OT, nor were they devoid of the ability to apply their knowledge. If they can be judged by the fragmentary defense recorded in Acts, they made so good a case for themselves that their opponents had no resort left to them but violence. Furthermore, by the time he wrote this Gospel, John had possibly fifty or more years' experience after his early appearances before the Jewish council. In that time he could have gained greatly in knowledge, depth of insight, and facility of expression.

Another objection—that John died as a martyr in the early years of the church—is based on a statement of Philip of Side, a church historian of the fifth century. He remarked that Papias, a disciple of John the Theologian, wrote in vol. 2 of his *Exposition of Dominical Oracles*, a five volume work, that "John the Theologian" and James his brother were put to death by the Jews. Papias's *Oracles* were a collection of unwritten traditions from around the first century; but, unfortunately, none of them survived. For what it is worth, Philip of Side was regarded by his contemporaries as a conceited and untrustworthy author whose writings were unreliable (Smith and Wace, 4:356). Furthermore, James the brother of John was executed by Herod, not by the Jews. And the statement is not even self-consistent because it asserts the early martyrdom of John while affirming that Papias had been his disciple. The evidence for the early decease of John is negligible.

Still another objection to the Johannine authorship is grounded on Eusebius's interpretation of a statement of Papias:

> And I shall not hesitate to append to the interpretations all that I ever learned well from the presbyters and remember well, for of their truth I am confident. For unlike most I did not rejoice in those who say much, but in those who teach the truth, nor in those who recount the commandments of others, but in those who repeated those given to the faith by the Lord and derived from the truth itself; but if ever anyone comes who followed the presbyters, I inquire into the words of the presbyters, what Andrew or Peter or Philip or Thomas or James or John or Matthew or any other of the Lord's disciples had said, and what Aristion and the presbyter John, the Lord's disciples, were saying [*legousin*, present tense, "are saying"]. For I did not suppose that information from books would help so much as the word of a living and surviving voice (*Historia Ecclesiastica* 3.39).

From this statement Eusebius deduced that there were two Johns, the former being the son of Zebedee and the latter the "presbyter John," to whom Eusebius ascribed the Book of Revelation. A different interpretation is possible, however. The two verbs "had said" and "are saying" imply that the former group of men mentioned by Papias had preceded his time; but with the latter two, Aristion and John, he apparently had some personal contact. He may have meant that the two Johns were identical, especially since the term *elder* (*presbyteros*) could have been applied to any of them and particularly to John the son of Zebedee, if he were the last survivor of the apostolic band. The fact that his great age is implied in the epilogue to the Gospel (John 21:23) and that "elder" is applied to the writer of the Second and Third Epistles (2 John 1; 3 John 1) tends to strengthen this conclusion. The witness of Irenaeus, who long preceded Eusebius, should take precedence over a quotation of Papias that is given out of context and that may have been garbled or misunderstood.

In summation, it may be said that while there have been objections to the traditional authorship, the more recent trend is toward a partial if not complete acceptance of the Johannine origin. At least, the basic content of the Gospel in early annals goes back to apostolic teaching. Morris, in his exhaustive commentary, says, "I accept the view that John the Apostle was the author of the Gospel. . . . This one seems to account for the facts best" (p. 30). Brown concludes: "When all is said and done, the combination of external and internal evidence associating the Fourth Gospel with John, son of Zebedee, makes this the strongest hypothesis, if one is prepared to give credence to the Gospel's claim of an eyewitness source" (p. xcviii).

4. Date

The date of the Gospel has been variously estimated at almost any point between 45, shortly after the dispersion of Christians from Jerusalem following the persecution under Paul (Acts 8:1–4), and the middle of the second century. The latter point was advocated by the Tübingen school in the early nineteenth century on the supposition that John represented a type of theological thinking that arose late in the first century or early in the second century and was not put in written form until approximately 150. The discovery of the Rylands fragment of John 18:31–33, 37–38, by C.H. Roberts about 1935, shows that this Gospel had been incorporated in a papyrus MS produced not later than 135. It must, therefore, originally have been written at some time prior to the date of the MS into which it was copied. The Egerton papyrus, which was written about the same time as the Rylands fragment, confirms this conclusion, for its phraseology incorporates unmistakable allusions to John (see Bell and Skeat, pp. 17–19, 42–51).

On the other hand, C.C. Torrey maintained that John was originally written in Aramaic and was later translated into Greek (p. 264). He openly challenged his colleagues to produce any direct evidence to the contrary. Although Torrey's contention that John was translated from Aramaic may be disputed, he seems to have demonstrated effectively that it may well be a product of a Palestinian Jew who wrote with firsthand knowledge of the land and who could have composed the Gospel earlier than the end of the first century. Several critics hold this viewpoint. E.R. Goodenough (2:145–82) argued that it could have been composed well before the destruction of Jerusalem in A.D. 70.[3] Albright stated that "the advanced teachings of Jesus as transmitted by the Gospel of John contain nothing that can be reasonably adduced as evidence of a late origin" ("Scrolls"). He also added that "the Gospel of John is not a product of the early second century A.D., but dates substantially, though not in its present form, from before A.D. 70."[4]

The explanation in ch. 21 concerning Jesus' words "If I want him to remain alive until I return, what is that to you?" (v.22) seemingly implies that "the disciple whom Jesus loved" must have attained a great age and must have been a contemporary of the second-generation church. Possibly so, but that would not have precluded his writing the Gospel at an earlier date. Nor, on the other hand, would it allow for a composition date later than the end of the first century. Most conservative scholars suggest a date around 85 to 90, when the author had achieved advanced age but was still in full possession of his memory and active in ministry. It may be, however, that the Gospel was composed at a fairly early date but that its "publication" or wide circulation began later.

If the Gospel were written before the end of the first century, or even by 85, it would still have been read by men only one generation removed from the contemporaries of

---

[3]Goodenough holds that the writer of the fourth Gospel was unacquainted with the synoptic Gospels. Some of his arguments are quite radical, but he has at least made the option of an early date possible.

[4]See also his *Archaeology of Palestine* (Baltimore: Penguin, 1951), pp. 239–49.

Jesus. Thus it could have been verified or contested by those who had authentic information concerning him. Brown states that "the positive arguments seem to point to 100–110 as the latest plausible date for the writing of the Gospel, with strong probability favoring the earlier limit of 100" (p. lxxxiii). He has set the latest limit, including redaction, at this point and suggests that the "first edition" may have been written prior to A.D. 70. Robinson does not believe that there is anything in the language of John that demands a composition date later than the 60s (pp. 259–85).

5. Place of Origin

The place of origin is uncertain. Tradition, based largely on the statements of Irenaeus (*Against Heresies* 3.1) and Eusebius (*Historia Ecclesiastica* 4.14.3–8) holds that John wrote from Ephesus, where he had settled after leaving Palestine subsequent to the war of 66–70. Ephesus was a large cosmopolitan center of the ancient world, where the cultures of East and West mingled. The apostle Paul previously had founded an active church in Ephesus (Acts 19:1–20), having spent more than two years there, during which time he evangelized most of the province of Asia (v.10).

A final decision on the matter of place cannot be reached on the basis of available evidence. The best that can be said is that Ephesus is as good a probability as any. It was one of the largest Christian centers in the Gentile world of the first century. The use of *logos* in John would appeal to the Greeks, and the direct allusion to the Greek interest in Jesus mentioned in John 12:20–22 may indicate that the Gospel was written with an eye on the Gentile world, though it cannot be attributed to a Greek writer.

6. Destination

The intended recipients of John's Gospel are not clearly identified. From the writer's habit of explaining Jewish usages, translating Jewish names, and locating Palestinian sites, it would seem that he was probably writing for a Gentile church outside Palestine. If the reading "believe" in John 20:31 is the present tense, it would imply that the Gospel was written to Christians who needed encouragement and deepening of their faith. If "believe" is in the aorist tense, it would suggest that the Gospel was addressed, at least in part, to a pagan constituency to bring them to belief in Jesus as Christ and the Son of God. The content of the Gospel does not give overwhelming support to either possibility. Its presentation of Jesus deals largely with the questioning of the Jews. But the language of the Prologue and the introduction of the Greeks in ch. 12 reveal the author's interest in Gentiles.

Probably it will not be too wrong to suggest that the Gospel of John was written for Gentile Christians who had already acquired a basic knowledge of the life and works of Jesus but who needed further confirmation of their faith. By the use of personal reminiscences interpreted in the light of a long life of devotion to Christ and by numerous episodes that generally had not been used in the Gospel tradition, whether written or oral, John created a new and different approach to understanding Jesus' person. John's readers were primarily second-generation Christians he was familiar with and to whom he seemed patriarchal. If the Johannine Epistles are any guide, the writer must have been a highly respected elder within the structure of the church. John considered himself responsible for its welfare and did not hesitate to assert his authority (2 John 1,

4, 8; 3 John 9–10). The doctrinal digressions implied by the counsel given in these Epistles indicate that the church was being imperiled, if not actually deceived, by false teachers who came in the guise of itinerant preachers.

There is no clue concerning the geographical location of the intended audience. If the Gospel was written at Ephesus, it could have been directed to the Christians of the province of Asia. There is no implication that it was written to a local church. Whether the recipients were Jews or Gentiles is not stated. John 20:31 is, as already noted, somewhat ambiguous because of alternate readings.

7. Occasion

We cannot discern any specific occasion for the composition of this Gospel. It lacks the personal preface of Luke. Neither does it seem to have been written simply as a piece of informative news like Mark. There is no personal dedication. It is not a complete narrative, nor is it an essay. It is not strongly historical in the sense that it reflects any particular time or place. Because of the rather defensive doctrinal position it takes, it may well have been written to combat the rising tide of Cerinthianism, which threatened the theological foundation of the church.

According to Irenaeus, Cerinthus was a teacher who contended that Jesus was merely a human personality who was possessed by the Christ-spirit at his baptism and who relinquished this spirit on the cross (*Against Heresies* 1.26.2). Contrary to this teaching, the Gospel asserts that the Word became flesh (John 1:14) and that the descent of the Holy Spirit on Jesus at the baptism was the proof of his mission, not the origin of it (1:32–34). The Cross did not terminate his ministry; it simply marked the end of one stage of it. The Son returned to the Father in person; he did not cease to be the Son by death. The stress on sonship throughout the Gospel conveys the idea that it was a live issue in the church; and that impression is strengthened by the warning "Such a man is the antichrist—he denies the Father and the Son. No one who denies the Son has the Father; whoever acknowledges the Son has the Father also" (1 John 2:22–23).

8. Purpose

John wrote this Gospel to meet the spiritual need of a church that had little background in the OT and that may have been endangered by the plausible contention of Cerinthus or men like him. John's intention is stated with perfect clarity: "These [signs] are written that you may believe that Jesus is the Christ, the Son of God, and that by believing you may have life in his name" (John 20:31). The total thesis of the Gospel is belief in the Son who came from the Father.

The Gospel gives an initial impression of discontinuity. Many of its episodes have little direct chronological or logical connection with one another. Nevertheless, they show a remarkable unity built on the one purpose of convincing the reader that Jesus was supernatural in his origin, powers, and goal. He was the *Logos* who had come into the world from another sphere (1:14). He performed miracles, or "signs," that illustrated his many-faceted powers, especially applied to human need. He died an unusual death, but he rose from the dead to send his disciples out on a universal mission. The last sentences of the Gospel imply the promise of his return. An entirely new revelation of the plan and power of God is latent in this Gospel (1:18).

9. Literary Form and Structure

The Gospel of John is a narrative composed of various scenes from the career of Jesus. It does not pretend to be a complete biography. The chronological gaps leave an impression of incompleteness for those expecting a complete chronicle of Jesus' career. Because the Gospel has an apologetic or possibly polemic purpose, it utilizes only the episodes that will best illustrate its presentation of Jesus as the object of faith. Nothing is said of Jesus' youth; the baptism is not described as it is in the Synoptics; the Galilean ministries with their parables and numerous miracles are not recounted in detail; the eschatological discourses and parables are missing. Much attention is given to aspects of Jesus' visits to Jerusalem, of which the Synoptics say relatively little.

On the other hand, certain personal interviews between Jesus and others are given at length. Dialogue and discourse between Jesus and his disciples are emphasized. Miracles are few and are selected for individual illustrative purpose. The vocabulary is distinctive and is limited to major ideas such as those expressed by the words *believe, witness, love, abide, the Father, the Son, the Counselor (paraklētēs,* referring to the Holy Spirit), *light, life, darkness, Word, glorify, true (alēthēs), real (alēthinos),* and others. Most of these are used metaphorically and represent the leading ideas of the Gospel. The peculiarities of vocabulary, which are evident in all the Gospels, are more pronounced in the Gospel of John. It is almost impossible to read a single paragraph in the fourth Gospel that does not identify itself as Johannine by at least one word or phrase.

The structure of this Gospel may be analyzed from various viewpoints. The author uses at least five different approaches to his subject: (1) a central theme, which can be traced through the progress of the narrative from beginning to end; (2) the phases of the ministry of Jesus, which are marked by growing tension between him and his opponents; (3) a chronological sequence, which is not perfectly defined but follows a general scheme, organized loosely around the feasts of the Jewish year; (4) a geographic allocation of activity between Galilee, where the first sign was performed, and Jerusalem, where the final action took place; and (5) the personal interviews that delineate so plainly Jesus' interest in different types of personality and his method of dealing with them.

a. Theme

The first of these criteria concerns the central theme "belief." The varied episodes and teachings of the Gospel are all subordinate to the definition and development of this concept. The Prologue introduces the ministry of John the Baptist by stating that "he came as a witness . . . so that through him all men might believe" (John 1:7). The closing words of the main narrative that precedes the Epilogue (ch. 21) declare that "these [things] are written that you may believe that Jesus is the Christ, the Son of God" (20:31). The word "believe" (*pisteuō*) appears ninety-eight times in the Gospel, more often than any other key word, and is obviously the major theme.

All the signs, teachings, and events in the Gospel are used to stimulate faith in Christ and are so ordered that they mark growth in this faith on the part of his disciples. Growth was not always uniform, as Simon Peter's experience shows, and generally was countered by a growth of unbelief, as seen in the conduct of Jesus' enemies. The conflict between belief and unbelief, exemplified in the actions and utterances of the main characters, forms the plot.

The development of "belief" in John's work affords one key to its interpretation and marks its progressive evangelistic appeal. The following outline shows its general progress:

1. The Prologue: The Proposal for Belief
   1:1–18
2. The Presentation for Belief
   1:19–4:54
3. The Reactions of Belief and Unbelief
   5:1–6:71
4. The Crystallization of Belief and Unbelief
   7:1–11:53
5. The Crisis of Belief and Unbelief
   11:54–12:50
6. The Assurance for Belief
   13:1–17:26
7. The Rejection by Unbelief
   18:1–19:42
8. The Vindication of Belief
   20:1–31
9. Epilogue: The Dedication of Belief
   21:1–25

The Johannine presentation of belief describes the nature of the person on whom belief is fixed. Each of the interviews in section 2 describes a different personality with a different need and a different challenge to faith. Section 3 gives further illustrations of belief and unbelief, accompanied by explanatory discourses that define the claims of Christ more exactly and intensify his personal appeal to his hearers. The feeding of the five thousand (6:1–69) marks the watershed of Jesus' ministry. At this point the popular following began to diminish, and the band of loyal disciples declared their settled purpose of adhering to him. Section 4 marks the fixation of these attitudes: the rulers became set in their hatred of Jesus and in their consequent resolve to remove him; the disciples, though somewhat uncertain of themselves, still clung to him and maintained their loyalty. Section 5, the Crisis, is concerned largely with Jesus' own reaction. Realizing that his hour had come, he accepted the will of the Father and resolutely moved toward the ultimate conflict. The ensuing action is twofold. The episode of the foot washing and the following long discourse (chs. 14–16) contain Jesus' confrontation with unbelief in his dismissing of Judas and his encouragement of the hesitant belief of the others by his attempt to prepare them for his own removal. The prayer to the Father (ch. 17) expresses Jesus' confidence in the sovereignty and purpose of his Father as related to himself, his disciples, and the world.

Section 7, which deals with Jesus' death, reveals the final division that belief and unbelief made in all those who knew him. His enemies were implacable, and their hatred, scorn, and utter rejection of him illustrate the real meaning of unbelief. Conversely, the loyalty of those who remained with him, however feeble, shows an attitude of trust in him, even though these disciples may not have fully comprehended the significance of the events they were involved in.

Sections 8 and 9 provide the vindication of the disciples' faith. The Resurrection dissolved their perplexity, dried their tears, and dispelled their doubts. The Epilogue launched the disciples on a new career as they followed a risen Christ to a larger life and a fuller ministry.

b. *Phases of Ministry*

The first approach to the ministry of Jesus is topical rather than biographical, though it is built on biographical episodes. The author is not so much concerned with a regular sequence of events as with the creation of a relationship. His main purpose is to involve his reader in an active faith in Jesus as the Christ, the Son of God; and the selection of events and teachings are shaped to this end.

Notwithstanding this fact, the Gospel is still strongly biographical. The phases of the ministry of Jesus follow a definite progression from the initial questioning of his authority down to its ultimate repudiation by his enemies. In the outline that follows this introduction five major divisions are noted:

I. The Prologue states the basic preparation for understanding the ministry of Jesus. "The Word became flesh and lived for a while among us" (1:14).

II. As in the Synoptics, Jesus is publicly introduced through the ministry of John the Baptist. The gaining of disciples, the miracles, the assertion of his authority and defense of his claims, and his rise to the peak of his popularity are keyed to specific "signs" (*sēmeia*) and claims that resulted in controversy. The decline that led directly to the Cross began at the highest point in Jesus' ministry, which John, along with the Synoptics, locates at the feeding of the five thousand. As Jesus' popularity waned, he became increasingly concerned for his disciples. When the multitude finally turned from him, and the power of his enemies increased, he gave more time to the needs of his disciples, until in his last hour his attention was concentrated on their future.

III. Chapters 13 through 17, which contain Jesus' farewell discourses in the Upper Room and his final prayer, occupy about 20 percent of the text. This section contains the teaching by which Jesus sought to prepare the disciples for the shock of his death and the responsibility that would fall to them. He showed no sense of defeat, nor did he anticipate that the disciples would fail in their mission. The prayer (ch. 17) that followed his counsel implies that he would achieve his objective even in death and that he would be reunited with the Father. Likewise he expected that the disciples would be preserved by divine power and that they would discharge their mission in the world adequately.

IV. The story of Jesus' death and resurrection is brief. John does not give an exhaustive account of its details. He does not include many of the events recorded in the Synoptics, such as the prayer in Gethsemane, the trial before the Sanhedrin, the suicide of Judas, the hearing before Herod Antipas, the utterances of the two brigands executed with him, the earthquake and darkness, the rending of the veil of the temple, and the comment of the centurion who commanded the execution squad. If John was absent from the scene long enough to take Jesus' mother to his home in Jerusalem, it is quite likely that he missed some of the action at the cross.

Had the Gospel ended with the burial of Jesus, it would have been a disastrous tragedy. His life would have become the supreme example of injustice because holiness would have been eclipsed by evil, truth would have succumbed to expediency, love would have been shattered by hatred, and life would have been extinguished by death. The Resurrection reversed all these possibilities. It authenticated Jesus' teaching, broke the power of evil, and brought hope out of despair. Jesus' postresurrection presence brought a new dimension to belief.

V. The Epilogue, possibly added as a postscript to the main body of the Gospel, solidifies the power and appeal of Jesus. Not only has he risen, but he calls his disciples to follow him to new conquests.

c. The Chronological Framework

The chronological framework of the Gospel is loose. The segment from John 1:19 to 2:11 represents the consecutive events of a few days, which are well marked by the phrase "the next day" (1:29, 35, 43), or some related expression. The major divisions of action following the initial sign (ch. 2) are indicated by the occurrences of feasts (2:13; 5:1; 6:4; 7:2, 14; 10:22; 12:1), one of which is not identified (5:1). The chief reason for mentioning them seems to be social, not chronological. They provide the historical association for understanding the meaning of Jesus' teaching or action. His offering of the water from within parallels the ceremonial outpouring of water at the Feast of Tabernacles (Dodd, pp. 348–49). The demand of the Jews for a declaration of messiahship at the Feast of Dedication (Hanukkah) reflects the desire for a renewal of political liberation such as the Maccabees had achieved (Lightfoot, pp. 45, 49). The Last Supper at the Passover season recalls Paul's statement "Christ, our Passover lamb, has been sacrificed" (1 Cor 5:7). Notwithstanding the difficulty of placing the events of this Gospel in a fixed chronological order, it is still true that John seems to have had a knowledge of such an order and that he adhered to it, allowing for gaps at those places where he chose to be silent.

The order of the last week begins with John 12. The opening verse says that Jesus arrived at Bethany "six days before the Passover" (12:1). On that day Mary and Martha gave a dinner for him. The crowd that came to see him was so large that the chief priests were alarmed, and they began to plot the destruction of both Jesus and Lazarus, whose raising had attracted much attention (vv.10–11).

On the next day, Jesus, mounted on a donkey, formally entered Jerusalem. The acclaim of the crowd further exasperated his enemies, who felt helpless in the face of Jesus' widespread popularity (12:12–19). John does not provide a complete sequence for the next few days. He mentions the inquiry of the Greeks concerning Jesus and says that after this discourse Jesus hid himself (v.36).

John resumes the narrative with the evening meal in the Upper Room, which was "just before the Passover Feast" (13:1). According to the sequence of the narrative, this took place on the same evening as the betrayal and arrest, with the hearings before Pilate and the Crucifixion following on the next morning. If so, Jesus must have eaten the Last Supper with the disciples on Thursday evening, which by Jewish reckoning would be the beginning of Friday. Therefore, the Crucifixion and interment would have been concluded just prior to Friday evening, the beginning of the Sabbath. This conclusion accords well with the statement that the interview with Pilate occurred on the "day of Preparation (*paraskeuē*) of Passover Week" (19:14), which would be Friday. Jesus' body was removed from the cross before sunset, since the next day was a "special Sabbath" because of the Passover (19:31). The Sabbath followed immediately.

Lightfoot says that the Last Supper in John is not the normal paschal meal; for upon the dismissal of Judas, the disciples thought Jesus wanted Judas to purchase what might be needed for the feast (13:29) (pp. 352–55). The ritual Passover Feast was eaten on Friday afternoon (18:28), but Jesus died at that time. Perhaps in his mind he was celebrating the Passover early because he knew that he would be arrested prior to the stated feast. Such an interpretation gives a more vivid understanding of Luke's report of Jesus' words: "I have eagerly desired to eat this Passover with you before I suffer" (Luke 22:15).

The tomb was found to be empty on "the first day of the week" (20:1); and in the afternoon of the same day Jesus appeared to the disciples in the Upper Room (v.19). Another manifestation occurred a week later in the same place (v.26). The episode by the Sea of Galilee, which belongs to the Epilogue, is somewhat indefinitely located "afterward" (21:1). John does not attempt a closed chronological system. He locates events by groups, not always completely stating their relation to each other. It would be unfair to say that his chronology is erroneous, though it was not completely systematic.

d. Geographical Structure

The Gospel's structure by location does not seem to follow any particular design, except that it emphasizes Jesus' activity in Jerusalem. He began his work in the region where John was baptizing, either at "Bethany on the other side of the Jordan," near the southern end of the Jordan River, a little north of the Dead Sea (John 1:28), or at Aenon (4:23), which has generally been located either at springs near Mount Gerizim, or at a site 8 miles south of Scythopolis (Beth-shean), on the west side of the Jordan.

There are three allusions to Galilee in the main narrative: (1) an indefinite stay in Capernaum, no particulars of which are chronicled (2:12); (2) the healing of the nobleman's son in Capernaum (4:43–54); and (3) the feeding of the five thousand at Bethsaida on the Sea of Galilee (6:1–15), followed by the address in the synagogue at Capernaum (vv.25–70). Except for the brief visit in Samaria (4:1–42) and in Ephraim (11:54), a city on the border of the Judean wilderness, the narrative of Jesus' action was centered in Jerusalem.

The main purpose of the fourth Gospel is to show, against the background of his opposition, who Jesus was, not to supply a full chronicle of his deeds. Since opposition seemed to come largely from the leaders of the Jewish hierarchy whose headquarters were in Jerusalem, the main scene is laid where the sharpest theological debates occurred and where the closing scenes of Jesus' life took place.

The apparent neglect of the Galilean ministry, with its extensive teaching, does not mean that the author of this Gospel was ignorant of it. Opinion has differed widely as to whether John was familiar with the Synoptic Gospels. Lightfoot declares that his commentary was "written in the belief that the evangelist knew not only the synoptic tradition, but the three Synoptic Gospels themselves" (p. 29). Whether or not John knew the Synoptics cannot be determined with certainty, and there seems to be no indisputable quotation from any of them in the text of his Gospel. On the other hand, there is a sense in which the fourth Gospel complements the others; and often it seems to begin its narrative at a point where the others have stopped, or to assume a knowledge they would supply. An instance of the former appears in the account of the Last Supper. John tells how the disciples reclined for the meal without the customary footwashing as they entered the room and how Jesus himself felt obligated to supply the lack of service (John 13:2–14). Luke tells us how on that occasion the disciples were bickering with one another for the highest place in the coming kingdom (Luke 22:24). If their attitude toward one another was rivalry for the best position in the coming rule of Jesus, it explains why no one was ready to wash the feet of the others.

e. Personal Interviews

One marked feature of John's Gospel is the partiality to personal interviews. The Synoptics emphasize Jesus' public ministry as he talked to the crowds, though they do lay considerable emphasis on the training of the disciples. Although the Gospel does on several occasions say that many believed in him in response to his public actions or appeals (2:23; 4:39; 7:31; 8:30; 10:42; 11:45; 12:11, 42), it records fewer of his general discourses. The personal interviews are rather widely distributed through the earlier part of the Gospel: Nicodemus in Jerusalem (3:1–15), the woman of Samaria (4:1–26), the nobleman of Cana (4:43–53), the paralytic in Jerusalem (5:1–15), the blind man (9:1–38), and Mary and Martha in Bethany (11:17–40). These interviews represent different classes of society, occur at different times during Jesus' career, and have different occasions followed by varying appeals. All of them, however, whether implicitly or explicitly, illustrate the nature and consequences of belief. Some, like the interview with Nicodemus, were with people who became Jesus' lasting followers; others, like the one with the paralytic, seem to have been wholly casual. Each interview is included in some narrative of action and the person interviewed is not simply a wooden figure or puppet used to make an abstract point. All of the interviews depict Jesus' personal concern for people.

The general interviews with groups are similar in content and teaching. In time and place they approximately parallel the individual interviews. "Many" listened to him in Jerusalem (2:23); "many of the Samaritans" received him willingly after his conversation with the woman (4:39); a crowd gathered to hear him in Capernaum after the feeding of the five thousand (6:24–40). And on his last visit to Jerusalem the pilgrims from Galilee (12:12), the followers who had come with him to the Passover (v.17), and the crowd in Jerusalem (vv.29–36) all gave him audience to the last day of his life. In no way does John minimize Jesus' universal appeal, though he says less about Jesus' continual itinerant ministry.

John gives a great deal of attention to Jesus' personal ministry to the disciples. Andrew (1:40; 6:8), Peter (1:42; 6:68; 13:6–9; 18:11; 21:15–22), Philip (1:43–44; 6:5; 12:22; 14:8–10), Nathanael (1:47–51; 21:2), Thomas (11:16; 14:5; 20:26–29), Judas Iscariot (12:4–8; 13:26–30), the other Judas (14:22–24), and Mary of Magdala (20:10–18) received Jesus' compassionate counsel. Although these disciples are not always mentioned by name, they reappear in the narrative frequently enough to show that Jesus had a continuing concern for them.

In contrast, John records interviews with hostile persons. At least six conflicts with "the Jews" are mentioned (2:18–20; 5:16–47; 6:41–59; 7:15–44; 8:31–58; 10:22–39). The title "The Jews" apparently is not given solely for the purpose of distinguishing their nationality from Samaritans or Gentiles but to identify Jesus' opponents. The Pharisees are included under this title in 8:13–29 and in the text of 8:3–9 also. Each of these instances indicates the progress of unbelief that leads to the climax of the Cross. The interview with Pilate is the only instance of a hostile individual confrontation in this Gospel, and Pilate's hostility is due more to his political dilemma than to personal enmity.

These personal interviews, with their varying degrees of success and their wide range of character, demonstrate the breadth of appeal of this Gospel and Jesus' technique in dealing with people. While the interviews do not in themselves constitute a consistent basis for outlining the progressive development of the Gospel, they illustrate it. Thus they serve much the same purpose as pictures in a book. The interviews clearly relate to the main theme and forcibly convey the revelation given through Christ and the effects of the power he exercised. They form a distinct thematic approach to the total teaching of the Gospel.

10. Theological Values

The Gospel of John is predominantly theological. Although all four Gospels present the person of Jesus from a theological viewpoint, John emphasizes it most strongly. His initial assertion—"In the beginning was the Word, and the Word was with God, and the Word was God. . . . The Word became flesh and lived for a while among us" (John 1:1, 14)—declares that Jesus was no ordinary person. He was the incarnation of the eternal God, who chose that means of revealing himself perfectly to men. This declaration is amplified by the further statement of John 1:18; "No one has ever seen God, but God the only [Son], who is at the Father's side, has made him known." Throughout the Gospel the essential deity of the Lord Jesus Christ is stressed.

A second theological aspect is the concept of atonement. Jesus was introduced by John the Baptist as the sacrificial "Lamb of God, who takes away the sin of the world" (John 1:29). Jesus told Nicodemus that "just as Moses lifted up the snake in the desert, so the Son of Man must be lifted up, that everyone who believes in him may have eternal life" (3:14–15). He spoke of his flesh, which he would "give for the life of the world" (6:51), and called himself "the good shepherd [who] lays down his life for the sheep" (10:11). The doctrine of the Atonement is not stated so explicitly as in some of the Pauline writings, but it is unmistakably latent in John's Gospel.

Another prominent theme is eternal life. Life in the sum of its total expression is a major subject of the Prologue: "In him was life, and that life was the light of men" (John 1:4). His gift to believers is eternal life (3:15–16; 10:10; 20:31), bestowed on those who commit themselves to him (3:36; 4:13; 5:21, 24; 8:12).

A very important body of teaching on the person and functions of the Holy Spirit appears in Jesus' farewell discourse to the disciples (John 14:25–26; 15:26; 16:7–15). His intermediary relation between Christ and the believer and his functional relation to God, the believer, and the world are plainly defined.

Perhaps the greatest theological contribution of the Gospel is a full discussion and demonstration of the nature of belief. Both by definition and by example its essence is described. Belief is equated with receiving (1:12), following (1:40), drinking (fig., 4:13), responding (4:51), eating (fig., 6:57), accepting (6:60, lit. "hear"), worship (9:38), obeying (11:39–41), and commitment (12:10–11). The lives of those who "believed" show both the method and result of their faith.

Numerous other theological topics mentioned in John will be discussed in the body of the text. Those that have been cited here suffice to show the wealth of material this Gospel contributes to Christian theology.

11. Canonicity

From a very early date the Gospel of John has been part of the NT canon. The Rylands fragment shows that the Gospel was circulated by the first third of the second century, and the allusions in the Egerton papyrus 2 confirm that conclusion. The Muratorian Canon, an incomplete list of accepted works dating from the second century (c. 170), included John and elaborated on a tradition concerning its origin. Tatian, a pupil of Justin Martyr who alluded to the "Memoirs of the Apostles" (*First Apology* 67), incorporated sections from it in his *Diatessaron,* a combined narrative of the four Gospels, which was widely used in the Syrian church in the second, third, and fourth centuries. Heracleon, a Gnostic, wrote a commentary on the Gospel about 170. He would scarcely have written a commentary on what he did not consider to be an authoritative work, though his personal beliefs were unorthodox. The Bodmer papyri of the early third century contain parts of two copies of this Gospel. The Fathers of the late second century—Irenaeus, Clement of Alexandria, and Tertullian—all accept it as authoritative. By the middle of the third century its place in the canon was fixed. Origen (c. 250) wrote an extensive commentary on it, and the subsequent church councils that had anything to say about the canon all recognized its authority. Eusebius, the church historian of the fourth century, classified the canon by (1) the acknowledged books, (2) the disputed books, and (3) the spurious works. John was classed among the undisputed works. Its canonicity was above question.

12. Text

The text of John is fairly stable. Most of the variants in the MS tradition are not important. There are, however, a few that deserve special comment. See the Notes for a discussion of them in loc.: 1:13; 1:18; 5:4; 7:53–8:11.

Numerous other readings are scattered throughout the text of John, some of which will be noted in the pages of this commentary. Those just mentioned, however, are of greater than average importance. On the whole, the Johannine text has fewer variants than most other NT books.

13. Special Problems

a. *The Relation of John to the Synoptics*

Since both the Gospel of John and the three other Gospels deal with narratives of the life of Jesus, the question of interrelationship naturally occurs. Matthew, Mark, and Luke distinctly resemble one another, not only in general subject and order of narrative but also in many instances of extended discourse. In some of these it would be difficult for anyone but a scholar to identify a given quotation as belonging to any one of the Synoptics, whereas the text of John differs radically in its form and content from the other Gospels.

The Gospel of John parallels the others in general order. It begins with the ministry of John the Baptist, narrates the early contacts with disciples, contains accounts of Jesus' conflicts with the scribes and Pharisees, and places the feeding of the five thousand and the walking on the water at the turning point of his ministry. The story of the Passion Week begins with the entry into Jerusalem and terminates with the Crucifixion and the Resurrection.

On the other hand, John the Baptist's introduction of Jesus to his disciples is highlighted rather than his general preaching-of-repentance ministry. Jesus' initial contact with the disciples is quite different from the calling of the first four disciples as reported elsewhere. The discourses of Jesus in John are mainly apologetic and theological rather than ethical and practical, as in the Sermon on the Mount. Only seven miracles are recounted, and of these only two duplicate those of the Synoptic Gospels. Chronological order is different, for John places a cleansing of the temple early in Jesus' ministry, whereas the Synoptics locate it in Passion Week. The events of the Last Supper, the betrayal, the hearing before Pilate, and the Crucifixion are reported quite differently from the other three Gospels; and the Resurrection account has only slight resemblance to the others.

These phenomena have evoked many questions, and various theories have been advanced to account for them. The similarities are sufficient to establish the identity of the

Jesus of John with the figure of the Synoptics, but the dissimilarities show that John did not lean on the written accounts of Matthew, Mark, and Luke. Whatever interrelationship may have existed between them, there is no convincing evidence that they affected John directly. Reconciliation of the chronological differences and the disparity of content and style may be difficult but it is not impossible. The best conclusion to be drawn is that John was written independently of the others, not simply because he used different sources, but because he had a different purpose in organizing his material. He wrote as a first-hand witness making a special presentation of Jesus. John possessed knowledge of many facts of Jesus' life mentioned in the Synoptics, but he also knew much they did not record. He utilized this material in a different way and shaped it for a different purpose. Each of the Gospel writers presented Jesus in accord with the needs of his readers and out of his own understanding of the Lord. All of them were drawing on the same sources of knowledge and were moved by the same Spirit.

The Johannine style is so different from that of the Synoptics that some scholars have repudiated the historical validity of the Gospel. F.C. Burkitt remarked:

> It is quite inconceivable that the historical Jesus of the Synoptic Gospels could have argued and quibbled with opponents as he is represented to have done in the Fourth Gospel. The only possibility is that the work is not history, but something else in historical form. . . . It is a deliberate sacrifice of historical truth, and as the evangelist is a serious person in deadly earnest, we must conclude that he cared less for truth than for something else (pp. 225, 228).

The current opinion concerning the historicity of John is not quite so drastic as that of Burkitt, whose conclusion overlooks the fact that a writer may have different styles for different occasions. The bulk of the teaching recorded in the first three Gospels was delivered to crowds that gathered to hear his words of wisdom or to opponents who contended with him. The larger part of the teaching in the fourth Gospel (e.g., John 14:17) was intended for the ears of his disciples only. A short passage in Matthew and another in Luke (Matt 11:25–30; Luke 10:21–22) are in similar style. Although these passages are brief, they are sufficient to show that Jesus could, and undoubtedly did, use both approaches in dealing with his contemporaries. Luke indicates that these words were spoken to the seventy-two disciples (NIV) after they had returned from a preaching tour rather than to the multitude at large.

b. Historical and Theological Interpretation

The interpretation of this Gospel has varied from regarding it as a historical narrative containing the *ipsissima verba* (very words) of Jesus to a mythological creation of an anonymous writer who used the name of Jesus to support his approach to Christianity. It may be conceded that the author's interest was primarily theological rather than biographical; indeed, all four Gospels contain theological interpretations of Jesus. The conclusions of any commentator on this aspect of John will be influenced as much by his personal suppositions as by the text. If he regards Jesus as merely a wandering Galilean prophet who happened to possess a singularly devout nature coupled with profound psychological insight, he would almost inevitably treat the Gospel as an allegory or fiction or both. If, on the other hand, he begins with the conviction of the author that "the Word became flesh and lived for a while among us" (John 1:14), he will conclude that the theological nature of the career of Jesus was inescapable and that there could be no other way of interpreting him or the Gospel. If Jesus was the Son of God, any attempted account of him would inevitably be theological; otherwise, it would not do him justice.

The author himself took this viewpoint when he stated that "these [things] are written that you may believe that Jesus is the Christ, the Son of God" (John 20:31). He did not, however, attempt to implement this purpose either by emotional appeal to imaginary scenes or by purely syllogistic reasoning. Like the Synoptics, John used occurrences in the life of Jesus to illustrate his teaching and gave no hint that they were imaginary. The events themselves are actual; the principles they exemplify may be abstract.

Furthermore, if the writer of the fourth Gospel did emphasize theology more than the authors of the Synoptics, he must have had a reason for doing so. The claims and deeds of Jesus, which John professes to have known and not to have fully recorded (John 20:30), demanded an explanation beyond ordinary cause and effect. Even if the author granted that the "signs" were narrated to illustrate some theological principle, it is still logical to believe they were selected because they had that inherent significance and were not composed for the occasion. The significance of the "signs" is determined by what Jesus actually said and did, not by the author's imagination.

While the intent of the author was neither to produce a complete biography of Jesus nor to recount all the miracles he did, there is no need to assume that he fabricated stories. As a matter of fact, the authors of the Synoptics also recount miracles; and while they do not always make their conclusions as explicit theologically as John does, their procedure is much the same. The events recorded in John are historical, though their exact sequence is not always clear. The deductions drawn from them are the basis for Johannine theology.

c. Displacement of Text

The existence of seeming gaps in the order of the fourth Gospel has led some scholars to speculate that the text may have suffered from disarrangement. For instance, some have suggested that the narrative makes better sense if chs. 5 and 6 are inverted. Chapter 6 opens with Jesus crossing "to the far shore of the Sea of Galilee," which had not been mentioned in the preceding context, the scene of which is laid in Jerusalem. John 5 begins with an unnamed feast in Jerusalem that Jesus attended. Since ch. 4 concludes in Galilee, there is a much more natural connection to another event in the same territory if ch. 6 follows at this point. Yet the same abruptness would appear if ch. 7 were to follow ch. 5 immediately. There is no hint in the MS tradition that such a displacement ever occurred. An arbitrary rearrangement of the text only creates another problem in the place of the one that it attempts to solve. Hunter remarks that, while scribal displacements might have occurred, "all such rearranging implies that we know the order John intended—a pretty big assumption" (p. 2).

A further difficulty arises from the size of the so-called displaced segments. If they were all the same length or multiples of the same length, the theory of wrongly arranged codex pages would be plausible. The segments, however, are of odd lengths that cannot be reduced to multiples of the same unit. It is, therefore, unlikely that any accidental dislocation would occur; and there is no convincing reason for concluding that the theoretical displacements were intended. If the author's order does not coincide with our theories, it is better to admit that he has simply utilized episodes without holding strictly to chronological or topographical sequence.

14. Bibliography

Commentaries

Barrett, C.K. *The Gospel According to John.* London: SPCK, 1958.
Bernard, J.H. *The Gospel of John.* ICC. 2 vols. New York: Scribner, 1929.
Brown, Raymond E. *The Gospel According to John.* AB. Vols. 29, 29A. Garden City, N.Y.: Doubleday, 1966, 1970.
Hendriksen, William. *Exposition of the Gospel According to John.* New Testament Commentary. 2 vols. Grand Rapids: Baker, 1953–54.
Hunter, A.M. *The Gospel According to John.* Cambridge Bible Commentary. Edited by P.R. Ackroyd, C.R.C. Leaney, J.W. Packer. Cambridge: Cambridge University, 1965.
Lightfoot, R.H. *St. John's Gospel: A Commentary.* Edited by C.F. Evans. London: Oxford University, 1969.
Lindars, Barnabas. *The Gospel of John.* NCB. London: Oliphants, 1972.
Marsh, John. *The Gospel of St. John.* Pelican New Testament Commentaries. Edited by D.E. Nineham. Hammondsworth, Middlesex, England: Penguin Books, 1972.
Morgan, G. Campbell. *The Gospel of John.* Old Tappan, N.J.: Revell, n.d.
Morris, Leon. *The Gospel According to St. John.* NIC. Grand Rapids: Eerdmans, 1971.
Sanders, J.M., and Mastin, B.A. *The Gospel According to St. John.* Black's New Testament Commentaries. London: Adam & Charles Black, 1968.
Turner, George A., and Mantey, J.R. *The Gospel According to St. John.* Evangelical Commentary. Grand Rapids: Eerdmans, 1964.
Westcott, B.F. *The Gospel According to St. John.* 2 vols. London: John Murray, 1908.

Special Studies

Boice, James. *Witness and Revelation in the Gospel of John.* Grand Rapids: Zondervan, 1970.
Dodd, C.H. *The Interpretation of the Fourth Gospel.* Cambridge: Cambridge University, 1965.
Edwards, H.E. *The Disciple Who Wrote These Things.* London: James Clarke & Co., 1953.
Gardner-Smith, P. *St. John and the Synoptic Gospels.* Cambridge: Cambridge University, 1938.
Headlam, A.C. *The Fourth Gospel as History.* Oxford: Basil Blackwell, 1948.
Higgins, A.J.B. *Jesus and the Son of Man.* Philadelphia: Fortress, 1964.
Hoare, F.R. *Original Order and Chapters of St. John's Gospel.* London: Burns, Oates, & Washbourne, 1944.
Macgregor, G.H.C., and Morton, A.Q. *The Structure of the Fourth Gospel.* Grand Rapids: Eerdmans, 1948.
Morris, Leon. *Studies in the Fourth Gospel.* Grand Rapids: Eerdmans, 1969.
Tenney, Merrill C. *John: The Gospel of Belief.* Grand Rapids: Eerdmans, 1948.

Articles

Albright, W.F. "The Dead Sea Scrolls." *The American Scholar* 23 (1952–53): 77–85. Washington, D.C.: United Chapters of Phi Beta Kappa.
———. "Recent Discoveries in Palestine and the Gospel of John" in *The Background of the New Testament and Its Eschatology,* edited by L.A. Davis and D. Daube. Cambridge: Cambridge University, 1956, pp. 153–71.
Goodenough, Erwin R. "John: A Primitive Gospel." JBL 64 (1945), Part II, 145–182.
Haas, N. "Anthropological Observations on the Skeletal Remains from Giv'at ha-Mivtar." IEJ 20 (1970): 49–59.
Hanhart, K. "The Structure of John 1:35–54." In *Studies in John: Presented to Dr. J.H. Sevenster on the Occasion of His Seventieth Birthday.* Leiden: Brill, 1970.

Hoehner, Harold. "The Significance of the Year of Our Lord's Crucifixion for NT Interpretation." In *New Dimensions in New Testament Study,* edited by R.N. Longenecker and M.C. Tenney. Grand Rapids: Zondervan, 1974, pp. 115–25.

Metzger, B.M. "On the Translation of John 1:1." ET 63 (1951–52): 125.

Tenney, Merrill C. "The Footnotes of John's Gospel." BS 117 (1960): 350–64.

General Works

Bell, H.I., and Skeat, T.C. *Fragments of an Unknown Gospel.* London: Trustees of the British Museum, 1935.

Burkitt, F.C. *The Gospel History and Its Transmission.* Edinburgh: T. & T. Clark, 1906.

Gaster, Theodor H., ed. *The Dead Sea Scriptures in English Translation.* Garden City, N.Y.: Doubleday, 1956.

Metzger, B.M. *A Textual Commentary on the Greek New Testament.* New York: UBS, 1971.

Roberts, C.H., ed. *An Unpublished Fragment of the Fourth Gospel.* Manchester: Manchester University, Press. 1935.

Robinson, J.A.T. *Redating the New Testament.* Philadelphia: Westminster, 1976.

Smith, William, and Wace, Henry. *A Dictionary of Biography.* 4 vols. London: John Murray, 1880.

Stauffer, Ethelbert. *Jesus and His Story.* New York: Alfred Knopf, 1959.

Torrey, C.C. *The Four Gospels.* New York: Harper, 1933.

Turner, C.H. *Historical Geography of the Holy Land.* Washington, D.C.: Canon Press. 1973.

15. Outline and Map

I. Prologue: Revelation of the Word (1:1–18)
   A. The Preincarnate Word (1:1–5)
   B. The Prophetic Announcement (1:6–8, 15)
   C. The Reception of the Word (1:9–13)
   D. The Incarnation of the Word (1:14, 16–18)

II. The Public Ministry of the Word (1:19–12:50)
   A. The Beginning Ministry (1:19–4:54)
      1. The witness of John the Baptist (1:19–34)
      2. The first disciples (1:35–51)
      3. The first sign (2:1–11)
      4. The interlude at Capernaum (2:12)
      5. The cleansing of the temple (2:13–22)
      6. The interview with Nicodemus (2:23–3:21)
         a. Nicodemus's visit (2:23–3:15)
         b. The author's comment (3:16–21)
      7. Further testimony of John the Baptist (3:22–36)
      8. The Samaritan ministry (4:1–42)
         a. The woman at the well (4:1–26)
         b. The return of the disciples (4:27–38)
         c. The faith of the Samaritans (4:39–42)
      9. The interview with the nobleman (4:43–54)
   B. The Rise of Controversy (5:1–47)
      1. The healing of the paralytic (5:1–15)
      2. Jesus' defense of his sonship (5:16–47)
         a. The prerogatives of sonship (5:16–30)
         b. The witnesses to his authority (5:31–47)
   C. The Beginning of Conflict (6:1–8:59)
      1. The feeding of the five thousand (6:1–15)
      2. The walking on the water (6:16–21)
      3. The address in the synagogue (6:22–59)
      4. The division among the disciples (6:60–71)
      5. The visit to Jerusalem (7:1–52)
         a. The journey (7:1–13)
         b. The popular debate (7:14–36)
         c. The climactic appeal (7:37–44)
         d. The rejection by the leaders (7:45–52)
      6. [The woman taken in adultery (7:53–8:11)]
   D. The Intensification of Controversy (8:12–59)
      1. Teaching in the temple area (8:12–30)
      2. The discourse to professed believers (8:31–47)
      3. The response of the unbelievers (8:48–59)
   E. The Manifestation of Opposition (9:1–11:57)
      1. The healing of the blind man (9:1–41)
         a. The healing (9:1–12)
         b. The consequences (9:13–41)
      2. The Good Shepherd discourse (10:1–21)
      3. The debate in Solomon's Colonnade (10:22–42)

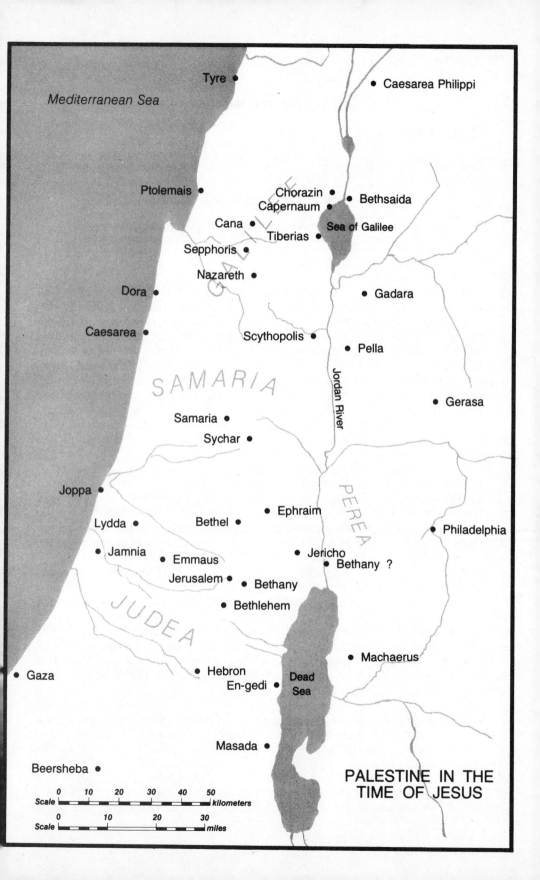

Mediterranean Sea

Tyre

Caesarea Philippi

Ptolemais

Chorazin
Capernaum
Bethsaida

Cana
Tiberias
Sea of Galilee

GALILEE

Sepphoris

Nazareth

Dora

Gadara

Caesarea

Scythopolis

Pella

SAMARIA

Jordan River

Gerasa

Samaria

Sychar

PEREA

Joppa

Bethel
Ephraim

Lydda

Philadelphia

Jamnia
Emmaus

Jericho
Bethany ?

Jerusalem
Bethany

Bethlehem

JUDEA

Machaerus

Gaza

Hebron
En-gedi
Dead
Sea

Masada

Beersheba

Scale 0 10 20 30 40 50 kilometers

Scale 0 10 20 30 miles

PALESTINE IN THE
TIME OF JESUS

Text and Exposition

I. Prologue: Revelation of the Word (1:1–18)

A. *The Preincarnate Word*

1:1–5

> [1]In the beginning was the Word, and the Word was with God, and the Word was God. [2]He was with God in the beginning.
> [3]Through him all things were made; without him nothing was made that has been made. [4]In him was life, and that life was the light of men. [5]The light shines in the darkness, but the darkness has not understood it.

1 "In the beginning" recalls the opening words of Genesis 1:1: "In the beginning God created the heavens and the earth." The expression does not refer to a particular moment of time but assumes a timeless eternity. "Word" is the Greek *logos*, which has several meanings. Ordinarily it refers to a spoken word, with emphasis on the meaning conveyed, not just the sound. *Logos*, therefore, is an expression of personality in communication. Scripture also tells us that it is creative in its power: "By the word [*logos*, LXX] of the Lord were the heavens made, their starry host by the breath of his mouth" (Ps 33:6). This verse clearly implies that the expression of God had creative power and called the universe into being. To the Hebrew "the word of God" was the self-assertion of the divine personality; to the Greek the formula denoted the rational mind that ruled the universe. John is asserting that the "Word" is the source of all that is visible and antedates the totality of the material world.

The use of *logos* implies that John was endeavoring to bring out the full significance of the Incarnation to the Gentile world as well as to the Jewish people. He does not adopt the Greek concept in its entirety, but he uses this term to indicate that Jesus had universal rather than local significance and that he spoke with ultimate authority. He was preexistent, involved in the act of creation, and therefore superior to all created beings. This presentation lifts Christ above the materialistic, pagan concept of deities just as the Incarnation brings the Hebrew concept of God into everyday life.

The preposition "with" in the phrase "the Word was with God" indicates both equality and distinction of identity along with association. The phrase can be rendered "face to face with." It may, therefore, imply personality, coexistence with the Creator, and yet be an expression of his creative being. The position of the noun *God* in the Greek text marks it as a predicate, stressing description rather than individualization. The "Word" was deity, one with God, rather than "a god" or another being of the same class. This is the real meaning of the phrase. Unity of nature rather than similarity or likeness is implied. The external coexistence and unity of the Word with God is unmistakably asserted.

2 This verse may seem to be repetitious, and it is just that, but with divine intent. John succinctly summarizes the great truths of v.1 by the effective means of restatement. The Word's preexistence, distinctiveness, and deity are brought out in the statement "he was with God in the beginning."

3 The word "made" (*egeneto*) has the meaning "became" rather than "constructed." The action refers to an event rather than a process. The visible universe with all its complexity owes its origin to the creative mind and power of God. Apart from his Word, existence is impossible. The pricrity of Christ over creation is taught here and it also is mentioned in Colossians 1:16 and Hebrews 1:2.

4 The term "life" (*zōē*) is uniformly used throughout the Gospel. Wherever it appears, it refers either to the principle of physical life (vitality) or, most often, to spiritual life. Frequently it is coupled with the adjective "eternal" to denote the quality and power of the believer's life. It occurs thirty-six times in John. The life was embodied in Christ, who demonstrated perfectly what eternal life is by his career (cf. John 14:6; 17:3). Christ is the "life" that is the "light of men." In him God's purpose and power are made available to men. He is their ultimate hope.

5 The metaphorical contrast between light and darkness as representing the powers of good and evil was common in John's day. The same imagery appears in the Qumran Scrolls, one of which is *The War of the Sons of Light and the Sons of Darkness*. A better translation of v.5b is "The darkness did not overcome it," for the underlying verb (*katelaben*) can be translated both ways. John, however, uses it elsewhere only in the sense of "overtake" or "overcome" (John 6:17; [8:3–4]; 12:35).

Notes

1 The preexistence of the Word is strongly brought out by the phrase Ἐν ἀρχῇ ἦν ὁ λόγος (*en archē ēn ho logos*, "in the beginning was the word"). Ἀρχῇ (*archē*) according to H. Bietenhard "is an important term in Gk. philosophy," which means, among other things, "starting point, original beginning" (DNTT, 1:164). By itself, this may not seem too significant, for few would debate that we are dealing with the "original beginning." It is the presence of the verb ἦν (*ēn*, "was") that brings out the importance of this phrase. Literally, it could and should be rendered "When the beginning began, the Word was already there." This is the sense of *ēn*, which is in the imperfect tense and implies continuing existence in the past. So before the beginning began, the Word was already in existence. This is tantamount to saying that the Word predates time or Creation.

The three statements of v.1 bring out three different aspects of the nature of the Word. The first speaks of his preexistence (see above). The second statement, "The Word was with God," is an assertion of the Word's distinctiveness. The preposition πρὸς (*pros*) indicates both equality and distinction of identity. Robertson says, "The literal idea comes out well, 'face to face with God'" (RHG, p. 623). Thus this implies personality and coexistence with God. Robertson says it bespeaks of "the fellowship between the Logos and God."

The third statement, "The Word was God," is especially significant. This is a clear statement of deity inasmuch as the noun θεός (*theos*, "God") is anarthrous; that is, it lacks the article. Much confusion has spawned over this point of Gr. grammar. Robertson et al. have aptly demonstrated that the lack of the article in the predicate is intentional so that the subject can be distinguished. In other words, in the phrase θεὸς ἦν ὁ λόγος (*theos ēn ho logos*, "God was the Word"), were it not for the article ὁ (*ho*) before the word λόγος (*logos*), the subject of the phrase would be indeterminate. But the presence of the article shows that it is the "Word" that is the subject. The fact that *theos* is a predicate shows that it is describing the nature of the Word; he is of the same nature and essence as the noun in the predicate; that is, the Word is divine (RHG, p. 767).

E.C. Colwell says that "a predicate nominative which precedes the verb cannot be translated as an indefinite or 'qualitative' noun solely because of the absence of the article; if the context suggests that the predicate is definite, it should be translated as a definite noun in spite of the absence of the article. In the case of a predicate noun which follows the verb the reverse is true; the absence of the article in this position is a much more reliable indication that the noun is indefinite" ("A Definite Rule for the Use of the Article in the Greek New Testament," JBL 52 [1933]: 20–21).

To say that the absence of the article bespeaks of the nonabsolute deity of the Word is sheer folly. There are many places in this Gospel where the anarthrous *theos* appears (e.g., 1:6, 12, 13, 18), and not once is the implication that this is referring to just "a god."

3 It is significant that the verb used three times in this v. is different from that used in the previous two vv. In vv.1–2 the verb is the imperfect of εἰμί (*eimi*, "to be"), ἦν (*ēn*, "was"), which is a verb describing a state of being. In v.3, however, the verb γίνομαι (*ginomai*, "to become") is used, which has the force of "coming into being." This, then, is another assertion of the deity of the Word. Through him all things "came into being," ἐγένετο (*egeneto*), but he always was (*ēn*). This latter truth is emphasized by the "I am's" of Christ mentioned throughout this Gospel.

5 Καταλαμβάνω (*katalambanō*, "overcome," which is the mg. reading in NIV) is a very forceful word. B. Siede says it "is used in the NT to designate the attack of evil powers. . . . The lad with epilepsy was attacked by a dumb spirit and dashed to the ground (Mark 9:18)" (TDNT, 3:750). Considering John's underlying concept of the battle between good and evil, perhaps "understood" is too mild a rendering. Metaphorically we have a preview of the triumph of light over darkness, which is later personified in Christ's work on the Cross.

B. *The Prophetic Announcement*

1:6–8, 15

> ⁶There came a man who was sent from God; his name was John. ⁷He came as a witness to testify concerning that light, so that through him all men might believe. ⁸He himself was not the light; he came only as a witness to the light.
> ¹⁵John testifies concerning him. He cries out, saying, "This was he of whom I said, 'He who comes after me has surpassed me because he was before me.'"

6 In vv.6–8 the human agent for introducing the Word to men is presented. This Gospel stresses the function of John the Baptist rather than his origin or character, as Luke does (Luke 1:5–24, 57–80). John takes for granted that the Baptist's identity was known by the reader. He states his importance as the forerunner of Christ but emphasizes his subordinate role (cf. John 3:22–30). Possibly this was directed toward the sect that survived John and perpetuated his teaching but had no knowledge of the completion of the work of Christ (Acts 18:24–25; 19:1–7). The important thing about John the Baptist was that he was "sent." The use of this word refers to the authority that commissioned him; the identification by name is incidental. John's function is defined in v.7.

7–8 "Witness" is distinctly a Johannine word. It is especially pertinent in this Gospel, which is an attempt to establish by adequate testimony the claims of Jesus as the Son of God. The preaching of John the Baptist, which must have been known to the readers of the fourth Gospel, was preparatory to the coming of the Christ. The Synoptics agree with John on this point (Matt 3:11–12; Mark 1:1–8; Luke 1:17; 3:15–17). John the Baptist told the crowds listening to him that he was only the forerunner of another who would confer on them the Holy Spirit and that they must repent, or change their attitude, in anticipation of meeting him. The author was careful to specify that John the Baptist was not the genuine light but that he came to attest it.

Although vv.6–8 seem alien to the general content of the text, they are not irrelevant. As the Word came to bring the heavenly light to humanity, so John came to speak from a human level and to awaken people to their need of God's revelation.

15 The author reverts to the witness of John the Baptist to explain further the Baptist's position as to Christ. The manifestation of Jesus came after John's appearance, but in importance Jesus took precedence over him. "Surpassed" (*emprosthen*) is the translation of an adverb that denotes positional precedence, whereas "before" (*prōtos*, lit. "first") refers to rank of importance. Jesus surpassed John because he was intrinsically greater.

Notes

6 Ἐγένετο (*egeneto*, "came") is the aorist of γίνομαι (*ginomai*), which was identified as a verb signifying "coming into being" (see Note on v.3). In the Gr. the contrast between the Word's state of always "being" and that of John the Baptist's "coming into being" is unmistakable. Morris says, "Jesus 'was' in the beginning. John 'came into existence'" (NIC, p. 88).

C. *The Reception of the Word*

   1:9-13

> [9]The true light that gives light to every man was coming into the world.
> [10]He was in the world, and though the world was made through him, the world did not recognize him. [11]He came to that which was his own, but his own did not receive him. [12]Yet to all who received him, to those who believed in his name, he gave the right to become children of God—[13]children born not of natural descent, nor of human decision or a husband's will, but born of God.

9 "True" (*alēthinon*) means "real" or "genuine" as opposed to "facsimile" or "secondary" rather than "false." Christ is the real light of humanity who was about to enter the world. The text should be understood to mean, not that he had already illumined everyone, but that his function would be to give the light of truth to all whom his ministry would affect, whether in greater or lesser degree. The translation is somewhat ambiguous because the participle "coming" used with the verb "was" may refer either to "light" or to "man." An alternate translation is "he was the real light that illuminates every man as he comes into the world." In this context the action of coming better fits the advent of the light than the arrival of every man.

10 "World" (*kosmos*) refers to the current organization or culture in which people live, whether applied to the natural environment (John 16:21) or to the present order as contrasted with the spiritual order (6:14; 9:39; 11:27; 16:28; 18:37). Here it plainly refers to the total environment that the Word created (1:3). The second part of the verse places the emphasis on the ancient world of men and women who did not recognize him. The aorist tense of the verb "know" (*egnō*) implies that there was no flash of awareness concerning his real person. Compare the statement of his opponents on a later occasion: "Isn't this the carpenter's son?" (Matt 13:55).

11 In the phrase "he came to that which was his own, but his own did not receive him," the former "own" refers to things; and the phrase may mean "his own property" or "his home" as in John 19:27. The latter "own" refers to "his own people," the nation he belonged to. Jesus came to the place he had created and had a right to possess. Those who inhabited it turned him away in rejection.

12–13 Just as there is a sharp antithesis in vv.4–5 between darkness and light, so here is an equally direct contrast between rejection and reception. In spite of the many who rejected the Word, there were some who received him. This provides the initial definition of "believe" by equating it with "receive." When we accept a gift, whether tangible or intangible, we thereby demonstrate our confidence in its reality and trustworthiness. We make it part of our own possessions. By being so received, Jesus gives to those who receive him a right to membership in the family of God.

"Become" indicates clearly that people are not the spiritual children of God by natural birth, for we cannot become what we already are. This verb implies a change of nature. The word *children* (*tekna*) is parallel to the Scottish *bairns*—"born ones." It emphasizes vital origin and is used as a term of endearment (cf. Luke 15:31). Believers are God's "little ones," related to him by birth. "Not of natural descent" excludes a purely physical process; "nor of human decision" rules out the result of any biological urge; "or a husband's will" shows that this kind of birth is not merely the outcome of a legal marriage. The relation is spiritual, not biological. NEB translates: ". . . not born of human stock, or by the fleshly desire of a human father." There is a connection with the concept of the new birth, elaborated in Jesus' conversation with Nicodemus (John 3:3–8). There also the writer lays the emphasis on believing, though his approach is different.

Notes

13 In a very few MSS the relative pronoun οἱ (*hoi*, which is rendered "children" in the NIV) and its following verb ἐγεννήθησαν (*egennēthēsan*) are singular ὃς ἐγεννήθη (*hos egennēthē*), not plural. In this case the passage should be translated: "Who was born not of natural descent, nor of human decision or of a husband's will, but born of God." The MS evidence is so slight and so late that it would probably never have been considered had not Tertullian, one of the Latin church fathers at the end of the second century, insisted that it was the correct reading (Tertullian *De Carne Christi* 19). A few quotations from the Latin fathers support his contention, but the reading does not occur in any Greek MSS and is, therefore, regarded as unauthentic.

D. *The Incarnation of the Word*

1:14, 16–18

14The Word became flesh and lived for a while among us. We have seen his glory, the glory of the one and only ⸌Son⸍, who came from the Father, full of grace and truth.
16From the fullness of his grace we have all received one blessing after another. 17For the law was given through Moses; grace and truth came through Jesus Christ. 18No one has ever seen God, but God the only ⸌Son⸍, who is at the Father's side, has made him known.

14 Verse 14 marks the fourth statement about the Word in this introduction to the presentation of Jesus. Note the contrast between vv.1 and 14. Verse 1 states that the Word "was," referring to its permanent condition or state, while v.14 states that the Word "became" flesh, involving a change in state. This is the basic statement of the Incarnation, for Christ entered into a new dimension of existence through the gateway of human birth and took up his residence among men. The verb translated "lived" means "to pitch a tent, to dwell temporarily" (BAG, p. 762). He left his usual place and accepted the conditions of human life and environment, with the attendant temporal limitations that all humans experience. Allusions to this appear elsewhere in various sections of the Gospel (3:17; 6:38–42, 51; 7:29; 8:23; 9:5; 10:36; 16:28).

John's presentation of Christ as the Word is not primarily metaphysical but practical (cf. comment in v.1). The term *Logos* was used by the philosophers of the day, particularly the Stoics, to express the central principle of the universe, the spirit that pervaded the world, or the ultimate Reason that controlled all things. John did not superimpose the philosophical concept on the person of Christ, but he adopted the Greek term as the best medium of expressing the nature of Christ. As the preexistent Son of God, he was the Creator of the world and the Executor of the will of the Father. As the incarnate Son of God, he exercised in his human existence these same powers and revealed effectively the person of the Father.

The writer indicates that he is not speculating on a philosophical concept but is bearing witness to an experiential reality. "We have seen his glory" implies a personal observation of a new reality. Probably there is an allusion to the Transfiguration (Matt 17:2–8; Mark 9:2–8; Luke 9:28–36), when Jesus appeared with a divine radiance and the voice of God acknowledged him as his beloved Son. His incarnation was the full manifestation of grace and truth because it was the greatest possible expression of God's compassion for people and the most perfect way of conveying the truth to their understanding.

The "one and only Son" represents the Greek *monogenēs*, which is derived from *genos*, which means "kind" or "species." It means "literally 'one of a kind,' 'only,' 'unique' (*unicus*), not 'only-begotten.' ... The emphasis is on the thought that, as the 'only' Son of God, He has no equal and is able fully to reveal the Father" (MM, pp. 416–17). God's personal revelation of himself in Christ has no parallel elsewhere, nor has it ever been repeated.

16 Verse 15 has already been discussed as part of the section concerning John the Baptist. Verse 16 connects directly with v.14, which says that the Son was full of the grace and truth of the Father. The writer reminds his readers that they have already experienced that grace in increasing measure. "One blessing after another" is an attempt to express in modern English the Greek phrase "grace in exchange for [*anti*] grace." When one supply of grace is exhausted, another is available.

17 The contrast between law and grace as methods of God's dealing with men is expressed here as plainly as in the Pauline writings (see Rom 5:20–21; Eph 2:8). The law represented God's standard of righteousness; grace exhibited his attitude to human beings who found that they could not keep the law. This attitude was depicted in the person and life of Jesus. This contrast has a parallel in the argument of Hebrews 3:5–6: "Moses was faithful as a servant in all God's house, testifying to what would be said in the future. But Christ is faithful as a son over God's house." Hebrews stresses the superiority of the Son to a servant. The servant can by his commission administer the law of the house correctly. The Son, who is the ruler of the house, can act with ultimate authority that surpasses the authority of the servant. Compare the words of Jesus in the Sermon on the Mount: "You have heard that it was said. . . . But I tell you" (Matt 5:21–22, 27–28, 33–34, 38–39, 43–44).

18 The noun *God* (*theon*) has no article in the Greek text, which indicates that the author is presenting God in his nature of being rather than as a person. "Deity" might be a more accurate rendering. The meaning is that no human has ever seen the essence of deity. God is invisible, not because he is unreal, but because physical eyes are incapable of detecting him. The infrared and ultraviolet rays of the light spectrum are invisible because the human eye is not sensitive enough to register them. However, photographic plates or a spectroscope can make them visible to us. Deity as a being is consequently known only through spiritual means that are able to receive its (his) communications.

"At the Father's side" is substantially the same expression as that used in John 13:23 concerning "the disciple whom Jesus loved," who "was reclining next to him." It shows intimate association, which presupposes close fellowship. As the confidant of the Father, Jesus is peculiarly qualified to act as the intermediary who can carry the knowledge of God to men. The word translated "is" is more accurately rendered "being," since it is a present participle. This implies constant relationship and presupposes preincarnate existence.

The phrase "has made him known" (*exēgēsato*) comes from the verb from which "exegesis" is derived, which means to "explain" or "interpret." The being and nature of God, which cannot be perceived directly by ordinary senses, has been adequately presented to us by the Incarnation. Obviously the author implies that his writing gives an adequate record of this revelation. The life and words of Jesus are more than an announcement; they are an explanation of God's attitude toward men and of his purpose for them.

Notes

14 Ὡς μονογενοῦς (*hōs monogenous*, "as an only begotten") is another controversial term. The critics of Christ's deity stress the "begotten" aspect, thus asserting that Christ was a "created" being, and this notwithstanding the strong statements to the contrary in vv.1–3. Marcus Dods decries the emphasis on the absoluteness of the phrase by saying, "Ὡς introduces an illustrative comparison, as is indicated by the anarthrous μονογενοῦς. Holtzmann expands thus: 'The impression which the glory made was so specific a character that it could be taken for nothing less than such a glory as an only son has from a father, that is, as the only one of its kind; for besides the μονογενής a father has no other sons' " (EGT, 1:690). Westcott says, "The thought in the original is centered in the personal Being of the Son and not in His generation. Christ is the One only Son, the One to whom the title belongs in a sense completely unique and singular" (p. 12).

18 The phrase "one and only Son" follows the majority of Gr. MSS, which read ὁ μονογενὴς υἱός (*ho monogenēs huios*). A number of MSS, including the two oldest papyri, read "only God" (μονογενὴς θεὸς, *monogenēs theos*). This is supported by a large number of quotations from the Fathers and several other MSS that also include the article ὁ (*ho*). If the rule is accepted that the more difficult reading is preferred—the latter reading in this case—there can be no doubt that this text also asserts the deity of Christ.

II. The Public Ministry of the Word (1:19–12:50)

Having introduced the figure of the incarnate Word by the Prologue, and having identified the forerunner by his name and by his mission, the author proceeds to present the ministry of the Word in some detail. Broadly, the book can be divided into two sections: the public and the private ministries of Christ. The former occupies the larger chronological section; the latter is brief and is closely related to the Passion, which concludes the narrative.

A. The Beginning Ministry (1:19–4:54)

1. The witness of John the Baptist

1:19–34

> [19]Now this was John's testimony when the Jews of Jerusalem sent priests and Levites to ask him who he was. [20]He did not fail to confess, but confessed freely, "I am not the Christ."
> [21]They asked him, "Then who are you? Are you Elijah?"
> He said, "I am not."
> "Are you the Prophet?"
> He answered, "No."
> [22]Finally they said, "Who are you? Give us an answer to take back to those who sent us. What do you say about yourself?"
> [23]John replied in the words of Isaiah the prophet, "I am the voice of one calling in the desert, 'Make straight the way for the Lord.'"
> [24]Now some Pharisees who had been sent [25]questioned him, "Why then do you baptize if you are not the Christ, nor Elijah, nor the Prophet?"
> [26]"I baptize with water," John replied, "but among you stands one you do not know. [27]He is the one who comes after me, the thongs of whose sandals I am not worthy to untie."
> [28]This all happened at Bethany on the other side of the Jordan, where John was baptizing.
> [29]The next day John saw Jesus coming toward him and said, "Look, the Lamb of God, who takes away the sin of the world! [30]This is the one I meant when I said, 'A man who comes after me has surpassed me because he was before me.' [31]I myself did not know him, but the reason I came baptizing with water was that he might be revealed to Israel."
> [32]Then John gave this testimony: "I saw the Spirit come down from heaven as a dove and remain on him. [33]I would not have known him, except that the one who sent me to baptize with water told me, 'The man on whom you see the Spirit come down and remain is he who will baptize with the Holy Spirit.' [34]I have seen and I testify that this is the Son of God."

19 The miracle of the Incarnation called for witnesses to substantiate its reality. First in order is that of John the Baptist. His preaching attracted such large crowds that the Jewish hierarchy in Jerusalem decided to investigate him. The priests represented the theological authorities of the nation; the Levites were concerned with the ritual and service of the temple. John did not seem to fit into any ecclesiastical category familiar to the Jewish authorities, and his unusual success demanded an explanation.

20 "Christ" is the Greek equivalent of the Hebrew "Messiah," meaning "Anointed." It was the title of the prophesied deliverer, who would bring renewal and political freedom to Israel (cf. John 4:25). John the Baptist disclaimed the title because it had political implications that would have made him appear to the Romans as a potential insurrectionist.

21-22 The suggestion that John the Baptist might be identified with Elijah reflected the Jewish expectation that the return of Elijah would precede the advent of the Messiah. Malachi had prophesied: "See, I will send you the prophet Elijah before that great and dreadful day of the Lord comes. He will turn the hearts of the fathers to their children, and the hearts of the children to their fathers; or else I will come and strike the land with a curse" (Mal 4:5-6). Because John's rough exterior and ascetic tendencies corresponded to Elijah's type of personality (cf. Mark 6:14), some identified him with the stormy prophet who had challenged Ahab (1 Kings 17-19). John rejected the suggestion and denied that he was Elijah raised from the dead. Again they asked, "Are you the Prophet?" referring probably to God's word to Moses: "The Lord your God will raise up for you a prophet like me from among your own brothers. You must listen to him" (Deut 18:15). The identity of "the Prophet" is not clear; and numerous speculations have been offered. Obviously the investigating committee was still uncertain of it. The populace of Jerusalem later ventured the same guess (John 7:40). Since the prophecy said that he would be like Moses, the Jews were inquiring whether Jesus would lead them in a new Exodus and overcome their enemies. When John disclaimed identity with all these persons, the delegation demanded in exasperation, "Who are you?"

23 The reference to Isaiah is taken from the opening words of the second section of the prophet's writing, which deals with the long-range prophecies of the future. It uses the figure of preparing a road for the king through open and uneven territory so that he may travel over a smooth highway. John the Baptist called himself the "roadbuilder" for one greater than he who would follow him with a fuller revelation. Isaiah said that "the glory of the Lord will be revealed, and all mankind together will see it" (Isa 40:5). This "glory" was revealed in the person of Jesus, of whom the writer of the Gospel said, "We have seen his glory" (1:14).

24-25 The Pharisees represented the strict interpreters of the Law and were particularly interested in examining the credentials of any new religious teacher in Judaism. John does not show unvarying hostility toward them. Nicodemus was a Pharisee and was apparently a sincere if unenlightened person. As a class, however, they were hostile toward Jesus because he did not observe traditional rules and because he openly rebuked their superficial and often hypocritical religiosity. When the delegates from the religious leaders in Jerusalem challenged John concerning his right to baptize, he stated that he did not profess to speak with ultimate authority. He was preaching repentance (Luke 3:3) and was calling for baptism as a confession of repentance in expectation of the greater person who was yet to appear.

26-27 It is not unlikely that John's baptism followed the pattern of proselyte baptism, which required a renunciation of all evil, complete immersion in water, and then reclothing as a member of the holy community of law-keepers.

John drew his reference to untying the sandals of his successor from the practice of using the lowest slave of a household to remove the sandals and wash the feet of guests. John's witness, therefore, reflected the exalted nature of Jesus and placed the latter far above himself.

28 "Bethany on the other side of Jordan" was so named to distinguish it from the Bethany near Jerusalem (see John 12:1). Its exact site is unknown. That it was located "on the other side" shows that the author must have been accustomed to thinking of the west side of the Jordan as his home territory.

29 The chronological scheme of this section is indicated by the reference to successive days: the first day, when the delegation from Jerusalem questioned John (1:19–28); the "next" (second) day, when John saw Jesus approaching (1:29–34); the "next" (third) day, when John pointed out Jesus to his disciples and when they visited him (1:35–42); and the "next" (fourth) day, when Jesus "decided to leave for Galilee" (1:43–50). A reference to the "third day" appears in John 2:1, suggesting a continuing sequence, but it seems ambiguous. If each of these "days" is regarded as one of a series, the "third day" will not fit the scheme since four days have already been mentioned. If the uses of "next" are all references to the same day, meaning "next after the first," they do not explain satisfactorily the differences in action. Perhaps the best solution is to interpret "the third day" as the third day after the departure to Cana. If Jesus were encountered first by the disciples on the east bank of the Jordan River somewhere opposite Jericho, the journey to Cana would have taken at least two days, if not a little longer.

The witness of John the Baptist was positive as well as negative and focused on Jesus rather than on himself. Verses 29–34 contain his presentation of the person of Jesus. Two aspects stand out in the titles by which he introduced Jesus. "The Lamb of God" reflects the sacrificial character of Christ's mission. The word here translated "Lamb" (*amnos*) appears in only four places in the NT: twice in this chapter (1:29, 36), once in Acts 8:32, and again in 1 Peter 1:19. The passage in 1 Peter is an allusion to Isaiah 53:7: "He was led like a lamb to the slaughter, and as a sheep before her shearers is silent, so he did not open his mouth." In the NT the quotations from Isaiah 53 apply directly to Christ (Matt 8:17; Luke 22:37; John 12:38; Acts 8:32–35; 1 Peter 2:22–24). These references assert the atoning work of Christ, who by one final sacrifice of himself removed the guilt of our sins and opened the way to God. John the Baptist limited his own function to introducing Jesus and declared that the latter could take away sin.

The sacrifice of a lamb to take away sin appears frequently in the OT. Offerings by Abel and Noah are mentioned (Gen 4:4; 8:20), but the first specific mention of a lamb is the offering of Isaac by Abraham (Gen 22:2–8). A lamb was prescribed as a guilt-offering (Lev 14:10–25) and as an accompaniment of taking the Nazirite vow (Num 6:1, 12). These have no direct messianic connection. But obviously the title used by John relates Jesus directly to an atoning ministry and death. In Revelation the same concept appears (Rev 5:6–13; 6:1–3, 5, 7; 7:9–10, 14, 17; 13:8; 14:1, 4, 9–10; 15:2–3; 19:7, 9; 21:9, 14, 22, 23; 22:1, 3), though the term for "Lamb" is different (*arnion*). Revelation employs this as a triumphal title, memorializing the completion of Christ's sacrificial work. It combines in one descriptive term the concepts of innocence, voluntary sacrifice, substitutionary atonement, effective obedience, and redemptive power like that of the Passover lamb (Exod 12:21–27). The theology of atonement is developed more fully in the First Epistle of John than in the Gospel (1 John 1:7; 2:2; 4:9–14), but the allusions to the atonement in the Gospel are unmistakable (1:29; 3:14; 6:51; 10:11; 11:49–52; 12:24; 18:11).

30 This verse is essentially a restatement of v.15. There is one significant addition, however. John says, "A man who comes after me." The Greek term *anēr* is introduced here; it means "man" with emphasis on maleness—an emphasis that is lost in the more generic *anthrōpos*. This use of *anēr* intimates the headship of Christ over his followers in the sense of the man-woman relationship in marriage (TDNT, 2:563).

31 The identity of the Messiah was unknown to John the Baptist. This does not mean, necessarily, that John did not know Jesus, for, after all, they were relatives (Luke 1:36). John's ministry was twofold: he sought to lead his hearers to repentance (Mark 1:4) and he was to reveal Messiah to Israel. Somehow John understood that the revelation of Messiah would take place in conjunction with his baptizing ministry; therefore, he remained faithful to his calling. However, even after Messiah had been revealed to Israel at the baptism of Jesus, John continued the other aspect of his ministry.

32-33 Another aspect of John's witness related to the work of the Holy Spirit, who both authenticated the mission of Jesus and was the seal of his work in individual lives. John did not pretend to impart the Spirit to his followers; he could only announce that Jesus would do so. To "baptize with the Holy Spirit" means that just as the common experience of baptism in water signified repentance and confession of sin, so the indwelling of the Holy Spirit is the seal and dynamic of the new life. Repentance and confession are the conditions on which the believer receives the gift of the Spirit (cf. Acts 2:38; Gal 3:2; 5:16-25).

The manifestation of the presence of the Spirit in Jesus' case was visible. The Gospel records the Baptist's subsequent reflection on the event. Luke's Gospel preserves the testimony of eyewitnesses who reproduced the actual scene. The phenomena of the descent of the Spirit and the voice from heaven identified Jesus unmistakably as the predicted Messiah and prompted another aspect of John's witness.

34 John the Baptist's solemn avowal that he had seen the descent of the Spirit on Jesus and that he is the Son of God is the climax of his testimony. The significance of the title can be best understood in the light of 1:18, which emphasized the revelatory function of sonship. Since Jesus shared the nature of the Father, he was able to reveal him understandably. Jesus is the final word from God, for nobody else has such a close relationship to deity, nor is there any other who has been similarly commissioned. The prophets spoke for God, but none of them could say that he came "from the bosom of the Father" (1:18, lit. Gr.). John's emphatic declaration was the reason why the disciples left him to follow Jesus.

Notes

1 The sequence of the "days" in John 1:19-2:1 is paralleled to some degree by the last week of Jesus' life introduced in John 12:1. The "days" of the first series begin with 1:19 and of the second series with 12:1.

Series 1	Series 2
1. Self-identification of John (1:19-28)	1. Presentation of Jesus at Bethany (12:1-11)
2. Announcement of the Son of God (1:29-34)	2. Entry into Jerusalem (12:12-50)
3. Introduction of first disciples (1:35-42)	3. Last Supper with disciples (chs. 13-17)

4. Nathanael: "The King of Israel" (1:43–51)

5. A day of silence

6. "The third day"—the wedding (2:1–5)

7. The first miracle (2:6–11)

4. Crucifixion: "The King of the Jews" (18–19: 37)

5. Burial and silence (19:38–42)

6. "The third day"—resurrection (ch. 20)

7. The last miracle (ch. 21)

---

2. The first disciples

1:35–51

35The next day John was there again with two of his disciples. 36When he saw Jesus passing by, he said, "Look, the Lamb of God!"

37When the two disciples heard him say this, they followed Jesus. 38Turning around, Jesus saw them following and asked, "What do you want?"

They said, "Rabbi" (which means Teacher), "where are you staying?"

39"Come," he replied, "and you will see."

So they went and saw where he was staying, and spent that day with him. It was about the tenth hour.

40Andrew, Simon Peter's brother, was one of the two who heard what John had said and who had followed Jesus. 41The first thing Andrew did was to find his brother Simon and tell him, "We have found the Messiah" (that is, the Christ).

42Then he brought Simon to Jesus, who looked at him and said, "You are Simon son of John. You will be called Cephas" (which, when translated, is Peter).

43The next day Jesus decided to leave for Galilee. Finding Philip, he said to him, "Follow me."

44Philip, like Andrew and Peter, was from the town of Bethsaida. 45Philip found Nathanael and told him, "We have found the one Moses wrote about in the Law, and about whom the prophets also wrote—Jesus of Nazareth, the son of Joseph."

46"Nazareth! Can anything good come from there?" Nathanael asked.

"Come and see," said Philip.

47When Jesus saw Nathanael approaching, he said of him, "Here is a true Israelite, in whom there is nothing false."

48"How do you know me?" Nathanael asked.

Jesus answered, "I saw you while you were still under the fig tree before Philip called you."

49Then Nathanael declared, "Rabbi, you are the Son of God; you are the King of Israel."

50Jesus said, "You believe because I told you I saw you under the fig tree. You shall see greater things than that." 51He then added, "I tell you the truth, you shall see heaven open, and the angels of God ascending and descending on the Son of Man."

35–36 The section immediately following John's testimony gives the response of Jesus' first disciples, who came to him largely because of John's influence. The whole section is tied together by a chronological framework that begins in v.29 of the preceding section and continues in the following section with a reference to "the third day" (John 2:1). The entire episode of John's introduction of Jesus and the opening of his public ministry is treated as a unit in the recollection of the writer. The first section deals with John's preparatory statement; the second, with the initial meeting between Jesus and his potential disciples; and the third, with the sign that demonstrated his power and confirmed their faith. The repeated allusion to the Lamb (*amnos*) of God focused the attention of John's disciples on Jesus as the basis for the divine forgiveness of sin and for the assurance that their repentance would be accepted. It stirred their interest and prompted them to investigate who Jesus was.

37–39 As John's disciples followed him, Jesus turned to challenge their motives by asking, "What do you want?" He probed them to find out whether they were motivated by idle curiosity or by a real desire to know him. Their reply was not merely an inquiry for his address but a courteous request for an interview. "Rabbi" was a term of respect accorded Jewish teachers (1:49). Literally, it means "Master." It was applied to John the Baptist (3:26), and in a longer form Mary Magdalene used it in addressing Jesus (20:16). Jesus encouraged the two disciples to become acquainted with him and to spend time with him. "The tenth hour" probably means about four o'clock in the afternoon, since Jewish time was ordinarily reckoned from sunrise. If "that day" implies any great length of time, the two disciples must have remained with Jesus overnight. "That day" would have to be interpreted loosely as including the next day, which by Jewish practice would begin at sunset.

40 Of the two disciples who heard John, only Andrew is named. The identity of the other is uncertain, though it may well have been the author himself. Throughout the Gospel it is obvious that he had an interest in Simon Peter. On this occasion the author wished to explain the origin of Simon's association with Jesus.

41 Andrew's testimony shows that the interview of the preceding hours must have been related to Jewish hopes and to Jesus' character. The statement "We have found the Messiah" does not necessarily imply an explicit claim by Jesus, but it does indicate a settled conclusion on the part of Andrew. Andrew's declaration does not imply that he had a correct concept of Jesus' messiahship. It only shows that he regarded Jesus as the candidate for that title. The expectation of a national deliverer was widespread in Judaism in the first third of the first century. Probably all the disciples expected that Jesus would fulfill their hopes for an independent kingdom and consequent political power for those who joined him (cf. Mark 10:28, 35–45).

42 The introduction of Peter to Jesus was brief but direct. The simple pronouncement " 'You are Simon son of John. You will be called Cephas' (which, when translated, is Peter)" was really a diagnosis of Peter's personality. Simon, or Simeon (cf. Acts 15:14), was the name of Jacob's second oldest son (Gen 29:33), who, with his brother Levi (29:34), had ruthlessly avenged the violation of their sister by one of the Canaanite princes (Gen 34:25–31). The rash and impulsive character of Simeon was mirrored in Simon, whose conduct as reported by all the Gospels reflects the same recklessness and tendency to violence (cf. John 18:10). Jesus accepted Simon as he was but promised that he should become Cephas, an Aramaic name, which, like the Greek "Peter," means "a rock." The development of Peter as recorded in this Gospel demonstrates the progress of that change.

43–45 Whereas the first disciples were introduced to Jesus by John the Baptist or by one of the other disciples, Jesus took the initiative in calling Philip. He, like Andrew and Peter, was a Galilean and quite likely a fisherman. The name Bethsaida, his hometown, means "house of fishing." Like Andrew, Philip found another, Nathanael, and by his witness brought him to Jesus. The identity of Nathanael is uncertain. Some have equated him with Bartholomew, others with Matthew. Since Bartholomew equals Bar-Tolmai, "son of Tolmai," it is not a proper name but merely indicates ancestry; and Nathanael Bar-Tolmai would be parallel to Simon Bar-Jona. The name Nathanael means "Gift of God." Since Matthew means "Gift of Jahweh," some have equated Nathanael and Matthew, but without convincing proof. Hanhart suggests that Nathanael represents Matthew and represents the first Gospel, with which John was familiar (pp. 22–24). Hanhart's argument is circuitous and seems fanciful.

Nathanael seems to have been a student of the Torah, or Pentateuch. Philip appealed to him on the basis of the prediction in the Law and the Prophets. Jesus' phrase "under the fig tree" (v.48) was used in rabbinic literature to describe meditation on the Law.

46 The response of Nathanael indicates that Nazareth did not enjoy a good reputation in Galilee. Perhaps Nathanael, who came from Bethsaida, looked down on Nazareth as a rival village, either poorer or morally worse than his own.

47–51 Jesus' comment on Nathanael suggests that the latter had been reading of Jacob's experience at Bethel (Gen 28:10–17). Jacob was filled with guile and had been forced to leave home because he had lied to his father and had swindled his brother. If under these circumstances Jacob was eligible for a revelation from God, would not Nathanael be even more worthy of such a blessing? Jesus said that Nathanael was free from guile (KJV) and used the imagery of Jacob's dream to describe the greater revelation he would give to Nathanael. Jesus implied that he himself would be the medium of that revelation, and his order of the angels' procedure implies that they rose from earth to heaven with their inquiries and then returned to earth with the answers. His mission is to answer human need and to make sure that the answers are proclaimed. The term "Son of Man" is used here for the first time in John's Gospel. According to all the Gospels, Jesus used it concerning himself to represent his relation with human affairs. For a fuller treatment of this title, see the comment on John 13:31.

3. The first sign

2:1–11

> [1]On the third day a wedding took place at Cana in Galilee. Jesus' mother was there, [2]and Jesus and his disciples had also been invited to the wedding. [3]When the wine was gone, Jesus' mother said to him, "They have no more wine."
>
> [4]"Dear woman, why do you involve me?" Jesus replied, "My time has not yet come."
>
> [5]His mother said to the servants, "Do whatever he tells you."
>
> [6]Nearby stood six stone water jars, the kind used by the Jews for ceremonial washing, each holding from twenty to thirty gallons.
>
> [7]Jesus said to the servants, "Fill the jars with water"; so they filled them to the brim.
>
> [8]Then he told them, "Now draw some out and take it to the master of the banquet."
>
> They did so, [9]and the master of the banquet tasted the water that had been turned into wine. He did not realize where it had come from, though the servants who had drawn the water knew. Then he called the bridegroom aside [10]and said, "Everyone brings out the choice wine first and then the cheaper wine after the guests have had too much to drink; but you have saved the best till now."
>
> [11]This, the first of his miraculous signs, Jesus performed in Cana of Galilee. He thus revealed his glory, and his disciples put their faith in him.

1 The wedding at Cana is linked to the preceding text by a chronological tie: "on the third day." Whether this means that "the next day" of vv.29, 35, and 43 refers to three events on the same day, or whether the "third day" means three days after Jesus' departure from the place of baptism, is not clear. The latter alternative seems more probable, for some time would be necessary for traveling; and Jesus with his new disciples could hardly have journeyed back to Cana in less than two days' time. The entire span between John's initial introduction of Jesus and the appearance at Cana can hardly have been less than a week.

Cana was a village in the hills of Galilee. Its exact location is disputed, but the best site seems to be that of Khirbet Qana, about nine miles north of Nazareth. It lay on a road that ran from Ptolemais on the Mediterranean coast southeastward to Sepphoris, the center of Roman administration in Galilee, and thence southward through Nazareth to Samaria and Jerusalem.

2-3 A wedding is always a gala occasion, and in a village like Cana it would be a community celebration. "Refreshments" were provided for all guests. Of these, wine was very important. To fail in providing adequately for the guests would involve social disgrace. In the closely knit communities of Jesus' day, such an error would never be forgotten and would haunt the newly married couple all their lives. The situation prompted Mary's urgency when she informed Jesus of the emergency.

4-5 Jesus' reply to Mary was not so abrupt as it seems. "Woman" (*gynai*) was a polite form of address. Jesus used it when he spoke to his mother from the cross (19:26) and also when he spoke to Mary Magdalene after the Resurrection (20:15). Two translations of Jesus' rejoinder to his mother are possible: (1) "What business is that of ours?" or (2) "What authority do you have over me?" The second alternative is based on the analogy of the question of the demoniac, "What do you want with us, Son of God?" (Matt 8:29), which employs exactly the same phraseology. Since Jesus' mother expressed neither surprise nor resentment, the former translation is probably more acceptable in this instance. She acknowledged that he should act independently, and she confidently told the servants to follow his orders. She fully expected that he would take appropriate action. He did indicate that he was no longer under her authority but that he was living by a new pattern timed by the purpose of God. Jesus had begun his miracles, not at the request of earthly parents whom he still respected, but according to the purpose of his heavenly Father. The "time" refers to the first hour when he manifested the real reason for which he came: "Father, the hour has come. Glorify your Son, that your Son may glorify you" (John 17:1).

6-7 The stone jars were large, containing about twenty gallons apiece. By the social rules of the day each guest was expected to wash his hands before eating, and a considerable amount of water would be needed for this. At the lowest estimate, 120 gallons of water would be available. If made into wine, it would supply approximately two thousand four-ounce glasses; and if, as was frequently customary, the wine was further diluted by three parts of water to one of wine, there would have been enough to last for several days.

8-10 The "master of the banquet" was not the host; he was the headwaiter or toastmaster. Usually he was called in to take care of the distribution of food and drink at a large social occasion. He was astounded by the high quality of the wine since generally a poorer quality was served once the taste of the guests became dulled.

11 The purpose of Jesus' first miracle after entering Galilee is not stated. In fact, for the most part its occurrence was unknown. The specific details of place and time emphasize the historicity of the miracle and lessen the likelihood that it should be interpreted allegorically. The nature of the miracle is very plain. Jesus had come to bring about conversion: water to wine, sinners to saints. And this latter miracle of transformation occurred in almost complete obscurity. Few know when or how it happened, but they know that it did happen.

The effect of this miracle is noteworthy. It marked the beginning of a ministry accompanied by supernatural power; and it proved so convincing to the new disciples that they "put their faith in him." The deed helped confirm the conclusion they had drawn from their previous interviews with him: Jesus must be the Messiah.

4. The interlude at Capernaum

2:12

> [12]After this he went down to Capernaum with his mother and brothers and his disciples. There they stayed for a few days.

12 This verse covers an unspecified period of time. It is introduced by the indefinite phrase "after this" and it says that Jesus' family and disciples stayed at Capernaum "for a few days." There is no clear indication that Jesus traveled in Galilee for some time between this sojourn and his trip to Jerusalem. Since the synoptic Gospels seem to imply that he had an early ministry in Galilee, it may fit at this point.

The allusion to Jesus' brothers recurs also in the synoptic Gospels. According to Mark 6:3, Jesus had four brothers and some sisters. Little is said about them in the Gospels; and only James appears later in the Book of Acts, as the moderator of the church in Jerusalem. Another allusion to them occurs in John 7:2–10. Several interpretations have been offered concerning Jesus' siblings: (1) they were children of Joseph by a previous marriage, (2) they were really Jesus' cousins, or (3) they were younger children of Joseph and Mary. The second view is probably incorrect since the word for cousin (*anepsios*) existed in the Greek language and could have been used if needed. The theory that they may have been stepbrothers of Jesus might be possible and might explain why Jesus did not bequeath the care of his mother to them at the time of his death. The most logical solution is to conclude that they were younger children of Joseph and Mary, born subsequent to Jesus. It accords with the implication of Matthew 1:24–25. The first or second view is supported by those who contend for the perpetual virginity of Mary.

5. The cleansing of the temple

2:13–22

> [13]When it was almost time for the Jewish Passover, Jesus went up to Jerusalem. [14]In the temple courts he found men selling cattle, sheep and doves, and others sitting at tables exchanging money. [15]So he made a whip out of cords, and drove all from the temple area, both sheep and cattle; he scattered the coins of the money changers and overturned their tables. [16]To those who sold doves he said, "Get these out of here! How dare you turn my Father's house into a market!"

¹⁷His disciples remembered that it is written: "Zeal for your house will consume me."
¹⁸Then the Jews demanded of him, "What miraculous sign can you show us to prove your authority to do all this?"
¹⁹Jesus answered them, "Destroy this temple, and I will raise it again in three days."
²⁰The Jews replied, "It has taken forty-six years to build this temple, and you are going to raise it in three days?" ²¹But the temple he had spoken of was his body. ²²After he was raised from the dead, his disciples recalled what he had said. Then they believed the Scripture and the words that Jesus had spoken.

13-14 About the time of the Passover, Jesus went up to Jerusalem from Galilee for the annual feast. The narrative poses a chronological puzzle, for the synoptic Gospels unitedly attach this event to Jesus' last visit to Jerusalem at the time of his death (see Matt 21:10-17; Mark 11:15-19; Luke 19:45-46). Either John is right and the Synoptics mistaken, or the Synoptics are right and John mistaken, or John has transplanted the account for topical or theological purposes, or there were *two* such occasions, only one of which was recorded by John and the other by the Synoptics. While each of these theories has been argued with some degree of logic, the last seems the best. The language of John and that of the Synoptics differ strongly. Sheep and oxen are not mentioned in the Synoptics; John does not allude to Jesus' command not to carry merchandise through the temple (Mark 11:16); the Synoptics do not mention Jesus' challenge, "Destroy this temple, and I will raise it again in three days" (John 2:19). Matthew and Mark, however, mention these words in connection with the trial before the Sanhedrin. Two witnesses appeared to testify that he had threatened to destroy the temple and to rebuild it in three days (Matt 26:61; Mark 14:57-58). Both mention that the accusation was repeated by the mob at the Crucifixion (Matt 27:39-40; Mark 15:29-30). Jesus' words must have impressed the crowd sufficiently so that they were remembered. It is not at all improbable that he may have cleansed the temple twice, two Passovers apart, and that the second so enraged the hierarchy that their animosity toward him exploded into drastic action. Interfering with their privileges once was impudent, twice would be inexcusable.

The sale of cattle and doves and the privilege of exchanging money were permitted in the temple court as a convenience for pilgrims who would need animals for sacrifice and temple shekels for their dues. Under the chief priests, however, the concessions had become merely a means of making money and had debased the temple into a commercial venture.

15-16 Jesus' action precipitated wild confusion. The animals would be bawling and running about aimlessly; the money changers would be scrambling for their coins in the dust and debris on the floor of the court; the officials would be arguing with Jesus about the rights of the case. Jesus' expression "my Father's house" reveals his feeling toward God. The merchandising of privilege was an insult to God and a desecration of the Father's house.

17 Jesus' vehemence revealed his inward passion for the Father and his jealous guardianship of the Father's interests. The Scripture brought to the disciples' minds is Psalm 69:9, from which other passages have been applied to Christ, dealing with his anguish of soul (vv.1-4), the gall and vinegar of the Cross (v.21), and his estrangement from his people (v.8).

18–21 The Jews' demand for a sign is quite in agreement with their general attitude toward Jesus during his lifetime. He commented on it at a later occasion when the Pharisees said, "Teacher, we want to see a miraculous sign from you" (Matt 12:38). He replied, "A wicked and adulterous generation asks for a miraculous sign! But none will be given it except the sign of the prophet Jonah" (v.39). Both Matthew and Mark cite a later instance that practically duplicates this one (Matt 16:1; Mark 8:11), and Luke adds one that may be still another (Luke 11:16). On this particular occasion, however, Jesus answered enigmatically, "Destroy this temple, and I will raise it in three days" (John 2:19). His critics assumed that he was speaking of Herod's temple, which had been in process of construction for forty-six years and was still incomplete. Jesus, says the author, really meant the temple of his body, which he would raise up in three days' time.

22 The author's comment indicates that from the first of his ministry Jesus had the end of it in view. One can hardly escape the conviction that the fourth Gospel depicts the career of Jesus as a voluntary progress toward a predetermined goal. The allusions to the destruction of the temple of his body (2:22), to the elevation on a cross (3:14; 12:32–33), to the giving of his flesh for the life of the world (6:51), to his burial (12:7), and the announcement of his betrayal and death to his disciples (13:19, 21) attest to his consciousness of the fate that awaited him in Jerusalem. Though the disciples did not comprehend the situation during Jesus' career, the Resurrection placed the memory of his sayings in a new perspective. The author's note illustrates the principle that the Gospel presents the life of Jesus in the light of the Resurrection and of the apostolic experience based on the results of that event.

Notes

19 The distinction in the words translated "temple" in vv.14 and 19–21 is worth noting. In v.14 the word is ἱερόν (*hieron*), which refers to a "shrine" or "holy building." This usage is consistent throughout the NT. The word ναός (*naos*) appears in vv.19–21 and signifies the "dwelling place" of deity. In the NT it is used metaphorically of the bodies of believers (1 Cor 3:16–17; 6:19). So whereas the Jews were thinking in terms of a physical building, Jesus was referring to his body. The apparent threat to destroy the temple was long remembered by Jesus' enemies. Not only did the false witnesses quote him at the time of his appearance before the Sanhedrin (Matt 26:60–61; Mark 14:57–58), but the same accusation was repeated at the arraignment of Stephen: "For we have heard him say that this Jesus of Nazareth will destroy this place [the temple] and change the customs Moses handed down to us" (Acts 6:14).

21–22 Jesus' technique of using a paradoxical statement to bewilder his enemies, which he subsequently explained for his disciples, frequently appears in John's Gospel. In this instance the disciples understood the enigma after the Resurrection and by their realization came to a fuller knowledge of the truth.

6. *The interview with Nicodemus* (2:23–3:21)

a. *Nicodemus's visit*

2:23–3:15

²³Now while he was in Jerusalem at the Passover Feast, many people saw the miraculous signs he was doing and believed in his name. ²⁴But Jesus would not

entrust himself to them, for he knew all men. 25He did not need man's testimony about man, for he knew what was in a man.

1Now there was a man of the Pharisees named Nicodemus, a member of the Jewish ruling council. 2He came to Jesus at night and said, "Rabbi, we know you are a teacher who has come from God. For no one could perform the miraculous signs you are doing if God were not with him."

3In reply Jesus declared, "I tell you the truth, unless a man is born again, he cannot see the kingdom of God."

4"How can a man be born when he is old?" Nicodemus asked. "Surely he cannot enter a second time into his mother's womb to be born!"

5Jesus answered, "I tell you the truth, unless a man is born of water and the Spirit, he cannot enter the kingdom of God. 6Flesh gives birth to flesh, but the Spirit gives birth to spirit. 7You should not be surprised at my saying, 'You must be born again.' 8The wind blows wherever it pleases. You hear its sound, but you cannot tell where it comes from or where it is going. So it is with everyone born of the Spirit."

9"How can this be?" Nicodemus asked.

10"You are Israel's teacher," said Jesus, "and do you not understand these things? 11I tell you the truth, we speak of what we know, and we testify to what we have seen, but still you people do not accept our testimony. 12I have spoken to you of earthly things and you do not believe; how then will you believe if I speak of heavenly things? 13No one has ever gone into heaven except the one who came from heaven—the Son of Man. 14Just as Moses lifted up the snake in the desert, so the Son of Man must be lifted up, 15that everyone who believes in him may have eternal life.

23–24 The interview with Nicodemus is connected with the first trip to Jerusalem. Jesus had already begun performing miraculous works. These signs attracted the attention of the crowd and brought many to a stage of belief parallel to that of the disciples (2:11). They reasoned that since Jesus possessed such power, he must have the favor of God—a line of reasoning followed later by the blind man (9:30–33). Jesus, however, was not satisfied with a superficial faith, even though it was genuine as far as it went. He did not trust himself to those who had professed belief only on the basis of his miracles.

25 Jesus had a thorough understanding of human nature. The principle stated here is basic to his dealing with all the personalities mentioned in the Gospel. He could read people more accurately than a doctor can read physical symptoms in diagnosing an illness. The prelude of these verses (23–25) is introductory to the three typical interviews in chs. 3 and 4: Nicodemus the Pharisee, the Samaritan woman, and the royal official at Cana.

3:1 Nicodemus was introduced as a man of the upper class, conservative in his beliefs, and definitely interested in Jesus' teaching. As a Pharisee he belonged to the strict religious sect of Judaism in contrast to the Sadducees, who were less rigid in their beliefs and were more politically minded. As a member of the ruling council or Sanhedrin, he would have been sensitive to the prevailing doctrinal trends of the time. His interest in Jesus had been prompted by the miracles he had witnessed, and he came for an interview to obtain more information. His approach shows that he was cautious, open-minded, and ready to receive a new revelation from God if he was sure of its genuineness.

2 The fact that Nicodemus came by night does not necessarily mean that he was timid, though in the light of the later references to him in this Gospel he does not seem to have been aggressive in his discipleship (7:45–52; 19:38–42). His salutation was courteous, and he showed no sign of hostility.

3 Jesus' reply was cryptic and abrupt. He informed Nicodemus that no man could even see the kingdom of God without a spiritual rebirth. Birth is our mode of entrance into the world and brings with it the potential equipment for adjustment to the world. To be born again, or "born from above," means a transformation of a person so that he is able to enter another world and adapt to its conditions. *Anōthen*, which NIV and many others translate as "again," in the Johannine writings normally means "from above," and it should be rendered thus here. To belong to the heavenly kingdom, one must be born into it.

4 Nicodemus's reply may be interpreted in two ways. At first sight he appears to be quite materialistic in his attitude, thinking that Jesus was advocating the impossibility of a second physical birth. On the other hand, he may not have so understood Jesus' statement. Perhaps he meant, "How can a man whose habits and ways of thinking have been fixed by age expect to change radically?" Physical rebirth is impossible, but is spiritual change any more feasible?

5 In response, Jesus repeated his solemn assertion, "I tell you the truth [KJV, 'verily, verily'], unless a man is born of water and the Spirit, he cannot enter the kingdom of God." Various interpretations have been suggested for the water. Does it refer to natural birth, which is accompanied by watery fluid? Or is it a symbol of the Spirit (John 7:37–39) so that "water" and "Spirit" are merely a hendiadys, two words referring to the same thing? Or is it a symbol of baptism? The best answer seems to be that if Jesus was attempting to clarify his teaching for Nicodemus, he would answer in familiar terms; and the author would want his readers to understand his phraseology. Since Jesus' ministry came shortly after that of John the Baptist, Jesus may have been referring to John's preaching, which dealt with the baptism of water, signifying repentance, and with the coming messenger of God who would endow men with the Holy Spirit (John 1:31–33). The new birth is conditioned on the repentance and confession of the individual in response to the appeal of God and by the transformation of life by the gift of the Holy Spirit.

6–8 Jesus asserted that the entrance into the kingdom of God that Nicodemus desired could not be achieved by legalism or outward conformity. It requires an inner change. Membership in the kingdom of God is not a prerogative of any particular race or culture, nor is it hereditary. It is given only by the direct act of God. The origin and the destination of the wind are unknown to the one who feels it and acknowledges its reality. Just so, the new life of one born of the Spirit is unexplainable by ordinary reasoning; and its outcome is unpredictable, though its actuality is undeniable.

9 Nicodemus's question "How can this be?" should not be interpreted as an exclamation expressing incredulity. Rather, it is a plea for direction. He wanted to know how this experience could become his. Nothing in the Judaism he knew offered anything like this. It is true that Jesus' words are paralleled by a promise in Ezekiel: "I will sprinkle clean water on you, and you will be clean; I will cleanse you from all your impurities and from all your idols. I will give you a new heart and put a new spirit in you; I will remove from you your heart of stone and give you a heart of flesh. And I will put my Spirit in you and move you to follow my decrees and be careful to keep my laws" (Ezek 36:25–28). The spiritual principle of these verses accords with that of the new birth that Jesus enunciated.

Proselytes to Judaism were washed completely, issued new clothing, and then received into the commonwealth of the people of God; but Israelites were regarded as sons of Abraham and children of God by covenant from birth. In effect, Jesus was telling Nicodemus that his descent from Abraham was not adequate ground for salvation. He would have to repent and begin a new life in the Spirit if he expected to enter the kingdom of God (cf. John 8:37–44).

Jesus illustrated his point by a play on words applicable both in Hebrew and Greek. The word for "spirit" (Heb., *rûah;* Gr., *pneuma*) is the word for "wind" in both languages and can be translated either way, depending on the context. Verse 8 could be rendered, "The Spirit breathes where he wills." NIV and other translations are undoubtedly correct, for the allusion to sound in the second sentence would not make much sense in sequence with "spirit." Possibly Nicodemus called on Jesus at the time when the evening wind was blowing through the city so that it was a ready illustration.

10 The Greek text uses the definite article with "teacher": "Are you *the* teacher of Israel?" (lit. tr.). Nicodemus's exact position in the theological circles of Israel is not defined, but the language suggests that he was a very important person. Jesus implies that as the outstanding teacher of the nation, Nicodemus should have been familiar with the teaching of the new birth. Evidently Jesus felt that since the OT contained this teaching in principle, those who read the Scriptures were responsible for knowing and believing the truth.

11 No doubt Nicodemus thought Jesus to be presumptuous when he said, "We speak of what we know." Jesus spoke with an air of authority. However, though the Pharisees spoke with a humanly imposed authority, Jesus spoke with an inherent authority. The use of "we" by Jesus is unusual. Perhaps his disciples were present and he was including them. Or Jesus may have been speaking as the earthly representative of the godhead. Throughout the years the "people" had rejected God's instruction as ministered through the prophets and the Scriptures. And things were no different now.

12–13 The "earthly things" Jesus alluded to were probably the phenomena he used for illustrations, such as the wind. If Nicodemus couldn't grasp the meaning of spiritual truth as conveyed by concrete analogy, how would he do so if it were couched in an abstract statement? No one had ever entered into heaven to experience its realities directly except Jesus himself, the Son of Man, who had come from heaven. Revelation, not discovery, is the basis for faith.

14–15 The reference to the Pentateuch (Num 21:4–9) would have been familiar to Nicodemus, for the Jewish scholars spent the larger part of each day in the study of Scripture and often memorized not only the Pentateuch but the entire OT. Although Jesus did not elaborate the details of this allusion, it has several applicable aspects:
1. The ancient Israelites were guilty of disobedience and a grumbling and unthankful spirit.
2. They were under the condemnation of God and were being punished for their sin.
3. The object elevated before them was the emblem of their judgment.

4. They were unable to rescue themselves.

5. The poison of the serpents was deadly, and there was no antidote for it.

6. They were urged to *look* at the serpent in order to receive life.

Jesus insisted that he would be "lifted up," a word used elsewhere for crucifixion (8:28; 12:32–34). There is a possibility that the Greek word *hypsoō* was used to translate the Aramaic term *z^eqap*, which could mean either "to elevate" or "to execute on a gibbet." It was a summons to receive Jesus as God's provision for the cure of sin and to place complete confidence in him for the future. Such confidence or belief would ensure partaking in the life of the age to come.

Notes

2:23–24 There is an interesting contrast here that is lost in the English translation. The same verb πιστεύω (*pisteuō*, "believe") is applied to the "many people" and to Jesus, but its first use is intransitive and the second use is transitive: literally, they "trusted in his name" (v. 23); and he did not "entrust himself to them" (v.24). Jesus would not believe in them unless they fully believed in him.

3:3 Should ἄνωθεν (*anōthen*) be rendered "again" or "from above"? It is used both ways in the NT. Luke at least once uses it to indicate "from time past" (Acts 26:5) and probably with the same meaning in Luke 1:3. James invariably has the meaning "from above" (James 1:17; 3:15, 17). Paul's use in Gal 4:9 accords more nearly with Luke's. The other instances in John unmistakably mean "from above" (3:31; 19:11, 23).

The infinitive ἰδεῖν (*idein*), translated "see," implies discernment or perception of meaning rather than simply registering a visual image, whereas βλέπω (*blepō*) means "to have the power of sight." The implication in John 3:3 is that without spiritual rebirth one cannot even perceive the reality of the kingdom of God.

9 The rabbis connected the concept of baptism with the ceremonial purification of complete immersion, basing it on the instructions for washing in Exod 19:10. The sprinkling of blood, immersion, and the submission to the Law (Exod 24:8) were the rites performed on proselytes "to bring them under the wings of the Shekinah." Baptism was not merely for the purpose of expiating special transgressions, as was the case chiefly in the violation of the so-called heretical laws of purity, but was the first step in a practice of holy living and a preparation for the attainment of a closer communion with God (cf. Jos. Antiq. 18. 5. 82). The Essenes followed the same practice. The purpose of baptizing the proselyte was for cleansing from the impurity of idolatry. The bathing in water constituted a rebirth and made him a "new creature" (cf. S. Kraus, "Baptism," JE I, pp. 499, 509; LTJM, 2:745–47).

14 Kittel, commenting on ὑψόω (*hypsoō*, "lift up") remarks: "In Jn. ὑψόω has intentionally a double sense in all the passages in which it occurs. . . . It means both exaltation on the cross and also exaltation to heaven" (TDNT, 8:610).

---

b. *The author's comment*

3:16–21

16"For God so loved the world that he gave his one and only Son, that whoever believes in him shall not perish but have eternal life. 17For God did not send his Son into the world to condemn the world, but to save the world through him. 18Whoever believes in him is not condemned, but whoever does not believe stands condemned already because he has not believed in the name of God's one and only Son. ¹⁹This is the verdict: Light has come into the world, but men loved darkness instead of light because their deeds were evil. ²⁰Everyone who does evil hates the light, and will not come into the light for fear that his deeds will be exposed. ²¹But whoever lives by the truth comes into the light, so that it may be seen plainly that what he has done has been done through God."

16 Commentators are divided as to whether vv.16–21 are a direct continuation of the conversation between Jesus and Nicodemus or whether they represent only the author's comment on Jesus' words. In either case, they express the most important message of the Gospel (emphasized elsewhere in many ways)—that salvation is a gift received only by believing God for it. The nature of belief is implied in the illustration of Moses lifting up the serpent in the wilderness (v.14). Belief consists of accepting something, not doing something. The result of belief is that one receives eternal life. He is freed from condemnation and lives in a relation of total honesty with God, for he does not fear having his real self exposed.

"Eternal," the new life God gives, refers not solely to the duration of existence but also to the quality of life as contrasted with futility. It is a deepening and growing experience. It can never be exhausted in any measurable span of time, but it introduces a totally new quality of life. The believer becomes imperishable; he is free from all condemnation; he is approved by God.

The verb "perish" depicts the opposite of salvation. It is used of death as opposed to life (Mark 3:6, transitive), "destroy" as opposed to preserve (1 Cor 1:19), "loss" as opposed to win or gain (2 John 8). It may be used of sheep that have gone astray (Matt 10:6) or a son who has wandered from his father's house (Luke 15:24). Its use here clearly implies that those without God are hopelessly confused in purpose, alienated from him in their affections, and futile in their efforts. Positive belief in Christ is necessary; all that one has to do to perish is nothing. To perish is to fail completely of fulfilling God's purpose and consequently to be excluded forever from his fellowship.

The presentation of the good news of God's love offers only two options: to believe or to perish. Eternal life, which is accepted by believing, is a gift of God and brings with it the fullest blessings God can bestow. To perish does not mean to cease to exist; it means to experience utter failure, futility, and loss of all that makes existence worthwhile. Its use with reference to Judas in John 17:12 is a vivid illustration.

17–18 Notwithstanding this gloomy picture of "lost" or "perish," God's purpose toward man is positive. God's attitude is not that of suspicion or hatred but of love. He is not seeking an excuse to condemn men but is rather endeavoring to save them. His purpose in sending Jesus into the world was to show his love and to draw men to himself. If they are lost, it is because they have not committed themselves to God, the only source of life. Beginning at this point, the contrast between belief and unbelief is increasingly exemplified. John has here defined the crux of belief and unbelief and has indicated the effects of each. The progress of both in the characters of those associated with Jesus becomes increasingly evident as the drama of this Gospel unfolds.

19–21 The difference between the believer and the unbeliever does not lie in the guilt or innocence of either; it lies in the different attitudes they take toward the "light." The unbeliever shrinks from the light because it exposes his sin; the believer willingly comes to the light so that his real motives may be revealed. This verse is paralleled by 1 John 1:8–9: "If we claim to be without sin, we deceive ourselves and the truth is not in us.

If we confess our sins, he is faithful and just and will forgive us our sins and purify us from all unrighteousness."

In John 1:5 we're told of the natural antipathy that exists between light and darkness. Verses 19–21 of ch. 3 lift this battle from the realm of the abstract to the concrete by showing that it is the love of evil deeds that keep men from responding to the light. There's no missing the fact that men are held accountable for their actions, and the choice is theirs: evil deeds or truth.

Notes

16 Morris says: "In the first century there were no devices such as inverted commas to show the precise limits of quoted speech. . . . Perhaps the dividing point comes at the end of v.15. . . . But in v.16 the death on the cross appears to be spoken of as past, and there are stylistic indications that John is speaking for himself " (NIC, p. 228).

7. Further testimony of John the Baptist

3:22–36

22After this, Jesus and his disciples went out into the Judean countryside, where he spent some time with them, and baptized. 23Now John also was baptizing at Aenon near Salim, because there was plenty of water, and people were constantly coming to be baptized. 24(This was before John was put in prison.) 25An argument developed between some of John's disciples and a certain Jew over the matter of ceremonial washing. 26They came to John and said to him, "Rabbi, that man who was with you on the other side of the Jordan—the one you testified about— well, he is baptizing, and everyone is going to him."

27To this John replied, "A man can receive only what is given him from heaven. 28You yourselves can testify that I said, 'I am not the Christ but am sent ahead of him.' 29The bride belongs to the bridegroom. The friend who attends the bridegroom waits and listens for him, and is full of joy when he hears the bridegroom's voice. That joy is mine, and it is now complete. 30He must become greater; I must become less.

31"The one who comes from above is above all; the one who is from the earth belongs to the earth, and speaks as one from the earth. The one who comes from heaven is above all. 32He testifies to what he has seen and heard, but no one accepts his testimony. 33The man who has accepted it has certified that God is truthful. 34For the one whom God has sent speaks the words of God; to him God gives the Spirit without limit. 35The Father loves the Son and has placed everything in his hands. 36Whoever believes in the Son has eternal life, but whoever rejects the Son will not see life, for God's wrath remains on him."

22–24 This period of Jesus' ministry in Judea is not paralleled by any account in the synoptic Gospels. It occurred before the arrest and imprisonment of John the Baptist, for he and Jesus were preaching and baptizing simultaneously. Mark begins the active ministry of Jesus after John's imprisonment (Mark 1:14) and states that Jesus summoned the disciples to follow him at that time. Matthew's account agrees with Mark's in substance (Matt 4:12–21). Luke does not specify that John's arrest preceded Jesus' ministry, though he mentions the imprisonment at the outset of his narrative (Luke 3:19). Both exercised a rural rather than urban ministry at this time. Jesus and his disciples remained in the Judean country; John was preaching farther north.

23 The exact location of Aenon is uncertain. Two sites are possible: one south of Beth-shan, where there were numerous springs; another a short distance from Shechem. Of the two, the former seems to be the better possibility. Eusebius and Jerome both mention it; and the ancient mosaic Madaba map of sacred sites depicts an "Aenon near to Salim" near the Jordan south of Scythopolis, the later name of Beth-shan. C.H. Turner observes that in this region John would have been in the territory of the Greek city of Scythopolis, outside the domain of Herod Antipas (p. 202).

25–26 The argument between a Jewish inquirer and the disciples of John indicates that there must have been confusion over the respective merits of Jesus and John. If both were baptizing, whose baptism was valid? By popular acclaim Jesus' influence was growing and John's was waning. John's interrogators felt that their friend and teacher had been eclipsed by Jesus' sudden popularity, and they wanted an explanation.

27–30 John showed no jealousy whatever; on the contrary, he reaffirmed his subordinate position. He would not claim for himself final authority but avowed that he had been sent in preparation for the Messiah. As the bridegroom is more important than the best man, or "friend" of the bridegroom who acted as the bridegroom's assistant, so he would be content to act as an assistant to Jesus.

Just how far the simile of bride and bridegroom should be pressed is questionable. Should the bride represent Israel, to whom the Messiah came, or the church? The imagery is applied to both (cf. Hos 2:19–20; Eph 5:32), but the focus of this passage is on the bridegroom, not the bride. The emphasis is on the relation of Jesus and John rather than on the relation of Jesus to Israel or to the church. To what extent this explanation of the relation of John the Baptist to Jesus was prompted by later conditions in the church is not stated. Adherents to John's preaching and baptism certainly existed in the middle of the first century and were widespread. Apollos of Alexandria, who ministered at Ephesus, was one of this company. Aquila and Priscilla later instructed him in the ministry of Christ (Acts 18:24–26). When Paul arrived at Ephesus, he found others who held the same belief. Paul himself brought them into a full understanding of the work of Christ (Acts 19:1–7). It is likely that this halfway understanding persisted among John's converts.

31–36 This paragraph, like vv.16–21, may be the author's reflection on what he had just written. Its phraseology accords better with the style of vv.16–21 than with that of John the Baptist. It is valuable as a testimony to the person of Christ in the light of what the author has just written. It declares in no uncertain terms that (1) Jesus came from heaven and spoke with a higher authority than that of earth; (2) that he spoke from observation, not from theory; (3) that he spoke the words of God; (4) that the Father's love had caused him to endow the Son with complete authority to execute his purpose. These qualities made Jesus superior in every way to John the Baptist, though the latter had an important and divinely authorized message. John spoke as one "from the earth." The Son, however, was not merely the messenger of God; he was the revealed object of faith. Once again the dividing line is affirmed. The believer in the Son has eternal life; the unbeliever will never possess that life, for he is already under condemnation. The wrath of God remains on him.

This is the only passage in the Johannine Gospel and Epistles in which "wrath" is mentioned. The word does not mean a sudden gust of passion or a burst of temper. Rather, it is the settled displeasure of God against sin. It is the divine allergy to moral evil, the reaction of righteousness to unrighteousness. God is neither easily angered nor vindictive. But by his very nature he is unalterably committed to opposing and judging all disobedience. The moral laws of the universe are as unvarying and unchangeable as its physical laws, and God cannot set aside either without violating his own nature. The rejection of his Son can be followed only by retribution. Acceptance of Christ is the personal appropriation of God's truth—an appropriation that might be compared to the practice of endorsing a check to cash it.

8. *The Samaritan ministry* (4:1–42)

a. *The woman at the well*

4:1–26

¹The Pharisees heard that Jesus was gaining and baptizing more disciples than John, ²although in fact it was not Jesus who baptized, but his disciples. ³When the Lord learned of this, he left Judea and went back once more to Galilee.

⁴Now he had to go through Samaria. ⁵So he came to a town in Samaria called Sychar, near the plot of ground Jacob had given to his son Joseph. ⁶Jacob's well was there, and Jesus, tired as he was from the journey, sat down by the well. It was about the sixth hour.

⁷When a Samaritan woman came to draw water, Jesus said to her, "Will you give me a drink?" ⁸(His disciples had gone into the town to buy food.)

⁹The Samaritan woman said to him, "You are a Jew and I am a Samaritan woman. How can you ask me for a drink?" (For Jews do not associate with Samaritans.)

¹⁰Jesus answered her, "If you knew the gift of God and who it is that asks you for a drink, you would have asked him and he would have given you living water."

¹¹"Sir," the woman said, "you have nothing to draw with and the well is deep. Where can you get this living water? ¹²Are you greater than our father Jacob, who gave us the well and drank from it himself, as did also his sons and his flocks and herds?"

¹³Jesus answered, "Everyone who drinks this water will be thirsty again, ¹⁴but whoever drinks the water I give him will never thirst. Indeed, the water I give him will become in him a spring of water welling up to eternal life."

¹⁵The woman said to him, "Sir, give me this water so that I won't get thirsty and have to keep coming here to draw water."

¹⁶He told her, "Go, call your husband and come back."

¹⁷"I have no husband," she replied.

Jesus said to her, "You are right when you say you have no husband. ¹⁸The fact is, you have had five husbands, and the man you now have is not your husband. What you have just said is quite true."

¹⁹"Sir," the woman said, "I can see that you are a prophet. ²⁰Our fathers worshiped on this mountain, but you Jews claim that the place where we must worship is in Jerusalem."

²¹Jesus declared, "Believe me, woman, a time is coming when you will worship the Father neither on this mountain nor in Jerusalem. ²²You Samaritans worship what you do not know; we worship what we do know, for salvation is from the Jews. ²³Yet a time is coming and has now come when the true worshipers will worship the Father in spirit and truth, for they are the kind of worshipers the Father seeks. ²⁴God is spirit, and his worshipers must worship in spirit and in truth."

²⁵The woman said, "I know that Messiah" (called Christ) "is coming. When he comes, he will explain everything to us."

²⁶Then Jesus declared, "I who speak to you am he."

1–3 Jesus' early ministry in the region of Judea was gaining increasing attention. The growing number of his disciples excited the curiosity of the Pharisees, who constituted the ruling religious class. The growth of any messianic movement could easily be interpreted as having political overtones, and Jesus did not want to become involved in any outward conflict with the state, whether Jewish or Roman. In order to avoid a direct clash, he left Judea and journeyed northward to Galilee.

4 The shortest route from Jerusalem to Galilee lay on the high road straight through Samaritan territory. Many Jews would not travel by that road, for they regarded any contact with Samaritans as defiling. Immediately after the fall of the northern kingdom in 722 B.C., the Assyrians had deported the Israelites from their land and had resettled it with captives from other countries. These had brought with them their own gods, whose worship they had combined with remnants of the worship of Jehovah and Baal in a mongrel type of religion. When the descendants of the southern captivity returned from Babylon in 539 B.C. to renew their worship under the Law, they found a complete rift between themselves and the inhabitants of Samaria, both religiously and politically. In the time of Nehemiah, the Samaritans opposed the rebuilding of the walls of Jerusalem (Neh 4:1–2); and later, in Maccabean times, they accepted the Hellenization of their religion when they dedicated their temple on Mount Gerizim to Zeus Xenios. By the time of Jesus a strong rivalry and hatred prevailed.

The words "had to" translate an expression of necessity. While the term speaks of general necessity rather than of personal obligation, in this instance it must refer to some compulsion other than mere convenience. As the Savior of all men, Jesus had to confront the smoldering suspicion and enmity between Jew and Samaritan by ministering to his enemies.

5 Sychar was a small village near Shechem, about half a mile from Jacob's well, which is located in the modern Shechem or Nablus. Opinion differs as to whether Sychar was the modern Askar or the Tell Balatah, where the old city of Shechem was found. El Askar is farther from the well than ancient Shechem and had a spring of its own. Although the old city had been largely destroyed by John Hyrcanus in 107 B.C., it is probable that some inhabitants remained in the vicinity and used this well for their water supply.

6 The well of Jacob lies at the foot of Mount Gerizim, the center of Samaritan worship. It is one of the historic sites in Palestine that we are reasonably certain of. The "sixth hour" would probably have been about noon, reckoning from daybreak. It was an unusual time for women to come to a village well for water. Perhaps the Samaritan woman had a sudden need, or perhaps she did not care to meet the other women of the community. In consideration of her general character, the other women may have shunned her.

7–8 Undoubtedly the woman was surprised to find a man sitting by the well and doubly surprised to be addressed by a Jew. Jesus' initial approach was by a simple request for water, which would presuppose a favorable response. One would hardly refuse a drink of cold water to a thirsty traveler in the heat of the day. The request did have a surprising element, however, for no Jewish rabbi would have volunteered to carry on a public conversation with a woman, nor would he have deigned to drink from a Samaritan's cup, as she implied by her answer.

9–10 There was a trace of sarcasm in the woman's reply, as if she meant, "We Samaritans are the dirt under your feet until you want something; then we are good enough!" Jesus paid no attention to her flippancy or to her bitterness. He was more interested in

54

winning the woman than in winning an argument. He appealed to her curiosity by the phrase "If you knew." He implied that because of the nature of his person he could bestow on her a gift of God that would be greater than any ordinary water. His allusion was intended to lift her level of thinking from that of material need to spiritual realities.

11 The woman heard his words but missed his meaning. "Living water" meant to her fresh spring water such as the well supplied. She could not understand how he could provide this water without having any means of drawing it from the well. Her comment was appropriate to one whose comprehension was tied to the earthy and material, for the well even today is over seventy-five feet deep; and "it has prob. been filled with much debris over the years since it was dug" (ZPEB, 3:388).

12 The woman's reference to "our father Jacob" was perhaps designed to bolster the importance of the Samaritans in the eyes of a Jewish rabbi. She was well aware of the low esteem the Jews had of her people. Josephus tells us that the Samaritans claimed their ancestry through Joseph and Ephraim and Manasseh (Antiq. 11.341).

13–15 Jesus' second reply emphasized the contrast between the water in the well and what he intended to give. The material water would allay thirst only temporarily; the spiritual water would quench the inner thirst forever. The water in the well had to be drawn up with hard labor; the spiritual water would bubble up from within. Because of her nonspiritual perspective, the woman's interests were very selfish. All she wanted was something to save the effort of the long, hot trip from the village.

16–17 Jesus' request to call her husband was both proper and strategic—proper because it was not regarded as good etiquette for a woman to talk with a man unless her husband were present; strategic because it placed her in a dilemma from which she could not free herself without admitting her need. She had no husband she could call, and she would not want to confess her sexual irregularities to a stranger. The abruptness of her reply shows that she was at last emotionally touched.

18 Jesus shocked the woman when he lifted the curtain on her past life. The conversation had passed from the small-talk stage to the personal. Her evil deeds were being exposed by the light, but was she willing to acknowledge the truth?

19–20 Realizing his superhuman knowledge, the woman called him a prophet; but then she tried to divert him. Since his probing was becoming uncomfortably personal, she began to argue a religious issue. She raised the old controversy between Jews and Samaritans, whether worship should be offered on Mount Gerizim, at the foot of which they stood, or at Jerusalem, where Solomon's temple had been built.

The Samaritans founded their claim on the historic fact that when Moses instructed the people concerning the entrance into the Promised Land, he commanded that they set up an altar on Mount Ebal and that the tribes should be divided, half on Ebal and half on Gerizim. As the Levites read the Law, the people responded antiphonally. Those on Gerizim pronounced the blessings of God and those on Ebal, the curses of God on sin (Deut 27:1–28:68). The Jews held that since Solomon had been commissioned to build the temple in Jerusalem, the center of worship would be located there. The controversy was endless, and Jesus did not intend to allow himself to be drawn into a futile discussion.

21-23 Jesus avoided the argument by elevating the issue above mere location. He made no concessions and intimated that the Samaritans' worship was confused: "You Samaritans worship what you do not know." Probably he was alluding to the error of the woman's ancestors, who had accepted a syncretism of foreign deities with the ancestral God of the Jewish faith. True worship is that of the spirit, which means that the worshiper must deal honestly and openly with God. She, on the contrary, had been furtive and unwilling to open her heart to God.

24 "God is spirit, and his worshipers must worship in spirit and in truth" carries one of the four descriptions of God found in the New Testament. The other three are "God is light" (1 John 1:5), "God is love" (1 John 4:8, 16), and "God is a consuming fire" (Heb 12:29). Jesus was endeavoring to convey to the woman that God cannot be confined to one place nor conceived of as a material being. He cannot be represented adequately by an abstract concept, which is intrinsically impersonal, nor can any idol depict his likeness since he is not material. Only "the Word become flesh" could represent him adequately.

25 Mystified by Jesus' words, the woman finally confessed her ignorance and at the same time expressed her longing: "I know that Messiah is coming. When he comes, he will explain everything to us." It was the one nebulous hope that she had of finding God, for she expected that the coming Messiah would explain the mysteries of life. There was a Samaritan tradition that the prophet predicted by Moses in Deuteronomy 18:15 would come to teach God's people all things. On this sincere though vague hope Jesus founded his appeal to her spiritual consciousness.

26 This is the one occasion when Jesus voluntarily declared his messiahship. The synoptic Gospels show that normally he did not make such a public claim; on the contrary, he urged his disciples to say nothing about it (Matt 16:20; Mark 8:29–30; Luke 9:20–21). In Galilee, where there were many would-be Messiahs and a constant unrest based on the messianic hope, such a claim would have been dangerous. In Samaria the concept would probably have been regarded more as religious than political and would have elicited a ready hearing for his teaching rather than a subversive revolt. Furthermore, this episode presumably occurred early in his ministry when he was not so well known.

Notes

6, 11-12 Two different words are translated "well" in this incident. The first, in v.6, is πηγή (pēgē), which refers to the source or spring discovered by Jacob. The second word, φρέαρ (phrear), used in vv.11-12, denotes the shaft dug into the ground to reach the water. The well tapped a subterranean spring that never ran dry. God supplied the water, but access to it was gained through a man. Now a greater than Jacob was offering through himself access to water that would satisfy throughout eternity.

24 The KJV rendering of πνεῦμα ὁ θεός (pneuma ho theos) as "God is a spirit" is misleading. Greek grammar has no indefinite article; its inclusion or exclusion is at the translators' discretion, whose decision, hopefully, is based on context and other Scripture. The point Jesus was trying to make here is not that God is one spirit among many. Rather, Jesus was seeking to lift the conversation

56

into the sphere of the spiritual and heavenly since the woman kept referring to human ancestry, Mount Gerizim, and traditional worship practices. The anarthrous construction and Gr. word order place the emphasis on the essential character of God; thus the essence of true worship must be on God's terms and in accord with his nature.

---

b. *The return of the disciples*

4:27–38

27Just then his disciples returned and were surprised to find him talking with a woman. But no one asked, "What do you want?" or "Why are you talking with her?"

28Then, leaving her water jar, the woman went back to the town and said to the people, 29"Come, see a man who told me everything I ever did. Could this be the Christ?" 30They came out of the town and made their way toward him.

31Meanwhile his disciples urged him, "Rabbi, eat something."

32But he said to them, "I have food to eat that you know nothing about."

33Then his disciples said to each other, "Could someone have brought him food?"

34"My food," said Jesus, "is to do the will of him who sent me and to finish his work. 35Do you not say, 'Four months more and then the harvest'? I tell you, open your eyes and look at the fields! They are ripe for harvest. 36Even now the reaper draws his wages, even now he harvests the crop for eternal life, so that the sower and the reaper may be glad together. 37Thus the saying, 'One sows and another reaps' is true. 38I sent you to reap what you have not worked for. Others have done the hard work, and you have reaped the benefits of their labor."

27 The disciples had left Jesus at the well. He was tired, and there would have been no need for him to have accompanied them into the town to buy food. They were surprised to find him talking with a woman—an apparent violation of custom—but they respected him too highly to question his behavior.

28–29 As the disciples approached, the woman made her way back to Sychar to report the interview to her fellow villagers. She was so excited that she forgot her water pot. At the village she was bold enough to suggest that perhaps the new person she had met might be the Messiah. "You don't suppose this could be the Messiah, do you?" would be a fair translation of her words.

30 It would be unlikely that the elders of Sychar would accept theological information from a woman of her reputation, and she did not venture to make a dogmatic pronouncement. Nevertheless, her manner was so sincere and her invitation so urgent that they immediately proceeded to the well to investigate.

31–34 The disciples were mainly interested in Jesus' physical welfare. He must have been exhausted by the travel of the morning. They were amazed that he was not hungry and wondered whether somebody else had given him food. He tried to tell them that the satisfaction of completing the work the Father had entrusted to him was greater than any food he might have been given. If the "had to" in v.4 reflects the plan of the Father for this trip, Jesus was telling the disciples that he did not live on bread alone but on every word that comes from the mouth of God (cf. Matt 4:4).

35 "Four months more and then the harvest" is probably a quotation of a current proverb. Having once sowed the grain, all the farmer needed to do was wait for it to ripen. Jesus was pointing out that the spiritual harvest is always ready and must be reaped before it spoils. As he was speaking, the Samaritans were leaving the town and coming across the fields toward him (v.30). The eagerness of the people the Jews regarded as alien and rejected showed that they were like grain ready for harvesting.

36–38 The disciples would not have to wait indefinitely for the result of their mission; the sowing and reaping could go on together. Jesus implied that they had already received a commission to reap for him and that they could benefit from the preparation he and the prophets had made. The reaping of people for the granary of God is not the task of any one group, nor is it confined to one era. Each reaps the benefit of its forerunners, and succeeding generations in turn gain from the accomplishments of their predecessors. As Paul said, "I planted the seed, Apollos watered it, but God made it grow" (1 Cor 3:6). Perhaps v.38 is an allusion to the preaching of John the Baptist, whose message of repentance had prepared the way for the disciples' preaching about Jesus.

c. The faith of the Samaritans

4:39–42

> ³⁹Many of the Samaritans from that town believed in him because of the woman's testimony, "He told me everything I ever did." ⁴⁰So when the Samaritans came to him they urged him to stay with them, and he stayed two days. ⁴¹And because of his words many more became believers.
> ⁴²They said to the woman, "We no longer believe just because of what you said; now we have heard for ourselves, and we know that this man really is the Savior of the world."

39–42 These few verses indicate two necessary and interrelated bases for belief: (1) the testimony of others and (2) personal contact with Jesus. This woman's witness opened the way to him for the villagers. If he could penetrate the shell of her materialism and present a message that would transform her, the Samaritans also could believe that he might be the Messiah. That stage of belief was only introductory, however. The second stage was hearing him for themselves, and it brought them to the settled conviction expressed in "we know" (v.42). "No longer" implies that they maintained their belief in him, but not solely on the basis of the woman's testimony. They had progressed from a faith built on the witness of another to a faith built on their own experience.

Notes

42 Two verbs may be translated "know": γινώσκω (ginōskō) and οἶδα (oida). The former usually implies knowledge by contact or experience; the second more generally denotes knowledge of facts or knowledge by intellectual process. While it would be precarious to contend that John always draws a sharp line between the two, the use of the latter in v.42 seems to fit the distinction, because it states a knowledge of fact that results in a settled conviction. The Samaritans are expressing assurance of a truth, not merely a progressive acquaintance with a person or situation.

9. *The interview with the nobleman*

4:43–54

⁴³After the two days he left for Galilee. ⁴⁴(Now Jesus himself had pointed out that a prophet has no honor in his own country.) ⁴⁵When he arrived in Galilee, the Galileans welcomed him. They had seen all that he had done in Jerusalem at the Passover Feast, for they also had been there.

⁴⁶Once more he visited Cana in Galilee, where he had turned the water into wine. And there was a certain royal official whose son lay sick at Capernaum. ⁴⁷When this man heard that Jesus had arrived in Galilee from Judea, he went to him and begged him to come and heal his son, who was close to death.

⁴⁸"Unless you people see miraculous signs and wonders," Jesus told him, "you will never believe."

⁴⁹The royal official said, "Sir, come down before my child dies."

⁵⁰Jesus replied, "You may go. Your son will live."

The man took Jesus at his word and departed. ⁵¹While he was still on the way, his servants met him with the news that his boy was living. ⁵²When he inquired as to the time when his son got better, they said to him, "The fever left him yesterday at the seventh hour."

⁵³Then the father realized that this was the exact time at which Jesus had said to him, "Your son will live." So he and all his household believed.

⁵⁴This was the second miraculous sign that Jesus performed, having come from Judea to Galilee.

43 The progress to Galilee is closely connected with the episode at Samaria. John seems to focus his Gospel on clusters of events. Compare 1:19, 29, 35, 43, and 2:1, as well as those chronological groupings that appear later.

44 The Johannine footnote "Now Jesus himself had pointed out that a prophet has no honor in his own country" is recorded also in Matthew 13:57 and Mark 6:4. Both of these express Jesus' reaction to the negative attitude the inhabitants of Nazareth in Galilee took toward him. Chronologically that episode occurred later than the visit to Galilee recorded in this chapter. The author was applying to the immediate situation a principle that Jesus stated on two other occasions. Did he intend to apply it to Judea or to Galilee? While the immediate context might be taken to relate to some previous experience in Judea, there is no indication that Jesus had at this time been the object of a wholesale rejection there, though some hostility may have been manifested by the Pharisees (4:1). In the light of Jesus' comment to the nobleman in v.48, it seems more likely that John was simply stating that Jesus had already been rebuffed in Galilee (cf. Luke 4:24–29) and that he was questioning the motives of the nobleman in the light of past experience. At this time the Galileans were somewhat more receptive because of the miracles they had witnessed at the Passover in Jerusalem. John says little in this Gospel about Jesus' Galilean activities, though he shows knowledge of them (2:1–11; 4:43–54; 6:1–7:13).

45 The Galileans hoped Jesus would duplicate the signs they had witnessed in Jerusalem while they were attending the Passover Feast. They were disappointed to discover that Jesus had no intention of exhibiting his powers to satisfy their curiosity. In Nazareth he performed few miracles, and it was probably the attitude of these people that caused him to rebuff the nobleman (v.48).

46 The reason for revisiting Cana is not given. It may be that Jesus expected to find some disciples who had believed on him after the miracle at the wedding. The royal official (*basilikos*) may have been a member of Herod's court. His son had been ill for some time and was not recovering from his sickness. Therefore, the father felt compelled to seek some further aid. It is possible that the official was a Gentile. If so, the three persons Jesus interviewed in this early ministry represented the Jews, the Samaritans, and the Gentiles —in short, the world he came to save. John's Gospel, though it chronicles chiefly the ministry of Jesus in Jerusalem, has a much wider horizon than the area of his residence.

47 The report that Jesus had healed people in Jerusalem must have reached this man's ears. Learning that Jesus had returned to Galilee, the man immediately sought Jesus out and urged him to heal his son, who was dangerously ill. The imperfect tense of the verb "begged" (*ērōta*, from *erōtaō*, to "ask" or "request") implies repeated or persistent action. The request was not casual but insistent.

48 The reply of Jesus seems like a heartless rejection. He seemed to insinuate that the official, like the rest of the Galileans, was only giving an excuse for eliciting a miracle from him. On the other hand, Jesus' words may express his hope more than his exasperation. He desired a belief characterized by dedication rather than amazement, and the second half of the episode shows that his aim was to inculcate a genuine commitment rather than merely to perform a cure.

49 The genuine distress of the father is demonstrated by his words: "Sir, come down at once before my little boy dies!" (lit. tr.). The use of the aorist tense of "die" (*apothanein*) to describe the impending crisis is in contrast with the present tense in v.47 (*apothnēskein*), which describes the progress of the illness. This indicates that the case was desperate.

50 Jesus' response still seems somewhat impersonal and casual. By dismissing the official with the statement that his son was alive, Jesus created a dilemma of faith. If the father refused to return to Capernaum without taking Jesus with him, he would show that he did not believe Jesus' word and would consequently receive no benefit because of his distrust. On the other hand, if he followed Jesus' order, he would be returning to the dying boy with no outward assurance that the lad would recover. He was forced to make the difficult choice between insisting on evidence and thus showing disbelief and of exercising faith without any tangible proof to encourage him. The official chose the second horn of the dilemma; he "took Jesus at his word" (ASV "believed the word") and set out on his return journey. He learned faith by the compulsion of necessity.

51–52 People are amazed by coincidences, but generally they do not attribute them to the direct activity of God. The official took a "chance" and went home as Jesus had commanded him to, and a miraculous report greeted him "while he was still on the way." There is an interesting progression in the description of the boy's condition. First the news came that "his boy was living." But more than that, the man was curious to know "the time when his son got better." Finally, he was told, "The fever left him yesterday at the seventh hour."

53–54 When the father considered the details of his meeting with Jesus and the good news concerning his son's recovery, he was convinced that it was more than coincidence at work. The timing was miraculous, and the boy's recovery was more than even circumstances could have brought about. "So he and his household believed."

The notation of succession in signs mentioned in v.54 is not repeated in the remainder of the Gospel. Though John says little about Jesus' Galilean ministry in general, he regarded it as important. If, as his footnote (v.44) implies, the Galileans were unlikely to believe on Jesus because he was well known to them, the convincing character of the two signs recorded here and the forceful demonstration of God's response to faith afforded by the second provided cogent illustrations for the main theme of belief.

Notes

49 "Little boy" is the translation of παιδίον (*paidion*), a diminutive that expresses the father's feelings more vividly than the more formal υἱός (*huios*, "son") of vv.46–47.

B. *The Rise of Controversy* (5:1–47)

1. *The healing of the paralytic*

5:1–15

¹Some time later, Jesus went up to Jerusalem for a feast of the Jews. ²Now there is in Jerusalem near the Sheep Gate a pool, which in Aramaic is called Bethesda and which is surrounded by five covered colonnades. ³Here a great number of disabled people used to lie—the blind, the lame, the paralyzed. ⁵One who was there had been an invalid for thirty-eight years. ⁶When Jesus saw him lying there and learned that he had been in this condition for a long time, he asked him, "Do you want to get well?"

⁷"Sir," the invalid replied, "I have no one to help me into the pool when the water is stirred. While I am trying to get in, someone else goes down ahead of me."

⁸Then Jesus said to him, "Get up! Pick up your mat and walk." ⁹At once the man was cured; he picked up his mat and walked.

The day on which this took place was a Sabbath, ¹⁰and so the Jews said to the man who had been healed, "It is the Sabbath; the law forbids you to carry your mat."

¹¹But he replied, "The man who made me well said to me, 'Pick up your mat and walk.' "

¹²So they asked him, "Who is this fellow who told you to pick it up and walk?"

¹³The man who was healed had no idea who it was, for Jesus had slipped away into the crowd that was there.

¹⁴Later Jesus found him at the temple and said to him, "See, you are well again. Stop sinning or something worse may happen to you." ¹⁵The man went away and told the Jews that it was Jesus who had made him well.

1 The words "some time later" mark a break in chronological sequence. Comparison with the Synoptic accounts shows that a measurable amount of time may have elapsed between the healing of the son of the royal official at Capernaum and the episode of the paralytic at the Pool of Bethesda. The reference to the feast does not define the time since the feast is unnamed. Some MSS employ the definite article, calling it "the feast." If this were the Passover, the time would be almost a year later than Jesus' arrival in Galilee as described in John 4:46. Apparently John was less interested in chronology than in following the trend of Jesus' conflict with unbelief.

2 The traditional location of the pool is beneath the present site of the Church of Saint Anne, on the northwest corner of Jerusalem and near the gate by the sheep market. Excavations have shown that it was surrounded by a colonnade on all four sides and down the middle of the pool, making five "porches" (ASV) in all.

The name of the section of the city where the pool was located is variously given in the MS tradition as Bethzatha, Bethesda, and Bethsaida. The various readings may arise from differing attempts to transliterate the Hebrew or Aramaic original. Bethesda (house of mercy) has the support of the majority of MSS and corresponds to the section of the city best suited to the description given by John.

3-4 Another problem arises from the absence of v.4 from the best MS texts. It is omitted by all MSS dated prior to the fourth century, though the rest generally include it with numerous variations. It is generally regarded as a gloss that was introduced to explain the intermittent agitation of the water, which the populace considered to be a potential source of healing. There is no question that they congregated at the pool, hoping to be cured of their ailments. The explanation of the moving of the water was probably added later.

5-6 Confinement to a bed for thirty-eight years would leave the sufferer so weak he would be unable to walk or even stand for any length of time. His case would be hopeless. Jesus selected for his attention the person who seemed most needy. Since he had been afflicted for thirty-eight years, he must have been well on in years. Jesus' question must have seemed rather naive to him. Who would not want to be healed from utter helplessness? Yet the question also implies an appeal to the will, which the long years of discouragement may have paralyzed. Jesus thus challenged the man's will to be cured.

7 The invalid's reply shows that he had lost his independent determination. He was waiting for somebody to assist him. Such efforts as he had been able to make had proved futile, and he was despairing of success.

8 The healing was not a response to a request, nor did it presuppose an expression of faith on the part of the man. Jesus asked him to do the impossible, to stand on his feet, pick up his bedroll, and go his way. Renewed by the miraculous influx of new power, the man responded at once and did so. Jesus supplied even the will to be cured!

9-10 The outcome of the miracle was twofold: the paralytic was healed and a controversy was precipitated. Since the healing took place on the Sabbath, it brought Jesus directly into conflict with the religious authorities. The rabbinic application of the fourth commandment involved all kinds of casuistic interpretation, much of which was overdrawn. The Synoptics record other occasions on which Jesus' activities on the Sabbath excited the criticism of his opponents (Matt 12:1–14; Mark 2:23–3:6; Luke 6:1–11). Jesus' healing on the Sabbath was one of the factors that brought him into disfavor with the religious leaders in Jerusalem.

11-12 The paralytic seems to have felt no particular gratitude to Jesus for his healing. He took no responsibility for the action on the Sabbath; and after Jesus had dealt with him the second time, he immediately informed the Jewish leaders who it was that had transgressed the Sabbath law. It seems quite unlikely that he would have been ignorant of the reason for their inquiry.

13 John indicates that on at least four occasions Jesus quietly withdrew from a scene of controversy. Each of these occurred after an argument with the Jews over his claims (8:59; 10:39; 12:36). All these reinforce the concept of the fourth Gospel that Jesus was immune to danger until the hour of his passion arrived (7:30; 8:20).

14–15 Jesus' interest in the man is implied in the word "find." Apparently Jesus searched for him because he was prompted by concern for his spiritual state as well as for his physical illness. The command "Stop sinning" presupposes the possibility that the man's affliction may have been caused by his own sin. There is no indication that this encounter strengthened the man's faith and attachment to Jesus; in fact, the contrary could easily be inferred. But he did confess Jesus as his healer.

Notes

---

1 External evidence favors the anarthrous use of ἐορτή (heortē, "feast") in "a feast of the Jews." The two oldest papyri texts, P[66, 75], and a number of other important MSS support this reading, though some add the definite article ἡ (hē). There may have been many speculations concerning which feast it might have been; and even with the article the conclusion would still be uncertain, though probably that would refer to the Passover. If it is the Passover, it affords a chronological basis for concluding that Jesus' ministry occupied three and a half years, on the assumption that each reference to the Passover represents a different year (2:13; 6:4; 11:55).

2 There seems to be no agreement among commentators on the proper transliteration of "Bethesda." Morris favors "Bethesda" (NIC, pp. 300–301); Hendriksen accepts "Bethzatha" (1:190); R. Brown agrees on "Bethesda" (29:206–7). J.T. Milik cites from 3Q15 (11.12–13, #57) an allusion to treasure buried on the eastern hill of Jerusalem "in Bet Esdatayin, in the pool at the entrance to its smaller basin" (Discoveries in the Judean Desert [Oxford: Oxford University, 1962], 3:271). "Bethsaida" is attested by P[66], but it is probably an assimilation to the name of the Galilean town mentioned earlier in John 1:44. Despite the ambiguity of the name as given in the MSS, the location seems now to be fairly well settled.

Turner and Mantey follow the older suggestion of Robinson, Schaff, and G.A. Smith that the pool should be identified with Gihon, which has intermittent action that would cause the water to be "stirred" (v.7) (pp. 129–31). However, current archaeological evidence has left this view with few advocates.

4 Verse 4 is omitted in the important, early MSS and by representatives of the versions. It is generally understood to be an explanatory gloss, dating probably from the late second century.

---

2. *Jesus' defense of his sonship* (5:16–47)

a. *The prerogatives of sonship*

5:16–30

> ¹⁶So, because Jesus was doing these things on the Sabbath, the Jews persecuted him. ¹⁷Jesus said to them, "My Father is always at his work to this very day, and I, too, am working." ¹⁸For this reason the Jews tried all the harder to kill him; not only was he breaking the Sabbath, but he was even calling God his own Father, making himself equal with God.
> ¹⁹Jesus gave them this answer: "I tell you the truth, the Son can do nothing by himself; he can do only what he sees his Father doing, because whatever the

Father does the Son also does. ²⁰For the Father loves the Son and shows him all he does. Yes, to your amazement he will show him even greater things than these. ²¹For just as the Father raises the dead and gives them life, even so the Son gives life to whom he is pleased to give it. ²²Moreover, the Father judges no one, but has entrusted all judgment to the Son, ²³that all may honor the Son just as they honor the Father. He who does not honor the Son does not honor the Father, who sent him.

²⁴"I tell you the truth, whoever hears my word and believes him who sent me has eternal life and will not be condemned; he has crossed over from death to life. ²⁵I tell you the truth, a time is coming and has now come when the dead will hear the voice of the Son of God and those who hear will live. ²⁶For as the Father has life in himself, so he has granted the Son to have life in himself. ²⁷And he has given him authority to judge because he is the Son of Man.

²⁸"Do not be amazed at this, for a time is coming when all who are in their graves will hear his voice ²⁹and come out—those who have done good will rise to live, and those who have done evil will rise to be condemned. ³⁰By myself I can do nothing; I judge only as I hear, and my judgment is just, for I seek not to please myself but him who sent me.

16 This verse introduces the element of controversy between Jesus and his opponents. The immediate cause was the healing on the Sabbath, which they interpreted as a violation of the fourth commandment: "Remember the Sabbath day by keeping it holy. . . . On it you shall not do any work" (Exod 20:8, 10). John records one other occasion when a healing was performed on the Sabbath for the same reason and with the same reaction. The synoptic Gospels also add other instances (Mark 2:23–28; 3:1–6; Luke 13:10–16; 14:1–6). The underlying provocation for the controversy was Jesus' attitude toward the Jewish traditions, which had grown up as interpretation of the Law and were often more rigid than the Law itself. Jesus contended that allaying human need was no violation of the Divine Law. He reminded his critics that if the Law allowed a man to rescue an animal from danger on a Sabbath day, the restoration of a man to health should certainly be permitted (Luke 14:5).

17 Jesus' argument for healing on the Sabbath was that God does not suspend his activities on the Sabbath. The laws of nature take no holiday. If a man cuts himself on the Sabbath, the healing process begins immediately. But more important than pointing out the unceasing laws of nature, Jesus identified his activities with those of the Father. Jesus claimed to be continuing the creative work of God.

18 The Jews were angry because of Jesus' violation of the Sabbath, but they were furious when he was so presumptuous as to claim equality with the Father. This claim of Jesus widened the breach between his critics and himself, for they understood that by it he was asserting his deity. His explanation shows that he did not claim identity with the Father as one person, but he asserted his unity with the Father in a relationship that could be described as sonship. This sonship has many facets, as shown in vv.19–24.

19 The Son is dependent on the Father. He does not act independently apart from the Father's will and purpose. Throughout this Gospel Jesus continually asserted that his work was to do the will of the Father (4:34; 5:30; 8:28; 12:50; 15:10). Equality of nature, identity of objective, and subordination of will are interrelated in Christ. John presents him as the Son, not as the slave, of God, yet as the perfect agent of the divine purpose and the complete revelation of the divine nature.

20 The Son is loved by the Father. The relationship is not that of master and slave, nor of employer and employee, but of a Father and a Son who are united by love. The Father has revealed to the Son the purpose and plan of his activity, much as the head of a family discusses with the others the plan he wishes to follow.

21 The Son is empowered by the Father. God is the source of life. He alone has power to reverse the processes of the material world and to bring life out of death. This supreme power the Father has conferred on the Son. The demonstration of this power appears in the later sign of the raising of Lazarus (John 11:41–44).

22–23 The Son is entrusted with the power of judgment. He possesses equal dignity with the Father and shares with him judicial as well as executive authority. Conversely, since the Son is equal in authority, he can rightly claim equal honor with God.

24 The Son is the arbiter of destiny. The determination of this destiny is immediate: "Whoever hears my word and believes him who sent me has eternal life and will not be condemned." Eternal life becomes the possession of the believer at the moment of acceptance; the future judgment will only confirm what has already taken place. The assurance of salvation does not begin at death or at a future judgment. "He has crossed over" is in the perfect tense, which indicates an accomplished transit and a settled state.

25 The phrase "and has now come" may refer to the present era that will terminate in the return of Christ and the resurrection of the dead, or it may refer to the power Jesus had to raise the dead during his lifetime, as in the case of Lazarus. There is another sense in which our Lord's words are true. As the source of life, he was promising to those who were spiritually dead, like the woman at the well, a new and eternal life if they would listen to his voice.

26 We do not have inherent life within us. Our life is derived from others. In the physical sense, our life is given to us by our parents. However, even that transaction is shrouded in deep mystery. Again Jesus claimed deity by saying he was not dependent on another for life just as the Father derived his life from no one. Jesus possesses inherent life, the power to create and the power to renew life that has been extinguished.

27 The title "Son of Man" has appeared twice previously in this Gospel: once in describing Jesus' function as a revelator of divine truth (1:51) and once in connection with his function as a Redeemer (3:14). Generally it is used only by Jesus concerning himself. As the Son of Man he is qualified to judge humanity because he belongs to it and can understand the needs and viewpoints of men. As the Epistle to the Hebrews states, "He had to be made like his brothers in every way, in order that he might become a merciful and faithful high priest in service to God, and that he might make atonement for the sins of the people" (Heb 2:17). Hebrews emphasizes Jesus' priestly function rather than his judicial position, but the underlying concept is the same.

28–29 This passage contains one of the few references to eschatology in John's Gospel. No chronological distinction is drawn here between the resurrection of the righteous and that of the wicked, neither is any such distinction excluded. John says little about a program, but he does emphasize the fact that Jesus will be the door to the eternal world.

The double resurrection assumes that both the righteous and the wicked will receive bodies in the future life and that presumably each body will express the character of the person who is resurrected. Some commentators claim that the resurrection of v.25 is wholly spiritual while that of vv.29 and 30 is physical and future. There seems to be an unnecessary distinction here, even though Jesus said that the time had already come when the dead would hear the voice of the Son of God, thus referring it to the present as he experienced it. The raising of Lazarus (ch. 11) can be taken as a demonstration of his meaning. Verses 29–30 are simply more explicit and completely future. Obviously spiritual resurrection from being dead in transgressions and sins (Eph 2:1) must precede physical resurrection.

30 Verse 30 marks a transition from self-affirmation to testimony. Jesus spoke with the confidence of being commissioned by the Father, not with the arrogance of self-assertion. Twenty-five times in this Gospel he asserts that he was sent by the Father. Two different words are used: *pempō*, which means to "send" in a broad or general sense, and *apostellō*, which has the additional connotation of "equip," "commission," or "delegate." In many of the occurrences in John these words seem to be used interchangeably since both are applied to the person of Christ. The former, however, is generally used descriptively in a participial form, "he who sent"; the latter is used as a finite verb in making an assertion of action. *Apostellō* is used exclusively in Jesus' prayer of John 17, where he speaks directly to the Father. Both appear in the last instance in John 20:21: "As the Father has sent (*apestalken*) me, I am sending (*pempō*) you." If any real difference can be detected, Jesus is saying, "In the same way that the Father commissioned me, so am I dispatching you on my errand." Perhaps it is better not to strain a point but merely to say that wherever either of these verbs is used concerning Jesus, it refers to his commission for the ministry, which distinguishes him as the Son of God.

b. *The witnesses to his authority*

5:31–47

31"If I testify about myself, my testimony is not valid. 32There is another who testifies in my favor, and I know that his testimony about me is valid.

33"You have sent to John and he has testified to the truth. 34Not that I accept human testimony; but I mention it that you may be saved. 35John was a lamp that burned and gave light, and you chose for a time to enjoy his light.

36"I have testimony weightier than that of John. For the very work that the Father has given me to finish, and which I am doing, testifies that the Father has sent me. 37And the Father who sent me has himself testified concerning me. You have never heard his voice nor seen his form, 38nor does his word dwell in you, for you do not believe the one he sent. 39You diligently study the Scriptures because you think that by them you possess eternal life. These are Scriptures that testify about me, 40yet you refuse to come to me to have life.

41"I do not accept praise from men, 42but I know you. I know that you do not have the love of God in your hearts. 43I have come in my Father's name, and you do not accept me; but if someone else comes in his own name, you will accept him. 44How can you believe if you accept praise from one another, yet make no effort to obtain the praise that comes from the only God?

45"But do not think I will accuse you before the Father. Your accuser is Moses, on whom your hopes are set. 46If you believed Moses, you would believe me, for he wrote about me. 47But since you do not believe what he wrote, how are you going to believe what I say?"

31 Because the authority of Jesus was questioned by his critics, he summoned witnesses to vouch for him. "Witness" or "testimony," whether verb or noun, is a common word

in this Gospel. The verb *martyreō* occurs thirty-three times. This term is used to describe the attestation of Jesus' character and power. Jesus gives five specific sources of testimony about himself.

Although Jesus discounts his own witness, "If I testify about myself," he still implies that it is valid. He said that it is "not valid" because under Jewish law the self-testimony of any man was not accepted in court. On another occasion he had said, "Even if I testify on my own behalf, my testimony is valid, for I know where I came from and where I am going" (John 8:14). The apparent contradiction can be resolved because the statement in John 5 is based on legal grounds whereas that in ch. 8 is based on personal knowledge. In consideration of Jesus' essential truthfulness, his witness concerning himself is sound, though in legal process it would not be admitted.

32 "There is another who testifies in my favor" could refer either to the Father or to John the Baptist, both of whom are mentioned in the context. The present tense of "testifies" (*martyrōn*), which implies continuing action in contrast to the perfect tense "has testified" (*memartyrēken*) applied to John the Baptist (v.33), favors the former view. Jesus was constantly conscious of the Father's confidence and support. On the other hand, the witness of John the Baptist follows immediately with v.33 and seems likely to be the elaboration of the statement in v.32.

33–34 "You have sent to John" is obviously a reference to the delegation sent from the Jewish rulers to John the Baptist when he was preaching in the Judean wilderness (1:19). The fact that they had already asked him for an explanation bound them to give proper consideration to his testimony. John had refused the title of Messiah but had predicted the coming of Jesus and had identified him at his appearance in such a way that his own disciples accepted Jesus as the Messiah (1:40). The testimony of John was effective; his preaching reached a wide audience of people and prepared the way for a further revelation of truth in the person of Jesus. Jesus appealed to the popular response that John elicited by pointing out that his audience had accepted John's message, which gave Jesus a place of ultimate authority. They could not consistently accept John's preaching and reject Jesus.

35 The content of the witness of John the Baptist has already been discussed in the comments on 1:19–34. He introduced Jesus to the public and to his disciples in particular as the Lamb of God and as the Son of God. John had burned himself out in his ministry. Possibly by this time he had been imprisoned; the past tense of the verb may imply that his ministry had closed. Jesus reminds his hearers that they had enjoyed John's preaching and had responded to it, but their response had been short lived and superficial. Now that Jesus had come with the fulfillment of John's message, they were paying scant attention to him.

36 Another witness is that of the works Jesus was doing. The Johannine use of this term "works" (*erga*) refers to those deeds that revealed Jesus' divine nature. As the quality of a man's deeds show his moral standards, skill, and personal competence, so Jesus' works marked him as superhuman in both his compassion and his power (cf. 3:19–21). He said later to those who questioned him, "The miracles I do in my Father's name speak for me" (10:25). In his final discourse to the disciples he asked them to believe him "on the evidence of the miracles [works] themselves" (14:11). Although he never performed miracles for the purpose of drawing attention to himself, he regarded them as valid proofs of his claims.

The Gospel lists seven of these works:
1. The turning of water into wine   (2:1–11)
2. The healing of the official's son   (4:43–54)
3. The healing of a paralytic   (5:1–15)
4. The feeding of the multitude   (6:1–14)
5. The walking on the water   (6:16–21)
6. The cure of the blind man   (9:1–41)
7. The raising of Lazarus   (11:1–44).

Each of these miracles demonstrated Jesus' power in a different area of human experience. They are called "signs" (*sēmeia*) because they point to something beyond themselves. Their significance does not lie in their extraordinary character but in the fact that Jesus was able to meet the emergencies of life directly and satisfactorily. It is noteworthy that they were generally followed by a confession of belief on the part of many of the spectators (2:11; 4:53; 6:66, 69; 9:38; 11:45).

37–38 The witness of the Father is distinguished from the works that the Father gave Jesus to perform. The allusion seems somewhat obscure, especially since Jesus disclaimed any visible or audible communication from God to the crowd in general. Nevertheless there were occasions on which a voice from heaven spoke, expressing approval of Jesus and affirming his sonship. The voice at the baptism and the utterance at the Transfiguration are recorded only by the Synoptics (see Matt 3:17; Mark 1:11; Luke 3:22; and Matt 17:5; Mark 9:7; Luke 9:35); the third appears in John 12:28. The first and third witnesses of the Father, though public, seem not to have been understood by the mixed crowd; the second was private. To a Jew, the voice from heaven would have meant the approval of God; yet this seems to have had little effect on the multitude. Jesus implies that his hearers had not apprehended the revelation of God because they had not believed him whom the Father had sent. Openness of belief must precede the reception of truth.

39–40 The verb "study" could be either an imperative, as KJV translates it, or an indicative, as in NIV. Probably the latter is the correct translation, for Jesus was stating a fact, not giving a command. After the destruction of the temple of Solomon in 586 B.C., the Jewish scholars of the Exile substituted the study of the Law for the observance of the temple ritual and sacrifices. They pored over the OT, endeavoring to extract the fullest possible meaning from its words, because they believed that the very study itself would bring them life. By so doing they missed the chief subject of the OT revelation. Jesus claimed the Law, the Prophets, and the Psalms (Writings) as witnesses to his person and claims (Luke 24:44). He rebuked his hearers for their inconsistency in studying the Scriptures so diligently while rejecting his claims, which were founded on those same Scriptures.

Jesus' statement reveals his attitude toward the OT. He accepted its divine authority and averred that its prophecies spoke of him (cf. Luke 24:27, 44). Not only did he affirm its predictive accuracy, but he also took both the principles and the predictions written in the Scriptures as a guide for his attitude and career. They prefigured his sacrifice (John 3:14–15), marked some of the events of the Passion (12:14–15; 18:9; 19:24, 28, 36), and seemed to be in the forefront of his thinking as the end approached.

41–42 The Scriptures are so designed that when people read them, they are to recognize and acknowledge God's glory. Even the Jews would agree to that. But Jesus said the people were incapable of both interpreting and applying the Scriptures, for as students of the Scriptures they should have known that they spoke of him. Because the Jews did not give "praise" (actually, the word is "glory" [*doxa*]) to Jesus, it was evident that they were spiritually unable to make the connection between the Scriptures and the Savior. But this came as no surprise to Jesus. The expression "I know you" is singularly forceful, for the perfect tense of the verb "know" (*egnōka*) implies a settled state of knowledge based on past experience (cf. John 2:24). Jesus would not entrust himself to those who responded solely on the basis of external circumstances, such as miracles. Outward adulation is of short duration.

43–44 Jesus expressed disappointment because the people would not accept his credentials though they would accept the personal claims of another who acted solely on his own authority. Jesus was not there as a representative of Caesar, or Zeus, or even himself. Men are more apt to receive other men than they are to receive one who comes in the name of God. Compare the choice of Barabbas over Jesus at the final trial (Luke 23:18–23). Verse 44 rebukes those students of the Scriptures who are more interested in establishing their competitive reputations for scholarship than in obeying the revelation of God so as to bring his approval.

45–47 Moses, the writer of the Law, was highly revered by the Jewish nation. The people would not knowingly do anything that would be contrary to the teaching of Moses and the Law. Their obedience to him was a source of pride. In fact, their very hope in securing God's favor and blessing lay in their relationship to Moses. Jesus' statement that their rejection of him would make them guilty before God even according to Moses was startling. Jesus told the people that the law of Moses would condemn them in their rejection of him because their failure to believe in him was essentially a rejection of Moses since Moses had prefigured him. Jesus said that a real belief in the revelation of the Law through Moses would lead to a belief in himself (cf. Luke 16:29–31).

Notes

---

36 Ἔργον (*ergon*, "work") appears twenty-seven times in the Gospel of John. In each instance the term implies the characteristic activity of the person it is ascribed to, whether men (3:19, 20, 21; 7:7; 8:39), God (4:34; 5:20; 6:28, 29; 9:3, 4; 10:37; 14:10), Satan (8:41), or Jesus (5:36; 7:3, 21; 10:25, 32–33, 38; 14:11, 12; 15:24; 17:4). Jesus referred several times to the work God had committed to him (4:34; 5:36; 9:3; 10:37; 17:4) and remarked that the Father was in him, doing his work (14:11). On a few occasions NIV translates ἔργον by "miracle" (7:3, 21; 10:25, 32, 38; 14:11; 15:24). While this is not a mistranslation since the "works" were in many instances miraculous, the stress lies more on the characteristic manifestations of Jesus' personality and commission than on the miraculous quality of his deeds. Not all were miracles, though the miracles should be included in the "works."

The application of the term ἔργον ("work") to Satan appears in the contrast Jesus drew between the works of Abraham and the works of his opponents' father. As a servant of God, Abraham set a standard for spiritual life his descendants had forgotten. Jesus reminded them that they were no longer walking in the steps of their forefather.

Jesus considered the "works" he performed to be one of the strongest witnesses to his claims (5:36; 14:10–11). They were not abnormal activities or special occasional miracles but were rather the usual mode of Jesus' activity when confronting a challenging situation. Because of this, the witness is doubly strong, for the "works" revealed the normal powers he exercised when they were needed.

42 The phrase τὴν ἀγάπην τοῦ θεοῦ (tēn agapēn tou theou, "the love of God") can denote either the "love from God" or the "love for God," depending on whether τοῦ θεοῦ (tou theou) is a subjective or objective genitive. In the former case it is God who supplies the love (cf. 1 John 4:7, 10, 19). Men do not respond to the person of Christ because they have not been the recipients of God's love. In the latter, the love is that which is directed towards God. Men do not love the Lord Jesus because they have no real love for God within them.

This is the first use of the noun ἀγάπη (agapē, "love") in the Gospel. John uses it seven times (13:35; 15:9, 10 bis, 13; 17:26), in addition to the copious use of the verb. As it is used in John, it speaks of a self-sacrificing, giving love (3:16). It is a love of action more than emotion and has in view the loved one's need.

C. The Beginning of Conflict (6:1–8:59)

Chapter 6 of John marks the watershed of Jesus' career. Up to this point his popularity had been increasing, in spite of the opposition of the leaders and the occasional grumbling of disaffected hearers or disciples. The interview with the disciples at Caesarea Philippi and the Transfiguration, which occurred shortly afterward, called for a new commitment on the part of the disciples and was followed by a new program on the part of Jesus. He openly declared to them that he would proceed to Jerusalem where he would be delivered up to death (Matt 16:13–17:13; Mark 8:27–32; Luke 9:18–36). John does not narrate these incidents, but his account parallels them to some degree. The feeding of the multitude is identical; there is an allusion to his impending death (John 6:51); and from that point the number of his disciples diminished (6:66), and the controversy with the Pharisees grew increasingly bitter.

1. The feeding of the five thousand

6:1–15

> [1]Some time after this, Jesus crossed to the far shore of the Sea of Galilee (that is, the Sea of Tiberias), [2]and a great crowd of people followed him because they saw the miraculous signs he had performed on the sick. [3]Then Jesus went up on the hillside and sat down with his disciples. [4]The Jewish Passover Feast was near.
>
> [5]When Jesus looked up and saw a great crowd coming toward him, he said to Philip, "Where shall we buy bread for these people to eat?" [6]He asked this only to test him, for he already had in mind what he was going to do.
>
> [7]Philip answered him, "Eight months' wages would not buy enough bread for each one to have a bite!"
>
> [8]Another of his disciples, Andrew, Simon Peter's brother, spoke up, [9]"Here is a boy with five small barley loaves and two small fish, but how far will they go among so many?"
>
> [10]Jesus said, "Have the people sit down." There was plenty of grass in that place, and the men sat down, about five thousand of them. [11]Jesus then took the loaves, gave thanks, and distributed to those who were seated as much as they wanted. He did the same with the fish.
>
> [12]When they had all had enough to eat, he said to his disciples, "Gather the pieces that are left over. Let nothing be wasted." [13]So they gathered them and filled twelve baskets with the pieces of the five barley loaves left over by those who had eaten.
>
> [14]After the people saw the miraculous sign that Jesus did, they began to say, "Surely this is the Prophet who is to come into the world." [15]Jesus, knowing that

they intended to come and make him king by force, withdrew again into the hills by himself.

1–4 This miracle is the only one that is mentioned in all the Gospels. This fact alone should alert us to its significance. The phrase "some time after this" shows that John does not specify the exact lapse of time between this event and the one previously recorded. The fact that Jesus was in Galilee may indicate that a segment of the Galilean ministry is presupposed as having already occurred. The feeding of the multitude took place in the spring shortly before the Passover (v.4). Perhaps some of the people belonged to a crowd of pilgrims who had come together from different parts of northern Galilee, in preparation for the annual pilgrimage to Jerusalem. Jesus was well known because of the miracles he had performed on sick people. John uses the word "signs" (*sēmeia*), though he gives no details of their character. His usage confirms his statement that Jesus performed "many other miraculous signs" during his ministry (20:30). The very fact that this one was selected enhances its importance.

The Synoptics indicate that Jesus had several motives in retreating to the north shore of the Sea of Galilee. The time had come to prepare the disciples for his death and to sort out those who would be loyal from those who would not. The determination of Jesus' enemies to remove him became known to him and to his disciples, and they had to confront this rapidly growing hostility. Furthermore, as the account shows, Jesus refused to take the part of a political Messiah or king. He was willing to meet basic needs but he would not assume the responsibility of leading a revolt or of creating a new nation. Knowing these things, he called the disciples together so that they could report on their recent ministries (Mark 6:30; Luke 9:10). Matthew adds that Jesus had just learned of the execution of John the Baptist (Matt 14:12–13) and that he withdrew to the wilderness with his disciples for consultation.

5–6 John's interest concentrates mainly on the relation of this occasion to the disciples. The crowd had come unbidden, prompted by curiosity and eagerness to share in Jesus' teaching and healing power. As the day declined, Jesus recognized that they were hungry. Desirous of involving the disciples in the responsibility for ministry, Jesus turned to Philip, asking, "Where shall we buy bread for these people to eat?" Jesus was not at a loss for a solution to the problem; he wished to educate the disciples by calling their attention to their responsibilities and by leading them to propose some plan of action.

7 Philip's reply shows that while he had a practical turn of mind, he was rather unimaginative. His calculations, however accurate, were futile, for he could only produce statistics to show what could not be done. The text translates "eight months' wages" rather than the literal "two hundred denarii" (*diakosiōn dēnariōn*). A denarius, which was worth approximately seventeen cents, was a day's wage for an unskilled laborer or soldier. If a man worked for six days a week, two hundred denarii would represent the pay for thirty-three weeks, which would be just about eight months. It would take a long time to save the equivalent of such a sum. No doubt none of the disciples would have enough money to subsidize the purchase of food for a crowd of approximately ten thousand persons, including women and children (Matt 14:21).

8–9 In contrast to Philip's pessimism, Andrew was more hopeful. He made the positive presentation of a boy's lunch: five small, flat barley cakes, made of the cheapest grain available, and the two fish, which probably were small pickled fish which served as hors d'oeuvres. Andrew doubted the value of his own suggestion, for he commented, "How far will they go among so many?"

10 The action of Jesus reveals both natural wisdom and supernatural power. His order to have the people sit down was necessary to stabilize the crowd so that there would not be a rush for the food. It also served to organize them in groups to facilitate serving. John mentions only the men, who numbered about five thousand; Matthew remarks that there were women and children also (Matt 14:21).

11 The multiplication of the food was obviously not done with great fanfare. As the disciples distributed it, Jesus seems to have increased it by breaking it indefinitely until all were satisfied.

12–13 In spite of the miraculous power that effectively produced the ample supply, Jesus permitted no waste of the surplus. Twelve baskets full of remnants were salvaged— possibly one for each of the disciples—and carried back to Capernaum. The term for "basket" (kophinos) usually denotes a large basket, such as might be used for fish or bulky objects. The detail of collecting the remaining fragments of bread and fish may have been introduced to emphasize the ample sufficiency that Jesus provided, or it may indicate that he combined generosity with economy.

14 The miracle excited the wonder of the people and compelled them to recognize that Jesus was an unusual person. The allusion to "the Prophet" is probably a reflection of Deuteronomy 18:15, Moses' prediction of a prophet like himself who would command their hearing. It gives an indication of the undercurrent of popular expectation that earlier appeared in the question of the Pharisees to John the Baptist (John 1:21) and also later in the discussion at the Feast of Tabernacles (7:40, 52 mg.). Since Moses had provided food and water in the desert (Exod 16:11–36; 17:1–6; Num 11:1–33; 20:2–11), the people expected that the Prophet like Moses would do likewise.

15 The desire of the multitude to make Jesus king marks both the height of his popularity and the moment of decision for him. They wanted someone to rule them who would feed them and guarantee their security; they had no comprehension of his spiritual mission or purpose. He, on the other hand, refused to become a political opportunist or dema-gogue. His kingdom could not be promoted by organizing a revolt against the existing political powers or by promising a dole to all who would join his banner.

2. The walking on the water

6:16–21

16When evening came, his disciples went down to the lake, 17where they got into a boat and set off across the lake for Capernaum. By now it was dark, and Jesus had not yet joined them. 18A strong wind was blowing and the waters grew rough. 19When they had rowed three or three and a half miles, they saw Jesus approaching the boat, walking on the water; and they were terrified. 20But he said to them, "It is I; don't be afraid." 21Then they were willing to take him into the boat, and immediately the boat reached the shore where they were heading.

16–17 "Evening" could be any time in the afternoon shortly before sunset. The disciples probably planned to cover the short distance between Bethsaida and Capernaum while daylight lasted. Twilight is brief in the Palestinian springtime, and they would naturally wish to reach home before dark. They actually "went down to the lake," for the terrain around the lake is hilly. For the feeding of the five thousand, the group had journeyed some distance inland. John states that darkness had already fallen before they actually began to cross the lake. The statement that "Jesus had not yet joined them" may imply that they half-expected him to do so and waited until the last minute, hoping that he would come.

18 The Sea of Galilee is six hundred feet below sea level, in a cuplike depression among the hills. When the sun sets, the air cools; and as the cooler air from the west rushes down over the hillside, the resultant wind churns the lake. Since the disciples were rowing toward Capernaum, they were heading into the wind; consequently, they made little progress.

19 "Three or three and a half miles" shows that the disciples were still a considerable distance from the shore at Capernaum. Mark says that "the boat was in the middle of the lake" (6:47). As the disciples looked back, they were terrified to see a human form coming toward them across the water. The hypothesis that Jesus was walking on the lake shore and only appeared to be walking on the water is scarcely adequate. The fishermen who were well acquainted with the Sea of Galilee would certainly be able to discern the difference between a person's walking on the shore and his walking on the surface of the water. Mark states that "they thought he was a ghost" (Mark 6:49), adding that "all saw him and were terrified."

20–21 Jesus calmed their fears by speaking to them. When they recognized his voice, they were willing to take him into the boat. The miracle was designed to demonstrate that Jesus could be with them under all circumstances. As the multiplication of the loaves and fishes showed his power over matter, so the walking on the water revealed his power over the forces of nature. It was one more step in the education of the disciples' faith.

3. The address in the synagogue

6:22–59

22The next day the crowd that had stayed on the opposite shore of the lake realized that only one boat had been there, and that Jesus had not entered it with his disciples, but that they had gone away alone. 23Then some boats from Tiberias landed near the place where the people had eaten the bread after the Lord had given thanks. 24Once the crowd realized that neither Jesus nor his disciples were there, they got into the boats and went to Capernaum in search of Jesus.

25When they found him on the other side of the lake, they asked him, "Rabbi, when did you get here?"

26Jesus answered, "I tell you the truth, you are looking for me, not because you saw miraculous signs but because you ate the loaves and had your fill. 27Do not work for food that spoils, but for food that endures to eternal life, which the Son of Man will give you. On him God the Father has placed his seal of approval."

28Then they asked him, "What must we do to do the works God requires?"

29Jesus answered, "The work of God is this: to believe in the one he has sent."

30So they asked him, "What miraculous sign then will you give that we may see it and believe you? What will you do? ³¹Our forefathers ate the manna in the desert; as it is written: 'He gave them bread from heaven to eat.' "

³²Jesus said to them, "I tell you the truth, it is not Moses who has given you the bread from heaven, but it is my Father who gives you the true bread from heaven. ³³For the bread of God is he who comes down from heaven and gives life to the world."

³⁴"Sir," they said, "from now on give us this bread."

³⁵Then Jesus declared, "I am the bread of life. He who comes to me will never go hungry, and he who believes in me will never be thirsty. ³⁶But as I told you, you have seen me and still you do not believe. ³⁷All that the Father gives me will come to me, and whoever comes to me I will never drive away. ³⁸For I have come down from heaven not to do my will but to do the will of him who sent me. ³⁹And this is the will of him who sent me, that I shall lose none of all that he has given me, but raise them up at the last day. ⁴⁰For my Father's will is that everyone who looks to the Son and believes in him shall have eternal life, and I will raise him up at the last day."

⁴¹At this the Jews began to grumble about him because he said, "I am the bread that came down from heaven." ⁴²They said, "Is this not Jesus, the son of Joseph, whose father and mother we know? How can he now say, 'I came down from heaven'?"

⁴³"Stop grumbling among yourselves," Jesus answered. ⁴⁴"No one can come to me unless the Father who sent me draws him, and I will raise him up at the last day. ⁴⁵It is written in the Prophets: 'They will all be taught by God.' Everyone who listens to the Father and learns from him comes to me. ⁴⁶No one has seen the Father except the one who is from God; only he has seen the Father. ⁴⁷I tell you the truth, he who believes has everlasting life. ⁴⁸I am the bread of life. ⁴⁹Your forefathers ate the manna in the desert, yet they died. ⁵⁰But here is the bread that comes down from heaven, which a man may eat and not die. ⁵¹I am the living bread that came down from heaven. If a man eats of this bread, he will live forever. This bread is my flesh, which I will give for the life of the world."

⁵²Then the Jews began to argue sharply among themselves, "How can this man give us his flesh to eat?"

⁵³Jesus said to them, "I tell you the truth, unless you eat the flesh of the Son of Man and drink his blood, you have no life in you. ⁵⁴Whoever eats my flesh and drinks my blood has eternal life, and I will raise him up at the last day. ⁵⁵For my flesh is real food and my blood is real drink. ⁵⁶Whoever eats my flesh and drinks my blood remains in me, and I in him. ⁵⁷Just as the living Father sent me and I live because of the Father, so the one who feeds on me will live because of me. ⁵⁸This is the bread that came down from heaven. Our forefathers ate ˌmanna, and died, but he who feeds on this bread will live forever." ⁵⁹He said this while teaching in the synagogue in Capernaum.

22–25 Although the people were unaware of Jesus' miracle of walking on the water, they knew that something had transpired. They knew that the disciples had used the lone boat and that Jesus had not departed with the disciples. The people were interested in seeing Jesus again, but they did not know where to find him. When boats became available (v.23) and the people came to the realization that Jesus and his disciples had departed, they "went to Capernaum in search of Jesus" (v.24). The crowd's surprise at finding Jesus with the disciples once again is evidenced by the statement, "When did you get here?" (v.25). Apparently Jesus' miracle of walking on the water was only for his disciples, for he did not tell the people how he had arrived at Capernaum.

26–27 Jesus was not flattered by the attention of the crowds, but immediately he began his instruction. The several answers he gave to their questions are mostly corrections of their opinions. The first is a reply to materialism: "You are looking for me, not because you saw miraculous signs but because you ate the loaves and had your fill" (v.26). His reply was "Do not work for food that spoils, but for food that endures to eternal life, which the Son of Man will give you" (v.27). This parallels his words to the Samaritan woman concerning the "living water" that did not come from the well. Like the Samaritan woman, the people could not lift their minds above the physical necessities of life. Jesus was not commanding them to stop working for a living, but he was saying that their main quest should not be for food that readily perishes. The "food that endures to eternal life" is himself, as the later mystical utterance in v.54 states.

28–29 The second question, "What must we do to do the works God requires?" implies both desire and a sense of self-sufficiency. The people seemed sure that if they wished to do so, they were capable of doing the works of God. As used in John, "works" (*erga*) refers to those acts that distinguish the peculiar abilities of some person (see Note on 5:36). In this setting it refers to the works God requires of those who please him. To Jewish questioners, obtaining eternal life consisted in finding the right formula for performing works to please God. Jesus directed them to the gift of God that could be obtained by faith in him. Again there is a similarity to his conversation with the Samaritan woman: "If you knew the gift of God" (John 4:10). Jesus contradicted directly the presuppositions of his interrogators.

30 The third question was "What miraculous sign then will you give that we may see it and believe you?" In consideration of the spectacular miracle he had performed on the preceding day, it seems incredible that they would have asked this question. The sequence of the text seems to indicate that those who looked for Jesus and then questioned him were part of the crowd who had eaten of the bread and fish he had multiplied. They were either forgetful or naive.

31 The best solution for this literary puzzle is that the crowd was, as usual, demanding a sign and had forgotten that the Lord had just provided one. They were attempting to evaluate him by the ministry of Moses, who had provided manna for their forefathers in the wilderness.

32–33 Jesus informed the people that Moses did not give them the real spiritual bread. The Greek word for "true" (*alēthinos*) means "genuine" or "original." Jesus did not mean that the manna had no food value; he meant it was not the means of sustaining spiritual life. He claimed to be the genuine and only source of spiritual nourishment. This may be an oblique reference to Deuteronomy 8:3: "Man does not live on bread alone but on every word that comes from the mouth of the LORD." As physical food is necessary for physical life, so spiritual food is necessary for spiritual life.

34–36 The request that Jesus should give the people the bread of life parallels the request of the Samaritan woman for the water of life (4:15). In both cases the petition indicates that the speaker did not understand Jesus' real meaning and reveals a materialistic frame of mind. Jesus had already startled the people by saying that Moses did not give them real bread from heaven. Now he shocked them a second time by announcing that he was the bread the Father had given. Jesus claimed to be the only permanent satisfaction for the human desire for life. The attainment of this satisfaction hinges on belief. The definition of this term varies between the people's use of it (v.30) and Jesus' (v.35). To them "belief" meant acceptance of his competence on the basis of miracles;

to him it meant commitment, not finally on the basis of the miracles, but on trust in his person. The assertion "I am the bread of life" is the first in a series of such declarations that are peculiar to this Gospel (8:12; 10:7, 11; 11:25; 14:6; 15:1). Each represents a particular relationship of Jesus to the spiritual needs of men: their light in darkness, their entrance into security and fellowship, their guide and protector in life, their hope in death, their certainty in perplexity, and their source of vitality for productiveness. He desired that men should receive him, not simply for what he might give them, but for what he might be to them. The use of the definite article "the" in "the life" (*tēs zōēs*) is definitive and restrictive. Jesus was talking about "the" bread that gives eternal life; but this was beyond their comprehension, just as the miracles Jesus had performed in their sight did not lead them to believe in him.

37 "All" (*pan*) is a neuter singular rather than a masculine plural and refers to everything the Father has put under Jesus' control (cf. John 5:19–27). It includes the people who are his. The paradox latent in this text has puzzled many. How can one be sure that the Father has really given him to Christ? Will he come only to be rebuffed? Jesus made plain that human salvation is no surprise to God. He summons men to himself by his Word and by his Spirit. They can come only at his invitation. The invitation, however, is not restricted to any particular time or place, nor is it exclusively for any one nation, race, or culture. No man needs to fear that he will come in vain, for Jesus said emphatically that he would not refuse anyone. Man does not make his opportunity for salvation; he accepts its free offer. A superficial attachment to God is not enough, for if the desire for salvation is not inspired by God, true salvation will not result.

38–40 Six times in this immediate context Jesus says that he "came down from heaven" (6:33, 38, 41, 50, 51, 58). His claim to heavenly origin is unmistakable. Jesus also repeatedly affirmed that he had come to do his Father's will. That will is made clear here: Jesus will "lose none of all that he has given" him (v.39). Not only does Jesus' keeping ministry apply to this life, but he will "raise them up at the last day." Jesus' constant allusion to the Father who gave him the believers, who sent him to give eternal life, and who draws believers to him indicates his close relationship with the Father. This relationship is not merely that of a prophet who speaks God's message; it is that of a Son who fulfills the Father's purpose (v.40). His prerogative of resurrection is the final proof of his authority.

41–42 "The Jews" in John usually represent those who are opposed to Jesus, not simply a group of Jewish origin (cf. 2:18, 20; 5:16). They might be called "the opposition party." In this instance they seem to be local persons, for they show some acquaintance with Jesus' family. They took for granted that he was the son of Joseph and Mary, whom they had known for several years. To them his claim of heavenly origin was incredible.

43–45 Jesus rebuked the people for their grumbling and told them that they would never come to him unless the Father initiated the action. Again Jesus spoke of the promise of resurrection for those who belonged to him (v.44; cf. v.39). Verse 45 indicates that God would do his drawing through the Scriptures and that those who were obedient to God's will as revealed in the Scriptures would come to Jesus. He had been delegated by the Father to have life, give life, secure life, and restore life.

46 Jesus' statement is the foundation for the assertion in John 1:18: "No one has ever seen God, but God the only Son, who is at the Father's side, has made him known." Jesus claimed authoritative knowledge of God such as a son could claim concerning his own father.

47 "I tell you the truth" is the NIV translation for the double *amēn* that prefaces Jesus' solemn assertions in this Gospel. As emphatically as he could, Jesus was saying that the one who believes in him has "everlasting life." The particular construction used here to describe the believer is a participle, which indicates that the person's life is characterized by belief in Jesus and does not just begin in faith.

48–50 Again Jesus says, "I am the bread of life" (cf. v.35). Before, he linked this statement with the supplying of man's basic needs; hunger and thirst would be permanently alleviated. This time Jesus links the statement to life itself. When the Jews ate the heavenly bread ("manna") in the wilderness, their physical needs were met. However, they still died (v.49). But Jesus said that he "is the bread that comes down from heaven, which a man may eat and not die" (v.50).

51 The key to a genuine experience with God lies in the sequence of statements in this verse. It is vested in the person of Christ, who descended from heaven to provide for man what his nature requires. To eat of this bread means to appropriate Christ as one's life. It is a figure of belief, for no one will eat what he cannot trust to be edible. To eat a meal implies that it is wholesome, nourishing, and real. This verse introduces the concept of Jesus' vicarious death, the sacrifice of his body for the sins of the world. (For a full discussion of the bread from heaven, see Morris, NIC, pp. 373–81.)

52 The last reaction of Jesus' opponents was prompted by the apparent impossibility of his statement. They took literally the figure of eating his flesh. Unless one has spiritual perception, spiritual truth makes no sense whatsoever. Nicodemus could not comprehend the new birth; so, too, now the Jews considered the Lord's words to be utter nonsense. It hardly seems possible that they misunderstood what he said, for they responded, "How can this man give us his flesh to eat?"

53–54 Jesus made himself perfectly clear. He repeated the statement with this added emphasis: "I tell you the truth." And with that, he added another aspect that was even more repulsive to the Jews: "Unless you eat the flesh of the Son of Man and *drink his blood*" (italics mine). If what Jesus said before was nonsense, this latter statement bordered on gross sin. The law of Moses expressly forbade any drinking of blood on penalty of being cut off from the people (Lev 17:10–14). Three times in this context Jesus refers to the importance of eating his flesh and drinking his blood. There could be no mistaking what he said now.

The progression in thought in vv.51–54 is significant. First, Christ said he gives his flesh "for the life of the world" (v.51). Then he says whoever has not partaken of his flesh and blood has "no life" in him (v.53). But then whoever eats his flesh and drinks his blood "has eternal life, and I will raise him up at the last day" (v.54). The Lord again gives the promise of resurrection to those who are associated with him (cf. vv.39–40, 44). If there were any Sadducees among the "Jews," they really would have been infuriated. They did not believe in resurrection, and Jesus was offering them something their theology denied.

55–57 Jesus explains what he means by his flesh and blood in these two verses. First of all, what he is talking about is as real to him as are the physical counterparts that his opponents had in mind. It is a real food and a real drink that produces a real life. To partake of the elements that Christ offers brings one into an abiding relationship with him. The reality of the Christ-imparted life has been attested to by the myriads of Christians throughout the age who have partaken of Christ's body and blood, in sweet communion with him. Jesus likened the relationship that believers would sustain with him to that existing between the Father and himself. The intimacy that the Son shared with the Father would be parallel to the intimacy between the Lord Jesus and his disciples.

58-59 Jesus climaxed his discourse by once more referring to the "bread that came down from heaven," the forefathers who ate it in the wilderness and died, and the promise of everlasting life to those who received him. Moses was great. It was through him that the people were sustained in the wilderness. But Jesus is far greater, for what he provides satisfies throughout all eternity. Ironically, this conversation took place at "the syngogue in Capernaum." What better place to promise eternal life than where people gather to seek that very thing through their religion!

Whether or not this text is sacramental in the sense that it is a Johannine substitute for the Synoptic account of the Lord's Supper has been argued at length. There are at least two factors that argue against the sacramental interpretation: (1) the equation of "eating" and "drinking" with belief, which is not a physical action, and (2) Jesus' own explanation to the disciples that his words "are spirit and life" (v.63). Undoubtedly the Lord's Supper as later established was intended to perpetuate the concept implied here, namely, that a constant renewal of faith and the outward confession of renewal should be expressed by participation in the bread and wine. There is no hint that Jesus was at this point instituting a sacrament or that the celebration of the Eucharist carried with it intrinsic saving power. Justin Martyr (c. 140) stated that no one was allowed to partake of it except (1) those who believed that the things Christians teach are true and (2) those who had already confessed their faith in baptism (*Apology* 1.66).

Notes

---

37 The Gr. construction employs the emphatic double negative: οὐ μὴ ἐκβάλω (*ou mē ekbalō*, "I will never drive away").

51, 53, 54, 56 The use of the aorist tense of ἐσθίω (*esthiō*, "to consume") in vv.51 and 53 implies a decisive action at the outset, an acceptance. The present tense of τρώγω (*trōgō*, "to gnaw" or "chew") refers to a progressive action that applies to the maintenance of a continuing state.

---

4. The division among the disciples

6:60-71

⁶⁰On hearing it, many of his disciples said, "This is a hard teaching. Who can accept it?"

⁶¹Aware that his disciples were grumbling about this, Jesus said to them, "Does this offend you? ⁶²What if you see the Son of Man ascend to where he was before! ⁶³The Spirit gives life; the flesh counts for nothing. The words I have spoken to you are spirit and they are life. ⁶⁴Yet there are some of you who do not believe." For Jesus had known from the beginning which of them did not believe and who would

betray him. 65He went on to say, "This is why I told you that no one can come to me unless the Father has enabled him."

66From this time many of his disciples turned back and no longer followed him.

67"You do not want to leave too, do you?" Jesus asked the Twelve.

68Simon Peter answered him, "Lord, to whom shall we go? You have the words of eternal life. 69We believe and know that you are the Holy One of God."

70Then Jesus replied, "Have I not chosen you, the Twelve? Yet one of you is a devil!" 71(He meant Judas, the son of Simon Iscariot, who, though one of the Twelve, was later to betray him.)

60 The enigmatic words of Jesus puzzled some of the disciples just as much as they did the mixed crowd. "Disciples" refers to the total group of adherents who had attached themselves to Jesus, however loosely, not solely to the Twelve. Those who could not understand him, or who were unwilling to trust him completely, withdrew. It was a turning point in their experience. They lacked the spiritual perception to grasp his meaning.

61 Jesus' inward knowledge of the disciples enabled him to detect their attitude. The language reemphasizes the principle stated in John 2:25: "He knew what was in a man." His questions reveal surprise that they were mystified. If they could not understand the meaning of eating his flesh and drinking his blood, how would they be able to interpret his resurrection (implied) and his ascension? If they were bewildered by his language, how much more difficult would they find the final event that would lead to his return to God?

62 This reference to the Ascension is one of several in the Gospel, though the act itself is not recorded (3:13; 8:21; 16:10; 17:11; 20:17). The disciples had complained that the concept of Jesus' being the true bread that comes down from heaven was incomprehensible. He intimated that if they witnessed his ascension, as he apparently expected, they would be even more astonished. They had difficulty in believing that he could belong to two different realms. When on the morning of his resurrection Mary grasped him in order to keep him in her existing world lest he should vanish again, he reassured her that he had not yet departed permanently to the Father (20:17). His intention of ultimate departure is clearly stated in John 14:3 and 17:11.

63 Jesus undoubtedly was referring to the Holy Spirit. The Spirit imparts life to the believer; it is not transmitted by the process of physical eating. Jesus was saddened by the dullness of some of his disciples that prevented their believing in the sense that they did not appropriate him.

64 Jesus' reference to those who did not believe is explained by his later allusion to Judas (v.70). Jesus had given ample opportunity for faith to all those who followed him; yet from the beginning his spiritual discernment made him aware of those whose faith was genuine and those whose attachment was only superficial.

65 Jesus strongly implied that faith is the result of God's enabling. Unbelief is natural to those who are selfish and alienated from God and who cannot accept the idea that he can do the impossible. Complete commitment to God is impossible for a selfish heart; the Holy Spirit must awaken and empower it to believe. This does not destroy the voluntary character of faith; it is rather in accord with the cry of the man who said to Jesus, "I do believe; help me overcome my unbelief " (Mark 9:24). Unbelief is part of the fabric of human mentality; the intervention of divine grace is necessary to transform it to faith.

66 "From this time" is a possible translation of *ek toutou*. It could also mean "Because of this [utterance]." The latter makes good sense because it was not simply the chronology that changed the disciples' attitude. It was the difficulty of comprehending Jesus' saying or the offense it gave to their self-sufficiency.

67 The desired response to a question can often be prompted by the way the question is framed. Our Lord ever wishes to encourage faith that is weak, and he had a great deal of concern and love for his disciples. That's why he asked, "You do not want to leave too, do you?"

68 The words of Simon Peter parallel those in the Great Confession given in the Synoptics (Matt 16:16; Mark 8:29; Luke 9:20). Peter spoke as the representative of the Twelve. He declared that nobody else had the life-giving message of Jesus and that there was no other source that would satisfy them. The statement reveals that, in spite of all his usual awkwardness, Simon's faith in Jesus was genuine; and he evidenced true spiritual sensitivity.

"Words of eternal life" refers to the nature of Jesus' teaching rather than to any specific formula he might have used. The Greek article, which marks definiteness, is lacking here. Simon Peter recognized the difference between the authoritative declaration of Jesus and the speculations of the religious teachers of his day. Peter's statement represents the spiritual discernment the disciples had developed during their association with Jesus.

69 The emphatic use of the first personal plural pronoun implies a contrast between the Twelve and those who had deserted Jesus: "*We* believe" (italics mine). Actually, the use of the perfect tense with the verbs "believe" and "know" indicates the verse should be translated "We have believed and have known." This shows a fixed and settled decision, which is expressed here by the English present tense. Peter is affirming that they have reached a final conviction that Jesus is indeed "the Holy One of God." This term is rare in the NT as a title of Jesus. It appears again in Peter's sermon at Pentecost, where he quotes Psalm 16:10 as a prophecy of Jesus' resurrection: "Nor will you let your Holy One see decay" (Acts 2:27), and also in his speech on Solomon's Colonnade: "You disowned the Holy and Righteous One" (Acts 3:14). It bears a strong resemblance to the expression "the Holy One of Israel," which occurs frequently in the prophecy of Isaiah (41:14; 43:3; 47:4; 48:17; and elsewhere).

70 Jesus indicated that his choice of the Twelve was conscious and deliberate; yet he included one he knew would be a traitor. Judas had no less opportunity than any of the others to know and serve Jesus; nor was he a victim of discrimination, for he was given a prominent place among them as treasurer of the group (John 12:6). He was dishonest in his financial administration and selfish in his attitude. In contrast with Simon Peter, who denied Jesus, it can be said that Judas acted by choice, Peter by impulse. Whereas Judas regarded Jesus as a means of attaining his ambition, Peter thought of Jesus as a friend. Judas was motivated by selfishness; Peter, by fear. The word "devil" (*diabolos*) means literally "slanderer." Generally it refers to Satan; only three times in the NT is it applied to human beings, twice in the Pastoral Epistles (2 Tim 3:3; Titus 2:3), where it is translated "slanderous" or "slanderer," and in this one instance in John. The two other instances in this Gospel unmistakably refer to Satan.

71 This verse reads like a footnote or side comment. Although the Gospels never indulge in lengthy denunciation of Judas, almost invariably his name is followed by the phrase "who betrayed him (Jesus)" (Matt 10:4; Mark 3:19; Luke 6:16; John 12:4; 18:2). "Iscariot" is derived from the transliteration *'îš qᵉrîyôṭ,* which means "man of Kerioth." Kerioth was a city in the southern part of Judah (Josh 15:25), south of Hebron in the dry Negeb. There was another city with the same name located in Moab, but the former seems more likely to have been the home of Judas.

5. *The visit to Jerusalem* (7:1–52)

a. *The journey*

7:1–13

> ¹After this, Jesus went around in Galilee, purposely staying away from Judea because the Jews there were waiting to take his life. ²But when the Jewish Feast of Tabernacles was near, ³Jesus' brothers said to him, "You ought to leave here and go to Judea, so that your disciples may see the miracles you do. ⁴No one who wants to become a public figure acts in secret. Since you are doing these things, show yourself to the world." ⁵For even his own brothers did not believe in him.
> ⁶Therefore Jesus told them, "The right time for me has not yet come; for you any time is right. ⁷The world cannot hate you, but it hates me because I testify that what it does is evil. ⁸You go to the Feast. I am not yet going up to this Feast, because for me the right time has not yet come." ⁹Having said this, he stayed in Galilee.
> ¹⁰However, after his brothers had left for the Feast, he went also, not publicly, but in secret. ¹¹Now at the Feast the Jews were watching for him and asking, "Where is that man?"
> ¹²Among the crowds there was widespread whispering about him. Some said, "He is a good man."
> Others replied, "No, he deceives the people." ¹³But no one would say anything publicly about him for fear of the Jews.

1 The chronological sequence is indicated by the indefinite reference "After this." The writer evidently knew of Jesus' later Galilean ministry but chose not to record it. He shows that Jesus did not return to Judea at once after the feeding of the multitude because his life would be in danger. Ever since the healing of the paralytic in Jersualem, his opponents had been attempting to kill him (5:18); and as time progressed, their hatred increased (7:19, 30, 32, 44; 8:59; 10:39; 11:8, 53) until they finally accomplished his death. From this point the opposition to Jesus becomes increasingly prominent in this Gospel.

2 The Feast of Tabernacles was celebrated in the autumn "on the fifteenth day of the seventh month" (Lev 23:34), which would compare roughly to the second week of October in our calendar. It began five days after the Day of Atonement (Yom Kippur) and lasted eight days (Lev 23:33–36; Deut 16:13–17). Each family constructed its own temporary shelter of branches to live in for the period of the feast. This typified the years of wandering in the desert before the people entered the Promised Land. The feast was joyful in character and was a time of thanksgiving for the harvest that marked the transition from nomadic poverty to stable affluence in their own land. It was one of the three annual feasts at which attendance was required of all Jewish men (Deut 16:16).

3–5 Because the gathering in Jerusalem brought together pilgrims from every section of Palestine, Jesus' brothers saw an excellent opportunity for him to acquire some publicity. Their advice to him was to join the crowds in Jerusalem so that he might enhance his reputation and gain more followers. Their suggestion may have been more sarcastic than serious, since they did not believe in him (v.5). To "believe in him" may carry with it a recognition of his purpose and sympathy with it, which his brothers did not have. Consequently their counsel may have been for him to abandon the idealism of teaching multitudes in obscurity and of risking death. If he possessed the powers his miracles seemed to imply, he should display them to the best advantage and capitalize on them.

6 Jesus' reply strongly resembles the one he gave his mother's request at the wedding in Cana of Galilee (2:4). He asserted that he was not living by the chance of casual opportunity but by a divine calendar predetermined by the Father. For this reason the world did not understand his action, and the difference in standards created both misunderstanding and hostility.

7 Again Jesus asserted that he did not belong to this world. The world regarded him as an alien and an antagonist because he condemned its evil works. The same idea is reiterated in the discourse to the disciples in John 15:18–21 and in the prayer to the Father in 17:14, 16. Jesus and the world at large lived in two different dimensions.

8–9 The word "yet" does not occur in many of the MSS, but it is included in the older papyri and in some of the older uncial MSS. The more difficult reading makes Jesus say, "I am not going up to this Feast." But v.10 tells us that afterwards "he went up also." Of course, Jesus' reference to "the right time" shows that the latter sense could be tenable. Morris (NIC, p. 401) notes that "not publicly" is the exact opposite to the brothers' suggestion (v.4). Jesus avoided all publicity and fanfare. He did not organize a delegation of disciples nor travel with a company of pilgrims.

10–11 The secret departure for Jerusalem was not an act of deception. It was an attempt to avoid unwelcome publicity. Jesus' enemies were watching for him, obviously for the purpose of arresting him (cf. v.1).

12–13 Public opinion was divided. The people who favored him were intimidated by the religious hierarchy, which was hostile toward Jesus. The atmosphere was tense, and Jesus did not wish to precipitate a crisis at this time.

Notes

8 The UBS text has οὐκ (ouk, "not") rather than οὔπω (oupō, "not yet"). The main support for the former is ℵ. The latter's main support is P$^{66, 75}$. B. Metzger states that "the reading οὔπω was

introduced at an early date ... in order to alleviate the inconsistency between ver. 8 and ver. 10" (*Textual Commentary*, p. 216). It might be harder to explain the substitution of *ouk* for *oupō* on textual grounds than the opposite; but it is still true that the older MSS contain the easier reading.

---

b. *The popular debate*

7:14–36

> ¹⁴Not until halfway through the Feast did Jesus go up to the temple courts and begin to teach. ¹⁵The Jews were amazed and asked, "How did this man get such learning without having studied?"
>
> ¹⁶Jesus answered, "My teaching is not my own. It comes from him who sent me. ¹⁷If any one chooses to do God's will, he will find out whether my teaching comes from God or whether I speak on my own. ¹⁸He who speaks on his own does so to gain honor for himself, but he who works for the honor of the one who sent him is a man of truth; there is nothing false about him. ¹⁹Has not Moses given you the law? Yet not one of you keeps the law. Why are you trying to kill me?"
>
> ²⁰"You are demon-possessed," the crowd answered. "Who is trying to kill you?"
>
> ²¹Jesus said to them, "I did one miracle, and you are all astonished. ²²Yet, because Moses gave you circumcision (though actually it did not come from Moses, but from the patriarchs), you circumcise a child on the Sabbath. ²³Now if a child can be circumcised on the Sabbath so that the law of Moses may not be broken, why are you angry with me for healing the whole man on the Sabbath? ²⁴Stop judging by mere appearances, and make a right judgment."
>
> ²⁵At that point some of the people of Jerusalem began to ask, "Isn't this the man they are trying to kill? ²⁶Here he is, speaking publicly, and they are not saying a word to him. Have the authorities really concluded that he is the Christ? ²⁷But we know where this man is from; when the Christ comes, no one will know where he is from."
>
> ²⁸Then Jesus, still teaching in the temple courts, cried out, "Yes, you know me, and you know where I am from. I am not here on my own, but he who sent me is true. You do not know him, ²⁹but I know him because I am from him and he sent me."
>
> ³⁰At this they tried to seize him, but no one laid a hand on him, because his time had not yet come. ³¹Still, many in the crowd put their faith in him. They said, "When the Christ comes, will he do more miraculous signs than this man?"
>
> ³²The Pharisees heard the crowd whispering such things about him. Then the chief priests and the Pharisees sent temple guards to arrest him.
>
> ³³Jesus said, "I am with you for only a short time, and then I go to the one who sent me. ³⁴You will look for me, but you will not find me; and where I am, you cannot come."
>
> ³⁵The Jews said to one another, "Where does this man intend to go that we cannot find him? Will he go where our people live scattered among the Greeks, and teach the Greeks? ³⁶What did he mean when he said, 'You will look for me, but you will not find me,' and 'Where I am, you cannot come'?"

14 Jesus remained in seclusion until the feast was half completed and then appeared in the temple court to teach. His absence during the first half of the week had aroused the curiosity of the pilgrims who had expected that he would come in order to take advantage of the eager crowds. From the following text one might suppose that the crowd at the feast was either critical or hostile. The atmosphere reflected the turn of events after the feeding of the five thousand, when many of Jesus' disciples turned from him. Although the final crisis had not come, he had passed the apex of his popular ministry.

15 Even Jesus' critics admitted his acumen and learning. They could not comprehend how he could have acquired such knowledge without engaging in formal rabbinical study. Their comment recalls that of Mark: "The people were amazed at his teaching, because he taught them as one who had authority, not as the teachers of the law" (Mark 1:22).

16 Jesus insisted that his teaching did not originate with himself but that the message and the power came from God. As the perfect man and messenger of God, he gave all credit to the Father who had "sent" him (see comment on 5:30).

17–18 "If any man chooses to do God's will" does not simply mean that if one happens to do God's will in the future he will know the origin of Jesus' teaching. Rather, it means there must be a definite act of the human will to do God's will, a settled, determined purpose to fulfill it. Spiritual understanding is not produced solely by learning facts or procedures, but rather it depends on obedience to known truth. Obedience to God's known will develops discernment between falsehood and truth.

19 Jesus accepted the fact that Moses transmitted the Law to Israel and acknowledged the authority of that Law. He accused his opponents, who claimed to be champions of the Law, with failing to keep it. His charge that they were plotting to kill him was amply substantiated by their action at the end of the feast (7:44–45). His charge should be interpreted in the light of his own teaching on the sixth commandment (Matt 5:21–22), in which he declared that the act of murder results from contempt and hatred of another personality.

20 The response of the crowd to Jesus' accusation shows that the decision of the rulers had not been widely publicized. The people were bewildered by Jesus' statement. Curiously the only allusions in John to demonic activity are accusations made against Jesus (8:48–52; 10:20). Miracles of healing demoniacs are not mentioned in this Gospel. The synoptic Gospels also record a similar accusation (Matt 9:34; 12:24; Mark 3:22; Luke 11:15), though they ascribe Jesus' powers to demonic influence rather than discounting his words as those of a disordered mind.

21–22 Jesus is not saying that he did only "one miracle." By this time he had performed several; but these were of little interest to the "Jews," even if they were aware of them. The reference to circumcision on the Sabbath shows that the issue of healing on the Sabbath was central to Jesus' controversy with the Jewish rulers. So, no doubt, the "one miracle" refers to the healing of the paralytic at the Pool of Bethesda (John 5:1–18), which initiated the hostile criticism of "the Jews."

23–24 Circumcision was initiated by Abraham (Gen 17:9–14) and explicitly commanded in the law of Moses (Lev 12:3). Because it had to be observed on the eighth day after birth, it was allowable on the Sabbath. Circumcision was emblematic of separation from all other peoples, who were consequently called "the uncircumcision" (Eph 2:11). Jesus argued that if a rite were permitted that marked purification by affecting only one member of the body, why should he not be allowed to make the entire man whole on the Sabbath? The translation "stop judging" correctly implies that his enemies should cease making superficial pronouncements on his work and that they should evaluate it objectively.

25–27 Generally, the people were confused about the conflict between Jesus and the religious authorities. They wondered why he wasn't censored if he was such a threat to the nation. The reason the authorities did not promptly have him arrested was that they were uncertain of the sentiments of the people. If they acted hastily, they feared an uprising among the people that would most assuredly bring disciplinary action from the Romans.

The people were uncertain of Jesus' real identity. They knew the authorities sought to kill him, but their reluctance to act led the people to conclude that perhaps there was some validity to Jesus' messianic claim. What further confused them, however, was that they believed the Messiah would rise up out of total obscurity, that no one would "know where he is from." But this attitude reflected an ignorance of the prophetic Scriptures. The priests were familiar with the prophecy that he would be born in Bethlehem (Matt 2:5). It may be, however, that popular legend asserted that the Messiah would suddenly appear out of obscurity.

28–29 In the midst of all this confusion, Jesus replied positively. His first statement may be ironic. It can be translated, "So you know me and where I am from, do you?" The people must have been aware of his boyhood in Nazareth and no doubt considered him to be the son of Joseph and Mary (6:42). Jesus' reply was a renewed affirmation of his origin in God and his divine commission. He had not undertaken his mission by his own volition, but he had been "sent." His assertion evoked the dual response of belief and unbelief. The popular misunderstanding prevailed through his contacts at the feast, for it reappeared in vv.41–44.

30 Jesus' enemies attempted to seize him, but they failed because the hour of crisis had not come. Not only did "the hour" restrain him from sudden independent action (2:4), but it assured him of divine protection until the moment for action came (cf. Luke 22:53).

31 The response of many was belief, though it was hesitant. They did not affirm that he was the Messiah but cautiously suggested that the Messiah would perform no more miracles than Jesus did. Consequently they tended to believe that he might be the promised leader they anticipated. An incidental implication of this statement is that Jesus had been performing miracles during his ministry in Jerusalem. No particulars are given, however.

32 The favorable reaction of those who believed prompted the chief priests and Pharisees to action. To delay longer might result in more people turning to Jesus. The arrest was made official since the temple guards constituted the arresting party.

33–35 Jesus' reply to the action gave an intimation of his coming death. The declaration that he would go where he could neither be followed nor found excited the curiosity of the crowd. They surmised that he expected to leave Palestine and minister among the Dispersion and the Gentiles.

At the time this Gospel was written, the message of Jesus had already been taken to the Gentiles by those who preached among the Jewish Diaspora and the Gentiles. An ironic touch is thus given to the speculation of the crowd, who had spoken of Jesus' going to the Gentiles as an improbability. The episode illustrates the exclusiveness of Judaism and implies the universality of the Gospel as the author saw it.

36 The perplexity of the crowd over Jesus' answer was echoed later by Simon Peter, who, upon hearing him speak similar words, said, "Lord, why can't I follow you now? I will lay down my life for you" (13:37). The crowd could not follow Jesus because of their ignorance of his identity and purpose; Simon was incapable because he lacked courage.

c. *The climactic appeal*

7:37–44

> 37On the last and greatest day of the Feast, Jesus stood and said in a loud voice, "If a man is thirsty, let him come to me and drink. 38Whoever believes in me, as the Scripture has said, streams of living water will flow from within him." 39By this he meant the Spirit, whom those who believed in him were later to receive. Up to that time the Spirit had not been given, since Jesus had not yet been glorified.
> 40On hearing his words, some of the people said, "Surely this man is the Prophet."
> 41Others said, "He is the Christ."
> Still others asked, "How can the Christ come from Galilee? 42Does not the Scripture say that the Christ will come from David's family and from Bethlehem, the town where David lived?" 43Thus the people were divided because of Jesus. 44Some wanted to seize him, but no one laid a hand on him.

37 The climax of the controversy came "on the last and greatest day of the Feast" of Tabernacles. According to the provision of the law, the feast was held for seven days, followed by an eighth day of spiritual observance, including an offering to God. The feast was established as a memorial to the wandering in the wilderness, where water and food were scarce. When the people emerged from the desert into the land of Canaan, they enjoyed regular rainfall and plentiful crops. The celebration of the Feast of Tabernacles included a daily procession of priests from the temple to the Pool of Siloam, from which they drew water that was poured out as a libation at the altar. This was accompanied by the recital of Isaiah 12:3: "With joy you will draw water from the wells of salvation."

Whether the "last day" of the feast was the seventh or the eighth day is not clear. Deuteronomy 16:13 calls for seven days; Leviticus 23:36 prescribes an eighth day, which follows the routine of the first seven. Josephus (Antiq. 3. 10. 4) says that on the eighth day there should be a sacrifice of a calf, a ram, seven lambs, and a kid in propitiation of sins. If "the last and greatest day of the Feast" refers to the eighth day, it makes the appeal of Jesus all the more meaningful. On that day Jesus took the opportunity to make a public announcement concerning himself. "Said in a loud voice" is the same verb translated "cried out" in v.28. He wanted to make himself and his claims known to the entire multitude present.

38 The offering of water memorialized God's provision for the thirsty people in the wilderness, but the water had been poured out and had left them unsatisfied. Now Jesus appeals to the individual: "Whoever believes in me." He was requiring an individual response of faith rather than a collective observance of a ritual. The marginal translation of this verse given in NIV, "If a man is thirsty, let him come to me. And let him drink, who believes in me," makes better poetic parallelism than the usual rendering; but it does not really solve the problem as to whether "from within him" refers to the believer or to Christ. The resultant punctuation would make the words beginning with "as the Scripture has said" an independent sentence. Verse 39 connects the manifestation of the Spirit with the believer rather than with Christ.

If "as the Scripture has said" refers to some particular passage, it is impossible to locate it. There are numerous allusions to water in the OT, but none accords exactly with this utterance. In the celebration of the feast, the words of Isaiah 12:3, quoted above, were employed as part of the ritual. Similar imagery with reference to "the pouring out" of the Holy Spirit occurs in Isaiah 32:15; 44:3; Ezekiel 39:29; Joel 2:28-32. Jesus took the symbolism of the OT and applied it to the gift he intended to bestow on the disciples after his passion was completed. He enlarged this teaching for them in his farewell discourse (14:16-17, 25-26; 15:26; 16:12-15).

39 John's statement shows that the passion of Christ was the important aspect of Jesus' revelation about the Holy Spirit, for it divided the era of law from that of the Spirit (John 1:17). The prophecy of Ezekiel concurs with this: "I will give you a new heart and put a new spirit in you; I will remove from you your heart of stone and give you a heart of flesh. And I will put my Spirit in you and move you to follow my decrees and be careful to keep my laws" (Ezek 36:26-27).

"Glorified" is the first use of this distinctly Johannine verb. It has varied meanings in this Gospel. It may refer to establishing status or to enhancing a reputation (8:54; 12:28; 13:32; 14:13; 15:8; 16:14; 17:1, 4, 5, 10; 21:19). In this particular context it refers to Jesus' death, which, despite all appearances, would be the entrance to glory for him (7:39; 11:4; 12:16, 23; 13:31). The death and resurrection of Jesus would demonstrate the perfection of God's love and power through humiliation. Compare the Pauline statement in Philippians 2:8-9: "He humbled himself and became obedient to death—even death on a cross! Therefore God exalted him to the highest place and gave him the name that is above every name, that at the name of Jesus every knee should bow, in heaven and on earth and under the earth."

40-41 "The Prophet" is presumably an allusion to the prediction of Moses that after him another prophet would appear who would command the attention of the people and who would bring them a further revelation from God (Deut 18:15). Moses explained that the prophet would not be accompanied by the frightening manifestations of Sinai, the great voice and the fire. He would rather be a fellow countryman, familiar to them, and one of their own level. Some so regarded Jesus; others suggested that he might be the Messiah.

42-44 The ignorance of the crowd in Jerusalem concerning Jesus is revealed by their uncertainty about his origin. On the basis of Scripture (Micah 5:2), they decided that Jesus could not be the Messiah since Micah's prophecy said the Messiah would come from Bethlehem and Jesus came from Nazareth. The confusion was such that no decision was made concerning his person and no action was taken to arrest him. Perhaps this is another illustration of Johannine irony, for Jesus *was* born in Bethlehem. The very passage that convinced his critics that he could not be the Messiah was one of the strongest to prove that he was.

d. *The rejection by the leaders*

7:45-52

⁴⁵Finally the temple guards went back to the chief priests and Pharisees, who asked them, "Why didn't you bring him in?"
⁴⁶"No one ever spoke the way this man does," the guards declared.

[47]"You mean he has deceived you also?" the Pharisees retorted. [48]"Has any of the rulers or of the Pharisees believed in him? [49]No! But this mob that knows nothing of the law—there is a curse on them."

[50]Nicodemus, who had gone to Jesus earlier and who was one of their own number, asked, [51]"Does our law condemn a man without first hearing him to find out what he is doing?"

[52]They replied, "Are you from Galilee, too? Look into it, and you will find that a prophet does not come out of Galilee."

45 Although the previous context states that there was no attempt to seize Jesus, it did not state that there was no official action. The phrase "the temple guards" shows that the chief priests and Pharisees had sent an arresting party, who failed in their mission. Since the high priest belonged to the Sadducean party, the coalition of the Pharisees and Sadducees was significant. The two groups were strongly opposed to each other in doctrine (Acts 23:7). In spite of their differences, their common animosity toward Jesus induced them to combine for action against him.

46 The report of the guards showed that Jesus had a strong influence on all who listened to him. Although they had been officially commissioned to arrest him, his teaching had so overawed them that they could not carry out their orders. "No one ever spoke the way this man does" could be translated stronger; for instead of a negative pronoun the text literally reads, "Never did any *man* talk in this fashion." In the Greek the word "man" (*anthrōpos*) occurs in the emphatic position at the end of the sentence and implies by contrast that he must be more than an ordinary human being.

47–49 The Pharisees were irate when the guards returned without Jesus. Their question, "Has any of the rulers or of the Pharisees believed in him?" opens with a particular construction that calls for a negative answer. It might be translated: "No one of the Pharisees has believed in him, has he?" The religious snobbishness of the rulers was revealed in their contemptuous dismissal of the guards' testimony. They assumed that nobody could be right except themselves. If they did not believe in Jesus, he must be unreliable and his claims must be fraudulent. They regarded the mass of the people as ignorant of the law and consequently incapable of any intelligent faith.

50–51 Nicodemus reappears in the Gospel at this point. John again explains that Nicodemus was a ruler of the Jews, "one of their own number." His tentative question, "Does our law condemn a man without first hearing him to find out what he is doing?" was not an open declaration that he had faith in Jesus. Rather, it was a protest raised on a legal technicality. Nicodemus may have felt that if he championed Jesus' cause unequivocally, he would lose his case; but if he raised a legitimate legal objection, he might prevent drastic action. This does imply that he was willing to defend Jesus' rights.

52 The scornful reply "Are you from Galilee, too?" intimates that Nicodemus was taking the stand of the crude and ignorant Galileans who were gullible enough to trust in the wandering prophet, Jesus. The rulers in Jerusalem had a dim view of the intellectual status of the Galileans. The statement "a prophet does not come out of Galilee" seems inconsistent with the fact that some of the OT prophets, like Jonah, did originate from northern Israel.

Notes

---

52 One of the oldest papyrus texts of John, P[66], which antedates the majority of the texts, reads "the prophet" (ὁ προφήτης, *ho prophētēs*). If that reading is correct, the statement of the Pharisees is probably a direct reference to "the prophet" mentioned in v.40 and would obviate the inconsistency mentioned above. The reading, however, is not otherwise attested; and there seems to be no particular reason in the OT for saying that "the prophet" could not come from Galilee. More probably the statement is simply the arbitrary rejection of all possibility that Jesus could be the Messiah or even a prophet.

---

6. *The woman taken in adultery*

7:53–8:11

> [53]Then each went to his own home.
> [1]But Jesus went to the Mount of Olives. [2]At dawn he appeared again in the temple courts, where all the people gathered around him, and he sat down to teach them. [3]The teachers of the law and the Pharisees brought in a woman caught in adultery. They made her stand before the group [4]and said to Jesus, "Teacher, this woman was caught in the act of adultery. [5]In the Law Moses commanded us to stone such women. Now what do you say?" [6]They were using this question as a trap, in order to have a basis for accusing him.
> But Jesus bent down and started to write on the ground with his finger. [7]When they kept on questioning him, he straightened up and said to them, "If any one of you is without sin, let him be the first to throw a stone at her." [8]Again he stooped down and wrote on the ground.
> [9]At this, those who heard began to go away one at a time, the older ones first, until only Jesus was left, with the woman still standing there. [10]Jesus straightened up and asked her, "Woman, where are they? Has no one condemned you?"
> [11]"No one, sir," she said.
> "Then neither do I condemn you," Jesus declared. "Go now and leave your life of sin."

Although this narrative is included in the sequence of the outline, it can hardly have belonged to the original text of this Gospel. It is absent from most of the oldest copies of the Gospel that precede the sixth century and from the works of the earliest commentators. To say that it does not belong in the Gospel is not identical with rejecting it as unhistorical. Its coherence and spirit show that it was preserved from a very early time, and it accords well with the known character of Jesus. It may be accepted as historical truth; but based on the information we now have, it was probably not a part of the original text.

7:53–8:1 The words "Then each went to his own home" show that the following account must have been related to some longer narrative of which it was a part. The subjects of this verse must be people at a gathering in the city of Jerusalem at which Jesus was present, for the next verse says, "But Jesus went to the Mount of Olives." "But" implies continuity with a mild contrast: the members of the group, whatever it was, went to their homes while Jesus made his way to the Mount of Olives, where he spent the night. This does not fit well with the preceding text because Jesus was not present at the meeting of the Sanhedrin to which the guards had reported. Furthermore, the withdrawal to the Mount of Olives would fit better the Passover season, when Jesus slept more than once under the shadow of the trees there. The reference to the temple courts (8:2) fits with his teaching described in 7:14, but this does not make convincing evidence. Since he used the Court of the Gentiles on numerous occasions, the event more probably occurred during one of his visits to Jerusalem during the last year of his life, either at the Feast of Dedication (10:22) or at the Final Passover (12:12).

2–3 The episode took place in the temple court at dawn. The entire affair had the appearance of trickery, a trap specially prepared to catch Jesus. The Sanhedrin would probably not have arisen early in the morning unless there was a special reason for doing so. They forced their way into the center of the group and interrupted Jesus' teaching by posing a question that created an apparently impossible dilemma for him.

4 The guilt of the woman was indisputable; she had been "caught in the act." There is no indication here that Jesus challenged the charge. He accepted the alternatives that it entailed.

5 The dilemma that the scribes and Pharisees posed was this: The woman was guilty, and under Mosaic law she would be condemned to death. The law's requirement was this: "If a man commits adultery with another man's wife—with the wife of his neighbor —both the adulterer and the adulteress must be put to death" (Lev 20:10). The nature of the penalty—stoning—was defined by the Deuteronomic law: "If a man is found sleeping with another man's wife . . . you shall take both of them to the gate of that town and stone them to death" (Deut 22:22–24). If, then, Jesus refused to confirm the death penalty, he could be charged with contradicting the law of God and would himself be liable to condemnation. If, on the other hand, he confirmed the verdict of the Pharisees, he would lose his reputation for compassion; and, as Morris suggests, he could have been reported to the Romans as inciting the Sanhedrin to independent exercise of the death penalty (NIC, p. 887).

6–8 The Pharisees' question was emphatic: "You, there! What do you say?" Jesus made no reply but "bent down and started to write on the ground with his finger." There have been several conjectures as to what he wrote. Some say he may have simply made marks in the dust to cover his embarrassment; or, as has also been suggested, he may have started to make a list of the sins of those who stood in front of him. It was, incidentally, the only occasion on record that refers to his writing. When his questioners kept pressing him for an answer, Jesus finally stood erect and replied, "If any one of you is without sin, let him be the first to throw a stone at her." Then he resumed his writing.

His reply put the dilemma back on his questioners. In this particular offense there would normally be no witnesses, since its nature would demand privacy. Either the witnesses became such by accident, which would be unusual; or they were present purposely to create the trap for Jesus, in which case they themselves were guilty; or they condoned the deed, and this would make them partners in it. According to Jewish law, in any case of capital punishment the witnesses must begin the stoning. Whether Jesus by his statement implied that they were guilty of condoning or of committing adultery with this woman, or whether he was speaking about past personal guilt is uncertain. In either case, each one of the accusers would either have to admit that he was guilty or else refrain from demanding the woman's death.

9 The accusers "began to go away one at a time, the older ones first." The older ones

either had more sins for which they were answerable or else had more sense than to make an impossible profession of righteousness. Finally the woman was left alone.

10 Jesus straightened up and addressed the woman: "Woman, where are they? Has no one condemned you?" His address was respectful (cf. 2:4; 20:13). Her accusers had made her the bait for a trap. They were more interested in destroying Jesus than in saving her. Their vicious hatred of him was as bad as her immorality. His rebuke had prevented their pronouncing sentence on her. Jesus did not pronounce sentence either. But neither did he proclaim her to be innocent.

11 Jesus dismissed the woman by saying, "Go now and leave your life of sin." Meeting a man who was interested in saving rather than exploiting and in forgiving rather than condemning must have been a new experience for her. Jesus' attitude provided both the motivation and the assurance she needed. Forgiveness demands a clean break with sin. That Jesus refrained from condemning her was a guarantee that he would support her.

Notes

The textual status of this passage is uncertain. It is lacking in the major papyri MSS of the early third century (P[66] and P[75]), in the great uncials that precede the sixth century (ℵ B probably A and C T W), in some of the later uncials (N X Θ Ψ), and in a considerable number of the best cursive MSS (33 157 565 and others). The oldest Syriac and Egyptian versions omit it, as do also the Georgian, Gothic, and some of the MSS of Old Latin. It is included by some of the representatives of the "Western" text (D G) and by a number of the later uncials and cursives (28 700 et al.). One MS (225) places it after John 7:36; a few, after 7:44; some uncials append it to the end of the Gospel; and one family of MSS, the Ferrar Group, place it after Luke 21:38. No early commentator contains it, nor is it quoted in any of the church fathers before Irenaeus, and then only in the Latin version, which was translated possibly as late as the fourth century. The multiplicity of small variants within this pericope indicate that it may have had a checkered literary history.

D. *The Intensification of Controversy* (8:12–59)

1. *Teaching in the temple area*

8:12–30

[12]When Jesus spoke again to the people, he said, "I am the light of the world. Whoever follows me will never walk in darkness, but will have the light of life." [13]The Pharisees challenged him, "Here you are, appearing as your own witness; your testimony is not valid." [14]Jesus answered, "Even if I testify on my own behalf, my testimony is valid, for I know where I came from and where I am going. But you have no idea where I come from or where I am going. [15]You judge by human standards; I pass judgment on no one. [16]But if I do judge, my decisions are right, because I am not alone. I stand with the Father who sent me. [17]In your own Law it is written that the testimony of two men is valid. [18]I am one who testifies for myself; my other witness is the one who sent me—the Father." [19]Then they asked him, "Where is your father?"

"You do not know me or my Father," Jesus replied. "If you knew me, you would know my Father also." [20]He spoke these words while teaching in the temple area near the place where the offerings were put. Yet no one seized him, because his time had not yet come.

[21]Once more Jesus said to them, "I am going away, and you will look for me, and you will die in your sin. Where I go, you cannot come."

[22]This made the Jews ask, "Will he kill himself? Is that why he says, 'Where I go, you cannot come'?"

[23]But he continued, "You are from below; I am from above. You are of this world; I am not of this world. [24]I told you that you would die in your sins; if you do not believe that I am ⸤the one I claim to be⸥, you will indeed die in your sins."

[25]"Who are you?" they asked.

"Just what I have been claiming all along," Jesus replied. [26]"I have much to say in judgment of you. But he who sent me is reliable, and what I have heard from him I tell the world."

[27]They did not understand that he was telling them about his Father. [28]So Jesus said, "When you have lifted up the Son of Man, then you will know who I am and that I do nothing on my own but speak just what the Father has taught me. [29]The one who sent me is with me; he has not left me alone, for I always do what pleases him." [30]Even as he spoke, many put their faith in him.

12 The segment that follows at this point is long and constitutes a chronological unit, though we have divided it for convenience in explaining the content. Precisely at what time during Jesus' visit to Jerusalem this took place, John does not say. It may have been shortly after the close of the Feast of Tabernacles, while Jesus was still in the city. This incident introduces the second of the great "I am's," "I am the light of the world." This recalls the statement of the Prologue: "In him was life, and that life was the light of men. The light shines in the darkness, but the darkness has not understood [overcome] it" (John 1:4–5). Jesus professed to be not only the inexhaustible source of spiritual nourishment, but he also was the genuine light by which truth and falsehood could be distinguished and by which direction could be established. Perhaps Jesus drew his illustration from the great candlestick or Menorah that was lighted during the Feast of Tabernacles and cast its light over the Court of the Women where Jesus was teaching. The Menorah was to be extinguished after the feast, but his light would remain.

13–14 As usual, the Pharisees challenged Jesus' claims. Legally his testimony concerning himself would be unacceptable because it would presumably be biased. Jesus had on a previous occasion admitted as much, for he had said, "If I testify about myself, my testimony is not valid" (5:31). Here he protested vigorously: "Even if I testify on my own behalf, my testimony is valid, for I know where I came from and where I am going." While a person's testimony about himself may be biased by self-interest, it is equally true that no one knows more about his own nature and experience than the person himself. No individual can be sure of his own origin apart from external testimony, nor can he be sure of his future circumstances. Jesus, however, possessed that knowledge concerning himself. When the final crisis of his life came, John says that Jesus knew "that he had come from God and was returning to God" (13:3). His testimony about himself was therefore more accurate than that of his opponents, for they had no idea of his origin or his destiny, as the confusion reported in ch. 7 shows (vv.25–44).

15–18 Jesus argued further that the Pharisees were not qualified to render a verdict on the validity of his witness because they used the wrong criterion: "You judge by human standards." To form a correct estimate of him, they must have the proper standard, and Christ is not measurable by "human standards." The actual word used here for "human standards" is "flesh" (*sarx*), which is used metaphorically to refer to the human nature. The ordinary categories for measuring personality would not apply to Jesus. He appealed to the rule of the law that prescribed two witnesses for an acceptable proposition (Deut 17:6). He would be qualified as one of the witnesses and his Father as the other. Jesus referred, of course, to God and emphasized again that the Father had "sent" him (cf. John 5:23–24, 37). Morris notes that "no human witness can authenticate a divine relationship. Jesus therefore appeals to the Father and Himself, and there is no other to whom He can appeal" (NIC, p. 443).

19 Whether the Pharisees' question is a bewildered inquiry or an intentional insult is hard to determine. In Western culture it would more likely be the former. In the East, to question a man's paternity is a definite slur on his legitimacy. It may be unwise to read into this question more hostility than is necessary; yet in the ensuing discussion the same idea recurs (v.41). Jesus was referring to God, and the Pharisees were unwilling to admit that he had so intimate a relation with God. Jesus asserted that the knowledge of the Father depended on knowing him. As the one whom the Father had sent (v.18), Jesus claimed to be an adequate and authoritative representative.

20 "Yet no one seized him, because his time had not yet come" is a footnote John adds that relates to the program of Jesus' life (see 2:4; 7:6, 30; 12:23, 27; 17:1). Jesus lived a protected life until his work was completed.

21-24 The following discourse marks the dual destiny of Jesus and his opponents: he would return to the Father, and they would die in their sins. Jesus claimed that he belonged to a totally different world from that of his questioners. To him the difference was natural; to them it was unnatural—something they could explain only by assuming that he belonged to the realm of the dead. He had come from the presence of God, and he asserted that only by faith could they attain his level. An insurmountable barrier separated them—unbelief (v.23). The attitude of unbelief is not simply unwillingness to accept a statement of fact; it is resistance to the revelation of God in Christ. Not only did they repudiate his claims, they completely rejected his person.

25 The question "Who are you, anyway?" shows the Pharisees' exasperation with Jesus' hints and seemingly extravagant claims. The crowd had ventured many guesses about his identity: "the Prophet" (7:40), "the Christ" (7:41), and others. The longer his explanation, the less satisfying it seemed to be. Jesus avoided making a direct claim to deity, but he relied on his works and character to speak for themselves. They witness to the fact that he had come from another world, that he was different from humanity in general, and that he had a unique mission to fulfill.

The translation of the second half of v.25 is difficult. The construction is unique to the Gospel of John. KJV renders it "Even the same that I said unto you from the beginning"; the Amplified Bible, "I am exactly what I have been telling you from the first"; NASB, "What have I been saying to you from the beginning?"; RSV, "Even what I have told you from the beginning"; NEB, "Why should I speak to you at all?"; Beck, "What should I tell you first?" The problem lies in the translation of the word *archēn*, which means literally "beginning." Its construction does not seem to fit the general sense of the passage, and there is no good analogy that can be used to explain it. The NIV rendering

—"Just what I have been claiming all along"—seems to be as satisfactory as any of the others.

26 Jesus certainly had enough accusations that he could have mustered forth to bring judgment on his accusers. The remainder of the verse implies that this judgment is tied to their unwillingness to acknowledge Jesus' relationship to the Father. Because he was speaking what the Father told him, the Father's judgment would come on them, too.

27-28 Jesus' questioners did not understand that he was speaking to them of God; so they missed the point of his peculiar relationship to the Father. Jesus asserted that when they had lifted him up, they would recognize him for what he was.

Two words in this context deserve special emphasis. "Lift up" (*hypsoō*) is used in John 3:14 to refer to the cross, which Jesus compared to the "banner-staff" on which the bronze serpent was elevated in the wilderness (Num 21:9). Usually the verb means "to set in a place of prominence," "to exalt." It may carry an additional meaning: that Jesus would be glorified by the cross. Such a concept goes well with his own statement in 12:23: "The hour has come for the Son of Man to be glorified," and its equal in 12:32: "But I, when I am lifted up from the earth, will draw all men to myself." The second word is "I am" in "then you will know that *I am*" (lit. trans.). "I am" (*egō eimi*) occurs three times in this discourse, in vv.24, 28, 58. It may be translated as in v.24, "I am [the one I claim to be]," that is, the Son of Man. Stauffer states that it may be the translation of "I AM," the title of God manifested (pp. 186–94). This title was revealed to Moses at the time of his commission to lead the people of Israel out of Egypt (Exod 3:14). The term predicates self-existence, eternal being. Along with this claim to divine nature, Jesus reaffirmed his subordination to the Father as the bearer of his message. Both his nature and his message come from God.

29 Four times in this discourse Jesus affirmed that he had been sent by the Father (vv.16, 18, 26, 29). He disclaimed originality for his message; he was simply conveying the truth of the one who had sent him and was carrying out his orders. His whole purpose was to please the Father. His utter devotion produced a life of complete holiness. This revelation forms a contrasting background to the slavery of sin that follows in the next paragraph.

30 The validity of the belief referred to here seems questionable. The people's lack of perception and shallowness of commitment are reflected in their response to Jesus' initial counsel. The following paragraphs begin with proud resentment on the part of the Jews and conclude with an attempted stoning.

2. *The discourse to professed believers*

8:31–47

> [31] To the Jews who had believed him, Jesus said, "If you hold to my teaching, you are really my disciples. [32] Then you will know the truth, and the truth will set you free."
>
> [33] They answered him, "We are Abraham's descendants and have never been slaves of anyone. How can you say that we shall be set free?"
>
> [34] Jesus replied, "I tell you the truth, everyone who sins is a slave to sin. [35] Now a slave has no permanent place in the family, but a son belongs to it forever. [36] So if the Son sets you free, you will be free indeed. [37] I know you are Abraham's descendants. Yet you are ready to kill me, because you have no room for my word.

38I am telling you what I have seen in the Father's presence, and you do what you have heard from your father."

39"Abraham is our father," they answered.

"If you were Abraham's children," said Jesus, "then you would do the things Abraham did. 40As it is, you are determined to kill me, a man who has told you the truth that I heard from God. Abraham did not do such things. 41You are doing the things your own father does."

"We are not illegitimate children," they protested. "The only Father we have is God himself."

42Jesus said to them, "If God were your Father, you would love me, for I came from God and now am here. I have not come on my own; but he sent me. 43Why is my language not clear to you? Because you are unable to hear what I say. 44You belong to your father, the devil, and you want to carry out your father's desire. He was a murderer from the beginning, not holding to the truth, for there is no truth in him. When he lies, he speaks his native language, for he is a liar and the father of lies. 45Yet because I tell the truth, you do not believe me! 46Can any of you prove me guilty of sin? If I am telling the truth, why don't you believe me? 47He who belongs to God hears what God says. The reason you do not hear is that you do not belong to God."

31 There must have been some sort of avowal of faith by the Jews that evoked the author's comment, "to the Jews who had believed him." Jesus evidently began his discourse with the assumption that they, having declared an initial faith, would proceed to a further commitment on the basis of his teaching. Receiving his teaching would mark them as genuine disciples and would lead them into a deeper experience of truth. The truth thus learned would liberate them from legalism and superstition, which had developed over the years. Jesus did not wish to break a bruised reed nor extinguish a smoldering wick of faith (cf. Matt 12:20), but he felt the necessity of making perfectly clear the conditions of discipleship.

32–33 The freedom Jesus spoke of was spiritual freedom from sin and its effects, as the following context shows. The Jews' response indicates that they were thinking of political freedom, since they spoke of being enslaved to persons (v.33). Their protest was ill-founded, for they forgot the slavery of Egypt, the numerous oppressions of the time of the Judges, the Exile in Babylon, and the current Roman domination of their land. Because they were descendants of Abraham, with whom God had established a permanent covenant (Gen 12:1–3; 15:1–21; 17:1–14, 19; 22:15–18), they considered themselves exempt from any spiritual danger.

34 Jesus' reply dealt with the spiritual aspect of freedom. Sin enslaves because every act of disobedience to God creates an atmosphere of alienation and a trend to further disobedience that inevitably makes escape impossible. Sin can possibly be overcome, but the attitude and habit of sin are inescapable. The participial construction "everyone who sins" is in the present tense, which implies a continual habit of sinning rather than an occasional lapse.

35–36 A slave has no security, for he can claim no family ties that entail an obligation toward him. The son of a family has permanent status within it. Jesus enlarged this analogy by stating that while a son is rightfully a partaker of family privileges, the Son can confer them. The hope for real freedom does not lie in the ancestry of Abraham but in the action of Christ.

37-38 The contrast between the attitude of Abraham and that of his self-styled descendants was proof that they were falsely claiming him as their spiritual ancestor. They were murderous in intent and impervious to revelation. Jesus had brought a message from the Father, and, unlike Abraham, they would not receive it. John the Baptist had made a similar observation in his preaching (Luke 3:8). Jesus' contrast of what he had "seen" and what they had "heard" reinforces the concept of authority implicit in his repeated claim to have been "sent" by the Father (John 8:29). He spoke from firsthand knowledge; they were acting on misinformation. They had been misled by Satan himself.

39 Contrary to the Jews' claim, Jesus insisted that they were not the true children of Abraham. Their hatred of Jesus, refusal to listen to truth, and lack of simple faith belied their profession.

40-41 The Jews' insistence that they were children of Abraham implied that they regarded their relationship to God as secure because of their lineal descent from the man with whom God had confirmed his covenant. While the covenant had not been abrogated, Jesus made it plain that his hearers needed to exercise individual faith to participate in it. His words give substance to his teaching on the new birth and are paralleled by Paul's explanation of Abraham's faith in Galatians 3:16-29. The heirs of Abraham are not merely those who are descended from him by blood but those who exercise his faith. The Jews' insistence that they were true descendants of Abraham brought Jesus' flat denial of their spiritual claims, and he attributed their attitude to another source. Their protest, "We are not illegitimate children," may carry the implication of a sneer: "*We* are not illegitimate children"—but you are! While John does not speak directly of the virgin birth, there may be hints that he knew of it and that some of the people knew that there was a mystery surrounding Jesus' origin. In any case, the Jews were unwilling to listen to Jesus' claims; yet, at the same time, they were insisting that they came from God.

42 Jesus gave another evidence of the Jews' hypocrisy. If they truly loved God, they would evidence that love by showing love to his Son. Love for God is a family affair; it involves loving all whom the Father has sent. This love should especially be manifested toward the Father's most beloved representative, his Son.

43-44 The people might have been confused as to why they did not love Jesus if he was indeed sent from the Father. Jesus spoke to that point with a rhetorical question: "Why is my language not clear to you?" The word "clear" really means "know" (*ginōskō*). In essence, Jesus was asking, "Why don't you know what I am saying?" Then he gave the answer: "You are unable to hear what I say." The word "unable" (*ou dynasthe*) speaks of an inherent inability. The reason the people didn't respond to Jesus' teaching was that they belonged to another. Their family association was wrong. Jesus said, "You belong to your father, the devil." And because of this family tie, they were inclined to carry out their father's desire, just as Jesus carried out his Father's desire. The devil is a murderer and a liar. He seeks to deprive life and distort truth. The Jews were merely demonstrating the truth of the adage "Like father, like son."

45 "Truth" is an abstract that is difficult for people to know and appreciate. Pilate had become so enmeshed in politics that he no longer knew what truth was (18:38). Jesus told the Jews that because they were children of their father, they didn't know what truth was. They lived in a world of lies, distortion, and falseness. In a sense, truth was a foreign language to them; their native language was lies.

46 Jesus' challenge "Can any of you prove me guilty of sin?" would have been impossible for anyone else to utter. No human being could risk making that challenge without many flaws in his character being made known. The verb "prove" (*elenchei*) implies more than an accusation; it is a conviction on the basis of evidence. Had Jesus not been sinless, someone in the hostile crowd would eagerly have charged him with at least one sin.

47 Jesus closed the argument by repeating that the Jews refused to hear him because they did not belong to God. Their bitterness toward him and their obtuseness toward his teaching contradicted their spiritual claims.

3. The response of the unbelievers

8:48–59

> 48The Jews answered him, "Aren't we right in saying that you are a Samaritan and demon-possessed?"
> 49"I am not possessed by a demon," said Jesus, "but I honor my Father and you dishonor me. 50I am not seeking glory for myself; but there is one who seeks it, and he is the judge. 51I tell you the truth, if a man keeps my word, he will never see death.
> 52At this the Jews exclaimed, "Now we know that you are demon-possessed! Abraham died and so did the prophets, yet you say that if a man keeps your word he will never taste death. 53Are you greater than our father Abraham? He died, and so did the prophets. Who do you think you are?"
> 54Jesus replied, "If I glorify myself, my glory means nothing. My Father, whom you claim as your God, is the one who glorifies me. 55Though you do not know him, I know him. If I said I did not, I would be a liar like you, but I do know him and keep his word. 56Your father Abraham rejoiced at the thought of seeing my day; he saw it and was glad."
> 57"You are not yet fifty years old," the Jews said to him, "and you have seen Abraham!"
> 58"I tell you the truth," Jesus answered, "before Abraham was born, I am!" 59At this, they picked up stones to stone him, but Jesus hid himself, slipping away from the temple grounds.

48 The hardened opposition to Jesus' claims appears in the accusation that he was "a Samaritan and demon-possessed." "Aren't we right in saying" may imply that this was an accusation frequently leveled at him. The Samaritans held many beliefs in common with the Jews, for they also relied on the Pentateuch as the supreme authority for their faith. They differed, however, in their interpretation of it and were much more lax in their attitude toward other religious influences. Since Jesus did not agree with all the traditional interpretations of the Law, the Jews may have classed him with the Samaritans as a heretic. According to John, demon-possession was attributed to Jesus on three occasions (7:20; 8:52; 10:20). In this context it is the equivalent of calling a man crazy, though the Gospels as a whole deal with demon-possession as an actual phenomenon. Demon-possession is characterized by both a disordered mind and definite control by evil.

49–50 Jesus denied the allegation and placed the burden of proof back on his adversaries. His aim was to honor the Father; theirs, to bring Jesus into disgrace. He disclaimed all selfish desire for prestige and relegated the final evaluation of his works to the judgment of God.

51 With the solemn affirmation "I tell you the truth," Jesus declared that any man who received his message would not experience death. It is a negative statement of a positive principle later declared by Jesus: "I have come that they may have life, and have it to the full" (John 10:10). It is the summary of his mission, for he came "to destroy the devil's work" (1 John 3:8) and to undo the penalty for sin pronounced in Eden: "You must not eat from the tree of the knowledge of good and evil, for when you eat of it you will surely die" (Gen 2:17). A fuller statement of this principle appears later in Jesus' promise to Martha: "I am the resurrection and the life. . . . whoever lives and believes in me will never die" (John 11:25).

52 To receive eternal life by keeping Jesus' word seemed to be the height of absurdity. The Jews felt that their charge of demon-possession was confirmed. If Abraham, the father of the nation, and the prophets, the accredited messengers of God, died, how could this obscure Galilean claim to have the power of life and death?

53 A better translation of this question would be "You are not greater than our father Abraham, are you?" A negative answer is assumed. Morris points out that Jesus' opponents frequently charged him with " 'making' Himself divine (5:18; 10:33; 19:7)" (NIC, p. 470). On the contrary, Jesus seldom asserted his deity, but he preferred so to live and act that men would observe his divine nature and confess it spontaneously (cf. Matt 16:13–17). He did not refuse such confessions, but he did not advertise himself.

54 Again Jesus referred his defense to the Father. God was responsible for Jesus' message and vindication. He reminded them that the God they claimed to be theirs was his Father. Their relation to God was formal; his was familial.

55 In this verse two different Greek words are used for "know." The word *ginōskō* is used in the phrase "you do not know him." The other word, *oida,* is used elsewhere in this verse. It may be that they do not really differ in meaning, since they appear in the same context and since the Johannine use of synonyms seems at times to observe no distinctions. But *ginōskō* implies a knowledge of experience whereas *oida* implies an instinctive perception of a fact. Jesus may have been saying, "You have not really attained an experience of God; I have a full consciousness of him." Jesus could not deny his knowledge without making himself a liar.

56 Jesus claimed that Abraham had a preview of his ministry and had rejoiced in it. This may refer to the promise God gave Abraham that his seed should become the channel of divine blessing to all the nations (Gen 12:3). By "my day" Jesus may have been referring to his redemptive work, which would summarize his career. Perhaps Isaac represented to Abraham the "seed" through which God would fulfill his promise: the miraculous birth of the son, his unquestioning trust in his father, his willingness to become a sacrifice to fulfill the command of God, and his deliverance from certain death. These may have spoken of the later Seed who cooperated in obedience to his Father, surrendered himself to the Father's will, and emerged victorious from death. Although this interpretation is not founded on any specific statement of Scripture, it would mean that Abraham's personal experience at the sacrifice of Isaac could have been an object lesson to him of the coming incarnation, death, and resurrection of the promised Seed (see Gen 22:1–18; Heb 11:17–19).

57 The Jews' retort that Jesus was "not yet fifty years old" affords an interesting side-light on Jesus' age. Fifty years was the limit observers would assign to him on the basis of appearance. If he were born between 6 and 4 B.C., and if the Crucifixion took place in A.D. 33, as Hoehner suggests (see note), Jesus would not have been older than his late thirties. Perhaps the tensions of his life had aged him prematurely, yet he was obviously less than fifty years of age. Luke says Jesus "was about thirty years old when he began his ministry" (Luke 3:23).

58 The rejoinder of Jesus, "Before Abraham was born, I am (*egō eimi*)" could only mean a claim to deity. "Was born" could be better translated "came into being" or "became," since the aorist tense of *ginomai* ("to become") is used. The same verb is used in John 1:14 to denote the Incarnation: "The Word became flesh." It implies the event of entering into a new state or condition of existence. "I am" implies continuous existence, including existence when Abraham appeared. Jesus was, therefore, asserting that at the time of Abraham's birth, he existed. Furthermore, I AM was recognized by the Jews as a title of deity. When God commissioned Moses to demand from Pharaoh the release of the Israelites, he said, "This is what you are to say to the Israelites: I AM has sent me to you" (Exod 3:14). Stauffer states that "the phrase harbors within itself the most authentic, the most audacious, and the most profound affirmation by Jesus of who he was" (p. 174). The same use of "I am" appears also in the theistic proclamations of the second half of Isaiah: "I, the Lord—with the first of them and with the last—I am he" (Isa 41:4; cf. 43:11–13; 44:6; 45:6, 18, 21; 48:17). The title became part of the liturgy of the Feast of Tabernacles, the time when this controversy recorded in John occurred. The phrase occurs in Jesus' response to the challenge of the high priest at his final hearing. When asked, "Are you the Christ, the Son of the Blessed One?" Jesus replied, "I am . . . and you will see the Son of Man sitting at the right hand of the Mighty One and coming on the clouds of heaven" (Mark 14:61–62). The violent reaction of the high priest in Mark 14:63 indicates that he regarded the use of the title as a blasphemous claim on Jesus' part to possess the quality of deity.

59 The crowd unmistakably understood Jesus' words as a blasphemous claim and immediately prepared to stone him. He did not protest their action as a mistake of judgment; he simply withdrew. How he managed to escape their wrath is not explained. He had done so on previous occasions, for "his time had not yet come" (John 7:30; cf. Luke 4:30).

Notes

57 Hoehner contends that the later date for the Crucifixion accords better with the known astronomical data and with the historical situation involving Pilate. The unwillingness of Pilate to risk the wrath of Tiberius may have been due to his appointment by Sejanus, prefect of the Praetorian Guard, who had fallen out of favor with the emperor. Sejanus had been executed, and Pilate did not wish to endanger his head and his career by a political misstep (pp. 115–26).

E. *The Manifestation of Opposition* (9:1–11:57)

The widening rift between belief and unbelief, which had become clearly apparent at the time of the feeding of the five thousand and was accentuated at the Feast of Tabernacles, at this point became an open breach. Not only had many of Jesus' disciples abandoned his cause (John 6:66), but the religious authorities also were becoming actively hostile (7:32). The last five or six months of Jesus' life were filled with controversy and with attempts on the part of the priests and scribes to trap him by his words or his actions. Jesus, however, being fully aware of their designs, maintained his usual ministry and became bolder in his resistance. John's Gospel deals with this period largely from the viewpoint of Jerusalem.

1. *The healing of the blind man* (9:1–41)

a. *The healing*

9:1–12

> [1]As he went along, he saw a man blind from birth. [2]His disciples asked him, "Rabbi, who sinned, this man or his parents, that he was born blind?"
>
> [3]"Neither this man nor his parents sinned," said Jesus, "but this happened so that the work of God might be displayed in his life. [4]As long as it is day, we must do the work of him who sent me. Night is coming, when no one can work. [5]While I am in the world, I am the light of the world."
>
> [6]Having said this, he spit on the ground, made some mud with the saliva, and put it on the man's eyes. [7]"Go," he told him, "wash in the pool of Siloam" (this word means Sent). So the man went and washed, and came home seeing.
>
> [8]His neighbors and those who had formerly seen him begging asked, "Isn't this the same man who used to sit and beg?" [9]Some claimed that he was.
>
> Others said, "No, he only looks like him."
>
> But he himself insisted, "I am the man."
>
> [10]"How then were your eyes opened?" they demanded.
>
> [11]He replied, "The man they call Jesus made some mud and put it on my eyes. He told me to go to Siloam and wash. So I went and washed, and then I could see."
>
> [12]"Where is this man?" they asked him.
>
> "I don't know," he said.

The cure of the blind man probably occurred shortly after the Feast of Tabernacles, while Jesus was still in Jerusalem. The episode is a unit by itself; it could easily be regarded as a story independent of its context. It is used as an illustration of Jesus' utterance recorded in 8:12: "I am the light of the world. Whoever follows me will never walk in darkness, but will have the light of life." The healing was not only a sample of Jesus' ability to restore sight to a man who was congenitally blind; but it also represented, figuratively, and for the blind man, experientially, the dawning of spiritual light. Furthermore, the healing brought new light to the disciples on one of the mysteries of life that had bewildered them.

1 Although Jesus had healed blind persons on other occasions (Matt 9:27–31; 12:22; 15:30; 21:14; Mark 8:22–26; 10:46–52), this "sign" was an outstanding case because the man had been born blind. Also, the sign was related to the issue of fate, which the disciples raised; and it illustrates the origination and development of faith, which is the theme of this Gospel. The encounter of Jesus and the blind man seems to have been

a casual one. Since blind beggars had little opportunity for employment, they were dependent on charity for their sustenance; and in a depressed economy, they usually fared rather badly.

2 The interest of the disciples was prompted by theological curiosity rather than compassion. For them the blind man was an unsolved riddle rather than a sufferer to be relieved. Their query, "Rabbi, who sinned, this man or his parents, that he was born blind?" was based on a principle stated in the law: "He [God] does not leave the guilty unpunished; he punishes the children and their children for the sin of the fathers to the third and fourth generation" (Exod 34:7). They construed this to mean that if a person suffered from any ailment, it must have been because his parents or grandparents had committed some sin against God (cf. Exod 20:5). To this they added the thought that perhaps he might have sinned before birth, whether as an embryo or in a preexistent state. Such a concept appears in the rabbinical writings.

3 Jesus refused to accept either alternative suggested by the disciples' question. He looked on the man's plight, not as retribution for some offense committed either by his parents or by himself, but as an opportunity to do God's work. Jesus did not consider the blindness as punishment or as a matter of irrational chance; it was a challenge to manifest God's healing power in the man's life.

4–5 The growing pressure of hostility rising from unbelief warned Jesus that his time was short. The twilight of his career was beginning and the darkness would soon fall. As all the Gospels show, Jesus was working under the shadow of the coming cross (Matt 16:21; Mark 8:31; Luke 9:22). While he had the opportunity, he must let his light shine on the darkness around him by healing both bodies and minds. The use of "we" shows that he included his disciples in his ministry. They also would pass through perils and opposition, but they would have the support of the Father who had sent him. "I am the light of the world" is a repetition of 8:12, but it is not superfluous. The healing of the blind man illustrates the positive and practical application of the principle. Jesus dealt not only in ideas but also in the application of them.

6 To make known his intention to the blind man, Jesus made clay from dust and spittle and placed it on the sightless eyes. Lindars suggests that the use of clay parallels the creative act of God in Genesis 2:7 (p. 343). Since the blindness was congenital, the healing would be creative rather than remedial. However, the emphasis of John seems to be on compassion rather than creation. The touch of a friendly hand would be reassuring. The weight of the clay would serve as an indicator to the blind man that something had been done to him, and it would be an inducement to obey Jesus' command.

7 The Pool of Siloam was located at the southern end of the city, probably a considerable distance from the place where the blind man was. The walk would call for some exertion. Certainly the man would not want to continue sitting by the roadside with mud smeared over his eyes. If his lifelong affliction had tended to make him apathetic, he now had at least one motive for obeying what must have seemed a foolish command. How could washing in a public pool restore the sight he never had? The trip the man made must have been a venture of faith. Jesus had not even told him that he would be healed but had merely commanded him to wash. If the man had overheard Jesus' conversation with

the disciples, he would have expected something to happen. Yet so extraordinary a miracle as giving sight to a man born blind would have seemed impossible.

8–9 The man's recovery of his sight created a genuine sensation. The effects of the miracle are described vividly by the responses of four groups or individuals: (1) the neighbors, (2) the Pharisees, (3) the parents, and (4) the man himself. The neighbors and acquaintances knew very well the man they had supported by their charity. To see him walking with normal sight was so incredible that they thought it must be a case of mistaken identity. He quickly settled the dispute by avowing that he was the man they had known.

10–12 The curiosity of the neighbors demanded an explanation. The man replied in matter-of-fact fashion, narrating the event just as it happened. His reply, however, indicates the first stage of faith: he accepted the fact. He made no attempt to evaluate Jesus' person but spoke of him simply as "the man they call Jesus." He showed no previous knowledge of him, nor had he bothered to investigate his person. In fact, the man was even unaware of Jesus' current whereabouts.

Notes

---

2 The Pharisees, Sadducees, and Essenes differed from one another on the concept of fate. The Pharisees held that all events are predestined but that some are conditioned by the human will. The Sadducees rejected any intervention of God in human affairs. The Essenes attributed all occurrences to divine predestination (see A. Broyde, "Fatalism," JE, 5:356). The debate must have been carried on in Jesus' day and must have provided a background for the disciples' query. R.H. Lightfoot states that "Jewish thought regarding even congenital defect as a punishment for sin, was inclined in such a case to explain it as having been committed in the womb, or in a previous existence, or by the parents" (p. 202).

3 The absence of a definite verb in the Greek text immediately before the "so that" (ἵνα, hina) clause raises a question of interpretation. Normally this type of clause expresses purpose. Should it therefore be interpreted to mean that the affliction of blindness was not a penalty for some sin of the past but was allowed that God might be glorified in the healing of the man? Such an explanation implies that years of misery were inflicted on him for the express purpose of demonstrating Jesus' power. Some expositors (e.g., G. Campbell Morgan, pp. 164–65) have suggested that the hina clause is dependent on the following verb rather than on the one preceding. The translation would then read: "But that the work of God might be displayed in his life, as long as it is day, we must do the work of him who sent me." In that case the purpose clause would express the intent of the definite verb "sent" in v.4 rather than the intent of the indefinite idea "this happened." Such a construction would be out of keeping with the general usage of this Gospel. Hina can express result as well as purpose and is so used elsewhere in John's writings (1 John 1:9). If it can be so interpreted here, it would mean that the blindness was not the divine purpose but that it was rather the accident of birth. The purpose was the healing, not the malady.

---

b. *The consequences*

9:13–41

¹³They brought to the Pharisees the man who had been blind. ¹⁴Now the day on which Jesus had made the mud and opened the man's eyes was a Sabbath.

¹⁵Therefore the Pharisees also asked him how he had received his sight. "He put mud on my eyes," the man replied, "and I washed, and now I see."

¹⁶Some of the Pharisees said, "This man is not from God, for he does not keep the Sabbath."

But others asked, "How can a sinner do such miraculous signs?" So they were divided.

¹⁷Finally they turned again to the blind man, "What have you to say about him? It was your eyes he opened."

The man replied, "He is a prophet."

¹⁸The Jews still did not believe that he had been blind and had received his sight until they sent for the man's parents. ¹⁹"Is this your son?" they asked. "Is this the one you say was born blind? How is it that now he can see?"

²⁰"We know he is our son," the parents answered, "and we know he was born blind. ²¹But how he can see now, or who opened his eyes, we don't know. Ask him. He is of age; he will speak for himself." ²²His parents said this because they were afraid of the Jews, for already the Jews had decided that anyone who acknowledged that Jesus was the Christ would be put out of the synagogue. ²³That was why his parents said, "He is of age; ask him."

²⁴A second time they summoned the man who had been blind. "Give glory to God," they said. "We know this man is a sinner."

²⁵He replied, "Whether he is a sinner or not, I don't know. One thing I do know. I was blind but now I see!"

²⁶Then they asked him, "What did he do to you? How did he open your eyes?"

²⁷He answered, "I have told you already and you did not listen. Why do you want to hear it again? Do you want to become his disciples, too?"

²⁸Then they hurled insults at him and said, "You are this fellow's disciple! We are disciples of Moses! ²⁹We know that God spoke to Moses, but as for this fellow, we don't even know where he comes from."

³⁰The man answered, "Now that is remarkable! You don't know where he comes from, yet he opened my eyes. ³¹We know that God does not listen to sinners. He listens to the godly man who does his will. ³²Nobody has ever heard of opening the eyes of a man born blind. ³³If this man were not from God, he could do nothing."

³⁴To this they replied, "You were steeped in sin at birth; how dare you lecture us!" And they threw him out.

³⁵Jesus heard that they had thrown him out, and when he found him, he said, "Do you believe in the Son of Man?"

³⁶"Who is he, sir?" the man asked. "Tell me so that I may believe in him."

³⁷Jesus said, "You have now seen him; in fact, he is the one speaking with you."

³⁸Then the man said, "Lord, I believe," and he worshiped him.

³⁹Jesus said, "For judgment I have come into this world, so that the blind will see and those who see will become blind."

⁴⁰Some Pharisees who were with him heard him say this and asked, "What? Are we blind too?"

⁴¹Jesus said, "If you were blind, you would not be guilty of sin; but now that you claim you can see, your guilt remains."

13–15 The case was so mysterious that the neighbors took the man to the religious authorities, the Pharisees, who supposedly would be able to offer an explanation. Since the day on which the miracle was performed was a Sabbath, the Sabbath law was involved. The Pharisees inquired how the man received his sight, and he repeated the story he had given first to the neighbors.

There are both parallels and contrasts between the healing in ch. 9 and that in ch. 5. Both occurred at a public pool; both concerned apparently incurable cases; and both occurred on the Sabbath, which precipitated the question of the Sabbath law. In the previous instance, however, the man healed reported voluntarily to the Pharisees and identified Jesus afterward. In this instance the man had no knowledge of Jesus' where-abouts, nor did he report the matter to the authorities. Furthermore, Jesus implied that the former man had sinned and adjured him to cease doing so (5:14); of this he stated that his condition was not the result of sin (9:3). There is no evidence that the former man became a believer whereas the man born blind demonstrated a growing faith.

16 The response of the Pharisees revealed reasoning from prejudice: "This man is not from God, for he does not keep the Sabbath." For the Pharisees there could be no other conclusion. Others, however, were hesitant and asked how a sinner could have the power to perform such miracles. The use of the plural "miraculous signs" (*sēmeia*) suggests that they knew other miracles of Jesus comparable to this one. The people took into consideration the source of the miracle, not simply this single instance. The contrast of these responses brings into focus an important principle of interpretation: Should Jesus be judged by an a priori application of the law or by an a posteriori consideration of his works?

The division among the Pharisees shows that there must have been at least a small minority who were not inflexibly hostile to Jesus. Perhaps Nicodemus and Joseph of Arimathea were among the number. The minority's question, "How can a sinner do such miraculous signs?" sounds much like Nicodemus's opening words to Jesus: "No one could perform the miraculous signs you are doing if God were not with him" (3:2).

17 Again the man himself was questioned to help bring a decision in the dispute. His verdict was more definite than the preceding one: "He is a prophet," the man said. The prophets were the agents of God, and in some instances they performed miracles; for example, Elisha (2 Kings 2:19–22; 4:18–44; 5:1–14). If, then, Jesus had performed an indisputable miracle, it was prima facie evidence that he must have a divine commission. As an emissary of God, he could be empowered to heal on the Sabbath, if necessary; and he would be above the jurisdiction of any human tribunal.

18–23 The evidence was still insufficient to remove the objections of "the Jews." In this context it seems that "the Jews" was synonymous with "the Pharisees." Unconvinced of the genuineness of the cure, they proceeded to query whether the man really had been born blind; for if he had not been blind from birth, the miracle could be disputed. They interrogated his parents, who, fearing excommunication from the synagogue, evaded the issue by stating that their son was an adult capable of answering for himself.

24 To the Jews there was only one solution. The Law forbade working on the Sabbath. Jesus had healed on the Sabbath; therefore, Jesus was a sinner. So the man was commanded to "give glory to God" for his healing.

25–27 The ensuing argument between the blind man and the Pharisees was a duel between an obvious fact and a legal syllogism. The fact of the healing was undeniable and was admitted by the blind man's opponents. Their incessant questioning exhausted his patience, and he indulged in some sarcasm by insinuating that their repeated inquiries showed an interest in becoming disciples of Jesus.

28–29 Such a response to learned rabbis on the part of an illiterate man was surely considered insulting. The Jews quickly retorted that they were abiding by the authority of Moses, whose law for centuries had been the standard of Israel's religion. Jesus they rejected as a nobody, a vagrant prophet who did not keep the law.

30–33 Again the blind man pressed the pragmatic argument, and he also employed an argument of his own. Since, according to the assumption of the Jews, "God does not listen to sinners" (cf. Ps 66:18; Prov 28:9; Isa 1:15), how could Jesus have performed this miracle if he were under divine condemnation? Rather, the man reasoned, the healing should be ample evidence that Jesus came from God.

34 To this argument the Jews had no real answer. So they attacked the man by character assassination and made him feel unworthy to answer on his behalf or Jesus'. Then they excommunicated him, thus isolating him from his family and friends and debarring him from employment.

35–36 In contrast to the negative result of rejection is the positive result of Jesus' response. "Found" implies that Jesus looked for the man so that he might confirm his faith by discipleship. The question "Do you believe in the Son of Man?" is a summons to commitment. The Greek pronoun *su* ("you") used with the verb makes the inquiry doubly emphatic. It demanded a personal decision in the face of opposition or rejection. Since the healing of the man occurred after Jesus' first interview, he would not have recognized Jesus by sight; and the question, couched in the third person, would not instantly identify the questioner as the object of faith. The change in reading from "Son of God" (KJV) to "Son of Man" is common to all modern versions. It seems less likely that "Son of God" should have been supplanted by "Son of Man" in the thinking of the early church than that the opposite should have occurred. Both terms were used of Christ to express his deity (see John 3:13; 5:27; 6:27; cf. Matt 26:63–64).

37–38 When Jesus said that the "Son of Man" was the person speaking, the man instantly responded by worshiping Jesus. He was ready to believe on the one who had healed him. His attitude was already positive. Probably he recognized Jesus as his healer by his voice. He needed only the identification to take the final step of faith. The progress in spiritual understanding of the person of Christ is marked by progressive descriptions: "The man they called Jesus" (v.11); "he is a prophet" (v.17); "from God" (v.33); "Son of Man" (v.35); and, lastly, "Lord" (v.38). This progression illustrates the man's movement from darkness to light, both physically and spiritually.

39–41 The negative result is illustrated by the Pharisees' response. Jesus' remark, "For judgment I have come into this world, so that the blind will see and those who see will become blind," makes him the pivot on which human destiny turns. The Pharisees, assuming that they could "see" without his intervention, asked in resentment, "Are we blind too?" Jesus' reply indicated that if they had acknowledged blindness, they could be freed from sin; but if they asserted that they could see when they were really blind, there would be no remedy for them. If they acted in ignorance of the light, they could not be held responsible for not knowing it; but if they claimed to understand it and still rejected it, they would be liable for judgment. Deliberate rejection of light means that "the light within . . . is darkness" (Matt 6:23).

Notes

34 Excommunication in this passage is not a late reflection of an ecclesiastical practice. Expulsion from the community of Israel was prescribed in the Mosaic law for a number of offenses, some ceremonial and some moral: eating leavened bread during the Feast of Unleavened Bread (Exod 12:15), misuse of holy oil (Exod 30:33), neglect of the Passover (Num 9:13), defilement by touching a corpse or neglect of purification afterwards (Num 19:3–20), eating flesh sacrificed in a peace offering (Lev 7:20), eating of blood (Lev 7:27; 17:10), slaughtering sacrifices outside the tabernacle (Lev 19:8), sexual abuses and perversions (Lev 18:29; 20:18), idolatry (20:3), and occult practices (20:6). There is a second allusion to the punishment in John 16:2, where it is mentioned as a possible danger for the disciples of Jesus.

The exact method of excommunication followed is not explained, and there seems to be little evidence concerning its usage either in the OT or in rabbinic teaching. It implied exclusion from all the fraternal benefits that the Jewish community could provide. Since the Jewish concept of salvation was built on membership in the covenant people, excommunication probably implied the loss of salvation as well. The Johannine usages (9:22; 12:42; 16:2) may relate to "The Heretical Blessings," the curse pronounced on "heretics," i.e., Jewish Christians, which would be relevant to Christians only after the destruction of the temple in A.D. 70 (Barrett, pp. 299–300). This view assumes that the Johannine narrative is interpreting the story of the blind man in the setting of the late first century, when the Gospel was presumably written. Since there is no explicit evidence concerning the practices of Judaism prior to A.D. 70, it may perhaps be assumed that the action against the blind man was taken on the basis of OT law: "Anyone who desecrates it [the Sabbath] must be put to death; whoever does any work on that day must be cut off from his people" (Exod 31:14).

35 Ἀνθρώπου (anthrōpou, "man") is the reading of the oldest MSS, some of the versions, and Chrysostom. The other sources read θεοῦ (theou, "God"). Both "Son of Man" and "Son of God" are used as titles of Jesus elsewhere in John; so the argument from style is indeterminate. Metzger remarks that "the external support for ἀνθρώπου . . . is so weighty, and the improbability of θεοῦ being altered to ἀνθρώπου is so great that the Committee regarded the reading adopted for the text as virtually certain" (Textual Commentary, pp. 228–29).

2. The Good Shepherd discourse

10:1-21

1"I tell you the truth, the man who does not enter the sheep pen by the gate, but climbs in by some other way, is a thief and a robber. 2The man who enters by the gate is the shepherd of his sheep. 3The watchman opens the gate for him, and the sheep listen to his voice. He calls his own sheep by name and leads them out. 4When he has brought out all his own, he goes on ahead of them, and his sheep follow him because they know his voice. 5But they will never follow a stranger; in fact, they will run away from him because they do not recognize a stranger's voice." 6Jesus used this figure of speech, but they did not understand what he was telling them.

7Therefore Jesus said again, "I tell you the truth, I am the gate for the sheep. 8All who ever came before me were thieves and robbers, but the sheep did not listen to them. 9I am the gate; whoever enters through me will be saved. He will come in and go out, and find pasture. 10The thief comes only to steal and kill and destroy; I have come that they may have life, and have it to the full.

11"I am the good shepherd. The good shepherd lays down his life for the sheep. 12The hired hand is not the shepherd who owns the sheep. So when he sees the wolf coming, he abandons the sheep and runs away. Then the wolf attacks the flock and scatters it. 13The man runs away because he is a hired hand and cares nothing for the sheep.

¹⁴"I am the good shepherd; I know my sheep and my sheep know me—¹⁵just as the Father knows me and I know the Father—and I lay down my life for the sheep. ¹⁶I have other sheep that are not of this sheep pen. I must bring them also. They too will listen to my voice, and there shall be one flock and one shepherd. ¹⁷The reason my Father loves me is that I lay down my life—only to take it up again. ¹⁸No one takes it from me, but I lay it down of my own accord. I have authority to lay it down and authority to take it up again. This command I received from my Father."

¹⁹At these words the Jews were again divided. ²⁰Many of them said, "He is demon-possessed and raving mad. Why listen to him?"

²¹But others said, "These are not the sayings of a man possessed by a demon. Can a demon open the eyes of the blind?"

Chapter 10 opens a new topic, the discourse on the Good Shepherd. It is seemingly unrelated to the previous narrative, though the reference in v.21 to opening the eyes of the blind shows that the author connected it with the preceding text. Whether the discourse was given at the Feast of Tabernacles (7:2, 14, 37), or whether it introduced the Feast of Dedication (10:22) is not made perfectly clear. The language of 10:22, "Then came the Feast of Dedication," would seemingly indicate a break in chronology at this point. The writer was drawing events from memory as they suited his purpose and recounting them in general chronological order, without supplying all the details of a continuing story.

The Good Shepherd discourse in some respects resembles the parables of the Synoptics. Matthew (18:12–14) and Luke (15:3–7) both cite a parable of a shepherd and his sheep; and all three Gospels (Matt, Luke, John) emphasize the aspect of careful concern that the shepherd feels for them. The Johannine presentation, however, is not concentrated on one point but utilizes the allegory with a wider meaning than do the Synoptics. The teaching is based on the practice of sheep herding, and several aspects are utilized to create a picture of the relation of Christ to his people.

1 "I tell you the truth" is a translation of the double use of the adverb "truly, truly" (amēn, amēn), or as in the KJV, "verily, verily." This is a phrase peculiar to the fourth Gospel, and it generally introduces a solemn asseveration about Jesus or his mission (cf. 1:51; 5:19, 24, 25; 6:26, 32, 47, 53; 8:34, 51, 58; 10:1, 7; 12:24; 13:16, 20, 21, 38; 14:12; 16:20, 23). In a few instances it refers either to a general principle of salvation or to the future action of a person (3:3, 5, 11; 21:18). Its use in this immediate context emphasizes the importance of the teaching the allegory contains, particularly as it represents the ministry of Jesus himself.

The imagery of the first two paragraphs is based on the concept of the "sheep pen." It was usually a rough stone or mud-brick structure, only partially roofed, if covered at all, or very often a cave in the hills. It had only one opening through which the sheep could pass when they came in for the night. The pen served for the protection of the sheep against thieves and wild beasts. The thief, who would not have any right of access by the gate, used other means of entrance. He would not follow the lawful method of approach.

"Thief " and "robber" are different in meaning. "Thief " (kleptēs) implies subtlety and trickery; "robber" (lēstēs) connotes violence and plundering. The latter term was sometimes used of bandits or guerrillas. The purpose of both was exploitation; neither was concerned for the welfare of the sheep.

2 The shepherd enters by the gate, which is the lawful method of entry. Jesus was contrasting himself with the false messiahs who by pretence or violence attempted to gain control of the people. He came as the legitimate heir of the chosen seed and claimed to be the fulfillment of the promises of the OT revelation.

3 The "watchman" cannot be identified with any particular person, but, rather, the word illustrates Jesus' coming at the right time and in the right way. He alone has the right to spiritual leadership of his people. This leadership of the sheep is self-authenticating. They "listen to his voice." The Oriental shepherd usually named his sheep and he could summon them by calling them.

4 A pen frequently held several flocks; and when the time came to go out to morning pasture, each shepherd separated his sheep from the others by his peculiar call. Instead of driving them, he led them so that they followed him as a unit. Wherever they went, the shepherd preceded them to provide guidance to the most advantageous pasturage and guardianship against possible danger.

5–6 The sheep refused to follow a stranger because his voice was unfamiliar. In fact, if a stranger should use the shepherd's call and imitate his tone, the flock would instantly detect the difference and would scatter in panic. Jesus used this figure to depict the relation between the disciples and himself.

In view of the fact that shepherds and sheep were so common in Palestine, it seems incredible that Jesus' metaphor should not be understood. His hearers, however, failed to comprehend his meaning because of their spiritual deadness. If they would not recognize his claims, they would not accept him as a shepherd; and their assumption that they were God's flock because they were descendants of Abraham (8:39) would eliminate the necessity of personal faith in Jesus for salvation.

7 The sudden shift of metaphor from shepherd to gate seems rather strange to us, but in reality it is not. When the sheep returned to the fold at night after a day of grazing, the shepherd stood in the doorway of the pen and inspected each one as it entered. If a sheep were scratched or wounded by thorns, the shepherd anointed it with oil to facilitate healing; if the sheep were thirsty, he gave them water. As Psalm 23:5–6 says, "You anoint my head with oil; my cup overflows." After all the sheep had been counted and brought into the pen, the shepherd lay down across the doorway so that no intruder —man or beast—could enter without his knowledge. The shepherd became the door. The emphatic singular pronoun "I" (*egō*) emphasizes that the shepherd is the sole determiner of who enters the fold and who is excluded. It parallels the later statement: "I am the way and the truth and the life. No one comes to the Father except through me" (John 14:16).

8 "All who ever came before me were thieves and robbers" cannot refer to the prophets who preceded Jesus. It must refer to the false messiahs and supposed deliverers of the people who had appeared in the period following the restoration from the Exile and especially in the century before Jesus' advent. After the death of Herod the Great in 4 B.C., there were many factions that contended for the leadership of the nation and attempted by violence to throw off the Roman yoke. Jesus' purpose was not political, as the emphasis of the discourse shows.

Hendriksen suggests that Jesus was referring to the religious leaders of the Jews as the "thieves and robbers" (2:308). They were attempting to gain the allegiance of the people and were not above using violence if it would serve their purpose (cf. John 8:59).

9–10 Jesus' main purpose was the salvation (health) of the sheep, which he defined as free access to pasture and fullness of life. Under his protection and by his gift they can experience the best life can offer. In the context of John's emphasis on eternal life, this statement takes on new significance. Jesus can give a whole new meaning to living because he provides full satisfaction and perfect guidance (cf. Ezek 34:15).

11 The concept of a divine shepherd goes back to the OT. Psalm 23 opens with the statement "The LORD is my shepherd" (v.1); Jeremiah speaks of gathering the nation as a flock of sheep that has been scattered (23:1–3); and Ezekiel prophesied: "As a shepherd looks after his scattered flock when he is with them, so will I look after my sheep. I will rescue them . . . I myself will tend my sheep and have them lie down" (34:12, 15). To the disciples the figure would have been specially apt since sheep herding was one of the major occupations in Palestine. It involved both protective concern and a sacrificial attitude. This latter is expressed in the words "the good shepherd lays down his life for the sheep." The phrase "lays down his life" is unique to the Johannine writings and means a voluntary sacrificial death (10:11, 17, 18; 13:37–38; 15:13; 1 John 3:16). The verb is used elsewhere in John to mean "lay aside, strip off " (13:4). In addition, the preposition *hyper*, translated "for," is generally used with a connotation of sacrifice (John 13:37; 15:13; cf. Luke 22:19; Rom 5:6–8; 1 Cor 15:3). "Life" (*psychē*) implies more than physical existence; it involves personality and is more frequently translated "soul." The good shepherd stands ready to sacrifice his total self for the sake of the sheep.

12 Jesus' statement "the hired hand is not the shepherd" indicates the difference between himself and the religious leaders of the day. The hireling, though not a brigand bent on the destruction of the sheep, is concerned more for his own safety than for that of the sheep. When the flock is attacked by a wolf, the hireling deserts them. The difference is not so much that of activity as of attitude. The hireling may guide the sheep to pasture, but he will not endanger himself for them. Without proper and courageous leadership, the sheep will be dispersed and easily made the victims of their enemies.

13 The hireling's main concern is his pay. This discourse anticipates Peter's words: "Be shepherds of God's flock that is under your care, serving as overseers—not because you must, but because you are willing, as God wants you to be; not greedy for money, but eager to serve; not lording it over those entrusted to you, but being examples to the flock" (1 Peter 5:2–3).

14–15 The reaffirmation "I am the good shepherd" is based on knowledge of the sheep. "Know" (*ginōskō*) in this Gospel connotes more than the cognizance of mere facts; it implies a relationship of trust and intimacy. The definitive analogy given here is drawn from Jesus' relation to the Father. The Shepherd is concerned for the sheep because they are his property and because he loves them individually.

16 The sheep "not of this sheep pen" probably refers to the Gentiles whom Jesus sent his disciples to (Matt 28:19) and whom he wished to include in his salvation. He stresses this idea of unity later in his farewell prayer (17:20).

17 The thrice-repeated allusion to laying down his life (10:11, 15, 17) gives the basis for Jesus' sacrifice as the means of our reconciliation both to God and to one another. See 1 John 3:16: "This is how we know what love is: Jesus Christ laid down his life for us. And we ought to lay down our lives for our brothers."

18 Two important aspects of Jesus' death are clarified by his authority. The first is that his death was wholly voluntary. His power was such that no human hand could have touched him had he not permitted it. The Gospel has already made clear that Jesus had avoided capture or execution (5:18; 7:44-45; 8:20, 59; 10:39; 11:53-54). Only when he declared that "the hour has come" (12:23) was it possible for his enemies to arrest him. The second aspect is his authority to lay down his life and take it up again. The death of Jesus, though voluntary, was not merely assent to being killed, a sort of indirect suicide; it was part of a plan to submit to death and then emerge from it victoriously alive. Anyone can lay down his life, if that means simply the termination of physical existence; but only the Son of the Father could at will resume his existence. He was acting in accord with a divine plan that involved a supreme sacrifice and a manifestation of divine power. The entire plan was motivated by his love for the Father and his readiness to carry out his Father's purpose. "Authority" means that he was not the helpless victim of his enemies' violence but that he had both the right and the power to become the instrument of reconciliation between man and God and between Jew and Gentile.

19-21 The reaction of the populace was divided. His enemies accused him of insanity for making a claim that seemed both unreasonable and impossible. The accusation of demon-possession had been leveled against him on other occasions (7:20; 8:48). His claims seemed so exaggerated and so contradictory to the popular understanding of the unity of God that they could be attributed only to the irrational and blasphemous utterance of a demoniac. Curiously, Johannine writings never mention any miracle of exorcism on Jesus' part but employ this language only to report the way his opponents described his utterances and behavior. On the contrary, many of the crowd regarded Jesus as sane. His words did not correspond to the ravings of a demoniac, nor did demoniacs cure the blind. The reference to the miracle narrated in ch. 9 shows that it must have left a strong impression in Jerusalem.

Notes

8 Josephus (Antiq. 17.10.4-8) describes in detail a number of these revolts and adds: "And so Judea was filled with brigandage. Anyone might make himself king as the head of a band of rebels ... and then would press on to the destruction of the community." In this category the revolts mentioned in Acts 5:36-37 fell.

16 The word translated "pen" (αὐλή, *aulē*) means a courtyard or "fold" (KJV), an enclosure open to the sky where sheep can be kept at night. The word "flock" (ποίμνη, *poimnē*) means the group as a unit and does not refer to the place where sheep are kept. The sheepfold or pen is the artificial means by which unity is established; the flock is determined by the nature of the animals. To speak of a flock immediately raises the question as to kind: sheep, goats, geese, or doves. A "pen" connotes a place where the "flock" is kept. The "flock" refers to the nation of Israel in distinction from all other groups because of their heritage and location. Ultimately the

sheep from another flock would be united with them to make one flock of the redeemed. The concept of the flock gathered from all nations pervades the Gospels. Matthew quotes Jesus as telling his disciples to make disciples "of all nations" (Matt 28:19); Mark records his command to herald the gospel "to all creation" (Mark 16:15); and Luke stresses his command that repentance and forgiveness of sins should be proclaimed in his name "to all nations" (Luke 24:47). The word translated "nations" (ἔθνη, *ethnē*) is also rendered "Gentiles." Jesus intended that his message should reach both the house of Israel and all the peoples of the earth and that both should be drawn together in him.

---

3. *The debate in Solomon's Colonnade*

10:22–42

22Then came the Feast of Dedication at Jerusalem. It was winter, 23and Jesus was in the temple area walking in Solomon's Colonnade. 24The Jews gathered around him, saying, "How long will you keep us in suspense? If you are the Christ, tell us plainly."

25Jesus answered, "I did tell you, but you do not believe. The miracles I do in my Father's name speak for me, 26but you do not believe because you are not my sheep. 27My sheep listen to my voice; I know them, and they follow me. 28I give them eternal life, and they shall never perish; no one can snatch them out of my hand. 29My Father, who has given them to me, is greater than all; no one can snatch them out of my Father's hand. 30I and the Father are one."

31Again the Jews picked up stones to stone him, 32but Jesus said to them, "I have shown you many great miracles from the Father. For which of these do you stone me?"

33"We are not stoning you for any of these," replied the Jews, "but for blasphemy, because you, a mere man, claim to be God."

34"Jesus answered them, "Is it not written in your Law, 'I have said you are gods'? 35If he called them 'gods,' to whom the word of God came—and the Scripture cannot be broken—36what about the one whom the Father set apart as his very own and sent into the world? Why then do you accuse me of blasphemy because I said, 'I am God's Son'? 37Do not believe me unless I do what my Father does. 38But if I do it, even though you do not believe me, believe the miracles, that you may learn and understand that the Father is in me, and I in the Father." 39Again they tried to seize him, but he escaped their grasp.

40Then Jesus went back across the Jordan to the place where John had been baptizing in the early days. Here he stayed 41and many people came to him. They said, "Though John never performed a miraculous sign, all that John said about this man was true." 42And in that place many believed in Jesus.

22–23 The Feast of Dedication, now known as Hanukkah, was established as a memorial to the purification and rededication of the temple by Judas Maccabeus on Kislev (December) 25, 165 B.C., after its profanation three years earlier by Antiochus IV Epiphanes. Antiochus, the king of Syria, had captured Jerusalem, plundered the temple treasury, and sacrificed a sow to Jupiter on the temple altar. His attempt to Hellenize Judea resulted in the Maccabean revolt, which, after three years, was successful in defeating the Syrian armies and liberating the Jewish people. Solomon's Colonnade (or Porch) was a long walkway covered by a roof supported on pillars on the east side of the temple, overlooking the Kidron Valley. The Colonnade served as a shelter from the heat of the sun in summer and from the cold rain in winter. Jesus used it as a center for informal teaching and preaching since there would almost always be some people present for worship at the temple.

24 The verb translated "gathered around him" (*ekyklōsan*) means "encircled" and implies that the Jews wanted to compel Jesus to make a categorical statement of his identity. Their demand, "How long will you keep us in suspense? If you are the Christ, tell us plainly," reveals their impatience. If he was the Messiah, they wanted him to fulfill his calling by achieving independence for the nation; if he was not the Messiah, they would look elsewhere. They could not escape the fact that his miracles (*erga*, "works") exceeded the powers of any ordinary man and that his teachings carried an authority greater than that of the established religious leaders. On the other hand, he had not formally presented himself as the Messiah, nor had he evinced any political ambitions. The crowd was demanding a declaration that would either dispel an illusion or enlist their allegiance.

25–26 Jesus' reply placed the burden of proof on his questioners. He reminded them that his previous sayings and works (*erga*) should be sufficient to establish his messianic mission (cf. John 5:16–47; 6:32–59; 7:14–30). He charged them with unbelief because they refused the evidence he had so plainly given them. He said the reason they did not believe was that they were not his sheep. By telling them that they did not belong to his flock, he implied that it was not descent from the chosen line that was the criterion of salvation. His sheep manifested their nature by following him. They enjoyed the favor of God. His immediate hearers refused to believe and thus cut themselves off from further revelation.

27–28 The sheep that belong to the Lord's flock are characterized by obedience, recognition of the shepherd, and allegiance to him. They are guaranteed eternal life and permanent protection. All the resources of God are committed to their preservation. Eternal life is given to them, not earned by them, and they themselves are given to Christ by the Father. Christ promises his personal protection to the sheep that the Father has given him: "No one can snatch them out of my hand."

29 The marginal reading of this verse, "What my Father has given me is greater than all," is probably the correct reading, though the MS evidence seems rather evenly divided. If so, the gift of the Father is the "sheep" viewed collectively. The Father assures their destiny, for nobody can wrest them from his hand. Throughout the preceding discourse, Jesus stressed his relationship with the Father, his intimate knowledge of the Father (10:15), and the love of the Father for him (v.17). He said that his miracles (*erga*, "works") were performed "in my Father's name" (v.25), which means that they were done by the power of the Father and for his honor. The final claim was "I and the Father are one" (v.30).

30 "I and the Father" preserves the separate individuality of the two Persons in the Godhead; the neuter pronoun "one" (*hen*) asserts unity of nature or equality (cf. 1 Cor 3:8). The Jews were quick to apprehend this statement and reacted by preparing to stone Jesus for blasphemy because he, a man, had asserted that he was one with God. For them Jesus' language did not mean simply agreement of thought or purpose but carried a metaphysical implication of deity. The Father and the Son functioned as one.

31 The verb translated "picked up" literally means "to carry." It is doubtful whether there were any loose stones in the paved courtyard of Solomon's Colonnade that could have been picked up. But not far off was the temple that was in the process of being

112

built, and certainly stones would have been readily available there. Stoning was the punishment prescribed for blasphemy according to the law of Moses (Lev 24:16), and the opponents of Jesus were preparing for just such an execution.

32 Jesus' question challenged the people's action on the ground that he had performed only helpful deeds. His question was designed to make them take stock of what he had done. Then they would see that stoning would be incongruous with his actions.

33 The Jews replied that the question was not the quality of his works but the nature of his claims, and they charged him with blasphemy. Had Jesus not meant to convey a claim to deity, he undoubtedly would have protested the action of the Jews by declaring that they had misunderstood him.

34-35 On the contrary, Jesus introduced an *a fortiori* argument from the Psalms to strengthen his statement. Psalm 82:6 represents God as addressing a group of beings whom he calls "gods" (Heb. *elōhîm*) and "sons of the Most High." If, then, these terms can be applied to ordinary mortals or even angels, how could Jesus be accused of blasphemy when he applied them to himself whom the Father set apart and sent into the world on a special mission? Jesus was not offering a false claim; he was merely asserting what he was by rights.

The parenthetic statement "and the Scripture cannot be broken" illustrates the high regard Jesus had for the OT. Throughout this Gospel the constant assumption is that the Scripture is the revelation of God, setting the timing, content, and character of Jesus' ministry. The Gospel quotes with approval Philip's words to Nathanael: "We have found the one Moses wrote about in the Law, and about whom the prophets wrote—Jesus of Nazareth, the son of Joseph" (1:45). The resurrection was explained for the disciples by Scripture and Jesus' words (2:22). Jesus used the episode of the bronze serpent (John 3:14-15; cf. Num 21:4-9) to illustrate for Nicodemus the meaning of his death and the power of faith. Jesus told his hearers plainly that the Scriptures bore witness to him (5:39). Scripture set the pattern Jesus followed in going to the Cross (12:14-16; 13:18; 19:18, 24, 28, 36). Whether all these other passages refer to Jesus' explicit statements or to the writer's explanation of his action, they presuppose a confidence in the authority and trustworthiness of Scripture that is in keeping with Jesus' attitude.

36 Jesus unmistakably referred to himself as the Son of God. To him it was not a strained assertion but a logical statement, for he was fully aware of his relation to the Father and to the responsibility the Father had committed to him. The accusation of blasphemy seems to be utterly unreasonable in the light of that relationship.

37-39 Jesus' appeal to his opponents summed up the attitude and method of his argument. He took his position, not on the basis of his personal authority, but on the attestation of his works. If they showed that he was demonstrating divine compassion and exercising divine authority over men and matter, he was divinely accredited. The word "miracles" (*erga*, "works") in John refers to those acts of Jesus that are peculiarly expressive of his nature and have evidential value. They especially reveal his personality and mission. For those who were predisposed not to believe in him, he offered pragmatic proof of his special relationship with God: "The Father is in me, and I in the Father." The appeal failed; and once again "they tried to seize him, but he escaped their grasp."

40–42 Having eluded their attempt to capture him, Jesus retreated to Perea, on the east side of the Jordan, where he would be comparatively safe from arrest. There he found a better reception, and again it is stated that "many believed on him." Perea was the domain of Herod Antipas, where the rulers in Jerusalem had no authority. Jesus thus would be safe from harassment there—at least temporarily.

The Jews' allusion to the testimony of John the Baptist indicates that his ministry had enduring influence, and they accepted Jesus on that basis. As in the case of the woman of Samaria, faith in Christ was preceded by the witness of another.

Notes

---

40 The place Jesus retired to may have been the "Bethany on the other side of the Jordan" (John 1:28), where John the Baptist was preaching when he first met Jesus. The exact location is unknown. It may have been just east of Jericho across the Jordan. Some, including Origen, identified it with Bethabara, about 10 miles south of the Sea of Galilee. The former option would be nearer to Jerusalem.

---

4. The miracle at Bethany (11:1–44)

a. The announcement of death

11:1–16

¹Now a man named Lazarus was sick. He was from Bethany, the village of Mary and her sister Martha. ²This Mary, whose brother Lazarus now lay sick, was the same one who poured perfume on the Lord and wiped his feet with her hair. ³So the sisters sent word to Jesus, "Lord, the one you love is sick."

⁴When he heard this, Jesus said, "This sickness will not end in death. No, it is for God's glory so that God's Son may be glorified through it." ⁵Jesus loved Martha and her sister and Lazarus. ⁶Yet when he heard that Lazarus was sick, he stayed where he was two more days.

⁷Then he said to his disciples, "Let us go back to Judea."

⁸"But Rabbi," they said, "a short while ago the Jews tried to stone you, and yet you are going back there?"

⁹Jesus answered, "Are there not twelve hours of daylight? A man who walks by day will not stumble, for he sees by this world's light. ¹⁰It is when he walks by night that he stumbles, for he has no light."

¹¹After he had said this, he went on to tell them, "Our friend Lazarus has fallen asleep; but I am going there to wake him up."

¹²His disciples replied, "Lord, if he sleeps, he will get better." ¹³Jesus had been speaking of his death, but his disciples thought he meant natural sleep.

¹⁴So then he told them plainly, "Lazarus is dead, ¹⁵and for your sake I am glad I was not there, so that you may believe. But let us go to him."

¹⁶Then Thomas (called Didymus) said to the rest of the disciples, "Let us also go, that we may die with him."

The account of the raising of Lazarus is the climactic sign in the Gospel of John. Each of the seven signs illustrates some particular aspect of Jesus' divine authority, but this one exemplifies his power over the last and most irresistible enemy of humanity—death.

For this reason it is given a prominent place in the Gospel. It is also extremely significant because it precipitated the decision of Jesus' enemies to do away with him. Furthermore, this episode contains a strong personal command to believe in Jesus in a crisis, when such belief would be most difficult. All that preceded is preparatory; all that follows it is the unfolding of a well-marked plot.

1–2 At this point Lazarus is introduced, though Mary and Martha are mentioned in Luke (10:38–42), with a possible allusion in Matthew (26:6–12) and Mark (14:3–9) that would correspond to the Johannine account. Apparently Jesus was frequently a guest in their home when he visited Jerusalem. Mark states that in the early days of the Passion Week Jesus "went out to Bethany with the Twelve" (11:11). Of Lazarus, however, nothing is known apart from the Johannine record. The identification of Mary by the action recorded later in this Gospel is unusual, unless the author presupposed some knowledge of her action on the reader's part. It seems probable that the story of Mary's anointing of Jesus may have been narrated in the church prior to the writing of this Gospel. John mentions it in order to identify Lazarus and to indicate Jesus' relations with the family.

3 Knowing Jesus' interest in them and the power of God to heal the sick, the sisters sent for him when Lazarus became ill. The malady must have been serious, for they were sufficiently alarmed to call Jesus back to the area where a price had been set on his head. The appeal was on the basis of love. The sisters' implication was that if Jesus loved Lazarus, he would return. They seemed quite confident that he would be prompt.

4–6 Jesus' reaction was optimistic and purposeful. He gave assurance to the disciples, and possibly a message to be sent back to the sisters, that Lazarus's illness would not terminate in death, and stated that Lazarus's illness would be an important aspect of his own glorification. Having said that, Jesus deliberately "stayed where he was two more days." His action may have appeared to the disciples, and almost certainly to the sisters, as unfeeling and selfish. Since he had the power to heal Lazarus, why should he not reply instantly? Perhaps the disciples were not particularly puzzled because their subsequent remarks indicated that they were well aware of the danger that threatened him in Jerusalem. His response, however, was quite different from that in the case of Jairus's daughter, when he acted promptly (Luke 8:41–42, 49–56), or in the case of the widow of Nain, whose son he raised when he met the funeral procession on the way to the burial ground (Luke 7:11–16).

7–8 His proposal to the disciples that they should return to Judea was not welcomed with enthusiasm. They remembered the previous conflicts with the rulers and feared for Jesus' life, and possibly for their own as well. The emphatic position of the adverb *there* at the end of the sentence gives the impression that they would be more willing to go with him if his destination were not Judea.

9–10 Jesus countered the disciples' objection with the following enigmatic statement: "Are there not twelve hours of daylight? A man who walks by day will not stumble, for he sees by the world's light. It is when he walks by night that he stumbles, for he has no light." The expression of Jesus may have been a current proverb like the one underlying the remark in John 9:4: "As long as it is day, we must do the work of him who sent me. Night is coming, when no one can work." In both instances, Jesus was thinking of his obligation to perform the work the Father had committed to him. Realizing that he was acting in accord with the purpose of the Father who had sent him and that he had clear illumination concerning his duty, Jesus resolutely decided to return to Jerusalem in spite of the peril. John in his First Epistle employed this same figure of speech: "If we claim to have fellowship with him yet walk in the darkness, we lie and do not live by the truth" (1 John 1:6). To digress from God's purpose is to walk in darkness; to remain in fellowship with God is to walk in the light. Jesus may have had the same concept in mind when he warned his disciples that the light would be with them only a little longer and that darkness would shortly overtake them (12:35). His presence was their illumination; when he was removed, they lost their sense of spiritual direction, as Peter's denial and Thomas's incredulity demonstrated.

11 In order to explain his action, Jesus informed his disciples that Lazarus was asleep and that he intended to wake him. The explanation was intended to be a part of the education of the disciples. Their interest and loyalty were plainly revealed by their willingness to listen to him and to move back into the area of danger if he so desired.

12–13 The disciples lacked imagination and took literally Jesus' announcement that Lazarus had fallen asleep. Assuming that "sleep" would mean that the fever had passed its crisis, they expressed their hope for Lazarus's recovery. Jesus, however, used the word *sleep* in a figurative sense, meaning "death." This does not mean that the dead are in a state of total unconsciousness, for Jesus' illustration of the rich man and the beggar predicates consciousness after death (Luke 16:19–31). It does show that Jesus looked on the death of Lazarus as a parenthesis after which there would be an awakening, not as a permanent removal from life.

14–15 Jesus' rejoinder to the disciples' comment made Lazarus's state unmistakable: "Lazarus is dead, and for your sake I am glad I was not there, so that you may believe. But let us go to him." Jesus' words seem strange. Why should he be glad that he was not present to save Lazarus from death, or to comfort the sisters, and why should Lazarus's death bring any benefit to the disciples? Jesus considered this an opportunity for a supreme demonstration of power that would certify the Father's accreditation of him as the Son and confirm the faith of the sisters and the disciples. He was certain of the outcome. He knew that positive belief and joy would be the result.

16 Thomas's comment marks his first appearance in this book. John's Gospel does not contain a complete list of the Twelve, though they are mentioned as a group on two occasions (6:67, 70–71; 20:24). Generally they are presented only as individuals and once in the Epilogue as a smaller group on the occasion of the fishing party in Galilee (21:1–2). Thomas appears four times: here, once in the discourse in the upper room (14:5), once after the Resurrection (20:24–29), and finally with the group described in the Epilogue (21:1). In the upper room incident, his attitude seems to be pessimistic and querulous. His comment in John 11:16 is paradoxical: "Let us also go, that we may die with him." "Him" no doubt refers to Jesus, not to Lazarus. Thomas expected that Jesus would be seized and executed and that his disciples would suffer with him. Notwithstanding this unhappy prospect, Thomas's loyalty is revealed by his readiness to share Jesus' peril. The skepticism that Thomas later evinced regarding the Resurrection was probably prompted by grief over Jesus' death rather than by disillusionment because of apparent failure.

Notes

11 Two words are used in the NT to express the idea of sleeping and/or death. Κοιμάω (koimaō), which appears in this passage in the perfect tense κεκοίμηται (kekoimētai), occurs eighteen times in the NT: in Matt, Luke, John, Acts, 1 Cor, 1 Thess, and 2 Peter. And except for three instances, it is uniformly a figurative description of death. The other word, καθεύδω (katheudō), appears in the Gospels sixteen times and in the Pauline Epistles four times and is invariably taken literally, with one possible exception (Eph 5:14), which is quoted in a fragment of Christian hymnody. Eph 5:14 appears to refer to death in terms of spiritual dullness rather than to physical disease.

There has been considerable controversy as to whether κοιμάω (koimaō) implies that the dead actually exist in a state of total unconsciousness until resurrection or whether it is merely a description of death based on the analogy of appearance. A person who is sleeping seems inert and unaffected by external stimuli. The use of this verb as a metaphor for death appears in the Greek classics, in the LXX, in the vernacular of the papyri, and in the patristic writings. In the light of such passages as Luke 23:43—the promise to the dying thief, "I tell you the truth, today you will be with me in paradise"— and Paul's declaration of his longing to "depart and be with Christ, which is better by far" (Phil 1:23), death for the child of God could hardly be an unconscious state. From Jesus' standpoint, Lazarus's death was comparable to a nap, which cut off consciousness of this world temporarily but did not mean a permanent severance.

b. *The conversation with Martha and Mary*

11:17–37

¹⁷On his arrival, Jesus found that Lazarus had already been in the tomb for four days. ¹⁸Bethany was less than two miles from Jerusalem, ¹⁹and many Jews had come to Martha and Mary to comfort them in the loss of their brother. ²⁰When Martha heard that Jesus was coming, she went out to meet him, but Mary stayed at home.

²¹"Lord," Martha said to Jesus, "if you had been here, my brother would not have died. ²²But I know that even now God will give you whatever you ask."

²³Jesus said to her, "Your brother will rise again."

²⁴Martha answered, "I know he will rise again in the resurrection at the last day."

²⁵Jesus said to her, "I am the resurrection and the life. He who believes in me will live, even though he dies; ²⁶and whoever lives and believes in me will never die. Do you believe this?"

²⁷"Yes, Lord," she told him, "I believe that you are the Christ, the Son of God, who was to come into the world."

²⁸And after she had said this, she went back and called her sister Mary aside. "The Teacher is here," she said, "and is asking for you." ²⁹When Mary heard this, she got up quickly and went to him. ³⁰Now Jesus had not yet entered the village, but was still at the place where Martha had met him. ³¹When the Jews who had been with Mary in the house, comforting her, noticed how quickly she got up and went out, they followed her, supposing she was going to the tomb to mourn there.

³²When Mary reached the place where Jesus was and saw him, she fell at his feet and said, "Lord, if you had been here, my brother would not have died."

³³When Jesus saw her weeping, and the Jews who had come along with her also weeping, he was deeply moved in spirit and troubled. ³⁴"Where have you laid him?" he asked.

"Come and see, Lord," they replied.

³⁵Jesus wept.

³⁶Then the Jews said, "See how he loved him!"

³⁷But some of them said, "Could not he who opened the eyes of the blind man have kept this man from dying?"

17-18 The time between Lazarus's death and Jesus' arrival at Bethany was four days. Presumably the time required for the journey of the messengers and the time needed for Jesus' return to Bethany would be approximately the same. Also, two full days intervened between their arrival where Jesus was and his departure for Bethany (v.6). So the death of Lazarus must have occurred not long after Jesus was first informed of his illness. The trip each way would have taken not much less than a day's travel since Bethany was more than twenty miles distant from Jesus' refuge in Perea (10:40–42). After three days all hope of resuscitation from a coma would be abandoned; and in the hot Palestinian climate, decay would have begun.

19 The family at Bethany must have been well known in Jerusalem, with connections within the Jewish hierarchy, since many "Jews" came to comfort Martha and Mary over the loss of Lazarus. A procession composed of relatives, friends, and sometimes hired mourners accompanied a body to the grave; and mourning usually lasted for several days afterward.

20 Martha, being more aggressive, "went out to meet" Jesus. Mary was quiet and contemplative: she "stayed at home." This portrayal of the sisters by John agrees with that found in Luke 10:38–42.

21-22 The words Martha addressed to Jesus express both a repressed reproach and a persistent faith. She was disappointed that Jesus had not responded to her first news of Lazarus's illness, but that did not lead her to break her relationship with him. Despite her remorse, she was confident that God would grant Jesus' desire in this matter.

23-26 Martha interpreted Jesus' promise (v.23) that her brother would rise again in terms of the expectation of a general resurrection. She may have taken his words as a conventional expression of comfort; he intended them to describe what he would do. Martha's reply indicates that she shared the Pharisaic belief in an ultimate resurrection for the just (Acts 23:7). By his reply, Jesus turned Martha's acceptance of a dogma into faith in his person. In what is surely one of his most majestic and comforting utterances, Jesus said that he embodied the vital power to bring the dead to life: "I am the resurrection and the life. He who believes in me will live, even though he dies; and whoever lives and believes in me will never die" (vv.25–26). The one who believes in Christ has eternal life that transcends physical death. If he is living and believing, he will never die but will make an instant transition from the old life to the new life. Jesus' words are amplified by Paul's statement in 1 Thessalonians 4:16–17: "The dead in Christ will rise first. After that, we who are still alive and are left will be caught up with them in the clouds to meet the Lord in the air." There is, however, no specific reference in John 11:25 to the second advent of Christ. Whether Jesus had this event in mind and whether Martha would so have understood his words is uncertain. In any case, Jesus was saying that he embodied the resurrection life that could overcome death and that believers would be assured of an inheritance in the age to come. On this basis, he asked her directly whether she believed.

27 Martha's commitment reveals a firm belief that Jesus was the Messiah, the Son of God, as preached by John the Baptist (1:34) and accepted by the disciples (1:49; 6:68), and the deliverer foretold by the prophets. Her language is emphatic: "Yes, Lord, . . . I believe."

28–30 The action of Mary, though less assertive, reveals a similar trust in Jesus. Martha told Mary that Jesus was asking for her. To Mary, this was equivalent to a command to come. Mary wasted no time in going to Jesus: "she got up quickly and went to him." Jesus had not entered the village. He was waiting for Mary to come to him. Perhaps he remained outside Bethany so as not to precipitate an argument in the event his enemies discovered him.

31 The Jews knew something was afoot when Mary left so hastily. Since they had come to mourn with the sisters, they thought it only fitting to follow her, supposing that she was going to the tomb.

32 Mary's greeting to Jesus was similar to Martha's; in fact, the words are identical except for their sequence. Martha's sentence, "Lord, if you had been here *my* brother would not have died" (italics added), puts the possessive pronoun at the end of the sentence in the Greek, while Mary's words, by their order, emphasize "my *brother*" (italics added). The difference is small and may simply be a result of rhetoric. But if the Greek order is taken to be significant, it may be that Martha was grieving because she had lost a precious possession while Mary was thinking of the life that had ended too soon. Morris says, "In view of John's habit of making slight alterations when statements are repeated these variations should not be regarded as significant" (NIC, p. 554, n. 62).

33–35 The response of Jesus to this calamity illustrates his human and divine natures. Up to this point he had been perfectly calm, assuring Martha that her brother would rise and asserting that he was the resurrection and the life. He was completely in command of the situation and challenged Martha's faith. But when Mary appeared, crushed with sorrow and accompanied by the waiting mourners, Jesus was moved with deep emotion. His feeling is expressed by three words: "deeply moved," "troubled" (v.33), and "wept" (v.35). The first of these (*enebrimēsato*) means literally "to snort like a horse" and generally connotes anger. It could not have indicated displeasure with the sisters whom he was trying to comfort and for whom he felt the strongest compassion. Perhaps it expressed his resentment against the ravages of death that had entered the human world because of sin.

The second word, "troubled" (*etaraxen*), expresses agitation, confusion, or disorganization. Here it implies agitation rather than complete confusion. Jesus was not apathetic or unnerved by the prevailing mood of sorrow. Lazarus had been a beloved friend, and Jesus shared in the common feeling of grief over his death. His human feelings were normal and are revealed by the crisis of the moment. Overcome by emotion, he gave way to weeping. Williams's translation reads: "Jesus burst into tears." His grief was spontaneous.

36–37 Jesus' true humanity was emphasized by the response of the people at Lazarus's tomb. Some were impressed by Jesus' open show of emotion and took it as an evident token of his love for Lazarus. Others, perhaps not so lovingly, wondered why Jesus had not prevented Lazarus's death by one of his miracles. The reference to the healing of the blind man shows that it must have created a sensation in Jerusalem since it was remembered several months after it had occurred.

Notes

---

27 The first person pronoun ἐγώ (*egō*, "I") used with the verb πεπίστευκα, (*pepisteuka*, "have believed") in the perfect tense gives added impact to Martha's personal conviction and implies not only a past decision but also a present state of mind. There could have hardly been a stronger expression of faith on her part.

33 Ἐνεβριμήσατο (*enebrimēsato*, "deeply moved") is used in Mark 14:5 to describe the attitude of the disciples toward Mary at the anointing in Bethany, and Matt 9:30, where it relates to Jesus' stern injunction to the blind men not to declare that he had healed them. The object of Jesus' anger is not stated.

The verb ταράσσω (*tarassō*, "troubled") is used to describe a sea in a storm (Isa 24:14 LXX) and the effect of fear or surprise on the human mind (Matt 2:3; 14:26; Luke 1:12; 24:38).

35 The third word, ἐδάκρυσεν (*edakrusen*, "wept"), means to shed tears quietly. It may be contrasted with the loud and ostentatious "weeping" (κλαίοντας, *klaiontas*) of the hired mourners (v.33), which was artificial.

36 The imperfect tense "were saying" (ἔλεγον, *elegon*) implies repeated or continued action. Jesus' sorrow impressed the onlookers with the depth of his concern.

---

c. The raising of Lazarus

11:38–44

> 38Jesus, once more deeply moved, came to the tomb. It was a cave with a stone laid across the entrance. 39"Take away the stone," he said.
>
> "But, Lord," said Martha, the sister of the dead man, "by this time there is a bad odor, for he has been there four days."
>
> 40Then Jesus said, "Did I not tell you that if you believed, you would see the glory of God?"
>
> 41So they took away the stone. Then Jesus looked up and said, "Father, I thank you that you have heard me. 42I knew that you always hear me, but I said this for the benefit of the people standing here, that they may believe that you sent me."
>
> 43When he had said this, Jesus called in a loud voice, "Lazarus, come out!" 44The dead man came out, his hands and feet wrapped with strips of linen, and a cloth around his face.
>
> Jesus said to them, "Take off the grave clothes and let him go."

38 The repetition of "deeply moved" (*embrimōmenos*), the present participle of the verb, shows that Jesus was still under the same emotional tension that his first contact with the mourners had aroused. He faced the necessity of fulfilling his prediction to the disciples that the outcome of Lazarus's death would be to the glory of God. He would also keep his promise to Martha that her brother should rise again. The burial place was a chamber cut in limestone rock and closed by a stone laid over the entrance.

39 Having challenged Martha's faith, Jesus now faced a challenge of his own. He ordered the covering stone to be removed. Martha's protest was natural. It would seem improper to expose a decaying corpse. She had to put faith in Jesus.

40 To Jesus the raising of Lazarus was no problem. The chief difficulty was to remove the uncertainty and hesitancy from Martha's attitude that the glory of God might be revealed to her and all present.

41–42 When Martha met his condition, which was the last step of faith she could take, Jesus took the next step. He did not ask God to raise Lazarus; he thanked him for having already answered. So great was Jesus' faith in the Father that he assumed this miracle that was necessary to his mission to be as good as done. Only raising Lazarus would complete the expectations Jesus had aroused in the disciples and in Mary and Martha. He said in his prayer that the transaction was already complete, but he asked for the raising of Lazarus as a convincing sign to the assembled people that he had been sent by the Father.

43–44 Having uttered this prayer, Jesus addressed the dead man. Jesus had said on a previous occasion that a time would come when all who were in their graves would hear his voice (John 5:28). This occasion was a single demonstration of that authority. The words spoken were brief, direct, and imperative and can be paraphrased, "Lazarus! This way out!" as if Jesus were directing someone lost in a gloomy dungeon. The creative power of God reversed the process of corruption and quickened the corpse into life. The effect was startling. The dead man appeared at the entrance to the tomb, still bound by the graveclothes that had been wound around him. Jesus then ordered that he be released from the wrappings and returned to normal life. It was a supreme demonstration of the power of eternal life that triumphed over death, corruption, and hopelessness.

5. The decision to kill Jesus

11:45–57

⁴⁵Therefore many of the Jews who had come to visit Mary, and had seen what Jesus did, put their faith in him. ⁴⁶But some of them went to the Pharisees and told them what Jesus had done. ⁴⁷Then the chief priests and the Pharisees called a meeting of the Sanhedrin.

"What are we accomplishing?" they asked. "Here is this man performing many miraculous signs. ⁴⁸If we let him go on like this, everyone will believe in him, and then the Romans will come and take away both our place and our nation."

⁴⁹Then one of them, named Caiaphas, who was high priest that year, spoke up, "You know nothing at all! ⁵⁰You do not realize that it is better for you that one man die for the people than that the whole nation perish."

⁵¹He did not say this on his own, but as high priest that year he prophesied that Jesus would die for the Jewish nation, ⁵²and not only for that nation but also for the scattered children of God, to bring them together and make them one. ⁵³So from that day on they plotted to take his life.

⁵⁴Therefore Jesus no longer moved about publicly among the Jews. Instead he withdrew to a region near the desert, to a village called Ephraim, where he stayed with his disciples.

⁵⁵When it was almost time for the Jewish Passover, many went up from the country to Jerusalem for their ceremonial cleansing before the Passover. ⁵⁶They kept looking for Jesus, and as they stood in the temple area they asked one another, "What do you think? Isn't he coming to the Feast at all?" ⁵⁷But the chief priests and Pharisees had given orders that if anyone found out where Jesus was, he should report it so that they might arrest him.

45–46 The response to the sign was twofold. "Many" of the Jews believed on the basis of the evidence they had seen, for the fact of Lazarus's restoration was incontrovertible. In contrast, others went to inform the religious leaders of Jesus' action, apparently as a gesture of disapproval. It seems unlikely that any of the believing Jews made up the delegation that went to the Pharisees. Those who believed would no doubt want to stay with Jesus, whereas the skeptics would be desirous of letting the religious authorities know what had happened so that they could take the necessary action.

47–48 The impact of Jesus' miracle in Bethany resulted in the calling of a meeting of the Sanhedrin. The council expressed not only disapproval but also frustration. They anticipated that the miracles of Jesus would bring such a wave of popular support that the Romans, fearing a revolution, would intervene by seizing complete authority, thus displacing the Jewish government and destroying the national identity. Their fears revealed a complete misunderstanding of the motives of Jesus, who had no political ambitions whatever. He had already indicated by his refusal to be made king that he had no intention of organizing a revolt against Rome. Jesus' reply concerning the lawfulness of paying tribute to Caesar, "Give to Caesar what is Caesar's, and to God what is God's" (Matt 22:21), confirmed that decision.

49–50 Caiaphas, the high priest, was the son-in-law of Annas, who is mentioned later in the account of Jesus' trial. Annas had been high priest from A.D. 7 to 14 and was succeeded by three of his sons and finally by Caiaphas from A.D. 18 to 36. The phrase "that year" may be an indirect allusion to the fact that the Roman government had changed the high priest so often that it became almost an annual appointment. That would not be true of Caiaphas, however, for he held office uninterruptedly for eighteen years; but in the long memory of the writer that year would have been outstanding as the year of Jesus' death. The utterance of Caiaphas reveals his cynicism and duplicity. He was contemptuous of the indecisive attitude of the Pharisees and recommended the elimination of Jesus rather than risking the possibility of a long contest with Rome.

51–52 John takes Caiaphas's statement as a kind of double entendre, an unconscious and involuntary prophecy that Jesus would become the sacrifice for the nation that it might not perish. The prophetic quality is attributed to Caiaphas's high priestly office rather than his personal character. Assuredly Caiaphas would not be reckoned among the prophets. The irony of the statement, which indirectly affirms the sacrificial aspect of Jesus' death, is paralleled by the record of the rulers' mockery of Jesus at the Crucifixion: "He saved others, but he can't save himself!" (Mark 15:31). In both instances the sneering remark expressed an unintended truth. The entire statement of Caiaphas is thus interpreted by the author and applied, not only to the nation of Israel, but also to the children of God who had been scattered throughout the world. These words might apply to the Jews of the Dispersion. But in the light of the universalism of this Gospel, they probably refer proleptically to the ingathering of the Gentiles, who become the children of God when they acknowledge the saviorhood of Christ (John 1:12; 10:16).

53 The growing hostility of the Pharisaic party and of the Sadducean priesthood had developed into a settled decision to do away with Jesus. Although the hierarchy feared a popular uprising in his support, they were resolute that he should die. John indicates that their opposition had reached the point of no return.

54 For this reason Jesus left Bethany, where danger threatened him, and removed to Ephraim, a village north of Jerusalem. Ephraim has been identified with Et Taiyibeh, a few miles northeast of Bethel. Perhaps it may be the city called Aphairema, mentioned in the account of the Maccabean wars (1 Macc 11:34). The town was on the edge of the Judean desert, into which Jesus could flee if necessary.

55-56 Just before the Passover, pilgrims from distant parts of the country began to assemble in Jerusalem. Ceremonial cleansing would take considerable time when a large crowd was involved, and the people wanted to be ready to participate in the sacred feast. Jesus had been present in Jerusalem at the Feasts of Tabernacles and Dedication and had been regularly engaged in teaching. Since the Passover would bring an even larger crowd to Jerusalem, the populace expected that Jesus would be there also. His previous visits had been accompanied by much controversy, and there had been several futile attempts to arrest or stone him (cf. John 5:18; 7:30, 44; 8:20, 59; 10:38). On each occasion, however, he had eluded his enemies, for "his time had not come." His foes were powerless to take him till he was ready to fulfill the final sacrifice of death (7:8, 30; 8:20, 59).

57 The high council of Judaism had issued a warrant for Jesus' arrest and had ordered that anyone who knew of his whereabouts should declare it. Silence meant complicity and could be punishable. In the light of this situation, it might be concluded that Judas was a messianist loyal to his nation and that his loyalty to the ruling priesthood took precedence over his personal loyalty to Jesus.

Notes

45 The UBS text has ἃ ἐποίησεν (ha epoiēsen, "[things] he did") rather than ὃ ἐποίησεν (ho epoiēsen, "[thing] he did"). Although the MSS evidence slightly favors the former, to us the latter seems more logical, since the context is focused on the one great sign of the raising of Lazarus rather than on a summary of miracles in general. Metzger favors the opposing view (*Textual Commentary*, p.235).

48 Morris suggests that "our place" probably refers to the temple (NIC, p. 566). Τόπος (topos) can be interpreted as "position" or "office" and is so used by Ignatius (*Smyrneans* 6:1) and Clement of Rome (1 Clement 40:5; 44:5). In every other instance in John the meaning is geographical.

F. *The Crisis of the Ministry* (12:1-50)

Chapter 12 of John is devoted to the crisis of Jesus' ministry that preceded its conclusion. As previously noted, the hostility of the religious authorities had been increasing and had intensified because they had been unable to entangle Jesus in any compromising dilemma or defeat him in public debate. Despite the fact that there had been a decline in his popularity because he refused to become involved in a political coup (6:15) and because some of his teaching was obscure to his listeners (6:52-66), he nevertheless retained a loyal group of disciples; and a large segment of the populace still regarded him with awe. They expected that he might still decide to use his miraculous powers on their behalf and establish a new political and economic order that would make Israel dominant among the nations. The division of attitudes prevailed both among the disciples and among the people.

For Jesus himself, the period was critical because the forces for and against him were crystallizing, and he had to make a decision as to which way he should turn. He had been living by a program established by the Father and outlined progressively by Scripture and by experience. No doubt the temptation to deviate from it for considerations of power or safety was always with him (Luke 4:13). Now, as the moment for the fulfillment of the divine purpose approached, the tension increased; and the indications that the climax was near multiplied.

John presents a series of events, each of which foreshadow the coming end. The first of these was the feast at the house of Mary and Martha.

1. The dinner at Bethany

12:1-11

> [1]Six days before the Passover, Jesus arrived at Bethany, where Lazarus lived, whom Jesus had raised from the dead. [2]Here a dinner was given in Jesus' honor. Martha served, while Lazarus was among those reclining at the table with him. [3]Then Mary took about a pint of pure nard, an expensive perfume; she poured it on Jesus' feet and wiped his feet with her hair. And the house was filled with the fragrance of the perfume.
>
> [4]But one of his disciples, Judas Iscariot, who was later to betray him, objected, [5]"Why wasn't this perfume sold and the money given to the poor? It was worth a year's wages." [6]He did not say this because he cared about the poor but because he was a thief; as keeper of the money bag, he used to help himself to what was put into it.
>
> [7]"Leave her alone," Jesus replied. "It was meant that she should save this perfume for the day of my burial. [8]You will always have the poor among you, but you will not always have me."
>
> [9]Meanwhile a large crowd of Jews found out that Jesus was there and came, not only because of him but also to see Lazarus, whom he had raised from the dead. [10]So the chief priests made plans to kill Lazarus as well, [11]for on account of him many of the Jews were going over to Jesus and putting their faith in him.

1 At this point the time schedule becomes more definite than previously. Although there are chronological references in this Gospel, there are also general gaps introduced by such expressions as "after this," "after these things" (2:12; 3:22; 5:1; 6:1; 7:1; 9:1; 10:40). While several of the events introduced by these rather vague expressions are connected with definite times and places, the intervals between them are not precisely measured. In this final period, however, the sequence is more definite.

The explanation that Bethany was the home of Lazarus, whom Jesus had raised from the dead, seems rather strange since the previous chapter had explained Jesus' relation to the family. Brown suggests that if this episode were incorporated into the text of John at a late date, the explanation would have been necessary to identify Bethany (29:446). On the other hand, if the Gospel were transcribed by a disciple of John from discourses that he gave at different times, a link would have been needed to resume the flow of narration.

2 The dinner was given for Jesus by Martha and Mary. The notation that Lazarus was among the guests seems unnecessary at first reading. If the dinner was an expression of gratitude for the restoration of Lazarus, he would naturally be expected to attend it. Perhaps the writer is giving a hint that after Lazarus's restoration to life he retired from any public appearance since he would be an object of general curiosity, as v.9 indicates. On this occasion Lazarus may have come out of seclusion to honor Jesus.

3 The anointing of Jesus' feet by Mary was not difficult because of the custom of reclining to eat instead of sitting at a table. Guests usually reclined on divans with their heads near the table. They leaned on cushions with one arm and ate with the other. Their

feet would project at the end of the divan away from the table. Mary could easily have slipped from her couch, walked around the other couches, and reached down to pour the ointment on Jesus' feet.

Spices and ointments were quite costly because they had to be imported. Frequently they were used as an investment because they occupied a small space, were portable, and were easily negotiable in the open market. Mary's offering was valued at three hundred denarii (v.5 Gr.), approximately a year's wages for an ordinary workingman. Perhaps it represented her life savings. She presented it as an offering of love and gratitude, prompted by Jesus' restoration of her brother to the family circle. Wiping his feet with her hair was a gesture of utmost devotion and reverence. The penetrative fragrance of the ointment that filled the house told all present of her sacrificial gift.

4–6 Judas Iscariot reappears here. He had been mentioned previously in a parenthetical statement appended to Jesus' comment on Simon Peter's confession of faith: "Have I not chosen you, the Twelve? Yet one of you is a devil" (6:70). Jesus knew Judas's tendencies and was well aware of his coming defection. Whereas many of Jesus' disciples deserted him (6:66), Judas remained to betray him. The others merely lost interest or were bewildered by his teaching and were reluctant to meet his moral demands. Judas determined to make Jesus serve his purpose—by treachery if necessary.

Judas had been appointed treasurer of the band of disciples; and, according to John, Judas used his office for his own enrichment. His remonstrance over the gift of the ointment revealed that he had a sharp sense of financial values and no appreciation of human values. Pouring the ointment on Jesus seemed to him an economic waste. Mary, on the contrary, was the only one who was sensitive to the impending death of Jesus and who was willing to give a material expression of her esteem for him.

7–8 Jesus' reply revealed his appreciation of Mary's act of devotion and the understanding it denoted. His words disclose also the current of his thought, for he was anticipating death. His comment on the poor was not a justification for tolerating unnecessary poverty; but it was a hint to Judas that if he were really concerned about the poor, he would never lack opportunity to aid them. The contrast of the attitude of Mary with that of Judas is unmistakable. Mary offered her best to Jesus in sacrificial love; Judas was coldly utilitarian. Jesus interested him only as a ladder for his ambitions.

The dinner marked the crisis of friendship with Jesus. Martha, Mary, and Lazarus risked all they had to do him honor and to demonstrate their loyalty in the face of approaching danger and death. Jesus' comment on Mary's action may or may not imply a premonition on her part of his approaching peril. In any event, her gift was an expression of the highest gratitude and devotion.

9–11 Quite simultaneously, the response of the crowds to Jesus brought another crisis to his enemies. So many became his followers that the priestly party was sure that their fears as expressed by Caiaphas were justified. Their resolution to destroy Jesus was strengthened, and in their wild madness of unbelief they even contemplated the possibility of removing Lazarus also, since his restoration to life was an undeniable witness to Jesus' power.

Notes

8 The latter half of v.8, μεθ᾽ ἑαυτῶν ... ἔχετε (*meth' heautōn ... echete,* "with you ... you have") is omitted by P[75], and the entire verse is omitted by the Western text. However, it is included by the majority of MSS. Brown states that "this verse in John is omitted by witnesses of the Western group, and the fact that it agrees with Matthew instead of with Mark suggests that it was a later scribal addition copied from the traditional Matthew" (29:449). Metzger, recognizing this problem, affirms that "the overwhelming manuscript support for the verse seemed to a majority of the Committee to justify retaining it in the text" (*Textual Commentary,* p. 237). While there are some problems in reconciling the Johannine account with those of Matt 26:6–13 and Mark 14:3–9, the placement of the accounts and the strong correspondence of most of the accompanying features reflect the same situation. Matthew and Mark say that the unnamed woman anointed Jesus' head; John says it was his feet. But this difference is scarcely sufficient to preclude identity. A similar episode mentioned in Luke 7:36–50 is probably not the same. The latter was located in Galilee; the woman involved was "a sinner"; and the discourse accompanying it was quite unlike that mentioned in John. Some commentaries, however, equate all these passages.

2. The entry into Jerusalem

12:12–19

¹²The next day the great crowd that had come for the Feast heard that Jesus was on his way to Jerusalem. ¹³They took palm branches and went out to meet him, shouting,

"Hosanna!"
"Blessed is he who comes in the name of the Lord!"
"Blessed is the King of Israel!"

¹⁴Jesus found a young donkey and sat upon it, as it is written,

¹⁵"Do not be afraid, O Daughter of Zion;
see, your king is coming,
seated on a donkey's colt."

¹⁶At first his disciples did not understand all this. Only after Jesus was glorified did they realize that these things had been written about him and that they had done these things to him.
¹⁷Now the crowd that was with him had continued to spread the word that he had called Lazarus from the tomb, raising him from the dead. ¹⁸Many people, because they had heard that he had given this miraculous sign, went out to meet him. ¹⁹So the Pharisees said to one another, "See, this is getting us nowhere. Look how the whole world has gone after him!"

12 Again John recounts a story that appears in all the synoptic Gospels (Matt 21:1–11; Mark 11:1–10; Luke 19:28–40). Although these accounts differ in details, they agree on the event itself and on the behavior of the crowds. John identifies two distinct multitudes: one composed of the "great crowd" of pilgrims who had come to Jerusalem for the Passover and were currently residing there (v.12) and the other composed of those who were traveling with Jesus and had witnessed the raising of Lazarus (v.17). The former multitude was probably larger, for John calls it "great."

13 If the former crowd came from Galilee, it would be well aware of Jesus' works there and would probably contain a number who had wished for a long time that he would declare himself as the expected Messiah. They applied to him the words of Psalm 118:25–26, one of the Songs of Degrees customarily sung by Passover pilgrims on their way to Jerusalem. These words ascribed to him a messianic title as the agent of the Lord, the coming king of Israel.

14 The entry into Jerusalem was Jesus' announcement that his hour had come and that he was ready for action, though not according to the expectation of the people. He did not come as a conqueror but as a messenger of peace. He rode on a donkey, not the steed of royalty, but that of a commoner on a business trip. John couples this entry with the prophecy of Zechariah (9:9), who announced that the king of Israel would appear in humility without pomp and ceremony. The pilgrims who had come to Jerusalem to attend the feast went out to greet Jesus; the other crowd gathered in his train. "Hosanna" is a Hebrew expression meaning literally "Save now!" It may be interpreted as a plea for immediate action on the part of the king. The blessing is the peoples' acclamation of him as the ruler of Israel (v.13).

15 The quotation from Zechariah 9:9 reads literally, "Cease from your fears, O daughter of Zion." "Daughter of Zion" is a personification of the city of Jerusalem; it occurs frequently in the OT, especially in the later prophets (Isa 1:8; 52:2; 62:11; Jer 4:31; 6:23; Lam 2:4, 8, 10, 13; Mic 4:8; Zeph 3:14; Zech 2:10).

16 This parenthetical statement by the author states that the disciples did not then understand the situation but that they later comprehended it. Similar parenthetical statements appear in John 2:17, 22. The author seems to be recalling the days of early discipleship and confessing how ignorant and obtuse he and his companions had been. His comments demonstrate that the Gospel must have been written when he and the others had attained a spiritual perception they did not possess in the years of their travels with Jesus. The Passion and the Resurrection were keys in unlocking the mystery of Jesus' person.

17–18 The second group in this account consists of those who were following Jesus, some of whom had witnessed the raising of Lazarus in Bethany. These people continued to publicize Jesus' miracle and aroused the curiosity of many in the city. These, in turn, joined the crowd that was on the way to meet Jesus as he neared Jerusalem.

19 The convergence of the pilgrims from a distance with Jesus' enthusiastic supporters from Jerusalem made a popular following that caused the rulers to become apprehensive. They felt that their attempts to stop Jesus were too few and too late.

Notes

17 The NIV follows the reading ὅτι (*hoti*, "that") rather than ὅτε (*hote*, "when"). Metzger observes that the reading ὅτε is preferable to ὅτι because it is supported by generally superior external testimony (*Textual Commentary*, p. 237). The Western reading, ὅτι, however, makes better sense of the passage and explains more adequately the pressure on the Pharisees.

3. *The response to the Greeks*

12:20–36

> [20]Now there were some Greeks among those who went up to worship at the Feast. [21]They came to Philip, who was from Bethsaida in Galilee, with a request. "Sir," they said, "we would like to see Jesus." [22]Philip went to tell Andrew; Andrew and Philip in turn told Jesus.
>
> [23]Jesus replied, "The hour has come for the Son of Man to be glorified. [24]I tell you the truth, unless a kernel of wheat falls to the ground and dies, it remains only a single seed. But if it dies, it produces many seeds. [25]The man who loves his life will lose it, while the man who hates his life in this world will keep it for eternal life. [26]Whoever serves me must follow me; and where I am, my servant also will be. My Father will honor the one who serves me.
>
> [27]"Now my heart is troubled, and what shall I say? 'Father, save me from this hour'? No, it was for this very reason I came to this hour. [28]Father, glorify your name!"
>
> Then a voice came from heaven, "I have glorified it, and will glorify it again." [29]The crowd that was there and heard it said it had thundered; others said an angel had spoken to him.
>
> [30]Jesus said, "This voice was for your benefit, not mine. [31]Now is the time for judgment on this world; now the prince of this world will be driven out. [32]But I, when I am lifted up from the earth, will draw all men to myself." [33]He said this to show the kind of death he was going to die.
>
> [34]The crowd spoke up, "We have heard from the Law that the Christ will remain forever, so how can you say, 'The Son of Man must be lifted up'? Who is this 'Son of Man'?"
>
> [35]Then Jesus told them, "You are going to have the light just a little while longer. Walk while you have the light, before darkness overtakes you. The man who walks in the dark does not know where he is going. [36]Put your trust in the light while you have it, so that you may become sons of light." When he had finished speaking, Jesus left and hid himself from them.

20 Another element that contributed to the crisis was the request of the Greeks to see Jesus. Their identity is uncertain, and they appear only briefly in the narrative. They were not Hellenistic Jews but Gentile Greeks who had joined the Jewish pilgrims to Jerusalem. Probably they were inquirers who had become interested in the Jewish faith but had not become full proselytes. They may have come from Galilee or the Decapolis, the ten Gentile cities generally east of Galilee and the Jordan, stretching from Damascus on the north to Philadelphia (Amman) on the south. Jesus had followers from these cities in his earlier ministry (Matt 4:25), and his reputation must have spread among their cities.

21–22 Just why these Greeks approached Philip rather than one of the other disciples is not stated. He had a Greek name, but this was not uncommon for Jews. Andrew's name also was of Greek origin. Philip in turn referred them to Andrew, and both of them carried the request to Jesus himself.

23 Curiously enough, there is no record that Jesus either gave these Greeks an audience or sent a reply back to them. The pronoun "them" in "Jesus answered them" (Gr.), which is omitted in NIV, could refer either to the Greeks themselves or to Andrew and Philip. In another sense, the action of Jesus is an answer to the Greeks' inquiry, because he announced openly that the great hour of his life had arrived. He felt the pressure of the Gentile world and realized that the time had come to open the way to God for the

Gentiles and to fuse Jewish and Gentile believers into one body. To accomplish this objective, he had to sacrifice himself (cf. John 10:16).

24 The likeness of the grain of wheat that is buried in the cold soil only to rise again multiplied for harvest is applicable to all believers in Christ. Until the seed is planted in the ground and dies, it bears no fruit; and if it is sacrificed, it produces a large crop.

25 The man who attempts to preserve his life will lose it, while the man who readily sacrifices his will keep it for eternal life. The two words translated "life" are different. The first, *psychē*, is generally rendered "soul" and denotes the individual personality, with all its related experiences and achievements. The second, *zōē*, in Johannine usage is usually coupled with the adjective *eternal* (*aiōnios*) and means the spiritual vitality that is the experience of God (John 17:3). Parallels to this statement appear in the synoptic Gospels (Matt 10:39; Mark 8:36; Luke 14:26). These were not all spoken on the same occasion. The statement in Matthew was part of a charge given to the disciples when Jesus sent them on a mission; that in Mark was given to them and a crowd that joined them (Mark 8:34); and the Lukan pronouncement was spoken to a mixed audience at an undefined point in Jesus' career, at some time within the last year of his life. Since this seems to have been a major principle of his teaching, its repetition at different times and under different circumstances is not at all unlikely.

The expression "who hates his life" need not be understood to mean a contempt for oneself or a suicidal impulse. Rather, it is a hyperbolic expression that means one is to base his priorities on that which is outside of himself. He is to place others or another above himself. In this instance, it is to make Christ the Master of one's life.

26 Jesus explained what it means to hate one's life by saying, "Whoever serves me must follow me; and where I am, my servant also will be." The impending Cross would involve the disciples in the same way it would involve Jesus, and he was informing them that he was the model for them to follow. He had already implied this in his discourse on the Good Shepherd, when he said, "When he has brought out all his own [out of the pen], he goes on ahead of them" (John 10:4). "Going ahead of them" implies that he does first what he asks them to do and that he confronts the dangers before they encounter them. Serving Christ implies the obligation of following him; conversely, he promised that wherever he might go, his servants would be privileged to accompany him and share his glory (cf. John 17:24).

27-28a Turning from the crisis as it would affect the disciples, Jesus revealed how it affected him. His dilemma corresponds to that in Gethsemane as recorded in the synoptic Gospels. There he shrank from a death that was imposed unjustly, executed cruelly, and could brand him as a rebel and a criminal. So he prayed, "My Father, if it is possible, may this cup be taken from me" (Matt 26:39; Mark 14:36; Luke 22:42). At the same time, he recognized that his death was necessary to carry out the divine program of redemption, for without the conflict there could be no conquest. Consequently he concluded his prayer by the resolute petition "Yet not as I will, but as you will" (Matt 26:39). John reveals that the prayer in Gethsemane, which he does not quote, was the culmination of a struggle that preceded it. In these words spoken publicly in the period of crisis, Jesus said, "Now my heart is troubled," or in a more literal rendering, "Now has my soul [*psychē*] been thrown into confusion." His language indicates that he is breaking under the strain of the crisis; its dangers and irrationality are overwhelming him. Should he ask the Father to spare him from the cataclysm that was so rapidly approaching? Had he done so, he might have averted seeming disaster at the price of failing to achieve his redemptive purpose. Nevertheless, he adhered boldly to his original purpose of completing the mission God had entrusted to him: "No, it was for this very reason that I came to this hour." The whole of his life's dedication is concentrated in this statement. The question was tentative; the resolution was final. He wanted the Father's name to be glorified, no matter what the cost!

28b–30 The voice from heaven is the third instance of its kind recorded in the Gospel narratives and the first such in John. On each occasion it was a public acknowledgment of the sonship and authority of Jesus and an endorsement of his work by the Father. John asserts unmistakably that the voice was a genuine, audible sound. It was not generally understood, however, for the crowd said that it had thundered. Others said that "an angel had spoken to him." The Father's audible commendation of Jesus appeared on three occasions: at his baptism, where Jesus commenced his career (Matt 3:17; Mark 1:11; Luke 3:21–22); at his transfiguration, which marked the turning point of his ministry (Matt 17:5; Mark 9:7; Luke 9:35); and at the conclusion of his ministry, as here. Jesus explained that the voice from heaven was intended to encourage the disciples and to inform the crowd, not to encourage him. If they did not understand it, the information would not benefit them greatly. Nevertheless, some did remember this occasion and found it helpful, as did John who recorded the event.

John does not tell his readers directly whether or not Jesus replied to the Greeks. The response, beginning in v.23, seems to have been directed to his disciples; and the words of vv.27–28 are more like a soliloquy.

31 Jesus recognized and announced unmistakably that the final crisis had arrived. Both the disciples and the more sympathetic segment of the crowd were uncertain of what his fate would be. For several months the prevailing attitude seems to have been uncertainty (John 6:60–66; 7:25–27, 40–44; 10:19–24; 11:55–56). Now he declared that a decisive action must follow. God's purpose is to glorify him. The hour for judgment has come, and the prince of the world must be exposed for what he is. "Judgment" does not imply that the final day of judgment has come or that only now is retribution for sin exercised. In the second commandment of the Mosaic law, God pronounced divine judgment by "punishing the children for the sin of the fathers to the third and fourth generation of those who hate me" (Exod 20:5). The moral and physical laws of God inevitably judge those who transgress them. Jesus conveyed the meaning that God, having now made his final revelation, must hold men responsible for their obedience or disobedience.

There is a parallel in Paul's address to the Athenians: "In the past God overlooked such ignorance, but now he commands all people everywhere to repent. For he has set a day when he will judge the world with justice by the man he has appointed" (Acts 17:30–31). Paul's outlook is more definitely eschatological than the Johannine presentation, but the essential idea is the same. The revelation of God in Christ is itself a disclosure of sin and a judgment on it.

"The prince of this world" can be none other than Satan. The same title is used in John 14:30 and 16:11. There are parallel expressions in the Pauline writings (2 Cor 4:4; Eph 2:2; 6:12). The Cross and the Resurrection spelled Satan's defeat. These events marked the glorification of all he renounced and the reversal of all he sought to attain. Satan was motivated by self-will; Jesus, by the will of the Father. Satan's power brought destruction and death; Jesus' power imparted renewal and life. Though Satan is still active, his action is only the desperation of futility (cf. Rev 12:12).

32–33 The preposition "from" (*ek*) in "lifted up from the earth" really means "out from" rather than "away from." It connotes not only being lifted or suspended above the earth, as on a cross, but being brought up out of the earth. Jesus had in mind not only the fact that he would be elevated on the cross but also that he would be exalted by the Resurrection. The verb *lifted up* (*hypsoō*) is used in John exclusively to refer to Jesus' death (John 3:14; 8:28; 12:32, 34), while elsewhere in the NT it means "exalt." It lends itself well to the double meaning of the method of death as specifically stated here (v.33) and the exaltation to spiritual sovereignty described in apostolic preaching (Acts 2:33; 5:31; Phil 2:9).

"All men" does not imply that all men will ultimately be saved; instead, it means that Christ draws men to himself indiscriminately, without regard to nationality, race, or status. Jesus' utterance was prompted by the presence of the Greek Gentiles and should be evaluated by the setting of the occasion. There is, however, a clear differentiation between believers and unbelievers, between the saved and the lost, in all the Johannine writings (John 1:11; 3:18, 36; 5:29; 6:40, 53, 64; 8:44; 1 John 3:10, 15; 5:12).

34 The crowd was puzzled by Jesus' prediction of his death. According to their understanding, the Messiah would be a supernatural person and would inaugurate his final and eternal reign as God's Anointed, the Son of David. In making the covenant with David, God promised him that his descendants would reign "forever" (2 Sam 7:12–13, 16). Psalm 89, a hymn in praise of God's favor to David, affirms the same thing (vv.26–29, 35–36). There is no specific passage in the Pentateuch that affirms the eternity of the Messiah, but if by "the Law" the people meant the OT in general, the Davidic Covenant may have been their source of information. The people were confused by Jesus' reference to the "Son of Man" and wanted to know who he was.

Although John 12:32 uses the first person pronoun "I" rather than "Son of Man," Jesus must have spoken of himself by this title. It appears frequently in the synoptic Gospels and also in John. If it was an apocalyptic title, the people did not understand that Jesus was so using the term. Their query, "Who is this 'Son of Man'?" implies that his concept of its meaning was different from theirs. The apocalyptic Son of Man would not die. Jesus enlarged the concept by applying it to the whole of his work: his true humanity, his suffering, his exaltation, and his judicial work. At this point he did not attempt a full answer to the questioning of the crowd. He adopted a pragmatic approach such as that given in John 7:17.

35–36 Jesus spoke with urgency. The light would not always be available, as he said to his disciples at the healing of the blind man: "Night is coming, when no one can work" (9:4). If his hearers wished to walk with certainty, they should act at once, for after his departure they might find themselves in the darkness. "Put your trust" (*pisteuete*) is continuative, similar to the command given later to the disciples in the upper room (John 14:1), and implies a persistent faith, not solely a momentary decision.

Notes

24 Blaiklock observes that the symbolism of the grain of wheat could have been especially significant to Greek Gentiles (E.M. Blaiklock, *Who Was Jesus?* Chicago: Moody, 1974, p. 56). The head of wheat was a common symbol for life in the Eleusinian mysteries. According to the myth that underlies the rites of this mystery religion, Demeter, the goddess of the earth, had lost her daughter to Hades, the king of death, who had abducted her to the underworld. In her distress, Demeter had been aided by Triptolemus, king of Eleusis. When Zeus intervened and compelled Hades to return his bride to her mother for six months each year, Demeter presented Triptolemus with a grain of wheat which, like her daughter, had to descend into darkness and later bear fruit. A dramatic representation of this event was part of the mystic ritual.

There is no indication that the Gospel of John was patterned after the myth or even paralleled it; but the concept of life in a seed that was buried and rose into a new life was common to both and is also developed in 1 Cor 15:37–38.

31 The word "world" is κόσμος (*kosmos*), which refers to the world system, not the created, material world. Satan is the prince of the present world system, but it has been judged and condemned; it will not lead to utopia. When Christ returns, he will set up the perfect world system, which he will rule in perfect righteousness.

4. *The response to unbelief*

12:37–50

37Even after Jesus had done all these miraculous signs in their presence, they still would not believe in him. 38This was to fulfill the word of Isaiah the prophet:

"Lord, who has believed our message
and to whom has the arm of the Lord been revealed?"

39For this reason they could not believe, because, as Isaiah says elsewhere:

40"He has blinded their eyes
and deadened their hearts,
so they can neither see with their eyes,
nor understand with their hearts,
nor turn—and I would heal them."

41Isaiah said this because he saw Jesus' glory and spoke about him.
42Yet at the same time many even among the leaders believed in him. But because of the Pharisees they would not confess their faith for fear they would be put out of the synagogue; 43for they loved praise from men more than praise from God.
44Then Jesus cried out, "When a man believes in me, he does not believe in me only, but in the one who sent me. 45When he looks at me, he sees the one who sent me. 46I have come into the world as a light, so that no one who believes in me should stay in darkness.
47"As for the person who hears my words but does not keep them, I do not judge him. For I did not come to judge the world, but to save it. 48There is a judge for the one who rejects me and does not accept my words; that very word which I spoke will condemn him at the last day. 49For I did not speak of my own accord, but the Father who sent me commanded me what to say and how to say it. 50I know that his command leads to eternal life. So whatever I say is just what the Father has told me to say."

Verses 37–50 are the author's explanation of the significance of his narrative up to this point. They focus on the conflict of belief and unbelief and include Jesus' final appeal for decision. The historical crisis must be resolved by immediate action that reveals either the belief or unbelief of those involved. The spiritual crisis that occurs when one confronts Christ is resolved through personal decision.

37–38 The author expresses surprise and regret that in spite of Jesus' numerous "signs" the people still obstinately refused to believe in him. Unbelief was rapidly approaching the climax attained in the rejection and crucifixion of Jesus. John connected this with the prophecy of Isaiah, thus plainly affirming that Jesus was the subject of the passage on the Suffering Servant (Isa 52:13–53:12). The implication of this identification extends beyond the immediate application. John refers simply to Isaiah 53:1, which by its rhetorical question implies that the Servant was not believed and that the revelation of God's power through him was not apprehended. The entire prophecy is quoted repeatedly in the NT and is an important basis for the doctrine of the Atonement. Prophecy played a large part in apostolic preaching. Peter in his address to the people after the healing of the lame man repeatedly alluded to the prophets: "But this is how God fulfilled what he had foretold through all the prophets, saying that his Christ would suffer" (Acts 3:18); "He must remain in heaven until the time comes for God to restore everything, as he promised long ago through his holy prophets" (v.21); "Indeed, all the prophets from Samuel on, as many as have spoken, have foretold these days" (v.24). Prophecy was the general foundation for the doctrine of the early church.

39–40 Not only did prophecy describe unbelief, it also explained it. Why should not the hearers of Jesus believe in him when the signs so unmistakably accredited his claims? John quotes from Isaiah 6 to show that unbelief is the result of the rejection of light, which act, by the sovereign law of God, gradually makes belief impossible. The antecedent text is taken from the commission of Isaiah. God appointed the prophet to preach to the inhabitants of Judah but warned him in advance that his mission would not be successful. The verbs as given in Isaiah 6:9–10 are imperatives. Isaiah was told to announce his message even though it merely hardened the hearts of those who heard him. God offered the opportunity of faith, but the very offer made the recipients of it more obstinate. John interprets the prophecy by its effect rather than by its intention. It was not God's desire to alienate his people; but without the offer of faith and repentance, they would never turn to him anyway. The cumulative effect of unbelief is a hardened attitude that becomes more impenetrable as time progresses.

41 The implication in this verse is startling. Isaiah 6 opens by saying, "In the year that King Uzziah died, I saw the Lord seated on a throne, high and exalted, and the train of his robe filled the temple." The prophet was looking at a manifestation of Deity and said, "My eyes have seen the King, the LORD Almighty" (6:5). John says that Isaiah saw Jesus and spoke of him. He identified Jesus with the Jehovah (Yahweh) of the OT.

42–43 John notes that many of the leaders believed. Probably Joseph of Arimathea and Nicodemus were among that number (John 19:38–39; cf. Mark 15:43; Luke 23:50–51). Possibly John learned of this movement among the national leaders through his acquaintance with Nicodemus. Since the attitude of the council as a whole would call for the excommunication of any avowed believers in Jesus (John 9:22), these remained silent. Though they did not agree with the attitude or action of the majority of the Sanhedrin, they still sought its approval.

44–46 Jesus equated belief in him with belief in God (cf. John 14:1). As John stated it in his First Epistle, "No one who denies the Son has the Father; whoever acknowledges the Son has the Father also" (1 John 2:23). The Father and the Son are inseparable; though they are two personalities, they work as one being. Jesus spoke of the Father as the one who had sent him, and he claimed to be the light that illumines the darkness of those who are without God.

47–50 Judgment on unbelief is not arbitrary but inevitable. The message of Christ when refused will become the condemnation of man in the last days since nobody who refused it can plead ignorance. The emphasis, however, is positive. Jesus' mission was intended to evoke belief and to rescue men from darkness. The Father's sovereign purpose is to lift men out of helplessness and death and give them eternal life. Because Jesus speaks the message the Father commanded him to speak, he is the Word of God.

At this point John closes the account of Jesus' public ministry of teaching. His subsequent teaching concerns only the disciples and their preparation for the final act of his life. Jesus' words before the chief priests and Pilate were defensive rather than didactic. Insofar as Jesus appeared publicly, he manifested the message of God to the world by what he did as well as by what he said.

III. The Private Ministry of the Word (13:1–17:26)

A. *The Last Supper* (13:1–30)

1. *The washing of feet*

13:1–20

> [1]It was just before the Passover Feast. Jesus knew that the time had come for him to leave this world and go to the Father. Having loved his own who were in the world, he now showed them the full extent of his love.
>
> [2]The evening meal was being served, and the devil had already prompted Judas Iscariot, son of Simon, to betray Jesus. [3]Jesus knew that the Father had put all things under his power, and that he had come from God and was returning to God; [4]so he got up from the meal, took off his outer clothing, and wrapped a towel around his waist. [5]After that, he poured water into a basin and began to wash his disciples' feet, drying them with the towel that was wrapped around him.
>
> [6]He came to Simon Peter, who said to him, "Lord, are you going to wash my feet?"
>
> [7]Jesus replied, "You do not realize now what I am doing, but later you will understand."
>
> [8]"No," said Peter, "you shall never wash my feet."
>
> Jesus answered, "Unless I wash you, you have no part with me."
>
> [9]"Then, Lord," Simon Peter replied, "not just my feet but my hands and my head as well!"
>
> [10]Jesus answered, "A person who has had a bath needs only to wash his feet; his whole body is clean. And you are clean, though not every one of you." [11]For he knew who was going to betray him, and that was why he said not every one was clean.
>
> [12]When he had finished washing their feet, he put on his clothes and returned to his place. "Do you understand what I have done for you?" he asked them. [13]"You call me 'Teacher' and 'Lord,' and rightly so, for that is what I am. [14]Now that I, your Lord and Teacher, have washed your feet, you also should wash one another's feet. [15]I have set you an example that you should do as I have done for you. [16]I tell you the truth, no servant is greater than his master, nor is a messenger greater than the one who sent him. [17]Now that you know these things, you will be blessed if you do them.

¹⁸"I am not referring to all of you; I know those I have chosen. But this is to fulfill the scripture: 'He who shares my bread has lifted up his heel against me.'
¹⁹"I am telling you now before it happens, so that when it does happen you will believe that I am He. ²⁰I tell you the truth, whoever accepts anyone I send accepts me; and whoever accepts me accepts the one who sent me."

1 The full Johannine account of the Passion begins at this point. The new stage of the conflict between belief and unbelief is marked by a chronological reference to the main feast of the year and by relation to the progress of the program of Jesus' life. John alludes to the nearness of the Passover as if to remind his reader that Jesus had been introduced by John the Baptist as the "Lamb of God, who takes away the sin of the world" (1:29). As the first Passover had been the turning point in the redemption of the people of God, so the Cross would be the opening of a new era for believers. John connects this with the manifestation of Jesus' love for his disciples. "To the fullest extent" is a better rendering of the original *eis telos* than KJV "unto the end." It does not mean that Jesus continued to love his disciples only up to the end of his career but that his love has no limits. "His own" refers to his disciples, of whom he had said that they were given him by the Father (10:29). Jesus had accepted the responsibility for them and was obliged to instruct and protect them (17:6–12).

2 Whether this meal was the actual Passover or not has been warmly debated. Yet it seems that it occurred on the same night as the arrest and betrayal. If so, it was presumably Thursday night; and the Crucifixion occurred on Friday, the day before the Passover, which would have begun on Friday evening. Luke states that when the day came on which the Passover lamb was to be sacrificed, Peter and John were sent to arrange the meal that the Lord and his disciples ate that evening (Luke 22:7–14). Matthew (26:17–20) and Mark (14:12–17) agree that the meal was on the day on which the Passover lamb was killed, which preceded the Passover itself. John stated later (18:28) that the Jewish delegates could not enter Pilate's hall on Friday morning because they would be defiled and unable to eat the Passover. In that case, the Last Supper must have preceded the Passover by twenty-four hours. If, then, the Passover began on Friday night, the meal could have taken place on Thursday night but would not have been the standard Passover Feast. The question is complicated by the fact that the Synoptics imply that Jesus did intend to eat the Passover with his disciples (Matt 26:18; Mark 14:14; Luke 22:11). No mention is made of the Passover lamb, however.

Several solutions for this impasse have been suggested, two of which may be plausible. One is that two calendars were in simultaneous use and one national group, using one calendar, ate the Passover on Thursday night whereas the other group, using the other calendar, ate the Passover on Friday night. There have been several variants of this theory: (1) one calendar was figured by the solar year, the other by the lunar year; (2) there was a difference between the time prescribed by the temple and that by the Qumran Essenes; or (3) Jesus, having been repudiated by the priesthood and consequently considered apostate, would not have been allowed to obtain a lamb for sacrifice and would have been compelled to celebrate the feast at a different time (see Stauffer, pp. 113–18). Whatever solution may be accepted, there seems to be no other conclusion than that Jesus did celebrate the meal with his disciples on Thursday night, that the hearing before Pilate and the Crucifixion took place on Friday, and that his body was placed in the tomb before sunset late that afternoon.

The focus of action lies in Jesus' washing the feet of the disciples. The circumstances are listed in detail. Judas had already determined to betray Jesus (13:2). His specific motive is not stated, and the impulse is attributed to satanic suggestion. The casual allusion to the devil at this point implies a deeper significance to the conflict than a mere political or theological squabble. The conflict was basically actuated by a rebellion against God, the absolute opposite of the attitude of Jesus. It is possible that Judas, realizing that Jesus' enemies were implacably hostile and that they were politically powerful, concluded that Jesus was foredoomed to lose in the struggle and so decided that he might as well gain immunity from sharing Jesus' fate. Judas could compensate himself by claiming the reward for betrayal. His act, however, was more serious than an incidental piece of treachery; he sold himself to the power of evil. As v.27 states, "Satan entered into him," and he came under the devil's control.

3-5 John emphasizes the fact that Jesus was not the innocent victim of a plot, unaware of what was transpiring around him. He knew "that the Father had put all things under his power, and that he had come from God and was returning to God." Jesus was fully aware of his authority, his divine origin, and his destiny. John says much more about the inner consciousness of Jesus than the Synoptics do, either because he was more observant or because Jesus confided in him. Furthermore, Jesus' inward awareness of his power and office did not deter his ministry to the men he had chosen and was trying to prepare for the final catastrophe.

The immediate situation was that they had come to the banquet room directly from the street. Ordinarily on such an occasion the host would have delegated a servant to the menial task of removing the sandals of the guests and washing their feet. Since the meeting was obviously intended to be secret, no servants were present. None of the disciples was ready to volunteer for such a task, for each would have considered it an admission of inferiority to all the others. John the Baptist had used the act of such a servant as his standard of the lowest and meanest kind of service that could be required of any man (John 1:27).

Sometime during the meal Jesus rose, removed his outer cloak, tied a towel around his waist, and began to perform the work of the servant who was not present. It was a voluntary humiliation that rebuked the pride of the disciples. Perhaps it accentuated the tension of the situation, because Luke notes that when the disciples entered the room, they had been arguing about who among them would be the greatest in the kingdom of heaven (Luke 22:24).

6-8a The response of Simon Peter may have been representative of the common feeling that Jesus ought not to demean himself by washing their feet. The emphatic use of pronouns in Peter's surprised question, "Lord! You [su] are washing my [mou] feet?" and his equally emphatic negative reply, "NEVER to all eternity shall you wash my feet!" (my trans.), reveal both the impetuousness of his disposition and the high regard he had for Jesus. Peter felt that Jesus should not degrade himself by assuming such a position.

8b Jesus' rejoinder, "Unless I wash you, you have no part with me," expresses the necessity, not only for the cleansing of Peter's feet to make him socially acceptable for the dinner, but also for the cleansing of his personality to make him fit for the kingdom of God. The external washing was intended to be a picture of spiritual cleansing from evil.

9–10 Peter, mistaking Jesus' veiled figure for the literal act, expressed his devotion by asking for a bath. Separation from Jesus was abhorrent to him. Jesus reminded him that a person once bathed needed to wash only his feet. "You are clean, though not every one of you" gives the clue to the interpretation of this action. One of the disciples had consistently refused Jesus' spiritual ministration. The others, who had been loyal though sometimes slow to understand, needed only occasional correction.

11 This Gospel emphasizes strongly the self-consciousness of Jesus concerning himself and his work. From the beginning of his ministry he had supernatural discernment of the potentialities of his disciples (1:42, 47–48, 51). He predicted his death and resurrection (2:19; 3:14; 6:51; 8:28; 10:18; 12:32). He claimed a peculiar relationship with God (5:19, 26; 10:38). Now, at the close of his ministry, the Gospel emphasizes even more strongly his supernatural awareness of the significance of what was occurring. Jesus realized that the time had come to leave his disciples (13:1), that the Father had committed all action to his authority (v.3), that the betrayer was already at hand (vv.10–11), that the identity of the chosen believers was settled (v.18), that the outcome of the existing situation was fixed (v.19; cf. 18:4), and, finally, that the moment of consummation had come (v.21; cf. 19:28). The progress of realization is reflected also in the synoptic Gospels, though not quite so definitely.

12–14 A second lesson Jesus wished to impart to the disciples by this act was one of love and humble service. His question, "Do you understand what I have done for you?" contrasts with his remonstrance of Peter: "You do not realize now what I am doing, but later you will understand" (v.7). The discernment of the disciples developed slowly. It took them a long time to begin to comprehend the intensity of Jesus' love for them and the nature of his humility in dealing with them. "Teacher" and "Lord" are both titles of respect that placed Jesus on a level above the disciples. Nicodemus, himself a teacher, had so greeted Jesus (John 3:2), and Jesus had returned the compliment (v.10). "Lord"— like the English "Mr.," an abbreviation of "Master"—was a common salutation, which could be both a greeting (John 4:11, 15, 19) or an acknowledgment of authority (13:6, 9). Jesus emphasized the fact that if he, whom they regarded as their leader, had stooped to serve their needs, they should do the same for one another. He made the action of necessity the pattern for dedicated living. For similar passages in the Synoptics, see Matthew 10:24, connected with the commission of the Twelve; Luke 6:40, a short discourse resembling the Sermon on the Mount; John 15:20, virtually a repetition of John 13:16. The concept of the servant-master relationship appeared frequently in Jesus' teaching.

15 The "example" does not necessarily imply the perpetuation of footwashing as an ordinance in the church. The only other allusion to footwashing in the NT occurs in 1 Timothy 5:10, where it does not refer to a regular custom but seems to allude to charitable ministrations to the poor. John calls this act an "example," which implies that the emphasis is on the inner attitude of humble and voluntary service for others. Perhaps it was the basis for the Pauline exhortation to the Philippians: "Your attitude should be the same as that of Christ Jesus, who, being in very nature God, did not consider equality with God something to be grasped, but made himself nothing, taking the very nature of a servant, . . . and became obedient to death—even death on a cross!" (Phil 2:5–8).

16–17 The recurrence of "sent" (*pempsantos*) at this point is a reminder that Jesus was constantly conscious of being commissioned by the Father. Jesus included his disciples in the commission and also included them in the action of servanthood. Jesus portrayed for them the true nature of Christian living: serving one another. And for those who would be willing to take this role on themselves, Jesus said there would be blessings.

18 Jesus' reason for washing the disciples' feet was not solely good manners and sanitation. The imminence of the betrayal was pressing in on him, and the resultant anguish was tearing at his heart. He knew that the disciples would fail at the crucial moment, but he despaired of none except Judas. While the lesson applied to all of them, it was particularly an appeal to Judas. The psalm Jesus quoted was attributed to David, who lamented the defection of a trusted confidant (Ps 41:9). A parallel occurs in Psalm 55:12–14. Quite probably it referred originally to Ahithophel, who had been David's counselor and diplomatic advisor but deserted him in Absalom's rebellion (2 Sam 15:12; 16:15–23; 17:4, 14, 23). Again this is an example of prophecy by parallelism.

19–20 Jesus was not merely asking for personal loyalty but for belief that he was the One sent by God ("I am He"). The expression is identical with that which he used in controversy with his enemies at the Feast of Tabernacles (8:24, 28, 58). He wanted the disciples to commit themselves to his claims before the events would seemingly invalidate them and before the Resurrection would confirm them (cf. John 2:22). He said that accepting the messenger whom he sent was equivalent to receiving him and that receiving him involved also receiving God. The language implies a close connection between the disciple and the master and an equally close connection between Jesus and God. As the disciples could claim to speak with Jesus' authority, so Jesus claimed to speak for God.

Notes

2 The reading γινομένου (*ginomenou*, "being"), the present participle, rather than γενομένου (*genomenou*, "having been"), the aorist participle, which indicates a past action, not only has better MS support but also fits better with the expression "he got up from the meal" (v.4), which implies an interruption. So, apparently, the meal was still in progress when Jesus got up.

10 The meaning of Jesus is clear in the choice of the words meaning "wash." Νίπτω (*niptō*, vv.5, 6, 8, 10) means to wash a part of the body; "bath" (v.10) is derived from the verb λούω (*louō*), which involves a complete washing. The difference between λελουμένος (*leloumenos*, "having been bathed") and νίψασθαι (*nipsasthai*, "to be washed") in v.10 is not only in their meaning but also in the tenses of the verbs. *Leloumenos* is a perfect tense, which implies a settled state; *nipsasthai* is an aorist, which refers to a single act. A parallel to this idea may be found in Hebrews 10:10: "And by that will, we have been made holy [ἡγιασμένοι, *hēgiasmenoi*, a perfect tense] through the sacrifice of the body of Jesus Christ once for all," and v.14: "Because by one sacrifice he has made perfect [τετελείωκεν, *teteleiōken*, perfect tense] forever those who are being made holy" (ἁγιαζομένους, *hagiazomenous*, a present tense). The work of Christ draws a permanent line between those who have been cleansed and those who are not clean. There is need, however, for washing from incidental defilement and for the Christian's continuing growth in grace.

11 The verb οἶδα (*oida*, "know") is generally used in John to denote certain knowledge of a fact rather than experiential acquaintance with a situation or person (cf. 14:4). It is connected with Jesus' supernatural knowledge of his origin, destiny, or circumstances. He *knew* that the witness

138

of John the Baptist was valid (5:32), what his procedure would be for the feeding of the five thousand (6:6), that his disciples were grumbling about his enigmatic speech (6:61), who really believed in him and who did not (6:64). He was sure of his origin with the Father who had sent him (7:29; 8:14, 55). These instances are multiplied in the account of the private ministry and the Passion. Jesus was conscious that his time had come (13:1) and that the Father had conveyed to him full authority to complete the mission for which he had come (v.3). He also knew the identity of the traitor (v.11) and he knew those who were loyal (v.18). He was well aware of the outcome of the impending events (18:4) and the prophetic program outlined for him in the Scriptures (19:28). The total impression given by this use of *oida* is that Jesus was living by a program he completely understood and that it was not simply a series of accidents he had to meet fortuitously. The concept fits with John's general picture of him as the divine Son of God, who came to perform the Father's will.

2. *The prediction of the betrayal*

13:21–30

²¹After he had said this, Jesus was troubled in spirit and testified, "I tell you the truth, one of you is going to betray me."

²²His disciples stared at one another, at a loss to know which of them he meant. ²³One of them, the disciple whom Jesus loved, was reclining next to him. ²⁴Simon Peter motioned to this disciple and said, "Ask him which one he means."

²⁵Leaning back against Jesus, he asked him, "Lord, who is it?"

²⁶Jesus answered, "It is the one to whom I will give this piece of bread when I have dipped it in the dish." Then, dipping the piece of bread, he gave it to Judas Iscariot, son of Simon. ²⁷As soon as Judas took the bread, Satan entered into him.

"What you are about to do, do quickly," Jesus told him, ²⁸but no one at the meal understood why Jesus said this to him. ²⁹Since Judas had charge of the money, some thought Jesus was telling him to buy what was needed for the Feast, or to give something to the poor. ³⁰As soon as Judas had taken the bread, he went out. And it was night.

21 Jesus was not surprised that Judas would betray him. He had announced it to the disciples at least a year earlier (John 6:70). Nevertheless, it still weighed heavily on his mind (13:18). The writer of the Gospel repeatedly mentions the betrayal when he alludes to Judas (12:4; 13:2). "Troubled" is the same verb used of Jesus' agitation at the grave of Lazarus (11:33) and at the request of the Greeks to see him (12:27). As "the hour" approached, the bitterness of the betrayal Jesus anticipated became known. The desertion by many of his disciples evoked an expression of disappointment; here, the injury was felt more poignantly. The quotation in v.18, which the author cites as prophetic of Jesus' feeling, contains in its context an allusion to "my close friend, whom I trusted" (Ps 41:9). Among the sorrows contributing to the agony of the Cross was the voluntary and selfish defection of Judas.

22 The announcement startled the disciples. Although Jesus had previously announced the betrayal, they had not taken it to heart. Now, realizing the hostility of the authorities in Jerusalem and knowing that Jesus' death might be imminent, the act that had seemed remote became an immediate possibility.

23–25 Simon Peter signaled to his friend who occupied the place next to Jesus, asking him to inquire who the traitor might be. Simon's inquiry demonstrated not only his persistent trait of curiosity but also his loyalty. He may have contemplated preventive action; for if he could know in advance who the person might be, he could intervene. "The disciple whom Jesus loved," presumably the author of the Gospel, made the inquiry.

26 Jesus gave no specific identification. He simply indicated that the offender would be the one to whom he would give the special morsel he had dipped into the dish. "Bread" in this context does not mean the modern spongy loaf used in most Western nations. It was probably a piece of flat bread, somewhat leathery in consistency, which could be used to scoop bits of meat taken from the pot in which they were cooked. For the host to select such a tidbit from the main dish and give it to a guest would be a mark of courtesy and esteem. The disciples, seeing this, would conclude only that Jesus regarded Judas as a friend he had confidence in. Perhaps he so favored others in turn. Jesus' reply would answer the question for the beloved disciple; but he could scarcely have communicated his knowledge to Peter at that moment without disturbing the peace of the group and violating the confidence of Jesus.

27a "Satan entered into him." This moment was Judas's last opportunity to renounce his treachery. If the other disciples were ignorant of Judas's intentions, he could change the course of his action without explanation, and none but Jesus would be the wiser. Once Judas left the room to seal his bargain with the priests, he would pass the point of no return. His yielding to selfish impulse opened the way to satanic control.

27b–28 "Quickly" (*tacheion*) is the comparative form of the adverb that means "fast," or, in this construction, "as fast as possible." Conscious that the time had come for his sacrifice (13:1), Jesus wished Judas to get on with his plot and leave. Once Judas had departed, Jesus would be able to continue his intimate ministry with his disciples in the upper room.

29 The reference to making a purchase for the Passover may corroborate the view that the Last Supper was held on the night preceding the killing of the Passover lamb. It seems unlikely that Jesus would wait until this moment to obtain the lamb; and the text says that the disciples didn't know the reason for Jesus' statement to Judas, which would hardly be the case if the lamb was missing.

30 The repetition of the phrase "As soon as Judas had taken the bread" (cf. v.27) indicates that Satan's control of Judas and Judas's departure from the group must have been simultaneous. There are depths of tragedy in the terse comment "And it was night." Perhaps as Judas opened the door to leave, John saw the city veiled in darkness. His four words correspond to Jesus' statement when Judas betrayed him: "This is your hour—when darkness reigns" (Luke 22:53).

John's comment "And it was night" heightens the implication that Jesus' life was one of conflict. The opposition of darkness and light is announced in the Prologue (1:5) and is illustrated by the growing hostility between Jesus and his enemies. As the conflict becomes more marked, Jesus says it reflects the contrast between what he had seen with his Father and what they had heard from theirs. When they protested, he declared plainly that God was his Father and that the devil was their father (8:38, 42–44). John notes the progress of the spiritual conflict in 13:27; 14:30; 17:15.

B. *The Last Discourse* (13:31–16:33)

With the departure of Judas, Jesus commenced the long farewell discourse to his disciples. At its beginning there is a prime example of wrong chapter division, for the unity of the text is not broken at 14:1. The dialogue comprising the first section really begins with Jesus' statement that his "glorification" is about to take place.

1. *Questions and answers* (13:31–14:31)

a. *The new commandment*

13:31–35

> [31]When he was gone, Jesus said, "Now is the Son of Man glorified and God is glorified in him. [32]If God is glorified in him, then God will glorify the Son in himself, and will glorify him at once.
> [33]"My children, I will be with you only a little longer. You will look for me, and just as I told the Jews, so I tell you now: Where I am going, you cannot come.
> [34]"A new commandment I give you: Love one another. As I have loved you, so you must love one another. [35]All men will know that you are my disciples if you love one another."

31 The title "Son of Man" appears twelve times in the Gospel of John, of which this is the last occurrence. As the "Son of Man," Jesus reveals divine truth (1:51); he has a supernatural origin (3:13; 6:62); his death by being "lifted up" achieves salvation for men (3:14; 8:28; 12:34); he exercises the prerogative of final judgment (5:27); he provides spiritual nourishment (6:27). This title is also used of his being "glorified" (12:23; 13:31), which John applies specifically to death and resurrection (7:39; 12:16). John does not emphasize the apocalyptic aspect of the title that appears in Matthew (Matt 16:27; 25:31), though it appears once in such a context (John 5:27). The sacrificial aspect of the title appears in Jesus' announcement of the betrayal given in the synoptic accounts of the Last Supper (Matt 26:24; Mark 14:21; Luke 22:22). In its general usage it is the title of the incarnate Christ who is the representative of humanity before God and the representative of deity in human life. In the perfection of Christ's humanity, God finds the fullness of his expression to men.

32 The Johannine use of "glorify" (*doxazō*) is peculiar. The word occurs five times in vv.31–32 in what seems to be unnecessary repetition. Intrinsically *doxazō* means "exaltation." But as Jesus used it, it relates to his death. He connected it with the accomplishment of his work and the fulfillment of the hour for which he had been destined (12:23). The Cross would become the supreme glory of God because the Son would completely obey the will of the Father. The meaning of "exalt" or "magnify" seems to fit better the last two uses in this verse: "God will glorify the Son in himself, and will glorify him at once." This dual dimension of "glorify" appears also in the prayer of ch. 17, in which Jesus reports that he has glorified the Father by completing the task that had been assigned to him (v.4) and then asks that he be restored to the glory he enjoyed with the Father in his preincarnate state (v.5). In this concept the Cross and the Resurrection are united as phases of a single redemptive event by which the purpose of God is completed and his righteousness vindicated. A similar presentation, though in different language, is Paul's description of the humiliation of Christ and his subsequent exaltation given in Philippians 2:4–11.

33 "My children" (*teknia*) is expressive of Jesus' love and concern for the Eleven, who must have seemed to him to be weak and immature. John uses the same term seven times in his First Epistle (2:1, 12, 28; 3:7, 18; 4:4; 5:21), generally to introduce an admonition, as Jesus does here. Jesus recalled to their memory his words to the Jews: "Where I go, you cannot come" (8:21). To the disciples he was speaking of the fact that they were unprepared to follow him but would rejoin him later (14:3). To the Jews he made no such promise; instead, he predicted that they would die in their sins because of their unbelief.

34–35 The most important instruction that Jesus left for the Eleven was this "new commandment" to love one another. "New" (*kainēn*) implies freshness, or the opposite of "outworn" rather than simply "recent" or "different." If their motive in following him had been to obtain a high place in the messianic kingdom (John 1:40, 49), Jesus knew that the spirit of rivalry would disrupt their fellowship before they could accomplish his commission to them. The attitude of love would be the bond that would keep them united and would be the convincing demonstration that they had partaken of his own spirit and purpose. He had loved them without reservation and without limit (13:1–5) and expected them to do the same.

b. *The question of Peter*

13:36–14:4

> ³⁶Simon Peter asked him, "Lord, where are you going?"
> Jesus replied, "Where I am going, you cannot follow now, but you will follow later."
> ³⁷Peter asked, "Lord, why can't I follow you now? I will lay down my life for you."
> ³⁸Then Jesus answered, "Will you really lay down your life for me? I tell you the truth, before the rooster crows, you will disown me three times!
> ¹"Do not let your hearts be troubled. Trust in God; trust also in me. ²In my Father's house are many rooms; if it were not so, I would have told you. I am going there to prepare a place for you. ³And if I go and prepare a place for you, I will come back and take you to be with me that you also may be where I am. ⁴You know the way to the place where I am going."

The structure of this dialogue offers a contrast between the attempt of Jesus to present some consecutive teaching in preparation of his departure and the nervous unrest of the disciples who were disconcerted by the awareness of impending danger. As usual, Simon Peter was the first to speak.

36 Unfortunately the written text cannot convey the tone of Peter's question; but if he said, "Where *are* you going?" he would have expressed bewilderment and perhaps slight exasperation. Jesus had previously spoken publicly of going away (8:21). On that occasion his enemies were mystified and wondered whether he was contemplating suicide. Now, in the intimacy of his inner circle, the disciples are equally puzzled, though conceivably less critical. Jesus' answer reflects Peter's underlying meaning, for Jesus' promise, "You will follow later," implies that Peter had asked the question so that he might go with him. Peter's affection for Jesus, though often expressed clumsily, was undeniably genuine.

37–38 Peter was impatient and avowed that he was ready to lay down his life. Jesus, who understood the situation as Peter did not, and who knew Peter's inner weakness, was gently incredulous. His answer, "Before the rooster crows, you will disown me three times," reveals his estimate of Peter. Cock-crow was reckoned as the watch between twelve midnight and three o'clock in the morning, when the light of dawn began to glimmer on the eastern horizon. When Peter heard this word, he must have been completely baffled. He would not question Jesus' authority. Yet he was so sure of his own devotion that he could not imagine such a failure.

14:1 Furthermore, the other disciples must have been equally perturbed, for Jesus added, "Do not let your hearts be troubled." At this point he began to address the entire company of disciples, as the plural pronoun *hymōn* ("your") indicates. The form of the imperative *mē tarassesthō* implies that they should "stop being troubled." "Set your heart at ease" would be a good translation. He urged them to maintain both their trust in God and in himself. The verb "trust" (*pisteuete*) could be either indicative or imperative; i.e., a statement, "You trust in God and also trust in me," or a command, as translated by NIV. This double imperative seems to be the better choice. The first part of the verse is unquestionably an imperative, and Jesus was plainly endeavoring to encourage the disciples to persist in faith. Their uncertainty and discouragement had weakened them, and he wanted to strengthen them against complete collapse in the imminent tragedy.

2 In spite of the threatening circumstances, Jesus spoke with calm assurance of the divine provision for them and took for granted that they would have a place in the eternal world. Jesus never speculated about a future life; he spoke as one who was as familiar with eternity as one is with his hometown. The imagery of a dwelling place ("rooms") is taken from the oriental house in which the sons and daughters have apartments under the same roof as their parents. The purpose of his departure was to make ready the place where he could welcome them permanently. Certainly he would not go to prepare for friends unless he expected that they would finally arrive. Although he was well aware of their weakness and impending failure, he took the responsibility of bringing them to the Father's house.

3 "I will come back" is one of the few eschatological allusions in this Gospel. Jesus was not speaking of a general resurrection but of his personal concern for his own disciples. Though he did not elaborate on the promise, the guarantee is unmistakable. His return is as certain as his departure, and he would take them with him to his Father's house. This promise does not refer to death. Jesus left by the road of death; he will return by the road of life, as he said later in this discourse: "Because I live, you also will live" (v.19).

4 Verses 1–4 not only contain Jesus' answer to Peter's question but also indicate an attempt on Jesus' part to return to the theme of the discourse he had first begun. He assumed that they knew the way to their destination; all they would need to do would be to follow the road. His sheep would follow him and find "the house of the Lord" at the end of their journey (Ps 23:6; John 10:27–28).

c. *The question of Thomas*

14:5–7

> ⁵Thomas said to him, "Lord, we don't know where you are going, so how can we know the way?"
> ⁶Jesus answered, "I am the way and the truth and the life. No one comes to the

Father except through me. ⁷If you really knew me, you would know my Father as well. From now on, you do know him and have seen him."

5 Thomas's abrupt question was like Peter's questions (13:6, 36–37), characteristic of its proponent. Thomas was utterly honest, pessimistic, and uninhibited. He did not suppress his feelings but voiced his despair. He had already declared his willingness to follow Jesus and to die with him if necessary when he proposed the journey to Bethany (John 11:16). Thomas despaired of ever learning the way and was not ready to accept a state of permanent bewilderment. His question revealed a man who was confused by life and felt that its riddles were insolvable.

6 Jesus' reply is the ultimate foundation for a satisfactory philosophy of life. First, it is personal. He did not claim merely to know the way, the truth, and the life as a formula he could impart to the ignorant; but he actually claimed to *be* the answer to human problems. Jesus' solution to perplexity is not a recipe; it is a relationship with him. Second, he did not counter Thomas's skepticism with an argument or a quotation drawn from his memory. He responded with an authoritative assertion as the master of life. He *is* the way to the Father because only he has an intimate knowledge of God unmarred by sin. He *is* the truth because he has the perfect power of making life one coherent experience irrespective of its ups and downs. He *is* the life because he was not subject to death but made it subject to him. He did not live with death as the ultimate end of his life; he died to demonstrate the power and continuity of his life. Because he is the way, the truth, and the life, he is the only means of reaching the Father. Jesus was not exhibiting a narrow arrogance. Rather, he was making the only possible deduction from the fact that he, the unique Son, was the sole means of access to the Father. Jesus' claim parallels the author's pronouncement: "No one has ever seen God, but God the only Son, who is at the Father's side, has made him known" (John 1:18). Jesus is the only authorized revelation of God in human form and he is the only authorized representative of humanity to God.

7 "If you really knew me" could probably be better rendered "If you have attained a realization of who I am, you will know my Father also." Jesus declared that he had adequately presented the Father in his own person. The statement has its parallel in Paul's teaching: "He is the image of the invisible God" (Col 1:15). "Knew" implies experience rather than intuition or theoretical knowledge. To the extent that the disciples had come to a satisfactory understanding of Jesus, they had a comprehension of the being of God.

Notes

7 Textual evidence for "knew" or "had known" is divided between ἐγνώκατέ (*egnōkate*) and ἐγνώκειτέ (*egnōkeite*). The former reading favors a first-class condition; the second reading, a second-class condition. The former assumes that they knew Jesus but had not realized his representation of the Father; the second is a contrary-to-fact condition.

d. *The request of Philip*

14:8–15

> [8]Philip said, "Lord, show us the Father and that will be enough for us."
> [9]Jesus answered: "Don't you know me, Philip, even after I have been among you such a long time? Anyone who has seen me has seen the Father. How can you say, 'Show us the Father'? [10]Don't you believe that I am in the Father, and that the Father is in me? The words I say to you are not just my own. Rather, it is the Father, living in me, who is doing his work. [11]Believe me when I say that I am in the Father and the Father is in me; or at least believe on the evidence of the miracles themselves. [12]I tell you the truth, anyone who has faith in me will do what I have been doing. He will do even greater things than these, because I am going to the Father. [13]And I will do whatever you ask in my name, so that the Son may bring glory to the Father. [14]You may ask me for anything in my name, and I will do it.
> [15]"If you love me, you will obey what I command."

8 If Thomas was a skeptic, Philip was a realist. Having determined in his thinking that the Father of whom Jesus spoke must be the Ultimate Absolute, Philip demanded that he and his associates might see him. Philip was materialistic; apparently abstractions meant little to him. Nevertheless he had a deep desire to experience God for himself. If he and the other disciples could only apprehend God with at least one of their senses, they would be satisfied. Perhaps he had in mind such a manifestation of God as "the angel of the Lord" who appeared to Jacob at Peniel (Gen 32:24, 30) and to the parents of Samson (Judg 13:3–22) or the experience of Moses on Mount Sinai (Exod 34:4–8).

9 Jesus was both pleased and saddened by Philip's request: pleased by his earnestness and saddened by his obtuseness. His union with the Father was so natural that he was astonished that Philip had not observed it. "I am in the Father, and . . . the Father is in me" (v.10) was his description of the relationship both in instructing the public and in his final prayer to the Father (cf. 10:38; 14:20; 17:21). For this reason he could say, "Anyone who has seen me has seen the Father." No material image or likeness can adequately depict God. Only a person can give knowledge of him since personality cannot be represented by an impersonal object.

10–11 Furthermore, if a personality must be employed to represent God, that personality cannot be less than God and do him justice, nor can it be so far above humanity that it cannot communicate God perfectly to men. For this reason John says that "the only Son, who is at the Father's side, has made him known" (John 1:18). The way Jesus made known the character and reality of the Father was by his words and works. The truth of God filled Jesus' words; the power of God produced his works.

12 Jesus again slowly resumed the main current of his teaching. He wanted to impress on the disciples that he was not disbanding them in anticipation of his departure but, rather, he was expecting them to continue his work and do even greater things than he had accomplished. Such an expectation seems impossible in the light of his character and power; yet, through the power of the Spirit whom Jesus sent after his ascension, there were more converts after the initial sermon of Peter at Pentecost than are recorded for Jesus during his entire career. The influence of the infant church covered the Roman world, whereas Jesus during his lifetime never traveled outside the boundaries of Pales-

tine. Through the disciples he multiplied his ministry after his departure. The Book of Acts is a continuous record of deeds that followed the precedent Jesus had set. As the living Lord he continued in his church what he had himself begun. He expected that the church would become the instrument by which he could manifest his salvation to all people.

13–15 The power of the disciples originated in prayer. Jesus could hardly have made more emphatic the declaration that whatever they should ask in his name, he would do. The phrase "in my name," however, is not a talisman for the command of supernatural energy. He did not wish it to be used as a magical charm like an Aladdin's lamp. It was both a guarantee, like the endorsement on a check, and a limitation on the petition; for he would grant only such petitions as could be presented consistently with his character and purpose. In prayer we call on him to work out his purpose, not simply to gratify our whims. The answer is promised so that the Son may bring glory to the Father. The disciples' obedience to him will be the test of their love.

e. The promise of the Spirit

14:16–21

> 16And I will ask the Father, and he will give you another Counselor to be with you forever—17the Spirit of truth. The world cannot accept him, because it neither sees him nor knows him. But you know him, for he lives with you and will be in you. 18I will not leave you as orphans; I will come to you. 19Before long, the world will not see me anymore, but you will see me. Because I live, you also will live. 20On that day you will realize that I am in my Father, and you are in me, and I am in you. 21Whoever has my commands and obeys them, he is the one who loves me. He who loves me will be loved by my Father, and I too will love him and show myself to him."

16–17 With the preceding words, Jesus returned from the answer to Philip's question to the more general theme of preparation for his departure. His absence would make more difficult the realization of the person of the Father whom he represented. In his place he promised to send the Holy Spirit, the "Counselor." "Counselor" is an attempted translation of the Greek *paraklētos*, which means literally "a person summoned to one's aid." It may refer to an advisor, a legal advocate, a mediator or intercessor (BAG, p. 623). In the First Epistle of John it is applied to Jesus' present ministry as "the one who speaks to the Father in our defense" (1 John 2:1). The Spirit's function is to represent God to the believer as Jesus did in his incarnate state. "Another" (*allon*) means another of the same kind, not of a different kind. The concept of the Holy Spirit was not new, for the Spirit of God was the active agent in creation (Gen 1:2) and in remonstrating with men who were sinning against God (Gen 6:3). He called and empowered men to do unusual deeds (Judg 3:10; 13:24–25; 14:6, 19; 15:14) and to prophesy (Zech 7:12). John the Baptist had predicted that Jesus would baptize with the Holy Spirit (Matt 3:11; Mark 1:8; Luke 3:16; John 1:33). In his discussion of the new birth, Jesus had already spoken to Nicodemus of the work of the Holy Spirit (John 3:5). The ministry of the Spirit, however, would be directed primarily to the disciples. He would direct their decisions, counsel them continually, and remain with them forever. He would be invisible to all and unapprehended by the world at large since the world would not recognize him. To use a modern metaphor, he would not operate on the world's wavelength. His presence was already *with* the disciples insofar as they were under his influence. Later, he would indwell them, when Jesus himself had departed. This distinction marks the difference between the Old Testament experience of the Holy Spirit and the post-Pentecostal experience of the church. The individual indwelling of the Spirit is the specific privilege of the Christian believer (see John 7:39).

18–19 Jesus' allusion to a return may refer to his reappearance after the Resurrection. He did reveal himself to his disciples in order to impart final instructions and comfort, but he did not remain visible for long. There was no public manifestation, as he intimated, and the private manifestation of the postresurrection appearances would verify his acceptance by the Father and his union with the Father. He would appear only to those who loved and obeyed him. The motive for these appearances was the need for reassuring the disciples, whom his departure would leave as helpless orphans in an unfriendly world. Jesus looked upon them as spiritual children (13:33) who needed the strong protection and guidance of a parent in order to survive. The resurrection of Jesus would also be the guarantee of life for the disciples. The eternal life that he would demonstrate is the same eternal life he promised to them.

20 The coming of the Spirit to indwell believers would bring the realization that the Father, Son, and Holy Spirit are united in purpose and operation and that there would be a new intimate relationship between them and believers. Furthermore, the Spirit's coming would be a confirmation of Jesus' exaltation to the Father's right hand to begin his present ministry as Advocate and Intercessor (John 15:26; Acts 2:33; 5:31–32).

21 Jesus reiterated the statement of v.15 because of its importance. Love is the basis of relationship with God. His love has been manifested in the gift of Jesus (1 John 4:9–10). Our love for him is manifested in obedience (1 John 5:3). Jesus said that there are great benefits for those who obey his commands, thus showing their love for him. Jesus said that the Father would love the obedient disciple, Jesus himself would love him, and Jesus would make himself known to him. Loving Christ pays unmatched dividends.

f. *The question of Judas (not Iscariot)*

14:22–24

> 22Then Judas (not Judas Iscariot) said, "But, Lord, why do you intend to show yourself to us and not to the world?"
> 23Jesus replied, "If anyone loves me, he will obey my teaching. My Father will love him, and we will come to him and make our home with him. 24He who does not love me will not obey my teaching. These words you hear are not my own; they belong to the Father who sent me.

22 The last question in this impromptu dialogue was posed by Judas (not Iscariot). Nothing is known of him beyond his name, unless he can be identified with Thaddaeus (Matt 10:3; Mark 3:18). Only Luke mentions a second disciple by this name (Luke 6:16; Acts 1:13). Judas could not understand how Jesus would appear to the disciples without being at the same time subject to public scrutiny. Either Jesus would be visible or he would not; for Judas there was no possibility of both.

23 Jesus in his reply did not discuss the question of postresurrection appearances. He focused the disciples' attention on the broader revelation that would come to them through obedience to his known teaching and through the work of the Holy Spirit. The reality of Jesus' and the Father's presence would be conditioned on obedience. The bond of love that would provide the atmosphere for the fellowship would be resultant rather than conditional, for obedience is the consequence of love. Obedience is not, however, the condition of God's love for men but the proof of their realization of his love and of their love for him.

24 Being obedient to Jesus' words extends beyond keeping the charges he personally delivered. Jesus equated his teaching with the Father's will. Thus, loving Jesus is demonstrated by one's obedience to the revealed will of God, the Bible.

g. *Parting comfort*

14:25-31

> 25"All this I have spoken while still with you. 26But the Counselor, the Holy Spirit, whom the Father will send in my name, will teach you all things and will remind you of everything I have said to you. 27Peace I leave with you; my peace I give you. I do not give to you as the world gives. Do not let your hearts be troubled and do not be afraid.
> 28"You heard me say, 'I am going away and I am coming back to you.' If you loved me, you would be glad that I am going to the Father, for the Father is greater than I. 29I have told you now before it happens, so that when it does happen you will believe. 30I will not speak with you much longer, for the prince of this world is coming. He has no hold on me, 31but the world must learn that I love the Father and that I do exactly what my Father has commanded me. Come now; let us leave.

25-26 Jesus resumed his teaching on the Holy Spirit because Judas's question evoked it. Through the Spirit Jesus' presence would be perpetuated among them. The phrase "in my name" used previously in vv.13, 14, means that the Spirit would be Jesus' officially delegated representative to act in his behalf. Just as Jesus himself demonstrated the personality and character of God to men, so after his departure the Holy Spirit would make the living Christ real to his followers. The function of the Spirit is teaching. He instructs from within and recalls to the memory what Jesus taught. The Spirit will, therefore, impress the commandments of Jesus on the minds of his disciples and thus prompt them to obedience.

27 The peace Jesus spoke of could not be exemption from conflict and trial. Jesus himself was "troubled" (12:27) by the impending Crucifixion. The peace he spoke of is the calmness of confidence in God. Jesus had this peace because he was sure of the Father's love and approval. The world can give only false peace, which mostly comes from the ignorance of peril or self-reliance. Jesus, fully aware of the distressing suffering confronting him, had such confidence in the purpose and power of the Father that he moved forward unhesitatingly to meet the crisis without fear. His peace would be the source of courage for the disciples. With his promise of peace, he repeated the words of comfort he had spoken in reply to Peter's question: "Do not let your hearts be troubled and do not be afraid" (cf. v.1). The disciples must have continued to show their dismay as they contemplated Jesus' departure.

28 In concluding this discourse, Jesus reminded them that he was about to return to the Father and that he had forewarned them so that their faith might not be disrupted by his removal. The statement "the Father is greater than I" refers to position rather than essence. Jesus was speaking from the standpoint of his humanity, the incarnate state he assumed in order to fulfill the purposes of redemption. He had already acknowledged that "the Son can do nothing by himself; he can do only what he sees his Father doing" (John 5:19). The numerous statements that the Father had sent him confirm that Jesus was acting under authority and was obligated to fulfill the Father's commands.

29 In this instance "believe" is Jesus' own word, not the author's interpretation. Throughout the Gospel the necessity of believing is emphasized (1:50; 3:12, 15; 4:21, 41; 5:24, 44, 46; 6:29, 35, 47, 64; 7:38; 8:24, 45; 9:35; 10:38; 11:25, 41; 12:37, 44; 13:19; 14:1, 11; 16:31; 17:20; 20:27). Jesus insisted that acceptance of his person is pivotal to spiritual experience.

"Believe" (*pisteusēte*) is an aorist subjunctive, which normally indicates the beginning of an action. After the previous statements that the disciples had believed (1:50; 2:11; 6:69), such a construction seems inconsistent. Nevertheless the final arrest and death they witnessed would undoubtedly shake their faith to its foundations, and Jesus wished to prepare them for the strain this crisis would place on them.

30–31 "The prince of this world" refers to Satan. Jesus was constantly aware of Satan's hostile presence and was preparing for his last attack. This Gospel makes no mention of the temptation of Jesus that is recorded in the Synoptics (Matt 4:1–11; Mark 1:12; Luke 4:1–13). Luke, however, indicates that the temptation was not Jesus' sole conflict with the devil, for he says, "When the devil had finished all this tempting, he left him until an opportune time" (Luke 4:13). Luke does not define what that "opportune time" was, but there could scarcely have been a more favorable moment for pressure than when Jesus was confronted with the final issue of his life. The betrayal by Judas, the frustration of human hopes, the disappointment of apparent failure, the agony of death—these would make him especially susceptible to suggestion or temptation. Jesus did not fear Satan because Satan had no claim on him. There was nothing in Jesus' character or action that could be used against him. Satan had no valid accusation that could be used as leverage to divert Jesus from the will of his Father. His obedience had been perfect, and he intended to complete the Father's purpose irrespective of what it might cost him.

At this point Jesus proposed leaving the upper room. Whether chs. 15–17 were spoken en route to Gethsemane or whether he and the disciples lingered while he finished the discussion is not plain; but in either case the words conclude the open dialogue.

Notes

30 The NIV translation "has no hold on me" does not seem to carry the full meaning of the text. The KJV "hath nothing in me" is absolutely literal, but it does not express the sense in modern idiom. "Has nothing on me" might be colloquial, but it would probably be a closer approximation to the meaning.

2. *The discourse on relations* (15:1–27)

In this section of the Farewell Discourse, Jesus dealt with three relationships that involve the disciples: (1) their relationship with him, (2) their relationship with one another, and (3) their relationship with the world around them. Jesus knew his disciples would constitute a distinct body or community with a definite function, and he wished to prepare them for the change his departure would make in their manner of living. Viewed from the standpoint of the writer and his time, this section previews the church and its development in the postresurrection period, though the word "church" does not appear here.

a. *The relation of the disciples to Christ*

15:1–11

> [1]"I am the true vine and my Father is the gardener. [2]He cuts off every branch in me that bears no fruit, while every branch that does bear fruit he trims clean so that it will be even more fruitful. [3]You are already clean because of the word I have spoken to you. [4]Remain in me, and I will remain in you. No branch can bear fruit by itself; it must remain in the vine. Neither can you bear fruit unless you remain in me.
>
> [5]"I am the vine; you are the branches. If a man remains in me and I in him, he will bear much fruit; apart from me you can do nothing. [6]If anyone does not remain in me, he is like a branch that is thrown away and withers; such branches are picked up, thrown into the fire and burned. [7]If you remain in me and my words remain in you, ask whatever you wish, and it will be given you. [8]This is to my Father's glory, that you bear much fruit, showing yourselves to be my disciples.
>
> [9]"As the Father has loved me, so have I loved you. Now remain in my love. [10]If you obey my commands, you will remain in my love, just as I have obeyed my Father's commands and remain in his love. [11]I have told you this so that my joy may be in you and that your joy may be complete.

The first of these relationships is primary, for the very existence of the group depended on the union of each individual with Christ. To illustrate it, Jesus used the analogy (or parable) of the vine. Viticulture was one of the common features of Palestinian life and would have been familiar to the disciples. It is possible that if the text of this discourse was spoken as they walked from the upper room in Jerusalem down into the Kidron Valley and across to the Mount of Olives, they could have seen the great golden vine, the national emblem of Israel, on the front of the temple. This symbolism has its precedent in the OT. Psalm 80 refers to Israel as a vine: "You brought a vine out of Egypt; you drove out the nations and planted it. You cleared the ground for it, and it took root and filled the land" (vv.8–9). An even better example is found in Isaiah 5:1–2, 7:

> My loved one had a vineyard
>   on a fertile hillside.
> He dug it up and cleared it of stones
>   and planted it with the choicest vines.
> He built a watchtower in it
>   and cut out a winepress as well.
> Then he looked for a crop of good grapes,
>   but it yielded only bad fruit. . . .
> The vineyard of the Lord Almighty
>   is the house of Israel,
> and the men of Judah
>   are the garden of his delight.

1 Jesus, using the vine metaphor, expanded its scope to all believers and individualized its application. In adapting it to the immediate situation, he stressed certain features. The first was that there is a genuine stock. The major essential in horticulture is to plant

the right kind of vine or tree in order to assure the proper quality of fruit. No fruit can be better than the vine that produces it. Jesus said, "I am the true vine." Unless the believer is vitally connected with him, the quality of his fruitfulness will be unacceptable. There may be many branches, but if they are to bear the right kind of fruit, they must be a part of the real vine.

The second feature is that God the Father is the gardener (*geōrgos*). The noun is quite general and really means "farmer," though here it is applied to an expert in growing grapes. Success in raising any crop depends largely on the skill of the farmer or gardener. The relation of the believer to God is that of the vine to the owner of the vineyard. He tends it, waters it, and endeavors to protect it and cultivate it so that it will produce its maximum yield.

2 Another emphasis is on pruning. Two aspects are noted: the removal of dead wood and the trimming of live wood so that its potential for fruitbearing will be improved. The verb translated "cut off" (*aireō*) means literally "to lift up" or "to take away"; the second, "trims clean" (*kathaireō*), a compound of the first, means "to cleanse" or "to purify." Here the translation "cut off" and "trim" is accurate, though it represents a special application of a more general term. Pruning is necessary for any vine. Dead wood is worse than fruitlessness, for dead wood can harbor disease and decay. An untrimmed vine will develop long rambling branches that produce little fruit because most of the strength of the vine is given to growing wood. The vine-grower is concerned that the vine be healthy and productive. The caring process is a picture of the divine dealing with human life. God removes the dead wood from his church and disciplines the life of the believer so that it is directed into fruitful activity.

3 "Clean" recalls Jesus' statement to the disciples at the footwashing: "And you are clean, though not every one of you" (John 13:10). There he singled out Judas, who was consciously and deliberately planning to betray him. Jesus did not equate "clean" with "perfect" but rather with sincere devotion that unites others to him as branches are united to the vine. Judas was an example of a branch that was cut off.

The means by which pruning or cleaning is done is the Word of God. It condemns sin; it inspires holiness; it promotes growth. As Jesus applied the words God gave him to the lives of the disciples, they underwent a pruning process that removed evil from them and conditioned them for further service.

4 Continued production depends on constant union with the source of fruitfulness. Branches that are severed from the parent stock may produce leaves temporarily, but inevitably they will wither because there is no source of life to sustain them; and they will never bear fruit. The effectiveness of the believer depends on his receiving the constant flow of life from Christ.

5 Fruitbearing is not only possible but certain if the branch remains in union with the vine. Uniformity of quantity and quality are not promised. But if the life of Christ permeates a disciple, fruit will be inevitable.

6 Failure to maintain a vital connection brings its own penalty—rejection and useless-ness. NIV translates this verse as most other versions do: "Like a branch that is thrown away." The Greek text contains the definite article: "Like *the* branch that is thrown away." Morris observes that the use of the definite article "the" (*to*) with "branch" (*klema*) may imply that it refers to the person who did not abide in the vine at the outset (NIC, p. 671, n. 17). Possibly it could be a reference to Judas Iscariot (cf. John 17:12). The indefiniteness of subject that characterizes the passive verb *exēranthē* ("withers" NIV) and the use of the plural "branches" in the second part of the sentence indicate Jesus' intent to show that fruitfulness is normal for believers. An absolutely fruitless life is prima facie evidence that one is not a believer. Jesus left no place among his followers for fruitless disciples. The aorist verbs translated "is thrown away" and "withers" refer to accomplished action in the past. They are used here to emphasize the immediacy and finality of action.

7 The connection is maintained by obedience and prayer. To remain in Christ and to allow his words to remain in oneself means a conscious acceptance of the authority of his word and a constant contact with him by prayer. The prayer request must be related to a definite need and must be for an object Jesus himself would desire. He was evidently referring back to the counsel in the preceding part of the discourse: "You may ask me for anything in my name, and I will do it" (John 14:14). He was not promising to gratify every chance whim. But so long as the believer was seeking the Lord's will in his life, Jesus would grant every request that would help accomplish this end.

8 The proof of discipleship is fruitbearing. This statement coincides with Jesus' teaching in the synoptic Gospels: "By their fruit you will recognize them" (Matt 7:20; cf. Luke 6:43–44). Just as Jesus glorified God by his life, so the disciples would glorify God by theirs.

9–11 Love is the relationship that unites the disciples to Christ as branches are united to a vine. Two results stem from this relationship: obedience and joy. Obedience marks the cause of their fruitfulness; joy is its result. Jesus intended that the disciples' lives should be both spontaneous and happy rather than burdensome and boring. Obedience in carrying out his purpose would be a guarantee of success, for Jesus never planned failure for his disciples. Joy logically follows when the disciples realize that the life of Christ in them is bringing fruit—something they could never produce in their own strength.

Notes

1 The adjective ἀληθινός (*alēthinos*) means "true" or "real" in the sense of original rather than derivative, or genuine rather than imitation. The related adjective ἀληθής (*alēthēs*) means "true" in opposition to that which is false or counterfeit. By this usage Jesus asserted that there may be other vines, but he is the only genuine and original stock.

b. *The relation of the disciples to one another*

15:12–17

12My command is this: Love each other as I have loved you. 13Greater love has no one than this, that one lay down his life for his friends. 14You are my friends if you do what I command. 15I no longer call you servants, because a servant does not know his master's business. Instead, I have called you friends, for everything that I learned from my Father I have made known to you. [16]You did not choose me, but I chose you to go and bear fruit—fruit that will last. Then the Father will give you whatever you ask in my name. [17]This is my command: Love each other.

12–13 Jesus repeated his command to "love each other" (cf. 13:34) because he knew that the future of the work among men depended on the disciples' attitude toward one another. His stress on love had been underscored earlier in this discourse (14:15, 21, 23, 28). Unity instead of rivalry, trust instead of suspicion, obedience instead of self-assertion must rule the disciples' common labors. The measure of their love for one another is that of his love for them (cf. 13:34), which would be further demonstrated by his forthcoming sacrifice. John caught the meaning of the statement and repeated it in his First Epistle: "This is how we know what love is: Jesus Christ laid down his life for us. And we ought to lay down our lives for our brothers" (1 John 3:16).

14–15 Again Jesus defined friendship in terms of obedience. Christian friendship is more than a casual acquaintance; it is a partnership of mutual esteem and affection (14:21). Jesus elevated the disciples above mere tools and made them partners in his work. A slave is never given a reason for the work assigned to him; he must perform it because he has no other choice. The friend is a confidant who shares the knowledge of his superior's purpose and voluntarily adopts it as his own. Jesus declared that he had revealed to the disciples all that the Father had given to him. The disclosure of the mind of God concerning his career and theirs would give them assurance that they were engaged in the right task and that God would ultimately bring it to a successful conclusion.

16–17 The disciples had not followed Jesus by some chance impulse; they had been chosen. He had invited them to interview him (1:39), he had promised to reshape them to his requirements (v.42), and he had summoned them to follow him (v.43). His miracles had clinched their original faith (2:11), and he had solicitously pleaded with them not to forsake him when many had departed from him (6:66–67). At that time he said that he had chosen them (v.70). He claimed them as his peculiar flock (10:27) and asserted that they would never perish (v.28). He expected that they would fulfill his purpose for them and that their work would be enduring. For this reason he urged them to maintain the relationship of love for one another that would facilitate the fulfullment of his hopes. Again he emphasized the need of prayer for the continuation of their mission: "Then the Father will give you whatever you ask in my name" (15:16; cf. 14:26). The effectiveness of prayer is linked to fruitbearing, which, in turn, is linked to obedience (vv.10, 14). He repeated the command to love one another, for in seeking to be obedient to the Lord and to be fruitful, it is possible to forget the brethren.

c. *The relation of the disciples to the world*

15:18–27

[18]"If the world hates you, keep in mind that it hated me first. [19]If you belonged to the world, it would love you as its own. As it is, you do not belong to the world, but I have chosen you out of the world. That is why the world hates you. [20]Remember the words I spoke to you: 'No servant is greater than his master.' If they persecuted me, they will persecute you also. If they obeyed my teaching, they will obey yours also. [21]They will treat you this way because of my name, for they do

not know the One who sent me. 22If I had not come and spoken to them, they would not be guilty of sin. Now, however, they have no excuse for their sin. 23He who hates me hates my Father as well. 24If I had not done among them what no one else did, they would not be guilty of sin. But now they have seen these miracles, and yet they have hated both me and my Father. 25But this is to fulfill what is written in their Law: 'They hated me without reason.'

26"When the Counselor comes, whom I will send to you from the Father, the Spirit of truth who goes out from the Father, he will testify about me; 27but you also must testify, for you have been with me from the beginning.

18 The term "world" (*kosmos*) has several uses in the Johannine writings. It may refer to the universe as the object of creation (1:10), the materialistic order that allures men from God (1 John 2:15–16), or mankind in general as the object of God's love (3:16). Here it refers to the mass of unbelievers who are indifferent or hostile to God and his people. Jesus reminded the disciples that in spite of the fact that he had come on an errand of love, the world at large hated him. The perfect tense of the verb "hate" (*memisēken*) implies that the world's hatred is a fixed attitude toward him—an attitude that carries over to his disciples as well. The world assumes this attitude because it rejects all who do not conform to its life style.

19–20 Jesus' choice of the disciples had set them apart for a different kind of life and for a different purpose. Therefore, the world would exclude them. Jesus' choice was also the guarantee that the lives of his disciples would have permanent value, but it did not guarantee immunity from attack. Jesus could promise them nothing more than what he himself had received.

21 There are two reasons for the obstinate attitude of the world. The first is ignorance: "They do not know the One who sent me." The world has no proper concept of (*ouk oidasin*, "they do not know") God. Consequently, the world cannot evaluate adequately the messenger whom he sent. Compare the statement of Paul: "Since they did not think it worthwhile to retain the knowledge of God, he gave them over to a depraved mind, to do what ought not to be done" (Rom 1:28). This ignorance is both intellectual and spiritual.

22 A second reason is resentment of Jesus' claims and standards. Both by his life and words he rebukes human sin and condemns it. He uncovers the inner corruption and hypocrisy of men, and they react violently to the disclosure. He strips away all excuses and exposes their selfishness and rebellion against God.

23 The connection between Jesus and the Father appears as strongly in this passage as it did in the argument of ch. 5. Jesus said that those who hated him would hate the Father, also. He and the Father belong in the same category; neither can be accepted or rejected without the other.

24 The sin of Jesus' enemies was both deliberate and inexcusable. Accredited by the miracles that he performed, he brought condemnation on them (cf. John 9:30–33, 39–41). His foes had heard his words and had witnessed his supporting miracles. Consequently, their reaction against him could not have been attributed to ignorance of his words or to lack of evidence substantiating them.

25 To explain his position and express his response, Jesus quoted from Psalm 69: "Those who hate me without reason outnumber the hairs of my head" (v.4). The quotation is partial. No doubt Jesus wished to emphasize only the phrase "without reason." The irony of his quotation is clear: the men who posed as the champions of the Law were fulfilling the prophecy concerning the enemies of God's servant.

26 In response to this attitude of hatred there must be a continuing witness to the love and grace of Christ. The last two verses of this chapter define the expected action of the disciples who will maintain the testimony of Jesus after he has left the earth. He completed the list of witnesses of ch. 5 (vv.31-40) by adding the witness of the Holy Spirit, whose ministry he had already partially described (14:16-17, 26), and also the witness of the disciples themselves.

27 The verb "testify" (*martureite*) could be indicative, as ASV translates it, or imperative, as NIV indicates by the insertion of "must." The latter translation is probably preferable since the whole discourse is instructional and preparatory to a new ministry for the disciples. "From the beginning" probably refers to the beginning of Jesus' public ministry.

Later, when the disciples felt that it was necessary to choose a successor for Judas Iscariot, one requirement was that of having belonged to the company of disciples "the whole time that the Lord Jesus went in and out among [them], beginning from John's baptism to the time when Jesus was taken up" (Acts 1:21-22). For the important task of witnessing to Jesus and his message, one must have complete experiential knowledge of his person. The apostles were committed to the transmission of sober facts; they were not creating a fictional legend. The coupling of the witness of the Spirit with that of the disciples defines their reciprocal relationship. Without the witness of the Spirit, the disciples' witness would be powerless; without the disciples' witness, the Spirit would be restricted in his means of expression.

3. The discourse on revelation (16:1-33)

a. The revelation of rejection

16:1-4

> ¹"All this I have told you so that you will not go astray. ²They will put you out of the synagogue; in fact, a time is coming when anyone who kills you will think he is offering a service to God. ³They will do such things because they have not known the Father or me. ⁴I have told you this, so that when the time comes you will remember that I warned you. I did not tell you this at first because I was with you.

1-2 Chapter 16 is a discussion of the revelation Jesus intended to give his disciples preparatory to their coming mission. He linked it with the preceding section of his final discourse by sharpening the warning he had already given to them concerning the hatred of the world. He applied this revelation particularly to their local conditions and predicted that they would suffer excommunication from the synagogue and even death. The episode of the healing of the blind man furnishes a graphic analogy, for he was expelled from the synagogue because of his defense of Jesus (9:22, 34). The raising of Lazarus so disturbed the Jews that they tried to kill both Jesus and Lazarus (12:10). While

Jesus was with the disciples, he could shelter and direct them. They needed to realize, however, that even his resurrection would not be sufficiently convincing to his enemies to remove the hatred that existed between them and his followers.

3 Jesus attributed the action of his foes to ignorance, not the ignorance of intellectual knowledge, but the lack of a personal experience of God and Christ. Their attitude was determined by who they thought Jesus was, and consequently by who they thought God was, rather than by actual contact with either. So warped had that attitude become that their contact with Jesus had generated hate for both himself and the Father (John 15:24). The principle is well summarized by Jesus' own words: "If then the light within you is darkness, how great is that darkness!" (Matt 6:23).

4 It may well be that this particular utterance of Jesus was reported by John because of the pressing need for courage in the church of his day. The Apocalypse indicates that there was a wide break between the church and the synagogue at the end of the first century (Rev 2:9; 3:9) and that those who professed to believe in Jesus were completely disowned by their Jewish compatriots. John's use of the term "the Jews" seems to confirm this.

b. *The revelation of the Holy Spirit*

16:5–15

> 5"Now I am going to him who sent me, yet none of you asks me, 'Where are you going?' 6Because I have said these things, you are filled with grief. 7But I tell you the truth: It is for your good that I am going away. Unless I go away, the Counselor will not come to you; but if I go, I will send him to you. 8When he comes, he will convict the world of guilt in regard to sin and righteousness and judgment: 9in regard to sin, because men do not believe in me; 10in regard to righteousness, because I am going to the Father, where you can see me no longer; 11and in regard to judgment, because the prince of this world now stands condemned.
> 12"I have much more to say to you, more than you can now bear. 13But when he, the Spirit of truth, comes, he will guide you into all truth. He will not speak on his own; he will speak only what he hears, and he will tell you what is yet to come. 14He will bring glory to me by taking from what is mine and making it known to you. 15All that belongs to the Father is mine. That is why I said the Spirit will take from what is mine and make it known to you.

5–6 The time had come for a new revelation. Previously Jesus had been with the disciples to counsel them and answer their questions. Now, in view of his imminent removal, they needed someone to take his place. He revealed to them the coming of the Holy Spirit, whom he had already mentioned in the general discourse (14:16–17, 26; 15:26). The statement "none of you asks me, 'Where are you going?' " seems incongruous with Peter's question in the earlier part of the discourse (13:36). At that point Peter's question was casual, and neither he nor the other disciples pressed the issue to ascertain what Jesus' plans really were. There was little concern about his future; they were interested mainly in their own future. They were sorrowful because they would lose him. So they made no inquiry about the reasons for his departure nor about the objectives he might wish to attain.

7 Jesus told the disciples that his separation from them was in their best interest. As long as he was with them in person, his work was localized; and it would be impossible to

communicate with them equally at all times and in all places. The coming of the "Counselor" would equip them for a wider and more potent ministry.

8 Three major aspects of the ministry of the Holy Spirit are described in vv.8-15:
1. To the world—conviction of sin, righteousness, and judgment.
2. To the disciples—direction and truth.
3. To Jesus—revealing him more perfectly to and through those who represent him.

The key to this first aspect of the Spirit's ministry is the word "convict" (*elenchō*). KJV translates it "reprove," but that rendering is not strong enough. The word is a legal term that means to pronounce a judicial verdict by which the guilt of the culprit at the bar of justice is defined and fixed. The Spirit does not merely accuse men of sin, he brings to them an inescapable sense of guilt so that they realize their shame and helplessness before God. This conviction applies to three particular areas: sin, righteousness, and judgment. The Spirit is the prosecuting attorney who presents God's case against humanity. He creates an inescapable awareness of sin so that it cannot be dismissed with an excuse or evaded by taking refuge in the fact that "everybody is doing it." The Spirit's function is like that of Nathan the prophet, who said to David, "You are the man" (2 Sam 12:7), and compelled him to acknowledge his misdeeds. David was so convicted that he was reduced to a state of complete penitence: "Against you, you only, have I sinned and done what is evil in your sight" (Ps 51:4).

9 The essence of sin is unbelief, which is not simply a casual incredulity nor a difference of opinion; rather, it is a total rejection of God's messenger and message. A court can convict a man of murder, but only the Spirit can convict him of unbelief. Jesus insisted that sin was fundamentally repudiation of his message and his mission.

10 The second area in which the Spirit convicts people is righteousness. He enforces the absolute standard of God's character, to which all thought and action must be compared. Apart from a standard of righteousness, there can be no sin; and there must be an awareness of the holiness of God before a person will realize his own deficiency. There is an infinite gap between the righteousness of God and the sinful state of man that man himself cannot bridge. The first step toward salvation must be the awareness that a divine mediatorship is necessary.

The connection between righteousness and Jesus' return to the Father is not immediately clear. Probably it should be interpreted as meaning that his return to the right hand of God was a complete vindication of all he had done and consequently established him as the standard for all human righteousness. Apostolic preaching conveyed this concept. Peter's statement in Acts 3:14-15 conveys much the same idea: "You disowned the Holy and Righteous One and asked that a murderer be released to you. You killed the author of life, but God raised him from the dead." Whereas righteousness had previously been defined by precepts, it now has been revealed in the incarnate Son, who exemplified it perfectly in all his relationships. John crystallized this thought in his First Epistle: "In him is no sin" (1 John 3:5).

11 Judgment always occurs when an act or thought is evaluated by an absolute principle. Actions are judged by their accord with law or by their lack of conformity to it. When human sin is confronted by the righteousness of Christ, its condemnation is self-evident. In this context "judgment" refers to the condemnation of satanic self-will and rebellion by the obedience and love toward the Father exhibited by Jesus. The Cross was the utter condemnation and defeat of the "prince of this world." "Condemned" is in the perfect tense (*kekritai*), which expresses a settled state. Satan is already under judgment; the sentence is fixed and permanent. (For discussion of "the prince of this world," see comments on 14:30.)

12–13 Jesus told his disciples directly that the revelation to date was incomplete. They were not sufficiently mature to understand all he wished to impart. A second function of the Holy Spirit would be to lead them into the full comprehension of all he could give them. The Spirit would not present an independent message, differing from what they had already learned from him. They would be led further into the realization of his person and in the development of the principles he had already laid down. They would also be enlightened about coming events. He would unfold the truth as the disciples grew in spiritual capacity and understanding. In this promise lies the germinal authority of the apostolic writings, which transmit the revelation of Christ through his disciples by the work of the Holy Spirit. He would conduct them (*hodēgeō*) into the unknown future as a guide directs those who follow him into unfamiliar territory.

14–15 The third function of the Spirit is to glorify Christ. His chief purpose is not to make himself prominent but to magnify the person of Jesus. The Spirit interprets and applies the character and teaching of Jesus to the disciples and by so doing makes him central to their thinking. He makes God a reality to people.

c. The revelation of Jesus' reappearance

16:16–24

> [16]"In a little while you will see me no more, and then after a little while you will see me."
> [17]Some of his disciples said to one another, "What does he mean by saying, 'In a little while you will see me no more, and then after a little while you will see me,' and 'Because I am going to the Father'?" [18]They kept asking, "What does he mean by 'a little while'? We don't understand what he is saying."
> [19]Jesus saw that they wanted to ask him about this, so he said to them, "Are you asking one another what I meant when I said, 'In a little while you will see me no more, and then after a little while you will see me'? [20]I tell you the truth, you will weep and mourn while the world rejoices. You will grieve, but your grief will turn to joy. [21]A woman giving birth to a child has pain because her time has come; but when her baby is born she forgets the anguish because of her joy that a child is born into the world. [22]So with you: Now is your time of grief, but I will see you again and you will rejoice, and no one will take away your joy. [23]In that day you will no longer ask me anything. I tell you the truth, my Father will give you whatever you ask in my name. [24]Until now you have not asked for anything in my name. Ask and you will receive, and your joy will be complete.

16 Jesus' remark "In a little while you will see me no more, and then after a little while you will see me" was obscure to his disciples and is still enigmatic to the reader of this Gospel. His prediction of disappearance refers to his death, but to what does the second appearance refer? He did not have in mind a coming in the person of the Holy Spirit because he had emphasized the distinction between himself and the Spirit and between their respective ministries. The disciples were confused by his language, both by the concept of his going to the Father and by the time element involved. The best solution seems to be that he was referring to the Resurrection, which would take place "a little while" after he had left them.

17–18 The two problems that vexed the disciples were the prediction of disappearance and then reappearance after a short interval and the concept of "going to the Father." The second was an allusion to his words recorded in John 14:28. The disciples had not yet established the mental perspective Jesus wished them to have and were thinking only in terms of the present situation. The use of the imperfect tense in "kept asking" (*elegon*) shows that they must have held a consultation among themselves about it and that the discourse did not proceed as an uninterrupted lecture. Apparently it was a casual conversation with periods of silence on Jesus' part.

19–22 The subsequent narrative develops the postresurrection period as a time in which the disciples' fears were quelled, their doubts dispelled, and their commission confirmed. Jesus compared their parting to the painful birth of a child, which, when fully accomplished, brings joy. The disciples were disappointed because the kingdom had not come; and they were distressed because of the calamity that was about to overtake Jesus, in which they all would share. The "world" would rejoice that he had been removed and would pride itself in a victory, but the disciples would mourn the untimely loss of their leader. In his resurrection, however, the conditions would be reversed, and their lamentations would be transformed into joy because he would return to them.

On the words "ask" and "asking," see Notes, p. 161.

23–24 The verb "ask" (*erōtaō*) in the phrase "in that day you will no longer ask me anything" means "to ask a question" rather than "to request a favor." While the sense is somewhat obscure, since the verb came to mean "to request of an equal," Jesus may have meant that at his reappearance after the Resurrection the truth of his claims and the status of his person would be self-evident. At that time the disciples would no longer question him as one of their number but would present their petitions to the Father in his name (cf. 14:13). As his disciples they would be eligible for the Father's response to their needs.

d. *The revelation of the Father*

16:25–33

> 25"Though I have been speaking figuratively, a time is coming when I will no longer use this kind of language but will tell you plainly about my Father. 26In that day you will ask in my name. I am not saying that I will ask the Father on your behalf. 27No, the Father himself loves you because you have loved me and have believed that I came from God. 28I came from the Father and entered the world; now I am leaving the world and going back to the Father."
>
> 29Then Jesus' disciples said, "Now you are speaking clearly and without figures of speech. 30Now we can see that you know all things and that you do not even need to have anyone ask you questions. This makes us believe that you came from God."
>
> 31"You believe at last!" Jesus answered. 32"But a time is coming, and has come, when you will be scattered, each to his own home. You will leave me all alone. Yet I am not alone, for my Father is with me.
>
> 33"I have told you these things, so that in me you may have peace. In this world you will have trouble. But take heart! I have overcome the world."

25 Jesus had used figurative or parabolic language to the disciples because of their spiritual immaturity. After the Resurrection, he would be at liberty to speak plainly about the Father. Little is said in the Gospels concerning the instruction Jesus imparted to the disciples during the forty days prior to his ascension. However, it is probable that during this period he gave them much of the teaching that was reflected in their later preaching and writing (Acts 1:3).

26–27 It would be unnecessary for Jesus to make requests on their behalf, for they would be able to present their own petitions. The phrase "in my name" recurs frequently in this farewell discourse (14:13–14, 26; 16:23–24, 26) and indicates Jesus' sponsorship of the disciples. Their standing with God will depend on his merits. Because of his work they will be able to approach the Father directly with their petitions. The relation Jesus had established with the disciples became the ground for their direct relationship with the Father. Because they had committed themselves to him and had "believed" (*pepisteukate*), the ground of this relationship was fixed.

28–30 Jesus' declaration that he had come from the Father and was about to return to the Father satisfied their inquiry. They felt that he was no longer talking in riddles. Their response to Jesus' straightforward declaration was a further confession of belief. They implied that their questions to him had been occasioned by their bewilderment over his figurative language. The direct statement he had just made clarified their understanding and eliminated the need for further questioning. In the light of that understanding they reaffirmed their belief that he had come from God.

31–32 Jesus was skeptical of the firmness of the disciples' avowed belief (NIV mg.). He was completely aware of their impending failure. Already he had expressed the same apprehension to Simon Peter, when the latter protested that he would be loyal regardless of whatever the other disciples did (John 13:37; cf. Matt 26:33–35; Mark 14:29–31; Luke 22:33–34). "You will leave me all alone" reveals Jesus' disappointment and emotional tension. The sympathy and support of these men, imperfect as they were, meant much to him. Nevertheless, his chief resource was the Father, whose purpose he came to fulfill and by whose power he was able to execute it.

33 Jesus imparted to his disciples the information concerning his death and his provision for them that they might be calm and confident in the face of disillusionment and apparent disaster. "Peace" reiterates the statement of John 14:27: "Peace I leave with you; my peace I give you." Even in the hour of his greatest suffering he had an unshakable confidence in the victorious purpose of God. Jesus did not overlook the trial that would affect them as well as himself, for that was inevitable in a world alienated from God. He did proclaim victory over it.

Notes

19–26 In this general passage the synonyms ἐρωτάω (*erōtaō*) and αἰτέω (*aiteō*) are used interchangeably.

16:19—"Jesus saw that they wanted to *ask* him about this" (ἐρωτᾶν, *erōtan*).

16:19—"Are you *asking* one another" (ζητεῖτε, *zēteite*).

16:23—"You will no longer *ask* me anything" (ἐρωτήσετε, *erōtēsete*).
16:23—"My Father will give you whatever you *ask*" (αἰτήσητε, *aitēsēte*).
16:24—"Until now you have not *asked* for anything" (ἠτήσατε, *ētēsate*).
16:24—"*Ask* and you will receive" (αἰτεῖτε, *aiteite*).
16:26—"In that day you will *ask* in my name" (αἰτήσεσθε, *aitēsesthe*).
16:26—"I am not saying that I will *ask* the Father" (ἐρωτήσω, *erōtēsō*).

Ζητεῖτε (*zēteite*, 16:19) means simply "to investigate" or "interrogate" and is often translated "seek." Sometimes it connotes an argument. Ἐρωτάω (*erōtaō*, 16:19, 23, 26) does not refer to making a petition but to simple questioning between those who stand on equal footing. It implies that Jesus, as a human being, was open to dialogue and inquiry with others. His use of the term concerning himself and the Father again implies equality since his removal from the world would elevate him to a new relationship with God. Αἰτέω (*aiteō*, 16:23–24, 26) refers to making a petition for a favor rather than for an answer to a question and implies that the request is addressed to a superior. (For a full discussion, see Trench, pp. 143–46.)

C. *The Last Prayer* (17:1–26)

The prayer of Jesus recorded in this chapter is not identical with the prayer in Gethsemane reported in the Passion narrative of the synoptic Gospels (Matt 26:36–45; Mark 14:32–41; Luke 22:39–46). Its content is closely linked to that of the preceding chapters, especially those reputedly spoken in the upper room. The vocabulary, which contains such Johannine terms as "glory," "glorify," "sent," "believe," "world," "love," connects its content with the same topics in preceding sections of the Gospel. And Jesus' concern for his disciples makes more lucid his attitude toward them on previous occasions. The prayer is intended to summarize in Jesus' own words his relationship with the Father and the relationship he wished his disciples to maintain with him and the Father.

The prayer is divisible into three parts: (1) Jesus' prayer concerning himself (1–5), (2) his prayer for the disciples (6–19), and (3) his prayer for all believers present and future (20–26). Apparently the prayer was spoken either just before the small company left the room where they had eaten together or as they made their way out of the city, across the Kidron Valley to Gethsemane.

1. *The prayer concerning himself*

17:1–5

> [1]After Jesus said this, he looked toward heaven and prayed:
> "Father, the time has come. Glorify your Son, that your Son may glorify you. [2]For you granted him authority over all people that he might give eternal life to all those you have given him. [3]Now this is eternal life: that they may know you, the only true God, and Jesus Christ, whom you have sent. [4]I have brought you glory on earth by completing the work you gave me to do. [5]And now, Father, glorify me in your presence with the glory I had with you before the world began.

1 John recorded even the gesture of Jesus: "He lifted up his eyes" (lit. Gr.). This was a typical Jewish gesture of prayer, whether offered to God or to idols (Ps 121:1; 123:1; Ezek 33:25; Dan 4:34; John 11:41). The general conversation ended as Jesus began to talk to the Father. The prayer began with the announcement "The time has come." Jesus' consciousness of living by a "calendar" was manifest from the beginning of the Gospel. When Mary spoke to him at the wedding of Cana, evidently suggesting that he should

intervene in the tense social situation by manifesting his power, he informed her that his time had not yet come, (2:4). He did not present himself as the Messiah, for though he did perform a miracle, few knew what had taken place or who was responsible for the new supply of wine. When his brothers urged him to go to Jerusalem to gain publicity for himself, he refused to do so because "the right time has not yet come" (7:8). Twice in the prolonged controversy with his enemies Jesus escaped death because "his time had not yet come" (7:30; 8:20); but now he acknowledged that the time of crisis had arrived (cf. 12:23; 13:1). This announcement enhances the significance of the prayer because it becomes Jesus' evaluation of the purpose of his life, death, resurrection, and ascension.

The word "glorify" should be applied to the total complex of these events as the climax of the Incarnation. The Son glorified the Father by revealing in this act the sovereignty of God over evil, the compassion of God for men, and the finality of redemption for believers. It is the Johannine parallel to what Paul called the "mind" of Christ (Phil 2:5 KJV, translated in NIV as "attitude"). Jesus focused his entire career on fulfilling the Father's purpose and on delivering the Father's message. He now petitioned the Father to glorify him by returning him to the place he had before the world was created (v.5). The words accord with the statement of John 1:18: "God the only Son, who is at the Father's side [lit. 'in the bosom of the Father'], has made him known."

2–3 The two sentences following the petition are parenthetical and explanatory. The first (v.2) indicates the scope of the authority Christ exercised in his incarnate state. He was empowered to impart eternal life to those who had been given to him. This Gospel is replete with assertions that life is in Christ: "In him was life, and that life was the light of men" (1:4). "The Son of Man must be lifted up, that everyone who believes in him may have eternal life" (3:15–16). "The water I give him will become in him [who drinks it] a spring of water welling up to eternal life" (4:14). See also 5:21, 26; 6:33, 54; 10:10; 11:25; 14:6. These words and others like them emphatically express the central purpose of Jesus: to glorify the Father by imparting life to men.

The second sentence (v.3) defines the nature of eternal life. It is not described in chronological terms but by a relationship. Life is active involvement with environment; death is the cessation of involvement with the environment, whether it be physical or personal. The highest kind of life is involvement with the highest kind of environment. A worm is content to live in soil; we need not only the wider environment of earth, sea, and sky but also contact with other human beings. For the complete fulfillment of our being, we must know God. This, said Jesus, constitutes eternal life. Not only is it endless, since the knowledge of God would require an eternity to develop fully, but qualitatively it must exist in an eternal dimension. As Jesus said farther on in this prayer, eternal life would ultimately bring his disciples to a lasting association with him in his divine glory (v.24).

4–5 Although the final act of his career remained to be performed, Jesus asserted that he had completed his task. He took for granted that the last step would be taken. A clue to the proleptic assertion may be found in John 12:27–28: "For this very reason I came to this hour. Father, glorify your name." Though he was aware that he had the option of refusing the Cross and so escaping death, he had resolved irrevocably to complete the work for which he had been sent. To all intents and purposes it was already done. Though the obstacles were many and though the prospect was terrifying, Jesus never once faltered from doing the Father's will. He had one main petition: that the Father would receive him back to the glory he had relinquished to accomplish his task. This petition for a return to his pristine glory implies unmistakably his preexistence and equality with the Father. It confirms his claim that he and the Father are one (John 10:30).

2. *The prayer concerning the disciples*

17:6–19

6"I have revealed you to those whom you gave me out of the world. They were yours, you gave them to me and they have obeyed your word. 7Now they know that everything you have given me comes from you. 8For I gave them the words you gave me and they accepted them. They knew with certainty that I came from you, and they believed that you sent me. 9I pray for them. I am not praying for the world, but for those you have given me, for they are yours. 10All I have is yours, and all you have is mine. And glory has come to me through them. 11I will remain in the world no longer, but they are still in the world, and I am coming to you. Holy Father, protect them by the power of your name—the name you gave me—so that they may be one as we are one. 12While I was with them, I protected them and kept them safe by that name you gave me. None has been lost except the one doomed to destruction so that Scripture would be fulfilled.

13"I am coming to you now, but I say these things while I am still in the world, so that they may have the full measure of my joy within them. 14I have given them your word and the world has hated them, for they are not of the world any more than I am of the world. 15My prayer is not that you take them out of the world but that you protect them from the evil one. 16They are not of the world, even as I am not of it. 17Sanctify them by the truth; your word is truth. 18As you sent me into the world, I have sent them into the world. 19For them I sanctify myself, that they too may be truly sanctified.

By far the largest part of Jesus' prayer relates to the disciples. He was much more concerned about them than about himself. He was sure of the suffering that was inevitable and the victory that was certain. The disciples, however, were a variable quantity; in themselves they were likely to fail. He had already predicted that they would desert him (Matt 26:31; John 16:32). Nevertheless, he prayed for them with confidence that they would be kept by the Father's power and presented for a future ministry. Jesus gives the reasons for his confidence in the next three verses.

6–8 The disciples had been given to Jesus by the Father. The gift was irrevocable and the Father was able to guarantee it. Jesus had no doubt of the final outcome. The disciples were obedient; they had accepted the message Jesus gave them. In spite of much misunderstanding on their part, there is no evidence that those who were with Jesus in the upper room had rejected or doubted the truth he imparted to them. They may not have comprehended it instantly, as the text of John shows (2:22; 20:9). They recognized that Jesus' message came from God; and they accepted him as a messenger of God, as their own confession declared (16:30). From the outset of his ministry, the disciples had received him as the Messiah, and their conviction of his messiahship had grown progressively during the period of association with him. Now that the supreme test of their faith was impending, Jesus prayed that they might be preserved against the persecution that could separate them from him and from one another.

9 At this point, Jesus' intercession was confined to the Eleven who were present with him. He reminded the Father that these men were under his peculiar care. As in his prayer at Lazarus's grave, Jesus took for granted the concern of the Father for the immediate need and the provision he had already made in order to meet it.

10 Jesus' statement "All I have is yours, and all you have is mine" assumes his equality with the Father. Each has full title to the possessions of the other; they share the same interests and responsibilities. Jesus' words are a sample of the continued intercession that constitutes his present ministry (Rom 8:34).

11 Jesus asked for the continuation of the Father's protection of the disciples in the period of danger that lay ahead of them. The title "Holy Father" is unusual and is comparable to the phrase "Righteous Father" that appears in v.25. The holiness of God contrasts with the selfishness and evil of the world that confronted the disciples. On the basis of the holiness of God's character, Jesus requested the Father to preserve the disciples. The verb "protect" (*tēreō*) is generally used in John to mean "obey" in the sense of keeping commandments (8:51–52, 55; 14:15) or to "observe" the Sabbath (9:16). Here (17:11–12, 15) it is applied to persons in the sense of "preserve," with an implication of defense. "Name" stands for the power of God manifested in his person (cf. 5:43; 10:25; 12:28; 17:6, 26), for a name represents authoritatively the person it describes.

The unity mentioned here is not simply a unity achieved by legislation. It is a unity of nature because it is comparable to that of the Son and the Father. The unity of the church must spring from the common life that is imparted to all believers by the new birth; and it is manifested in their common love for Christ and for one another as they face a hostile world. The unity of the Son and the Father was manifested in the deep love that each sustained for the other and by the perfect obedience of the Son to the Father and the perfect response of the Father to the Son.

12 Jesus' request for the protection of the disciples was occasioned by the prospect of his leaving the world. They would still be remaining in it, exposed to its temptations and hostility. In reviewing his care of them to date, he used two different words: "protected" and "kept them safe." The former (*tēreō*) has been defined in the comment on the preceding verse; the latter (*phylassō*) means "to guard," "protect," or "observe conventions." Like other Johannine synonyms, the two may at times be used interchangeably, but there is a slight difference between them. *Tēreō* has the sense of protection by conservation; *phylassō*, by defense against external attack. Jesus stated that he had kept safely all the disciples except Judas. "The one doomed to destruction" (lit. "son of perdition") is a phrase used in only one other passage in the NT. In 2 Thessalonians 2:3 it is applied to the Antichrist. Because of this singular coincidence, some have assumed that the Antichrist will be Judas resurrected! More likely this phrase was a common Semitism denoting an abandoned character, one utterly lost and given over to evil. The language does not imply that Judas was a helpless victim who was destined to perdition against his will. Rather, it implies that, having made his decision, he had passed the point of no return; and, by so doing, he carried out what the Scriptures had indicated would happen. John does not identify the specific passage Jesus had in mind. A comparison with Peter's statement in Acts 1:20, after Judas's death, suggests that it was probably Psalm 69:25 or Psalm 109:6–8.

13 Jesus prayed not only for the safety of the disciples but also that they might have joy in spite of the coming conflict. The same sentiment had been expressed in the dialogue with them (15:11; 16:22, 24). There would be nothing in the attitude of the world to promote their joy; but, as with Jesus, their awareness of the approval of the Father and the consciousness of a task accomplished and the expectancy of glory would create true joy for them.

14 The very fact that the disciples received the message of God from Jesus differentiated them from the world at large. They had a different nature and a different affiliation. Such a radical contrast drew the hatred of the world, which always demands conformity to its viewpoint and practices. They had taken their stand with Jesus and would therefore be susceptible to the same rejection he had experienced.

15–16 Jesus did not, however, ask that they be removed from a disagreeable and dangerous environment. Like him, they had a mission to discharge and must remain to fulfill it, however perilous it might be. He did ask for protection for them from the evil one.

The declaration that "they are not of the world" gives the negative aspect of the previous prayer that they may be one as Jesus and the Father are one. The disciples' unity binds them to Christ and at the same time separates them from the world. John stresses the separation that results from difference of nature. This principle appears in the separation of antichrists from believers: "They went out from us, but they did not really belong to us" (1 John 2:19). The separation is inherent, not artificial.

17 "Sanctify" (*hagiazō*) means "to separate" or "to set apart," usually for some specially good purpose or use. Its derivative meaning thus becomes "dedicate" or "consecrate" and then "to revere" or "to purify." The believer is so changed by the working of God's Word in his life that he is separated from evil and to God. This new devotion, which results in separation from evil, produces purification of life and consecration to God's service. Since the Word of God is truth, it provides the unchanging standard for the course and character of life. The form of the expression "your word" raises the possibility that Jesus may have been referring to himself when he spoke. He had said that he was "the truth" (14:6); so as the Logos of God he embodied truth in its totality.

18 "Sent" implies equipment for a definite mission. Jesus united the disciples with himself in the work he began and expected them to continue. Just as the Father sent him with authority, so he gave them authority (cf. Matt 28:18–20); as he had come with a message of God's love and forgiveness, so they should proclaim the same; as he had come into danger and peril of death, so they would encounter the same problems; and as the Father had sent him to the victory of the Resurrection, so they could expect the same. His words include warning, commission, and encouragement.

19 In keeping with his words in v.17, Jesus did not mean that he intended to make himself more holy than he already was, when he said, "For their sakes I sanctify myself." Rather, he was devoting himself to God in the interest of his work for the disciples. His example of dedication to the will of the Father, demonstrated in his unswerving acceptance of the Cross, would be the standard for their sanctification.

The petitions of Jesus' prayer for the disciples define certain aspects of eternal life. The first is the authentic revelation of the Father in contrast to erroneous information or delusive myth. Jesus reinforced his claim to be the authorized revealer of the true God (v.6; cf. 1:18; 14:9–11). As his revelation was accepted, the disciples progressed to a knowledge of the Father and to a solid faith (v.8; cf. 16:25). This faith united them with Jesus so that they came under his protection and experienced security that eternal life imparts (v.12; cf. 10:28–29). Eternal life also implies sanctification—being set apart for the service of God.

Notes

15 The substantival adjective πονηροῦ (ponērou, "evil") may be either masculine or neuter. If the former, it means "from the evil person"; if the latter, "from the evil thing," or from evil as a principle. The allusions in the general context to Satan (13:2, 27; 14:30; 16:11) make the former rendering seem more fitting to this occasion.

17 "Your word" (ὁ λόγος ὁ σός, ho logos ho sos) is an unusual construction. Instead of using the genitive of the personal pronoun to express the idea of "your," the personal possessive pronoun is used, which generally emphasizes quality rather than possession alone. It implies that the "word" is peculiarly God's; it originates from him and is qualified by his personality rather than being a message that might originate with anyone but which he happened to give. If "word" (λόγος, logos) in this phrase is applied to Christ, the expression would be singularly appropriate because Jesus was the full and original expression of the Father's nature and mind and could have come only from him.

17, 19 Only the verb "sanctify" (ἁγιάζω, hagiazō) is used in John, perhaps because this Gospel emphasizes the act of sanctification rather than the process or quality. The verb (ἁγίασον, hagiason) in v.17 is aorist imperative, which speaks of an initial, and presumably complete, separation. In v.19 ἡγιασμένοι (hēgiasmenoi, "have been sanctified") is a perfect passive participle, which implies a fixed and final state. As Jesus used the word concerning himself, he may have been referring to the settled determination he had from eternity past (Rev 13:8) to carry out the Father's will, even to death. This act of sanctification by Christ would set apart his followers for all eternity.

3. The prayer concerning future believers

17:20–26

20"My prayer is not for them alone. I pray also for those who will believe in me through their message, 21that all of them may be one, Father, just as you are in me and I am in you. May they also be in us so that the world may believe that you have sent me. 22I have given them the glory that you gave me, that they may be one as we are one: 23I in them and you in me. May they be brought to complete unity to let the world know that you sent me and have loved them even as you have loved me.

24"Father, I want those you have given me to be with me where I am, and to see my glory, the glory you have given me because you loved me before the creation of the world.

25"Righteous Father, though the world does not know you, I know you, and they know that you have sent me. 26I have made you known to them, and will continue to make you known in order that the love you have for me may be in them and that I myself may be in them."

20 The last section of Jesus' prayer shows that he expected the failure of the disciples to be only temporary. The entire tone of the farewell discourse is built on the assumption that after the Resurrection they would renew their faith and carry on a new ministry in the power of the Holy Spirit. The provisions and warnings of the upper room discourse presuppose the continuation of Jesus' work through these men. It illumines his declara-

tion recorded by Matthew: "I will build my church" (Matt 16:18). Jesus expected the ministry of the Spirit in the disciples to result in adding more believers to their number. So his prayer includes all believers in all ages.

21 At this point, the burden of the prayer is for unity. Jesus had already stressed the need for mutual love that would bind them together for their common task. Now, foreseeing the addition of many more who would increase the diversity of temperaments, backgrounds, and interests, he made a special plea that all might be one. The standard is not an institutional but a personal unity: "Just as you are in me and I am in you. . . . that they may be one as we are one" (vv.21-22). He was not calling for uniformity, since he and the Father are distinct from each other and have different functions; nor was he calling for agreement in external opinion. He predicated that the unity would be one of nature; for he and the Father, while distinguishable in person, are one being. As previously stated, the new birth brings believers into the family of God by spiritual generation (1:12-13). The concept parallels the Pauline teaching on the body of Christ, that all believers belong by a vital rather than merely a formal relationship (1 Cor 12:12-13). The Johannine symbol of the vine in ch. 15 contains the same idea of a vital unity in which every separate branch is still an integral part of the one vine. The purpose of this unity is the maintenance of a convincing testimony before the world to the revelation of God in Christ and to his love for the disciples. Through the common witness and experience of the disciples, Jesus wished to establish the fact of his divine origin and of the love of God for men. The unity is another aspect of eternal life because where there is a common source of life there must be a common likeness of expression. As the central life of the vine appears in all the branches and makes them fruitful, so genuine eternal life imparted by Christ will unify his people.

22-23 The "glory" the Father had given Jesus was the triumphant task of redeeming men to God. As Hebrews states, he was "crowned with glory and honor because he suffered death" in the process of "bringing many sons to glory" (Heb 2:9-10). By sharing in his calling, they participate in his glory and are united with him and with one another. God and man are together involved in bringing the new creation into being. The effect of this united testimony is a confirmation of the divine mission of Jesus and of God's love for believers.

24 The final aspect of eternal life relates to ultimate destiny. The final attainment would be to be with Christ (cf. 14:3) and to see his glory. "See" (*theōrōsin*) in this context means more than to recognize by form; "observe" would be a better translation. The disciples had witnessed his incarnate life, which was a humiliation, voluntarily accepted for their sakes. Its process was epitomized by Jesus' action at the Last Supper, when he took the place of a servant to wash the disciples' feet (13:1-15). Now, on the eve of being "glorified," he desired that the disciples might see him as he really was. Perhaps the writer had this in mind when he wrote in his First Epistle, "'We shall be like him, for we shall see him as he is" (1 John 3:2). "Before the creation of the world" is a further assertion of Christ's preexistence. This shows that the binding power of unity in the Triune God is love.

25-26 The title "Righteous Father" parallels the title "Holy Father" in v.11. Both are unique and appear only in this prayer. The entire prayer is based on the righteousness of God, who will vindicate the Son by glorifying him. Jesus' revelation of God was

167

founded on personal knowledge and personal communion. When he spoke of God, it was on the basis of intimate acquaintance and not philosophical speculation. The essence of the revelation lay in the love of God, which Jesus exhibited toward the disciples. His purpose was to perfect his union with them, that they in turn might know the Father. Jesus wanted to include them in the inner fellowship of the Triune God.

IV. The Passion of the Word (18:1–20:31)

A. *The Arrest in Gethsemane*

18:1–11

> ¹When he had finished praying, Jesus left with his disciples and crossed the Kidron Valley. On the other side there was an olive grove, and he and his disciples went into it.
> ²Now Judas, who betrayed him, knew the place, because Jesus had often met there with his disciples. ³So Judas came to the grove, guiding a detachment of soldiers and some officials from the chief priests and Pharisees. They were carrying torches, lanterns and weapons.
> ⁴Jesus, knowing all that was going to happen to him, went out and asked them, "Who is it you want?"
> ⁵"Jesus of Nazareth," they replied.
> "I am he," Jesus said. (And Judas the traitor was standing there with them.) ⁶When Jesus said, "I am he," they drew back and fell to the ground.
> ⁷Again he asked them, "Who is it you want?"
> And they said, "Jesus of Nazareth."
> ⁸"I told you that I am he," Jesus answered. "If you are looking for me, then let these men go." ⁹This happened so that the words he had spoken would be fulfilled: "I have not lost one of those you gave me."
> ¹⁰Then Simon Peter, who had a sword, drew it and struck the high priest's servant, cutting off his right ear. (The servant's name was Malchus.)
> ¹¹Jesus commanded Peter, "Put your sword away! Shall I not drink the cup the Father has given me?"

1 Jesus and the disciples left the room where they had convened, descended from the city, crossed the Kidron Valley, and made their way up the lower slope of the Mount of Olives, which lay to the east of Jerusalem. The Kidron River is a winter torrent, dry in the summer, but a flowing stream during the winter and spring rains. It runs southward along the east side of the city and joins the Valley of Hinnom and the Tyropoeon Valley south of Jerusalem. Gethsemane, the name assigned to the olive grove on the side of the mountain where Jesus and his disciples went, means "oil press." The city was filled with visitors at the Passover season and would have had little room for lodging within its walls. Neither Jesus nor the disciples were wealthy; so they probably camped outdoors during their visit to the temple for the Passover Week. The site of the garden is still marked by a small grove of ancient trees.

2 Jesus often used the Garden of Gethsemane as a meeting place with his disciples (cf. Luke 22:39). Judas, probably having attempted to find Jesus at the house where he and the others ate the Last Supper, went to Gethsemane, expecting to locate him there.

3 The Greek word for "detachment of soldiers" (*speira*) has been traditionally rendered "cohort," from the Latin *cohors*, which denotes a tenth of a legion, or about six hundred men. The noun is accompanied by the definite article, which refers to some particular

168

band of men, perhaps the detachment connected with the Castle of Antonia, the Roman barracks in Jerusalem. The synoptic Gospels agree that the arrest was effected by a "crowd" (*ochlos*), which connotes an armed mob rather than an organized military guard (Matt 26:47; Mark 14:43). Luke uses the phrase "officers of the temple guard" (Luke 22:52), which would refer to the temple police rather than to Roman legionnaires. It is not impossible that the hysterical alarm of the priests caused them to ask aid from Pilate in arresting Jesus, since the temple police had failed on a previous occasion (John 7:32, 45–47). Pilate, knowing the volatile character of the Passover pilgrims, would probably have been disposed to granting such a request, though a full complement of six hundred men would hardly seem necessary. The torches and the lanterns were needed, as the arrest took place at night and would require a search in the darkness of the olive grove.

4–6 The author lays great emphasis on Jesus' consciousness of surrounding circumstances and his own destiny (cf. John 6:64; 13:1, 3, 11, 18). He was not taken unwillingly or by surprise. For a long time he had been aware of the plot against his life and, had he wished, he could have escaped. On at least two previous occasions he had withdrawn from the danger zone: once when he retreated beyond the Jordan into Perea (John 10:40) and again after the raising of Lazarus, when he moved into the desert region (11:54). Now "the time" had come (cf. 17:1). He did not wait to be apprehended but voluntarily confronted his enemies.

In the darkness of the garden they were not sure which man they wanted. So in answer to his question they replied, "Jesus of Nazareth." John omits the signal of Judas and mentions only Jesus' own statement for the identification. Jesus' reply startled the arresting party by its openness and readiness and possibly because it was like the claim he had made previously: "I am" (8:24, 28, 58). If it were intended as an assertion of deity, his calm demeanor and commanding presence temporarily unnerved his captors.

7–9 Jesus' chief intent seems not to have been to advance a claim but rather to shield the disciples. In a sense, he sacrificed himself for their safety. He had promised the Father that he would protect them (17:12), and he fulfilled his guarantee in the voluntary surrender of his life. The utterance in v.8 is a graphic illustration of the principle of substitutionary atonement that pervades this Gospel (cf. 1:29; 3:14–16; 10:11, 15–18; 12:32; 17:19).

10 The action of Peter illustrates the curious combination of loyalty and obtuseness that characterized him. Realizing that Jesus was endangered, Peter was courageous enough to come to his defense and risk his own safety by doing so. To this extent he justified his boastful promise that if all others should forsake Jesus, he would not (John 13:37; cf. Mark 14:29–31). Evidently Peter was excited and missed his aim, for he cut off the right ear of Malchus, the high priest's servant. The use of the definite article "the" with "servant" may indicate that Malchus was the special deputy of the high priest in this action and that he was in the forefront of confrontation. Someone in the apostolic band, presumably the writer, remembered the man and his name. This incidental recollection is a hint that the Johannine account rests on eyewitness testimony.

11 Jesus' command to Peter declared his disapproval of Peter's sudden and violent intervention. Had Jesus desired defense, he could have summoned angelic aid, but he did not do so (cf. Matt 26:52–53). "Shall I not drink the cup the Father has given me?" expresses both the necessity of his suffering and his absolute commitment to the fulfillment of the Father's purpose. The word "cup" connects this statement with the prayer in Gethsemane, which only the Synoptics record (Matt 26:42; Mark 14:36; Luke 22:42). Though the writer must have known of Jesus' struggle, he recorded only the outcome. Jesus accepted the Father's will and calmly moved on to its fulfillment.

B. *The Hearing Before Annas*

18:12-14, 19-24

12Then the detachment of soldiers with its commander and the Jewish officials arrested Jesus. They bound him 13and brought him first to Annas, who was the father-in-law of Caiaphas, the high priest that year. 14Caiaphas was the one who had advised the Jews that it would be good if one man died for the people.

19Meanwhile, the high priest questioned Jesus about his disciples and his teaching.

20"I have spoken openly to the world," Jesus replied. "I always taught in synagogues or at the temple, where all the Jews come together. I said nothing in secret. 21Why question me? Ask those who heard me. Surely they know what I said."

22When Jesus said this, one of the officials nearby struck him in the face. "Is that any way to answer the high priest?" he demanded.

23"If I said something wrong," Jesus replied, "testify as to what is wrong. But if I spoke the truth, why did you strike me?" 24Then Annas sent him, still bound, to Caiaphas the high priest.

12-14 With the willing surrender of Jesus, the arrest was complete. The "commander" (*chiliarchos*) was the officer in charge, possibly the executive of the Roman garrison in Jerusalem (cf. the use of the same term in Acts 22:24, 26, 27, 28; 23:17, 19, 22). The technical expression strengthens the impression that the Romans supported the action of the Jewish hierarchy. Jesus was taken at once to the residence of the high priest. Tradition places it on the south side of Jerusalem, just west of the Tyropoeon valley and not far from the city wall. Annas had served as high priest from A.D. 6 to 15, when he was deposed by the Roman procurator, Valerius Gratus. Four of Annas's sons were among those who succeeded him. His son-in-law, Caiaphas, held office from A.D. 18 until A.D. 36, within which period Jesus' active ministry occurred. Although others held the priestly office, Annas seems to have been the elder statesman and advisor, particularly for Caiaphas.

John's Gospel alone takes note of Christ's appearance before Annas. Luke suggests that some time may have elapsed between the interview with Annas and the confrontation with Caiaphas and the council because he locates the latter at "daybreak" (Luke 22:66). If Jesus were held in custody till the elders could be summoned to a meeting in the morning, it is quite possible that he was somewhere in the house of the high priest. The main hearing seems to have followed in the early hours of the morning, before the members of the Jewish tribunal. The hearing before Annas was probably a preliminary attempt to evaluate the case and enable them to formulate some sort of charge to lay before Pilate. As the elder statesman, Annas was regarded with great respect by his contemporaries and must have been considered an expert in religious matters. If it is assumed that the text is in its original order (see note), he is called "high priest" (as also is Caiaphas, 18:24). Since Luke speaks of "the high priesthood of Annas and Caiaphas" (Luke 3:2), it may be that while Caiaphas was the official priest recognized by the Roman government, Annas remained "the power behind the throne."

19 The questioning focused on Jesus' disciples and his teaching. The number and activity of the former would be important if subversion was suspected, and the teaching would be scrutinized for possible revolutionary elements.

20–21 Jesus had nothing to hide. He had so frequently and openly declared the principles of his kingdom that there would be many witnesses who could narrate in detail what he had taught. The interrogation by Annas was unnecessary because public testimony to Jesus' teaching and attitude would be easily available, especially in Jerusalem, where he had been speaking to crowds for several days.

22–24 Jesus' answer impressed one of the retainers as disrespectful to the high priest, and he struck Jesus in the face. The act was illegal. No sentence had been passed, and a prisoner was not subject to abuse, especially when uncondemned. In spite of Jesus' protest, nothing was done; and he was sent bound to Caiaphas. Just how far Jesus had to be transported from Annas to Caiaphas is not known. It is possible that they occupied rooms in the same building, in which case little time would be required for the transfer. John says nothing about the hearing before Caiaphas. The Synoptics indicate that it included an appearance before the council of the elders, who must have been specially summoned for the occasion (Matt 26:57–68; Mark 14:53–65: Luke 22:66–71).

Notes

12–27 The Sinaitic Syriac changes the order of these verses to vv.12–13, 24, 14–15, 19–23, 16–18, 25–27; a somewhat similar arrangement occurs in the Palestinian Syriac. Although this change of order would simplify the account and facilitate harmonization with the Synoptics, the textual evidence is not sufficient to support it. Morris comments that a general corruption of the original text into its present form is quite unlikely and that the change in the Sinaitic Syriac is probably a harmonizing expedient. The existing text does present a difficulty, but it is not insuperable (NIC, pp. 748–49).

C. *The Denial by Peter*

18:15–18, 25–27

[15]Simon Peter and another disciple were following Jesus. Because this disciple was known to the high priest, he went with Jesus into the high priest's courtyard, [16]but Peter had to wait outside at the door. The other disciple, who was known to the high priest, came back, spoke to the girl on duty there and brought Peter in.
[17]"Surely you are not another of this man's disciples?" the girl at the door asked Peter.
He replied, "I am not."
[18]It was cold, and the servants and officials stood around a fire they had made to keep warm. Peter also was standing with them, warming himself.
[25]As Simon Peter stood warming himself, he was asked, "Surely you are not another of his disciples?"
He denied it, saying, "I am not."
[26]One of the high priest's servants, a relative of the man whose ear Peter had cut off, challenged him, "Didn't I see you with him in the olive grove?" [27]Again Peter denied it, and at that moment a rooster began to crow.

15–16 The imperfect tense of the verb "to follow" (*ēkolouthei*) is descriptive. It implies that Peter and an unnamed disciple had traced Jesus and his captors back from Gethsemane over the Kidron Valley to the residence of the high priest in Jerusalem. The identity of the other disciple is not disclosed, nor does the account specify that it was "the disciple whom Jesus loved" (cf. 13:23; 19:26; 20:2–3; 21:20, 24). The association of the two, however, would favor that view since they appear together both at the Last Supper (13:23–24) and on the morning of the Resurrection (20:2–3). This anonymous disciple was known to the household of the high priest and readily obtained access for himself and Peter. The basis for this acquaintance is not explained. On the assumption that this disciple was John, it may be that the family had connections with the priesthood, either by business relationships or possibly by marital ties. Salome, the mother of John, was a sister of Mary, Jesus' mother (cf. John 19:25 with Mark 15:40), and would have been equally related to Elizabeth, whose husband, Zechariah, was a priest (Luke 1:36). The evidence is tenuous, but the author does exhibit a considerable knowledge of Jerusalem and the events that took place there. "Courtyard" is a translation of the Greek *aulē*, which could be rendered "palace" (cf. Note on 10:16). The former rendering (NIV) is preferable here in view of the fact that Peter was not in an inner assembly room but was standing with servants and retainers by a fire (v.18).

17 Apparently Peter's first statement of denial accompanied his admittance to the courtyard; the last occurred somewhat later, perhaps just as Jesus was about to be taken to the council chamber. There are minor differences in all four accounts of the denial, but there are broad general agreements. The first denial was a reply to a question asked by the girl who tended the gate and granted access to Peter and the other disciple. The wording of the Greek text, *me kai su* ("are you not?"), implies that the girl recognized both the unnamed disciple and Peter as followers of Jesus. Matthew and Mark agree that the first questioner was a servant girl (Matt 26:69; Mark 14:66), but they do not connect her with the disciples' entrance into the courtyard. Luke agrees that the first accuser was a servant girl who thought Peter was one of Jesus' disciples (Luke 22:56).

18 Jerusalem is twenty-six hundred feet above sea level, and on a spring night the air is chilly. The servants had lighted a charcoal fire (*anthrakian*), which would warm only those near it and would not give off a great deal of light. Peter must have edged toward it, hoping to absorb some warmth, yet not wishing to make himself visible. He certainly did not want to be recognized again!

25 The focus of attention on Peter is interrupted by the author's reversion to the interrogation of Jesus by the high priest (vv.19–24). Matthew and Mark agree that the second interrogator was a girl; Luke, however, does not state whether it was a man or a woman (Matt 26:71; Mark 14:69; Luke 22:58). The first two questions were introduced by the particle *mē*, which calls for a negative answer. Peter's answer to this suggested negative drew him into a position he could not escape from and caused him to make an emphatic denial: "I am not."

26–27 The third question, according to John, was raised by a relative of Malchus and was worded in such a way as to expect an affirmative answer. He was sure that he had seen Peter in the olive grove. Matthew and Mark agree that the questioner identified Peter as Galilean (Matt 26:73; Mark 14:70), and Luke agrees with them at this point (Luke 22:59). As the questioning proceeded from suspicion to reasonable certainty,

Peter became more nervous. With increasing vehemence he disavowed any connection with Jesus, and on the third occasion the rooster crowed. The shrill sound must have recalled Jesus' words spoken a few hours before: "Before the rooster crows, you will disown me three times" (John 13:38). The author adds no further comment at this point, but the fact that he recorded the denial implies that it was a turning point in Peter's experience. It was a revelation of his own weakness that he could not escape. It no doubt prompted self-examination, and Peter's response was exactly the opposite of that of Judas. Judas in his failure fell into despair; Peter returned to Christ.

D. *The Trial Before Pilate*

18:28–19:16

28Then the Jews led Jesus from Caiaphas to the palace of the Roman governor. By now it was early morning, and to avoid ceremonial uncleanness the Jews did not enter the palace; they wanted to be able to eat the Passover. 29So Pilate came out to them and asked, "What charges are you bringing against this man?"

30"If he were not a criminal," they replied, "we would not have handed him over to you."

31Pilate said, "Take him yourselves and judge him by your own law."

"But we have no right to execute anyone," the Jews objected. 32This happened so that the words Jesus had spoken indicating the kind of death he was going to die would be fulfilled.

33Pilate then went back inside the palace, summoned Jesus and asked him, "Are you the king of the Jews?"

34"Is that your own idea," Jesus asked, "or did others talk to you about me?"

35"Do you think I am a Jew?" Pilate replied. "It was your people and your chief priests who handed you over to me. What is it you have done?"

36Jesus said, "My kingdom is not of this world. If it were, my servants would fight to prevent my arrest by the Jews. But now my kingdom is from another place."

37"You are a king, then!" said Pilate.

Jesus answered, "You are right in saying I am a king. In fact, for this reason I was born, and for this I came into the world, to testify to the truth. Everyone on the side of truth listens to me."

38"What is truth?" Pilate asked. With this he went out again to the Jews and said, "I find no basis for a charge against him. 39But it is your custom for me to release to you one prisoner at the time of the Passover. Do you want me to release 'the king of the Jews'?"

40They shouted back, "No, not him! Give us Barabbas!" Now Barabbas had taken part in a rebellion.

19:1Then Pilate took Jesus and had him flogged. 2The soldiers twisted together a crown of thorns and put it on his head. They clothed him in a purple robe 3and went up to him again and again, saying, "Hail, O king of the Jews!" And they struck him in the face.

4Once more Pilate came out and said to the Jews, "Look, I am bringing him out to you to let you know that I find no basis for a charge against him." 5When Jesus came out wearing the crown of thorns and the purple robe, Pilate said to them, "Here is the man!"

6As soon as the chief priests and their officials saw him, they shouted, "Crucify! Crucify!"

But Pilate answered, "You take him and crucify him. As for me, I find no basis for a charge against him."

7The Jews insisted, "We have a law, and according to that law he must die, because he claimed to be the Son of God."

8When Pilate heard this, he was even more afraid, 9and he went back inside the palace. "Where do you come from?" he asked Jesus, but Jesus gave him no answer. 10"Do you refuse to speak to me?" Pilate said. "Don't you realize I have power either to free you or to crucify you?"

¹¹Jesus answered, "You would have no power over me if it were not given to you from above. Therefore the one who handed me over to you is guilty of a greater sin."

¹²From then on, Pilate tried to set Jesus free, but the Jews kept shouting, "If you let this man go, you are no friend of Caesar. Anyone who claims to be a king opposes Caesar."

¹³When Pilate heard this, he brought Jesus out and sat down on the judge's seat at a place known as The Stone Pavement (which in Aramaic is Gabbatha). ¹⁴It was the day of Preparation of Passover Week, about the sixth hour.

"Here is your king," Pilate said to the Jews.

¹⁵But they shouted, "Take him away! Take him away! Crucify him!"

"Shall I crucify your king?" Pilate asked.

"We have no king but Caesar," the chief priests answered.

¹⁶Finally Pilate handed him over to them to be crucified. So the soldiers took charge of Jesus.

This account of Jesus' trial before Pilate is the longest in the four Gospels. Whereas the other three accounts deal largely with the legal charges, John's narrative places more importance on Jesus' concern with Pilate and on Pilate's shifting attitude. Its psychological portrait of Pilate is comparable to that of the Samaritan woman at the well of Sychar (ch. 4) or that of the blind man (ch. 9). The Johannine presentation makes it more of an interview than a trial, though some of the legal details are plainly described.

28 John does not describe the early morning session of the council. There Caiaphas put Jesus on oath to declare whether or not he was the Son of God; and on his assertion that he was, Jesus was condemned on a charge of blasphemy (Mark 14:60–64). The penalty under Jewish law was death. But because the high priest had no authority to execute a death sentence, it was necessary to transfer the case to the Roman prefect, Pontius Pilate. He was in Jerusalem at that time, for the Passover Week was always a period when Jewish nationalistic sentiment ran high and uprisings were likely to occur. In order to keep close control of the city, Pilate and his troops were there to handle any emergency that might arise.

After the verdict of the Sanhedrin, the prisoner was moved to Pilate's residence. The location is uncertain. It may have been the palace of Herod, on the west side of the city, near the present Jaffa gate; or it may have been the Tower of Antonia, on the north side of the temple enclosure, where the Roman barracks were located.

"Early morning" would probably mean about seven or eight o'clock. There may have been time for the last session of the Jewish council after sunrise since it was illegal to pronounce a death sentence at night. The Jewish delegation did not enter into the courtroom because entering a Gentile home or business room entailed seven days' defilement. Inasmuch as the Passover was imminent, they did not wish to be excluded from the feast for ceremonial uncleanness.

29–30 Pilate's initial question was the normal opening inquiry of a trial: "What charges are you bringing against this man?" Pilate was proceeding by the usual routine of Roman law and would not automatically pronounce a sentence without knowing the alleged crime. The answer was elusive. The high priest no doubt knew that Jesus was not guilty of any crime under Roman law and that there was no evidence to support a charge.

31 Pilate took much the same position Gallio did at Paul's arrest in Corinth (Acts 18:12–16). An argument about the ceremonial requirements of Jewish law had no standing in a Roman court, and Pilate was ready to dismiss the case. There is a possibility that he had already been approached by the priest concerning the arrest of Jesus and was unconvinced of the justice of their case. He may have been suspicious of the legality of of their action and would not want to do anything that would place his rulership in jeopardy. The Jews' admission that they could not execute the prisoner was a confession of their intention. Pilate was shrewd enough to realize that their motive was not a sincere desire to remove a dangerous revolutionary. Matthew states that Pilate "knew that it was out of envy that they had handed Jesus over to him" (Matt 27:18).

32 The introduction of Roman action at this point insured death by crucifixion, if the Jews could persuade Pilate to render a verdict against Jesus. Jewish capital punishment was inflicted by stoning; but crucifixion would place Jesus under the curse of God (Deut 21:22–23; cf. Gal 3:13). His messianic claims would be discredited, and the rejection would be justified. The manner of death is explicitly connected with Jesus' own prophecy (John 3:14; 12:32–33). Ironically, the death that the Jewish hierarchy regarded as a final negation of Jesus' claims became the means of justification apart from the law (Gal 3:13).

33 Puzzled by the Jewish attitude, Pilate withdrew to the audience chamber within the building and summoned Jesus. His question to Jesus was emphatic: "Are *you* the king of the Jews?" (italics mine), as if he were asking for a straightforward answer because he did not trust the priests. The sentence could be translated as an exclamation: "So *you* are the king of the Jews, are you!" Pilate may also have been expressing his surprise that Jesus did not look like a pretender to the vacant throne of Judaism and seemed much less assertive than such persons usually are. Pilate had expected to meet a sullen or belligerent rebel and met instead the calm majesty of confident superiority. He could not reconcile the character of the prisoner with the charge brought against him.

34 Jesus' reply irritated Pilate, for he was accustomed to receiving answers to his questions, not challenges. Since he had shown sufficient interest in Jesus to confer with him personally, Jesus began to probe him to ascertain how sincere that interest might be. Was Pilate asking for information on his own initiative, or was he merely following a legal procedure at the instigation of the Jewish hierarchy?

35 Pilate's reply was a question that expressed his indignation. Literally, he asked, "I am not a Jew am I?" His question is introduced by the particle *mēti*, which calls for a negative answer. The response conveys the feeling that Pilate did not want to be classified as a Jew. He insisted that he was merely endeavoring to find the key to the puzzling case the Jewish leaders had brought before him. He had not originated the accusation, but he wanted to know what Jesus had done to arouse their hatred.

36 Jesus' answer to this question bewildered Pilate. Jesus asserted that his kingdom was not of this world because he had no military support and did not relate to any geographic locality. He did not, however, deny that "king" could be his proper title. He affirmed that his kingdom had a different origin and a different character from any Pilate knew. Those who served Jesus were not fighting men. Had he been an ordinary revolutionary, he would have offered armed resistance to those who took him captive.

37 Without attempting to argue about an abstraction that must have seemed irrational to him, Pilate came back to the central question: "So you are a king, then, aren't you?" (my translation). Jesus assented by confirming Pilate's conclusion. Then Jesus declared that his purpose was to bear testimony to truth, and he intimated that anyone who was devoted to truth would listen to him. The obvious inference from his words would be that he came into the world from another realm, that whoever did not listen to him would not be characterized by truth, and that if Pilate really wanted to know what truth was, he would give Jesus his earnest attention. Jesus was more interested in appealing to Pilate than in defending himself. This method appears in all of his other interviews in this Gospel. In each of them Jesus' focus was on reaching the heart of the person he addressed, not simply in magnifying himself. He made an appeal to Pilate, not for acquittal or mercy, but for recognition of truth.

The combined statement, "For this reason I was born, and for this I came into the world" can be linked with John 1. Morris points out that this expression is a peculiar combination (NIC, p. 771). It reinforces Jesus' statement in this Gospel that he was fully aware of both his origin and destiny (John 8:14). Jesus must have meant that he had existed in a preincarnate state. Instead of advertising his deity, Jesus simply took it for granted.

38 Pilate's reply, "What is truth?" is difficult to interpret. Was it facetious, scornful, impatient, despairing, or sincere? Even from the context it is not possible to be sure what he meant. Pilate's immediate response was to declare Jesus innocent of any crime. He may have regarded him as a harmless philosopher or as an impractical dreamer. Certainly he did not look on Jesus as a dangerous subversive. His language does not imply that he attributed moral perfection to Jesus but only that Jesus had not transgressed any law that would have made him liable to punishment.

39 Aware, however, that there were political overtones in the situation that called for some sort of action, Pilate groped for a solution that would be satisfactory to all concerned. Although no other record of it can be found, there must have been the custom of releasing one prisoner at every Passover as a means of placating the Jewish population. Pilate seized on the opportunity to appeal to the masses and suggested that he would release Jesus if they demanded it. His proposal assumed that Jesus was popular with the general crowd, who did not always favor the hierarchy. Pilate may also have been indulging in finely honed sarcasm when he referred to Jesus as "the king of the Jews." If Jesus were not released, the people would be guilty of the death of the one they called their king.

40 Pilate miscalculated the attitude of the crowd at this point. They had been instructed by the priests to ask for the death of Jesus; so instead of his release, they demanded that of a brigand named Barabbas. Quite likely Barabbas was a guerrilla "resistance fighter" who had been captured by the Romans and was being held for execution. In the eyes of the people, he was considered a champion of a free Israel and possibly something of a hero. The word applied to him (*lēstēs*) does not refer to a thief in the ordinary sense but to an outlaw or insurrectionist. The name Barabbas is Aramaic, meaning "son of the father." By a strange irony the pseudo-son of the father was released, but the real Son of the Father was crucified.

19:1 The scourging of Jesus was the usual accompaniment of crucifixion. The Roman scourge consisted of a wooden handle to which several rawhide thongs were fastened. Into each thong small butterfly shaped pieces of metal or bone were fixed. Wielded by a powerful arm, the scourge was a deadly weapon, which in a few strokes would strip the flesh from a man's back. Frequently death followed immediately so that the victim did not survive for crucifixion. Evidently Pilate intended to make an appeal to the sympathy of the mob, in hope that they would be satisfied with the scourging and would call for Jesus' release.

2-3 The legionnaires who had been detailed to administer the scourging amused them-selves by a crude joke. Knowing that Jesus was called "king of the Jews," they threw a scarlet cloak about his shoulders, twisted a crown from a thorny vine that grew in the vicinity, and mocked him with the salutation "Hail, O king of the Jews!" as they slapped his face.

4-5 As the soldiers brought him out to the view of the crowd, Pilate, having once more declared Jesus' innocence, said, "Here is the man!" Pilate may have thought that the ironic spectacle of a king whose crown was thorns, his robe a cast-off cloak, and his status a prisoner would change their attitude. If so, he was speedily disillusioned.

6-7 The Jewish officials demanded crucifixion for no good reason Pilate could deter-mine. In disgust he told them to crucify him themselves, for no charge could be brought against him. Pilate must have realized that the Sanhedrin could not execute the sentence. His apparent relegation of Jesus to them was an act of sarcasm. The Jews knew this and made a new approach to Pilate, claiming that by their law Jesus was worthy of death for blasphemy because he claimed to be the Son of God. Their charge corroborates the fact that he had claimed to be the Son of God (see comments on 10:34–38). So they invoked the law of blasphemy (Lev 24:16) as the ground for their insistence on Jesus' crucifixion.

8-9 To the Jews, Jesus' claim was the height of sacrilege. For Pilate, however, it had a different meaning. In pagan mythology the Olympian deities frequently consorted with men and women, and their semi-divine offspring, such as Hercules, had appeared on the earth and performed miraculous deeds. Hardened as he was, Pilate feared lest he should offend one of these visitors. His further questioning of Jesus was an attempt to ascertain who Jesus was. If Jesus really was a supernatural being, Pilate did not wish to be responsible for mistreating him. Divine judgment would certainly be the inevitable consequence. The silence of Jesus, like his silence in the presence of Herod (Luke 23:6–11), meant that he could accomplish nothing with a trifler. Pilate had already pronounced Jesus innocent; so the case resolved itself to the alternative of release or a gross perversion of justice.

10 Jesus' refusal to answer him angered Pilate, whose conceit and arrogance were shown by his question: "Don't you realize I have power either to free you or to crucify you?" He was insulted because Jesus had not shown him more deference. Pilate's asser-tion of authority seems almost ridiculous in contrast with the weakness and indecision he exhibited in this case. Jesus, who could view the situation in its true light, knew that though Pilate had the legal authority of which he boasted, he was really hampered by political pressures.

11 Jesus looked on Pilate as checked by the hand of God. Pilate was simply an instru-ment in the divine purpose. The real guilt lay with those who had delivered Jesus to Pilate in the first place. The reference is to Caiaphas and the Jewish hierarchy who had initiated the trial.

12 Jesus' penetrating analysis of the situation made Pilate more eager than ever to release him. But the popular pressure was too strong. The cry "If you let this man go, you are no friend of Caesar" carried the day. The phrase "a friend of Caesar" was more than a casual allusion to Roman patriotism. It usually denoted a supporter or associate of the emperor, a member of the important inner circle. The cry was a veiled threat: if Pilate exonerated Jesus, the high priest would report to Rome that Pilate had refused to bring a rival pretender to justice and was perhaps plotting to establish a new political alliance of his own. Tiberius, the reigning emperor, was notoriously bitter and suspicious of rivals. If such a report were sent to him, he would instantly end Pilate's political career and probably his life, too.

13 Jesus' analysis of Pilate's situation accentuated the dilemma he found himself entangled in. If he condemned Jesus to satisfy the Jewish hierarchy, he would be making a travesty of Roman justice. If he released Jesus, he would add to his contention with the hierarchy and would endanger his already shaky political future.

The decision could no longer be deferred. "The Stone Pavement" could have been in the Castle of Antonia, which housed the Roman garrison in Jerusalem. The castle stood on a rocky height of land, which accords with the Aramaic "Gabbatha," meaning "ridge" or "height."

14–15 The time in view here depends on the method of reckoning "the sixth hour." If it were reckoned from midnight, it would be about six o'clock in the morning; if from sunrise, which accords better with John's general procedure, it would be about noon. The problem is further complicated by the testimony of Mark, who states that the Crucifixion took place at "the third hour" (Mark 15:25). Perhaps the best solution is that Mark indicates that the trial came early and that the execution occurred on mid-morning, while John stresses the fact that it was accomplished before noon. The expressions of time are approximations rather than precise statements of hours; John qualified his expression by saying "about."

Pilate presented the bleeding, disheveled figure to the crowd with these words: "Here is your king." In their bitter irony, these words show Pilate's contempt for the Jews. As the people clamored for Jesus' crucifixion, Pilate scornfully asked, "Shall I crucify your king?" The reply of the chief priests is astonishing: "We have no king but Caesar." The official heads of the nation, who would gladly have welcomed independence, put themselves on record as subjects of the pagan emperor. Even allowing for the fact that the Sadducean priesthood was willing to compromise with the Romans for the sake of political advantage, nothing revealed their lack of spiritual principles so vividly as this act of betrayal. It was the final step in the process initially described in the Prologue: "He came to that which was his own, but his own [people] did not receive him" (John 1:11).

16 Realizing that the priests were implacable and that resisting them would only endanger his career. Pilate finally gave in and ordered the Crucifixion. Certain features of Pilate's examination of Jesus are significant. Pilate's behavior shows that he was apprehensive of trouble. From the outset he was uncertain of his position. He oscillated between public confrontation with the Jewish mob and private interrogation of Jesus. Seven times in this brief narrative the author says or implies that Pilate "went out" or "went in" (18:29, 33, 38; 19:1, 4, 9, 13). Beneath his arrogant manner, there was an uncertainty that came from the conflict between Pilate the Roman judge and Pilate the politician. He finally succumbed to expediency.

From the standpoint of Jesus, Pilate was a person in need; and Jesus gave him the opportunity of receiving truth if he would have it. Jesus made a greater effort to penetrate Pilate's mind than to defend himself. When Pilate asked, "What is truth?" (18:38), he was near to the kingdom of God because incarnate truth was standing before him. Pilate sacrificed truth for what he thought was security and lost both.

Notes

18:28 In the phrase "to the palace of the Roman governor" (εἰς τὸ πραιτώριον, *eis to praitōrion*), the words "of the Roman governor" are possibly a correct interpretation; but they are not found in the Greek text. The exact title of Pilate is uncertain. Matthew 20:8 and Luke 8:3 use the term ἐπίτροπος (*epitropos*), the Greek equivalent of the Latin "procurator," a title generally held by the governors of Judea in the reign of Claudius (A.D. 41–54) or afterwards. Josephus states that Pilate was sent by Tiberius as procurator to Judea (Wars 2. 9. 2). A fragmentary Latin inscription discovered in Caesarea in 1961 calls Pontius Pilate the prefect of Judea. Under Augustus (27 B.C.–A.D. 14) the prefect was an officer, sometimes chosen from the privileged class of the equites (the elite Roman calvary) and possibly even a freedman, appointed by the emperor to a position of authority. (See Jerry Vardaman, "A New Inscription Which Mentions Pilate as a Prefect," JBL 81 [1962]: 70–71, and also A.N. Sherwin-White, *Roman Society and Roman Law in the New Testament* [Oxford: Clarendon, 1963], pp. 6–7, 12.) Pilate was subordinate to Vitellius, the governor of Syria, who later dismissed him and sent him to Rome to be examined by the emperor for misconduct in office (Jos. Antiq. 18. 4. 2). Only the death of Tiberius saved him from disgrace.

The place Jesus was taken is identified in John 19:13 as "The Stone Pavement," or "'Gabbatha," the Aramaic name for "The Ridge." In the basement of the Convent of the Sisters of Zion an extensive pavement has been excavated, consisting of massive slabs of stone, laid over subterranean cisterns and grooved to allow for the entrance of horses. Carved rudely on some of these slabs are gameboards at which the Roman soldiers amused themselves while off duty. This site seems to fit John's description better than Herod's palace.

Technically, πρωί (*prōi*, "early morning") refers to the fourth watch of the night between 3 A.M. and sunrise (BAG, p. 732). It seems rather improbable that the meaning should be confined to the technical sense since it is unlikely that Pilate would have been available before dawn.

37 The Greek οὐκοῦν (*oukoun*, "so") calls for a positive answer. Jesus' reply, Σὺ λέγεις ὅτι βασιλεύς εἰμι (*Su legeis hoti basileus eimi*, "You say that I am a king"), is really an affirmative assent. A comparison of the same construction in Matthew 26:64 with the parallel passage in Mark 14:62 (ἐγώ εἰμι, *egō eimi*) demonstrates that it was equivalent to the personal statement "I am." It is similar to the English slang "You said it!"

19:2 The crown of thorns (στέφανος ἐξ ἀκανθῶν, *stephanos ex akanthōn*) was possibly an attempt to mock the radiate crown that appeared on the heads of the emperors in the Roman coinage of that time (see H. St. John Hart, JTS III, [1952], 66–75). The radiate crown was the symbol of the emperor's divinity and would thus express even more strongly the derision of the soldiers. Furthermore, if John intended this connotation, it showed another stroke of irony in which the guards' crude jest was truer than they realized.

3 In the phrase "they kept coming (ἤρχοντο, *erchonto*) and saying (ἔλεγον, *elegon*)," the verbs are in the imperfect tense, which implies repeated action, as NIV shows.

6 The right of the Jewish council to inflict the death penalty was limited to the execution of Gentiles who intruded into the sacred enclosure of the temple. They had no right to execute criminals. Rome reserved that power (the *ius gladii*) for itself in order to strengthen the control over subject provinces or client kingdoms. It was, however, within the power of the Roman prefect to accept the sentence of the Sanhedrin, whether on the basis of a political or religious charge (see Sherwin-White, *Roman Law*, pp. 32–47).

E. *The Crucifixion*

19:17–27

> [17]Carrying his own cross, he went out to The Place of the Skull (which in Aramaic is called Golgotha). [18]Here they crucified him, and with him two others—one on each side and Jesus in the middle.
> [19]Pilate had a notice prepared and fastened to the cross. It read, Jesus of Nazareth, The King of the Jews. [20]Many of the Jews read this sign, for the place where Jesus was crucified was near the city, and the sign was written in Aramaic, Latin and Greek. [21]The chief priests of the Jews protested to Pilate, "Do not write 'The King of the Jews,' but that this man claimed to be king of the Jews."
> [22]Pilate answered, "What I have written, I have written."
> [23]When the soldiers crucified Jesus, they took his clothes, dividing them into four shares, one for each of them, with the undergarment remaining. This garment was seamless, woven in one piece from top to bottom.
> [24]"Let's not tear it," they said to one another. "Let's decide by lot who will get it."
> This happened that the Scripture might be fulfilled which said,
>
> > "They divided my garments among them
> > and cast lots for my clothing."
>
> So this is what the soldiers did.
> [25]Near the cross of Jesus stood his mother, his mother's sister, Mary the wife of Clopas, and Mary of Magdala. [26]When Jesus saw his mother there, and the disciple whom he loved standing nearby, he said to his mother, "Dear woman, here is your son," [27]and to the disciple, "Here is your mother." From that time on, this disciple took her into his home.

17 Under Pilate's orders, Jesus was turned over to the execution squad, which normally consisted of four legionnaires and a centurion. Whether more were involved as a precaution against violence because of the popular tumult is not stated. The division of Jesus' garments (v.23) seems to show that only four legionnaires were involved. It was customary for the condemned person to wear a placard (v.20) giving his name and the nature of his crime and to carry the transverse beam of his cross. The procession moved from Pilate's judgment seat to a place outside the city called "The Place of the Skull." Contrary to current hymnology, there is no evidence that it was a hill. The reason for its name is uncertain. It is unlikely that skulls were left on the ground, which would be an affront to Jewish custom, or that the topography resembled a skull. The exact location is unknown.

18 Apart from this simple statement, the writer makes no attempt to describe the process of crucifixion, probably because it was well known to the readers and he did not want to dwell on the physical horror of the Cross. The victim carried the crossbeam to the place of execution (cf. v.17), where he was affixed to the cross by nails driven through the hands or wrists and through the feet. Generally, a rope was tied around the chest, knotted between the shoulders, and then tied to the wooden stake behind the body to prevent its falling forward as fatigue weakened the muscles. A peg was set in the upright stake to act as a supporting seat. The victim was stripped of his clothing and left shamefully naked, exposed to the mocking people, the heat of the sun by day, and the chill and dampness of night, which in the spring at the altitude of Jerusalem might drop to 40 or 50 degrees Fahrenheit.

An ossuary unearthed near Jerusalem in Giv'at ha-Mivtar revealed the only known instance of the skeleton of a man who had been crucified. It showed that the feet had been nailed sideways to the cross whereas the body had been facing forward. Such a position would create a twist of about ninety degrees at the waist. The unnatural position, growing thirst, exposure to the weather, some loss of blood, and impaired breathing contributed to bring about a lingering and painful death. The tension on the arms prevented normal breathing, which caused the lungs to slowly fill with moisture. The victim drowned slowly by internal accumulation of fluid. The action of the heart was seriously affected. Frequently a crucified man might live as long as thirty-six hours, or even longer in an increasing agony, unless by exhaustion or dementia he finally lapsed into unconsciousness. Crucifixion was probably the most diabolical form of death ever invented. Paul, in writing of the humiliation of Christ, says, "He humbled himself and became obedient to [the point of] death—*even death on a cross*" (Phil 2:8, italics mine). Paul's statement reveals the feeling toward death by this method. Death for Jesus was unbelievable, but crucifixion was unthinkable.

John gives no details concerning the two others crucified with Jesus. The synoptic accounts describe them as "robbers" or brigands (Matt 27:38; Mark 15:27; Luke 23:32–33, 39) like Barabbas (cf. comment on 18:40). It may be that these two and Barabbas were guerrilla fighters captured by the Romans in some skirmish in Galilee. Anti-Roman unrest was rife at this time, and the rebels often replenished their food supplies or treasury by robbery of wealthy landholders. Jesus was classed with subversives and criminals.

19–22 The placard on the cross was the conventional announcement of the offense the victim had committed. The languages were intended to make the inscription plain to all: Aramaic, for the local inhabitants; Latin, for the officials; Greek, the lingua franca of the eastern Mediterranean world. Its content was Pilate's psychological revenge on the Jewish hierarchy for forcing his decision. It proclaimed loudly to all passers-by that Rome had crucified the king of the Jews as a common criminal. Stung by the insult, the priests remonstrated, asking that Pilate make clear that it was Jesus' claim to be King of the Jews, not that it was in fact true. Having succeeded by his unjust compromise in removing any possible ground of accusation that he was derelict in his duty to the Roman state, Pilate resumed his haughty attitude and refused to change the wording. "What I have written, I have written" means essentially, "Take it and like it!"

23–24 Usually the clothing of a crucified man became the property of the executioners. Jesus' simple wardrobe was composed of five items: a turban or headdress; an outer robe; a sash or girdle, the folds of which would provide pockets; sandals; and a fairly long tunic, woven in one piece, that was an undergarment. The first four were easily divided among the four legionnaires, but the fifth would be of no value if cut into four parts. Gambling was as well known in the Roman army as it is among soldiers today. So the tunic was awarded to one of them at the cast of the dice. John's reason for mentioning this episode was its illustration or fulfillment of the prophecy of Psalm 22. Psalm 22 is a startling picture of the Crucifixion, which begins with Christ's fourth word from the cross: "My God, my God, why have you forsaken me?" (Matt 27:46; Mark 15:34). If Pilate's inscription shows that he exploited Jesus' crucifixion as a means of psychological vengeance, the gambling of the legionnaires shows their callous and mercenary attitude.

25-27 The harsh brutality of the scene is softened by the allusion to Jesus' care for his mother. Four women are mentioned here: Mary, the wife of Clopas; Mary Magdalene; Mary, the mother of Jesus; and his mother's sister, who was presumably Salome, the mother of James and John (cf. Matt 27:56; Mark 10:35; 15:40). The identity of Mary of Clopas is uncertain. She may have been the wife or daughter of Clopas. If she were the former, a question arises whether Clopas and Alphaeus, who was the father of James the younger (Mark 3:18), were identical. Most of these women were related in some way to the Twelve and were among Jesus' most loyal followers. Mary of Magdala appears in Luke's list of those who helped support Jesus by their contributions (Luke 8:2). There is nothing in the NT to imply that she was of loose moral character. "Magdalene" refers to her home in Magdala, a town on the western side of the Sea of Galilee, named probably from the Hebrew *migdol*, or "watchtower."

The anguish and terror of Jesus' mother at the Crucifixion must have been indescribable. His tender concern for her in the hour of his mortal agony illustrates his true humanity and compassion. On the assumption that John was "the disciple whom he loved," it could well be that Jesus consigned his mother to John's care because none of his brothers was present and because John was the nearest available relative. Apparently John removed Mary from the scene at once and took her to his home in Jerusalem. There could not have been time to go to Galilee, for the writer resumes his narrative at the close of the Crucifixion. His temporary absence may account for the omission of some of the details found in the Synoptics, including Jesus' dialogue with the criminals who were crucified with him. Mary must have remained in Jerusalem for a time since she was present at the session of prayer that preceded Pentecost.

Notes

17 Two places have been claimed as the site of the Crucifixion. One is at the present site of the Church of the Holy Sepulchre, which was built in honor of Helen, the mother of Constantine, in the fourth century, after an attempt to identify the original site. The devastation of the city after the first and second revolts destroyed all landmarks or buried them so deeply under rubble that they cannot now be identified. The second place is Gordon's Calvary, located outside the present wall, north of the Damascus Gate on the Nablus Road. It is now a Muslim cemetery on the brow of a ridge that encircles the northern wall. While the rocky eminence and the adjacent garden containing an ancient tomb seem to fit the description of the Gospels, it is doubtful whether either would have been used before A.D. 70. Until the location of the "Second Wall" that bounded the northwest side of the city in Jesus' time can be settled, the exact location of Calvary will be debatable. The data of the Gospels are not specific; all that can be known is that the Crucifixion took place outside the city walls, not far from one of the main roads.

18 The process of crucifixion has been vividly illustrated by the discovery of the remains of a man executed in this manner. In 1968 a number of ossuaries were found in burial caves during a building project at Giv'at ha-Mivtar in northeast Jerusalem, slightly to the northwest of Mount Scopus. A full report on "Anthropological Observations on the Skeletal Remains from Giv'at

ha-Mivtar" was published in IEJ, vol. 20, nos. 1, 2 (1970). The analysis of the remains of the crucified man is on pp. 49–59 of the report. The body had been affixed to a cross by nails through the wrists between the ulna and the radius; the feet had been transfixed by a single spike through a wooden cleat, the right side of the right heel and the right side of the left heel, and then into the upright stem of the cross. The latter was made of olive wood that was so hard that the tip of the spike was bent and could not be extracted from the bones through which it had been driven. The resultant position of the body was such that the knees were bent to the left while the torso was fixed at a ninety-degree angle to the thigh bones. The lower legs had been shattered by a single blow that had crushed the right leg and cracked the left leg against the edge of the upright of the cross. The body had been supported by a peg or cleat in the cross under the left hip. The identity of the victim is unknown. Apparently he died at the time of the Fall of Jerusalem in A.D. 70, or possibly earlier. This is the only known archaeological evidence of the practice of crucifixion.

27 The phrase "into his home" is the Greek εἰς τὰ ἴδια (eis ta idia), the same phrase that appears in John 1:11. It means "the things peculiarly one's own," hence, "one's home." The entire Gospel indicates that the "disciple whom he [Jesus] loved" was well acquainted with Jerusalem and that it was the center of action for much of his narrative. Even if he were Galilean by origin, he may well have been living in the city at times. It has been suggested that he may have been the Jerusalem agent for Zebedee & Sons, Fishmongers!

F. *The Death of Jesus*

19:28–37

28Later, knowing that all was now completed, and so that the Scripture would be fulfilled, Jesus said, "I am thirsty." 29A jar of wine vinegar was there, so they soaked a sponge in it, put the sponge on a stalk of the hyssop plant, and lifted it to Jesus' lips. 30When he had received the drink, Jesus said, "It is finished." With that, he bowed his head and gave up his spirit.

31Now it was the day of Preparation, and the next day was to be a special Sabbath. Because the Jews did not want the bodies left on the crosses during the Sabbath, they asked Pilate to have the legs broken and the bodies taken down. 32The soldiers therefore came and broke the legs of the first man who had been crucified with Jesus, and then those of the other. 33But when they came to Jesus and found that he was already dead, they did not break his legs. 34Instead, one of the soldiers pierced Jesus' side with a spear, bringing a sudden flow of blood and water. 35The man who saw it has given testimony, and his testimony is true. He knows that he tells the truth, and he testifies so that you also may believe. 36These things happened so that the Scripture would be fulfilled: "Not one of his bones will be broken," 37and, as another Scripture says, "They will look on the one they have pierced."

28 The phrases preceding Jesus' last request (his sixth word from the cross) show that he was consciously fulfilling the program the Father had set for him. "Knowing that all was now completed" accords with the declaration in his prayer: "I have brought you glory on earth by completing the work you gave me to do" (17:4). Unerringly and methodically Jesus carried out the commission the Father had assigned to him. To some extent this commission had been prescribed by OT prophecy. The phrase "I am thirsty" recalls Psalm 69:21: "They put gall in my food and gave me vinegar for my thirst." Jesus' loss of blood, his nervous tension, and his exposure to the weather had generated a raging thirst.

29 The "vinegar" was probably the cheap sour wine the legionnaires drank. Though it provided some refreshment, it was a strong astringent that could contract the throat muscles and prevent the condemned victim from crying out with pain. Just what is meant by "hyssop" is uncertain. The word may describe more than one plant. It could have been a brush used for sprinkling (Exod 12:22), which has been identified with sorghum grass. This, however, did not grow a stalk of sufficient rigidity to act as a rod for supporting a sponge. It has been suggested that there is a primitive error in the text. Instead of reading *hyssōpō* with the majority of the MSS, it should read *hyssō*, meaning "javelin." If so, one of the soldiers could easily have impaled a sponge filled with the vinegar on the end of his javelin and reached it up to moisten Jesus' lips. This reading, however, occurs in only one MS (1242) of late date. In four MSS of the Old Latin it is rendered *perticae*, meaning "a long pole." Although this is a tempting speculative emendation, the evidence is not sufficient to sustain it. The elevation of the body on the cross would not be at a very great height, and the stalk of a plant growing nearby would be sufficient to support a light sponge. W.E. Shewell-Cooper states that "it could easily be the *Capparis sicula*," which "is found in the Sinai desert, and grows on the walls of Jerusalem" (ZPEB, 3:235). The thirst consummated Jesus' physical suffering. Having passed that stage, he had completed his work and was ready to end his mission.

30 The use of the perfect tense in "It is finished" (*tetelestai*) signifies full completion of Jesus' work and the establishment of a basis for faith. Nothing further needed to be done. Jesus' act was voluntary and confident, for he had discharged perfectly the Father's purpose and was leaving the scene of his human struggle. The expression may be interpreted in various ways: as a cry of relief, because suffering is ending; as a cry of anguish, because his ministry has ended in failure; or as a shout of victory, because the purpose of God has triumphed in his death. The last of these seems to be the author's intent. He makes it the final report of Jesus to the Father, who will now exalt him to glory. The final word says that "he bowed his head and gave up his spirit." It could also be translated "he laid his head to rest and dismissed his spirit." Jesus retained consciousness and command of himself till the very end.

31-32 Mark (15:42) agrees with John that Jesus died on the day preceding the Sabbath, hence, on Friday, "the day of Preparation." The day began at sunset on Thursday and ended at sunset on Friday. The meal Jesus and his disciples ate must have been on Thursday night, which would actually fall on the Passover since the day began in the evening, not in the morning, as in the Western calendar. The removal of bodies from the cross was a concession to Jewish religious scruples. The Romans usually left the bodies of criminals on their crosses as a warning to potential offenders, much as pirates in the eighteenth century were hung in chains so that passing ships might see their fate. The Jewish law forbade leaving hanged bodies on a gallows overnight (Deut 21:22–23; Josh 8:29). The soldiers broke the legs of the living victims to hasten death. The only way a crucified man could obtain a full breath of air was to raise himself by means of his legs to ease the tension on his arms and chest muscles. If the legs were broken, he could not possibly do so; and death would follow shortly because of lack of oxygen.

33 The execution squad was well acquainted with the signs of death. Consequently, not fracturing Jesus' legs shows that the squad considered him to be already dead. Jesus' swift death marks either the climax of inner tension, the fatal results of the scourging, or, as the text seems to indicate, a voluntary ending of his life because his work was ended. He had said of himself that he could lay down his life that he might take it again (10:17).

34–37 One of the soldiers pierced Jesus' side with his spear, probably to see whether there would be any reaction. The flow of "blood and water" has been variously explained. Ordinarily dead bodies do not bleed because there is no action of the heart to produce arterial pressure. One suggestion is that since the body was erect, the flow was due to gravity and that the crassamentum (the heavy, red corpuscles) and the serum (the yellowish white aqueous part) of the blood had already begun to separate. Another is that either the stomach or the lungs contained water that flowed with the blood. The author places great importance on the fact, emphasizing that he had witnessed it for himself and that he was telling the truth. He connected it with OT prophecy. The bones of the Passover lamb were left unbroken (Exod 12:46), and the divine protection of a righteous man guarantees that God "protects all his bones, not one of them will be broken" (Ps 34:20). The prophetic significance of the pierced side is referred to in Zechariah 12:10, where it is related to the final manifestation of the Lord to Israel. Verses 35–37 are a footnote giving the author's viewpoint in the third person, a usage in keeping with his practice throughout the Gospel (cf. M.C. Tenney, "Footnotes," pp. 350–64).

Notes

---

30 The verb τελέω (teleō, "to finish") was used in the first and second centuries in the sense of "fulfilling" or "paying" a debt and often appeared in receipts. Jesus' statement "It is finished" (τετέλεσται, tetelestai) could be interpreted as "Paid in full," or, as the words of a gospel hymn read, "Jesus paid it all" (see MM, p. 630).

The verb κλίνω (klinō, "bow," "rest") used in the phrase κλίνας τὴν κεφαλὴν, (klinas tēn kephalēn, "bowed his head"), appears also in Matt 8:20 and Luke 9:58. The world afforded Jesus only a cross on which to lay his head.

G. *The Burial of Jesus*

19:38–42

> [38]Later, Joseph of Arimathea asked Pilate for the body of Jesus. Now Joseph was a disciple of Jesus, but secretly because he feared the Jews. With Pilate's permission, he came and took the body. [39]He was accompanied by Nicodemus, the man who earlier had visited Jesus at night. Nicodemus brought a mixture of myrrh and aloes, about seventy-five pounds. [40]Taking Jesus' body, the two of them wrapped it, with the spices, in strips of linen. This was in accordance with Jewish burial customs. [41]At the place where Jesus was crucified, there was a garden, and in the garden a new tomb, in which no one had ever been laid. [42]Because it was the Jewish day of Preparation and since the tomb was nearby, they laid Jesus there.

38 Burial in the Middle East usually takes place within twenty-four hours after death. In this case, the body of Jesus would probably have been flung into a common pit with the bodies of the two other victims, had not his friends intervened. Jesus had no estate of his own from which to pay for his burial, and his relatives were either too poor or too afraid of the authorities to assume responsibility for it. Joseph of Arimathea is mentioned in all four Gospels (Matt 27:57–60; Mark 15:42–46; Luke 23:50–56). Matthew says he was wealthy; Mark, that he was a member of the Sanhedrin ("Council") and was "waiting for the kingdom of God"; Luke, that he had not concurred in the vote of the council to condemn Jesus. Joseph's action was courageous, for his petition was a tacit admission that he was a friend of Jesus and consequently an associate in whatever supposed subversion Jesus might have advocated. Joseph took the initiative and petitioned Pilate for permission to remove the body. His request was an open confession of his faith, for up to this time he had been a secret believer.

39 Nicodemus, another distinguished member of the Jewish aristocracy, shared the responsibility for receiving Jesus' body with Joseph. This marks Nicodemus's third appearance in the Gospel: one at his initial interview with Jesus (ch. 3), the second at his defense of Jesus before the council (7:45–52), and finally at the burial. Like Joseph, Nicodemus was a secret disciple whose faith grew slowly. As a member of the Sanhedrin, he had more at stake than the Galilean fishermen who had become followers of Jesus early in his career. His cooperation with Joseph in the burial shows that his faith had finally matured. Neither of these men appears in the Jewish records or traditions of the time. For that reason some have regarded them as legendary; but were that so, there is no obvious reason for introducing them gratuitously into the narrative. If they had been regarded by their Sanhedrin contemporaries as traitors to Judaism, their names would have been erased from the records.

The mixture of spices that Nicodemus provided was a very large quantity. Spices were generally imported and were very expensive. Myrrh is a gum exuded by a tree that grows in Arabia and is prized for its perfume. It was one of the gifts of the wise men to Jesus (Matt 2:11). Aloes are derived from the pulp in the leaves of a plant that belongs to the lily family. The spice is fragrant and bitter to the taste. Used with myrrh, it acts as a drying agent; and the fragrance would counteract the odor of decaying flesh. The quantity of one hundred Roman pounds (75 lbs. avdp.) revealed both Nicodemus's wealth and his appreciation of Jesus.

40 The burial of the body was hasty and had to be completed before sundown. The process is uncertain. The spices, being of somewhat gummy character, may have been laid in the folds of the cloth to provide a rigid casing for the body, or they may have been ground and mixed with oil to form an ointment to rub on the body. The former procedure agrees better with the text. "Strips of linen" is a translation of *othoniois*. Later usage in the koine Greek made the term a generic equivalent of clothes (cf. MM, p. 439). In the case of Lazarus, the graveclothes were wrapped around him in such a way that he had to be released after he was raised. The entire process was really the preparation of the body for instant burial rather than final interment.

41 The place of burial was a private garden, not a public cemetery. The privacy of this garden allowed the women to visit the tomb. No doubt they would have been hesitant to enter a public cemetery at any time—especially before daylight. Matthew states that the burial place was Joseph's own rock-hewed tomb (Matt 27:60). The location was near the place of execution and was probably just outside the Second North Wall of the city. Brown states that the tombs of the Hasmonean high priests John Hyrcanus and Alexander Jannaeus were located in this general vicinity (29a: 941–43). Joseph, as a wealthy member of the Sanhedrin, apparently owned property in this area.

42 The allusion to the "day of Preparation," which was ending, creates the impression that the burial was hasty. The amount of spices used militates against an expected temporary burial; it is more likely that as far as Joseph and Nicodemus were concerned, it was final. On the other hand, they may not have completed all they wished to do. The women had observed the place of the entombment. Consequently they knew where to go in order to fulfill their desire for a part in the burial of Jesus.

Notes

40 Ἐνταφιάζειν (*entaphiazein*, "to prepare for burial") refers to laying out a body and anointing it rather than to the actual burial (cf. MM, p. 217).

H. *The Resurrection* (20:1–29)

If the narrative of John had ended with ch. 19, it would not have been exceptional; all human biographies end with death. The picture of Jesus would have been that of a man of exceptional character, who made extraordinary claims, and whose sincerity could not be reasonably doubted. Nevertheless, the main narrative would have been closed with a sense of frustration. His claims would have been negated, his aspirations would have been unrealized, and his teaching would have seemed too lofty to be true. The major difference between the life and teachings of Jesus and those of any other great religious leader lies in the fact that Jesus rose from the dead and the others did not, however persistent their influence may be.

In presenting the evidence for Jesus' resurrection, John deals more with its effect on human personality than with the material proofs the Western mind would prefer. He assumes the fact and then shows how it influenced certain disciples in such a way that its reality becomes indisputable.

1. *The witness of Peter and John*

20:1–9

> [1]Early on the first day of the week, while it was still dark, Mary of Magdala went to the tomb and saw that the stone had been removed from the entrance. [2]So she came running to Simon Peter and the other disciple, the one Jesus loved, and said, "They have taken the Lord out of the tomb, and we don't know where they have put him!"
>
> [3]So Peter and the other disciple started for the tomb. [4]Both were running, but the other disciple outran Peter and reached the tomb first. [5]He bent over and looked in at the strips of linen lying there but did not go in. [6]Then Simon Peter, who was behind him, arrived and went into the tomb. He saw the strips of linen lying there, [7]as well as the burial cloth that had been around Jesus' head. The cloth was folded up by itself, separate from the linen. [8]Finally the other disciple, who had reached the tomb first, also went inside. He saw and believed. [9](They still did not understand from Scripture that Jesus had to rise from the dead.)

1 "The first day of the week" would be the day after the Sabbath. In the Jewish method of reckoning time, it would begin with sundown on Saturday and continue until sundown on Sunday. The text seems to indicate, however, that the visit of the women to the tomb occurred early on Sunday morning. Only Mary Magdalene is mentioned by name, but others are listed in the synoptic Gospels (Matt 28:1; Mark 16:1; Luke 24:10). Quite likely Mary Magdalene, noticing that the stone had been rolled away from the door of the tomb, ran to warn the disciples while the others investigated further.

2 Mary hastened to find Peter and John, the leaders of the Twelve, and announced that the body was missing from the tomb: "They have taken the Lord." No identification is given for "they." Either the word is an impersonal plural or else, as is more likely, it is an oblique reference to the Jewish hierarchy who had designed Jesus' death. Obviously Mary thought the body had been secretly removed by Jesus' enemies.

3 The quick response of Peter and the other disciple shows that the disciples were not responsible for removing the body. Had they been aware of an official removal, or had some of their own number been involved in a conspiracy, they would not have been so concerned.

4 Both Peter and the other disciple "ran" to the tomb. The only other passage in the NT that refers to running, apart from metaphorical use or to an athletic contest, is Matthew 28:8, which describes how the women "ran" to bring the disciples the news. The disciples' running shows they were activated by a powerful emotion, possibly either consternation, as in the case of Mary, or joy, as with the women. Peter, perhaps being the older and heavier of the two, was unable to maintain as swift a pace as his companion. The unnamed disciple arrived first but did not venture to enter the tomb.

5 Having seen that the graveclothes were still within, the other disciple probably concluded that the body was also there and so refrained from entering. Either he felt that he should not enter the tomb out of respect for the dead, or else he feared the ceremonial defilement of touching a corpse.

6-7 Peter, who by this time had overtaken his partner, had no such inhibitions. He entered directly into the tomb. He also saw the graveclothes and observed that the headcloth was not lying with the other pieces but was rolled up in a place by itself. This means the headcloth still retained the shape the contour of Jesus' head had given it and that it was still separated from the other wrappings by a space that suggested the distance between the neck of the deceased and the upper chest, where the wrappings of the body would have begun. Peter must have been wondering why the graveclothes were left in this position if the body had been stolen. A robber would not have left them in good order. He would have stripped the body completely, leaving the clothing in a disorderly heap; or he would have taken the body, graveclothes and all.

8 At this point, the "other disciple" summoned up courage to enter the tomb, perhaps wondering what had reduced Peter to silence. The disciple saw the meaning of the empty graveclothes and "believed." The unique phenomenon of the graveclothes looking as if the body were in them when no body was there undoubtedly recalled Jesus' previous words (cf. John 2:22; 11:25; 16:22).

9 The teaching of Scripture, however, was not yet clear to the disciples, and they required fuller explanation by Jesus (cf. Luke 24:25-27, 44-47). To what "Scripture"

does this passage refer? There is a parallel in John 2:21, which asserts that the disciples understood Jesus' statement about raising the temple of his body in connection with Scripture. The Gospel of John contains no specific text that might be interpreted as a prediction of the Resurrection. Perhaps Psalm 16:10, quoted by Peter in his address on the Day of Pentecost (Acts 2:24–31), is the best possibility for the "Scripture." For these two key disciples, the realization of the truth of the Resurrection began with material evidence, the significance of which dawned on them slowly. Their eagerness to visit the tomb showed their concern for Jesus. Had they dismissed him from their consciousness after his death, they would not have exerted themselves by running to Joseph's garden early in the morning. Their understanding, however, was slow in spite of Jesus' repeated predictions of his passion and resurrection.

Notes

5 Three words are used in this account to denote the visual perception of the disciples. In v.5, John "looked in at" (βλέπει, blepei) the linen clothes, implying that he had a clear picture of them and did not act on hearsay. In v.6, Peter "saw" (θεωρεῖ, theōrei), or "contemplated," "observed," the strips of linen, implying that he scrutinized them carefully but did not know how to interpret the phenomenon. In v.8, the "other disciple ... saw" (εἶδεν, eiden), meaning that he perceived the significance of what registered on the retina of his eyes. The first two verbs are not always distinguishable in meaning, though in Johannine usage the second seems to denote studying a person or thing for its significance (cf. 2:23; 4:19; 7:3; 12:19).

7 The participle ἐντετυλιγμένον (entetyligmenon), translated "wrapped up by itself," comes from the word ἐντυλίσσω (entylissō), which means "to wrap up" or "to roll up." It is used in the papyri to refer to fettering prisoners, wrapping children in clothes, or entangling fish in a net (MM, p. 219). It implies that the cloth had been wound around the head into the shape of a sphere and not folded flat like a table napkin. In the NT this word is used only in the description of Jesus' entombment (cf. Matt 27:59; Luke 23:53).

2. The appearance to Mary Magdalene

20:10–18

¹⁰Then the disciples went back to their homes, ¹¹but Mary stood outside the tomb crying. As she wept, she bent over to look into the tomb ¹²and saw two angels in white, seated where Jesus' body had been, one at the head and the other at the foot.

¹³They asked her, "Woman, why are you crying?"

"They have taken my Lord away," she said, "and I don't know where they have put him." ¹⁴At this, she turned around and saw Jesus standing there, but she did not realize that it was Jesus.

¹⁵"Woman," he said, "why are you crying? Who is it you are looking for?"

Thinking he was the gardener, she said, "Sir, if you have carried him away, tell me where you have put him, and I will get him."

¹⁶Jesus said to her, "Mary."

She turned toward him and cried out in Aramaic, "Rabboni!" (which means Teacher).

¹⁷Jesus said, "Do not hold on to me, for I have not yet returned to the Father. Go instead to my brothers and tell them, 'I am returning to my Father and your Father, to my God and your God.'"

¹⁸Mary of Magdala went to the disciples with the news: "I have seen the Lord!" And she told them that he had said these things to her.

10 Puzzled but convinced that something unusual had occurred at the tomb, Peter and the other disciple returned to their lodgings in Jerusalem. The phraseology seems to indicate that they had a fixed place where they were staying, possibly the "upper room," or perhaps the same place the unnamed disciple took Mary at the time of the Crucifixion. No details are given in the Gospels.

11 Mary Magdalene had returned to the tomb and stood outside, wailing for the loss of Jesus. On looking into the tomb, she saw two figures in white seated on the shelf where the body of Jesus had been lying, one at the foot and the other at the head. Presumably the position of the graveclothes indicated which was the foot and which was the head of the burial position. The tomb was a horizontal chamber cut through the soft limestone rock that Jerusalem was built on. Usually such tombs had a small antechamber into which the low entrance opened and from which the burial chambers radiated. Some were cut to contain only one body; others were rooms in which a family might be buried. This tomb seems to have been large enough to accommodate several living persons in addition to the burial cells.

12 No description is given of the angels. When angels appear in the Bible, they are usually recognized by their powers rather than by any significant difference from human form. Mary did not respond to them in any unusual way, possibly because her eyes were clouded with tears, or because she was preoccupied with the loss of Jesus' body. The sole feature noted in the text is that the angels were clothed in white. This parallels Luke's description of the men who appeared at the ascension of Jesus (cf. Acts 1:10).

13 The question the angels asked Mary brought from her only an expression of grief and frustration. The death of Jesus, which she had witnessed, was in itself distressing and unnerving; the disappearance of the body from the place of burial would add apprehension and mystery to her grief. She had hoped for the sad consolation of completing the burial, and even that had been taken from her.

14 As Mary turned back toward the outside of the tomb, she saw a person standing there whom she took for the keeper of the garden. She was aware of his presence, but she did not recognize him. The same two words are used here that occur in the preceding section (cf. vv.5–6, 8): Peter "saw" or "observed" the content of the tomb, but John "perceived" its meaning. Mary likewise "observed" the figure standing before her, but at first she paid scant attention to him because of her overwhelming concern for the body of Jesus.

15 The person addressed her first as a stranger, using the polite salutation "Woman" and asking the reason for her grief. From her lamentations one would conclude that she had lost some possession or some person. Thinking that Jesus was the keeper of the garden, she assumed that he would know she was looking for a body. So she requested that if he had removed it, he would tell her where she might find it that she might take it for final burial. Her words reveal her devotion. She never paused to consider how she would carry the corpse of a full-grown man or how she would explain her possession of it.

16 Only one thing was necessary to establish Jesus' identity—his uttering her name. One of the strange commonplaces of life is that the most penetrating utterance one can understand, no matter by whom spoken, is his personal name. Furthermore, the way it is spoken often identifies the speaker. No gardener would ever know her name, and no one else would pronounce it the way Jesus did. Turning again for a second look, she addressed him in Aramaic as "Rabboni." Strictly it means "my dear lord," but John defines it in this instance as "Teacher." In this ecstatic moment of recognition, Mary must have prostrated herself before him and clasped his feet, as the other women did according to Matthew's report (Matt 28:9).

17 In reply to her action, Jesus said, "Do not hold onto me." He was not refusing to be touched but was making clear that she did not need to detain him, for he had not yet ascended to the Father. He planned to remain with the disciples for a little while; she need not fear that he would vanish immediately. Ultimately he would return to God, and he urged her to tell the disciples that he would do so. The use of the word "brothers" includes more than the members of his immediate family. It placed the disciples on a new plane of relationship with himself. Having passed through death and resurrection, Jesus had become the representative man, the Lord from heaven, who "is not ashamed to call them brothers" (Heb 2:11). During his early ministry, Jesus expressed the same feeling. When his mother and brothers came to summon him from his preaching, he replied, "Who are my mother and my brothers?" (Mark 3:33). Then he answered his own question, "Whoever does God's will is my brother and sister and mother" (v.34).

The way Jesus stated his destination is illuminating: "I am returning to my Father and your Father, to my God and your God." Nowhere in the Gospels did Jesus himself address God as "our Father" or "our God." One seeming exception is the prayer Jesus taught his disciples, which is commonly referred to as the Lord's Prayer (Matt 6:9–13; Luke 11:2–4). But in that prayer Jesus was teaching the disciples to address God and was not necessarily including himself in the petition. The reason for the distinction in his word to Mary was not, of course, that there were two gods but rather that her relationship with God was different from his. He is the eternal Son of the Father; she, as well as all the disciples, had become a member of the family by receiving him (cf. John 1:12). Both relationships concerned only one God.

18 Mary's announcement to the disciples that she had seen the Lord was an additional confirmation of the belief that rested on inference from material evidence. The beloved disciple had believed, but he had not yet personally seen the risen Lord Jesus. Mary brought the witness of her experience to corroborate his deduction.

Notes

11 The Greek word κλαίω, (klaiō, "to cry") is the same one used concerning the mourners at Lazarus's death (John 11:31, 33) and at the death of Jairus's daughter (Luke 8:52). It represents loud and uncontrollable wailing.

12 Apart from the disputed verse of John 5:4, angels are mentioned only three times in this Gospel: in John 1:51, in 12:29, and again in 20:12. The first is an allusion to Genesis 28:12; the second is a casual reference to angelic intervention to explain a mysterious phenomenon; the third speaks directly of an angelic appearance. According to Luke, angels appeared in connection

with the annunciation of the births of John the Baptist and Jesus (Luke 1:11–20, 26–38), the suffering of Jesus in Gethsemane (22:43), and the Resurrection (24:4, 23). The angels seem to have appeared and disappeared at will; they delivered information and provided protection. They excel mankind in intelligence, strength, and duration. Hebrews 1:14 describes their function: "Are not all angels ministering spirits sent to serve those who will inherit salvation?"

17 The NIV translation "Do not hold on to me" is accurate. The verb ἅπτω (haptō) does not mean to touch with the tip of a finger to test whether an object is real or not but to "clutch" or "grip." Jesus was not protesting that Mary should not touch him lest he be defiled, but he was admonishing her not to detain him because he would see her and the disciples again. The use of the particle μή (mē, "not") with the present imperative means to stop an action already begun rather than to avoid starting it.

"Returned" is the translation of ἀναβέβηκα (anabebēka), the perfect tense of ἀναβαίνω (anabainō), and implies a state rather than an action. In essence, Jesus was saying, "I have not yet entered into an ascended state." The Gospel of John makes several allusions to the Ascension. The use of ἀναβέβηκεν (anabebēken, "has . . . gone" NIV) in John 3:13 does not speak directly of Jesus' ascension. It merely asserts that no man has ever ascended directly into the presence of God. A more direct implication lies in the question Jesus addressed to his querulous disciples: "What if you see the Son of Man ascend to where he was before!" (6:62). They were complaining that his assertion about eating his flesh and drinking his blood was too difficult to understand. He countered by asking them what they would say if they saw him ascend. Luke uses plainer language concerning the Ascension (Luke 9:51; 24:51; Acts 1:9; 2:33–34), though he makes no attempt to explain its mystery. The concept seems to imply the entrance into a new dimension of living rather than a mechanical change of location.

---

3. The appearance to the disciples

20:19–23

> [19]On the evening of that first day of the week, when the disciples were together, with the doors locked for fear of the Jews, Jesus came and stood among them and said, "Peace be with you!" [20]After he said this, he showed them his hands and side. The disciples were overjoyed when they saw the Lord.
> [21]Again Jesus said, "Peace be with you! As the Father has sent me, I am sending you." [22]And with that he breathed on them and said, "Receive the Holy Spirit. [23]If you forgive anyone his sins, they are forgiven; if you do not forgive them, they are not forgiven."

19–20 The third episode came in the evening of the first day. John does not cite the appearances to Simon and to the travelers on the road to Emmaus that appear in the Lukan account (Luke 24:13–35). This appearance came to the collective group for the purpose of allaying their fears. They had narrowly escaped arrest with Jesus in Gethsemane; they realized that as the disciples of one who was regarded as a dangerous agitator they would be under suspicion; and they were probably holding a consultation on the best method of withdrawing from the city without attracting the notice of the temple police or the Roman authorities. The doors were locked for fear that the Jews would send an arresting detachment for them as they had for Jesus.

The appearance of Jesus in the room excited both amazement and fear. The implication is clear that Jesus was not impeded by locked doors. The resurrection body has properties different from the body of flesh; yet it is not ethereal. There was a definite continuity between the physical body of Jesus' earthly career and the new body since his hands and side still showed the scars that identified him. His greeting of "Peace" and the assurance of his identity calmed their fears and demonstrated by unmistakable proof that he was alive. They were overjoyed, not only to see him again, but also to realize that he was undefeated by death and that his claims were validated.

21 The repetition of the common greeting "Peace" (Gr. *eirēnē*; Heb. *šalôm*) reassured the disciples of his real presence. Not only did his appearance renew their devotion and their hopes, but it also renewed their commission as disciples. Had there been no Resurrection, there would have been little motive for them to undertake a mission in his name. But since he had risen, the old commitment was even more compelling. "As the Father has sent me," he said, "I am sending you." He had come into the world to fulfill the Father's purpose and had completed his task. Now he expected them to continue his work in his absence. As the Father had sent him to speak his words, to do his works, and to lay down his life for the salvation of men, so he expected them to deliver his message (15:27), to do greater works than he had done (14:12), and to give their lives in his service. They would have all the privileges, all the protection, and all the responsibilities that he had during his ministry.

22–23 For this ministry Jesus provided the Holy Spirit and the commission to proclaim the forgiveness of sins. These are linked together for a new ministry. This was the initial announcement of which Pentecost was the historic fulfillment. The descent of the Spirit on the church at Pentecost brought the proclamation by Peter to his hearers: "Repent and be baptized, every one of you, in the name of Jesus Christ so that your sins may be forgiven" (Acts 2:38). The words of Jesus emphasize that the Holy Spirit is not bestowed on the church as an ornament but to empower an effective application of the work of Christ to all men.

The commission to forgive sins is phrased in an unusual construction. Literally, it is: "Those whose sins you forgive have already been forgiven; those whose sins you do not forgive have not been forgiven." The first verbs in the two clauses are aorists, which imply the action of an instant; the second verbs are perfects, which imply an abiding state that began before the action of the first verbs. God does not forgive men's sins because we decide to do so nor withhold forgiveness because we will not grant it. We announce it; we do not create it. This is the essence of salvation. And all who proclaim the gospel are in effect forgiving or not forgiving sins, depending on whether the hearer accepts or rejects the Lord Jesus as the Sin-Bearer.

Notes

19 For a discussion of the meaning of κεκλεισμένων (*kekleismenōn*), translated "locked" in NIV, see LSJ, p. 957. KJV renders the word "shut," but the sense of the passage is clearer if Jesus entered when the doors were impassable by ordinary means of access.

22 There is no definite article with "Holy Spirit" (πνεῦμα ἅγιον, *pneuma hagion*) in the Greek text; but in the light of Jesus' instruction in the Upper Room Discourse, the disciples could not have mistaken his meaning. "Breathed on" (ἐνεφύσησεν, *enephysēsen*) appears in a similar construction elsewhere only in the LXX of Gen 2:7, with reference to the creation of man. God formed man from the dust of the earth and then "breathed into" him the breath of life so that

he became a living being. Jesus "breathed" into the disciples the breath of the new creation that gave them spiritual vitality. The first man was given responsibility for the material creation, but the disciples were to have responsibility for the new creation.

23 A similar expression occurs in Jesus' commission to Peter: "Whatever you bind on earth will be bound in heaven, and whatever you loose on earth will be loosed in heaven" (Matt 16:19). In both statements the Greek verb of the second clause is a periphrastic future perfect (ἔσται δεδεμένον, *estai dedemenon*, "will be bound"; ἔσται λελυμένον, *estai lelumenon*, "will be loosed"), a rare form in koine Greek. Generally it is explained as an alternative for the simple future passive, having lost its original force. Apparently, however, in this instance it may retain the meaning of the future perfect, which implies that its action precedes that of the first verb of each sentence. As in English today, the future perfect was a dying tense that ultimately disappeared from common usage. The appearance of the form is therefore all the more significant. The delegation of power to the disciples to forgive or to retain the guilt of sin thus depends on the previous forgiveness by God. Perhaps this concept underlies Paul's verdict on the man in the church at Corinth who was guilty of gross immorality and seemed unrepentant (1 Cor 5:1-5). For a discussion of the grammatical problem involved, see J.R. Mantey, "The Mistranslation of the Perfect Tense in John 20:23, Matt 10:19, and Matt 18:18" in JBL 58 (1939): 243–49. Mantey points out that the Greek fathers never quoted this passage in support of absolution. In the Matthean passages the future perfect is translated as a simple future passive, but properly the distinction of completed action should have been retained. The distinction between the periphrastic and the nonperiphrastic use is that in the periphrastic the participles and auxiliary have nothing between them except postpositives: note, e.g., the nonperiphrastic instances in Gen 41:36 (LXX); Exod 12:6 (LXX); Luke 12:52; and the periphrastic instances in Matt 10:22; John 6:31; 16:24; 19:19; Eph 5:5; James 5:15.

---

4. The confession of Thomas

20:24-29

24Now Thomas (called Didymus), one of the Twelve, was not with the disciples when Jesus came. 25When the other disciples told him that they had seen the Lord, he declared, "Unless I see the nail marks in his hands and put my finger where the nails were, and put my hand into his side, I will not believe it."

26A week later his disciples were in the house again, and Thomas was with them. Though the doors were locked, Jesus came and stood among them and said, "Peace be with you!" 27Then he said to Thomas, "Put your finger here; see my hands. Reach out your hand and put it into my side. Stop doubting and believe."

28Thomas said to him, "My Lord and my God!"

29Then Jesus told him, "Because you have seen me, you have believed; blessed are those who have not seen and yet have believed."

24 Thomas is singled out for special treatment because his confession provides a climactic illustration of the triumph of belief. His name is the Aramaic term for "twin," of which Didymus is the Greek equivalent (cf. John 11:16; 21:2). In some of the Syrian MSS he is called Judas Thomas and identified with "Judas, not Iscariot" of John 14:22. It seems hardly credible that two names should be used for the same man in the same context. A Syrian tradition identified Thomas with the Judas of Mark 6:3 and made him the twin brother of Jesus, a conclusion which seems impossible in the light of the Gospel accounts of the birth of Jesus. In John 11:16 and 14:5 Thomas appears as a loyal, outspoken, and rather pessimistic person who was uncertain of the future but closely attached to Jesus. Much the same picture emerges from the episode presented here. He was absent from the gathering on the first day of the week, though he must have been in contact with the rest of the disciples afterwards.

25 In spite of the repeated assurances of his colleagues that Jesus had risen (*elegon*, "they kept saying," is the imperfect tense of repeated action), Thomas was obstinate. He was so certain of the death of Jesus that he would not credit the report of his reappearance and insisted that he would not believe unless he could actually touch Jesus' body. Thomas would be satisfied by nothing less than material evidence. His incredulity is testimony to the fact that the resurrection appearances were not illusions induced by wishful thinking.

26 "A week later" literally reads "after eight days" in the Greek text. In reckoning of a span of time, the days on both ends of the span were counted. The appearance to Thomas occurred on the evening of the Sunday one week after the Resurrection. The disciples had remained in Jerusalem during that time. On this occasion Thomas was present. He must have recovered somewhat from the original shock of Jesus' death and was willing to rejoin his old associates. It may well be that the depth of his grief and his inability to reconcile the death of Jesus with the raising of Lazarus hindered him from rejoining the others on the occasion of the previous week. The reappearance of Jesus took place under the same conditions as the previous appearance, which the disciples had described to Thomas. Therefore, he could not charge them with having fabricated their report when Jesus greeted them in the same manner as before.

27 Jesus' appeal to Thomas shows that he knew what Thomas had said to his colleagues when they told him of the first appearance. Since Jesus had not been visibly present to hear his reaction to their report, Thomas must have been startled to hear Jesus quote his very words. Jesus did not immediately upbraid him for his doubts, but he challenged him to make the test that he had suggested. Jesus' words can be translated "Stop becoming an unbeliever and become a believer." Jesus halted Thomas on the road to a despairing unbelief and offered him the positive evidence he could build an enduring faith on.

28 Thomas was disposed to believe in Jesus by his personal attachment to him, as he demonstrated previously by his resolute adherence in impending danger (11:16). Jesus may have felt that the faith of all the disciples was fragile, for he told them explicitly that the raising of Lazarus was designed to give them a solid basis for a continuing faith (11:15). Now, having been challenged to make a personal test of Jesus' reality, Thomas expressed fullest faith in him. For a Jew to call another human associate "my Lord and my God" would be almost incredible. The Jewish law was strictly monotheistic; so the deification of any man would be regarded as blasphemy (10:33). Thomas, in the light of the Resurrection, applied to Jesus the titles of Lord (*kyrios*) and God (*theos*), both of which were titles of deity.

29 Jesus' commendation of Thomas was extended to all others who, like Thomas, would place a final faith in him and who, unlike Thomas, would have no opportunity to see him in his postresurrection form. Thomas's declaration is the last assertion of personal faith recorded in this Gospel. It marks the climax of the book because it presents Christ as the risen Lord, victorious over sin, sorrow, doubt, and death. It also presents the faith that accepts not only the truth of what Jesus said but also the actuality of what he was—the Son of God. In the experience of Thomas, the writer has shown how belief comes to maturity and how it changes the entire direction of an individual life.

Notes

---

27 "Stop" is a translation of μὴ γίνου (*mē ginou*), the present middle imperative of γίνομαι (*ginomai*, "to become"). The construction parallels that of ἅπτου (*haptou*, "hold") in v.17 and means to discontinue what has already begun. Jesus wished to stop the already evident failure of Thomas's faith.

I. Statement of Purpose

20:30–31

> [30]Jesus did many other miraculous signs in the presence of his disciples, which are not recorded in this book. [31]But these are written that you may believe that Jesus is the Christ, the Son of God, and that by believing you may have life in his name.

30–31 The last two verses of this chapter are really the conclusion of the Gospel. They summarize its strategy, subject, and purpose. The strategy is to use selected works of Jesus as "signs" (*sēmeia*) that illustrate his character, demonstrate his power, and relate him to human need. Seven of these signs have been narrated, exclusive of the final sign, the Resurrection. Each one involved a human personality and showed how the power of Jesus can be applied to human emergencies. These signs were performed in the presence of the disciples so that they were attested by sympathetic and competent witnesses as well as by those who happened to be present at the time, whether friendly or hostile to Jesus. The criteria for selection seems to be magnitude, varied individual significance, and effect both on the disciples and the public.

The signs, however, are not of primary intrinsic importance. The chief subject of the Gospel is the Lord Jesus Christ, whom the author desires to present as the Christ (Messiah), the Son of God. Christ (Gr. *Christos*; Heb. *Māšiah*) means "Anointed One" and refers primarily to the deliverer appointed by God, who would come to free the nation from bondage and restore the Davidic kingdom. Jesus was given this title by the earliest disciples (1:41), but it appears seldom in the Gospel; and Jesus did not use it concerning himself because it had political implications he did not intend to fulfill at the time. He told Pilate that his kingdom was not of this world (18:36), and he made no attempt to inaugurate a revolutionary movement. "Messiah," however, did represent the deliverer from sin promised in the Old Testament as the fulfillment of the covenants with the patriarchs and David and who would consummate God's purpose for the nation and the world. At that time the Jewish nation was still looking for the Messiah; John asserts that he had already come.

The title "Son of God" appears at intervals in the text of this Gospel. John the Baptist introduced Jesus by this title (1:34); Nathanael applied it to him (1:49); and on several occasions Jesus applied it to himself (5:25; 9:35, a questionable reading; 10:36; 11:4). "Son of God" would appeal to the Gentile world rather than to the Jew, for the Gentiles did not have the same reservations about it as the Jews did. The title does not, of course, imply biological descent like that of the Greco-Roman demigods; but the metaphor of sonship expresses the unity of nature, close fellowship, and unique intimacy between Jesus and the Father. Human fatherhood and sonship are only a faint copy of the relation between God the Father and God the Son. To believe that Jesus is the Christ (Messiah) and the Son of God involves the total acceptance of the revelation of God that he offers, the acknowledgment of his divine authority, and the fulfillment of the commission he entrusted to his disciples. The total scope of this belief is illustrated in the narrative of this Gospel. Its result is eternal life, a new and enduring experience of God by the believer. This conclusion ties together the three persistent themes of the Gospel: the "signs" that demonstrate Christ's nature and power; the response of "belief" that is exemplified in the crises and growth in the lives of the disciples; and the new "life" that is found in the relationship with Christ.

Notes

---

31 The mg. rendering of NIV, "may continue to believe," rests on the present subjunctive πιστεύητε (pisteuēte, "believe"). The reading followed by the main text is the aorist subjunctive πιστεύσητε (pisteusēte, "may believe"), which refers to an initial or single act of belief, and which is supported by a wider range of MS evidence. While the latter affords a broader range of testimony dating from the fifth century, the former is older, beginning with the third century, if P66 has been correctly interpreted. Metzger says that it is difficult to choose between the two readings (*Textual Commentary*, p. 256). If the author was exact in his usage, the former would refer to the maintenance of faith by Christians, the latter to the initial commitment of nonbelievers.

V. The Epilogue (21:1–25)

Chapter 21 of John is a postscript to the main development of the book. It is not irrelevant to the preceding text; in fact, it completes it by illustrating the result of belief. It reads like a reminiscence that the author might have added subsequent to the composition of the first part by dictation to an assistant or scribe who added his own comment in the last two verses. The language bears a strong likeness both to the Synoptics and to other sections of John. The miracle of the catch of fish resembles the initial episode related to the call of the disciples (Luke 5:1–11); the action of Simon Peter is completely in character with other representations of his tendency toward impulsive speech or action (Matt 16:21–23; 26:33–35; John 13:36–38; 18:10–11, 15–18, 25–27; 20:6); the allusion to "sheep" follows the figure of 10:1–18; and v.19 uses phraseology concerning Peter that is applied to Jesus in 12:33. Apart from its relation to the themes and language of the main body of this Gospel, it owes its origin to the need for dispelling a false legend that had become current concerning Jesus' supposed prediction that the author of John would not die before Jesus' return.

There is no textual evidence for considering John 21 as a late addition to the main body of the Gospel. Every complete MS of John contains it. Evidently it is integral to the Gospel as a whole, though it may have been written as a special section.

A. *The Appearance at the Sea*

21:1–14

¹Afterward Jesus appeared again to his disciples by the Sea of Tiberias. It happened this way: ²Simon Peter, Thomas (called Didymus), Nathanael from

Cana in Galilee, the sons of Zebedee, and two other disciples were together. ³"I'm going out to fish," Simon Peter told them, and they said, "We'll go with you." So they went out and got into the boat, but that night they caught nothing.

⁴Early in the morning, Jesus stood on the shore, but the disciples did not realize that it was Jesus.

⁵He called out to them, "Friends, haven't you any fish?"

"No," they answered.

⁶He said, "Throw your net on the right side of the boat and you will find some." When they did, they were unable to haul the net in because of the large number of fish.

⁷Then the disciple whom Jesus loved said to Peter, "It is the Lord!" As soon as Simon Peter heard him say, "It is the Lord," he wrapped his outer garment around him (for he had taken it off) and jumped into the water. ⁸The other disciples followed in the boat, towing the net full of fish, for they were not far from shore, about a hundred yards. ⁹When they landed, they saw a fire of burning coals there with fish on it, and some bread.

¹⁰Jesus said to them, "Bring some of the fish you have just caught."

¹¹Simon Peter climbed aboard and dragged the net ashore. It was full of large fish, 153, but even with so many the net was not torn. ¹²Jesus said to them, "Come and have breakfast." None of the disciples dared ask him, "Who are you?" They knew it was the Lord. ¹³Jesus came, took the bread and gave it to them, and did the same with the fish. ¹⁴This was now the third time Jesus appeared to his disciples after he was raised from the dead.

1 "Afterward" implies an indefinite lapse of time (cf. 2:12; 3:22; 5:1, 14; 6:1; 7:1; 11:7, 11; 13:7; 19:28, 38), but not always a long time. Since this event is categorized as Jesus' third appearance to the disciples after the Resurrection (v.14), it must have taken place between the beginning of the second week and the Ascension. According to Luke, the Ascension took place outside Jerusalem near Bethany (Luke 24:50–53; cf. Acts 1:1–12). The account in Mark 16:19 does not specify the place of the Ascension. Matthew states only that the Great Commission was given to the disciples in Galilee, but he does not mention the Ascension. Paul speaks of Jesus' meeting with five hundred brethren at once, which was probably in Galilee (cf. Matt 28:7, 10; 1 Cor 15:6). The record of Jesus' postresurrection ministry is as fragmentary as that of his career prior to the Resurrection, and the Gospel emphases on it differ. Matthew, Mark, and John 21 speak of a Galilean manifestation; Luke and John 20 deal only with Jerusalem.

John is the only NT writer to use the name "Sea of Tiberias" for the Sea of Galilee, as it is called in the other Gospels (Matt 4:18; 15:29; Mark 1:16; 7:31), or the Lake of Gennesaret (Luke 5:1). John speaks once of the "Sea of Galilee" but qualifies it: "that is, the Sea of Tiberias" (6:1).

"Appeared," translated as "happened" at its second occurrence in this verse, is a characteristic Johannine word. It was the most frequently used to denote the self-revelation of Christ (1:31; 2:11; 9:3). It occurs three times in the Epilogue (21:1 bis, 14) in preparation for the final revelation of Jesus regarding the commissioning of Peter for his coming ministry. The First Epistle of John uses the term in the same way concerning both the incarnate Christ (1:2; 3:5, 8; 4:9) and his return (2:28; 3:2). Not only was this occasion an appearance of Christ after his resurrection, but it was also a disclosure of his purpose for the disciples.

2 The seven disciples who were present include several previously named in this Gospel: Simon Peter (1:40–42, 44; 6:8, 68; 13:6–9, 24, 36–38; 18:10–11, 15–18, 25–27;

20:2–7); Thomas (11:16; 14:5–6; 20:24–29); Nathanael (1:45–50); the sons of Zebedee, who are not mentioned directly in this Gospel; and two others, who could have been Philip (1:43–46; 6:5–7; 12:21–22; 14:8–10) and Andrew (1:40–42, 44; 6:8; 12:22). The identity of the last two is uncertain, for no names are given. The reason for the disciples' return to Galilee may have been to escape scrutiny and criticism by the mob in Jerusalem or to obey the command of Jesus (Matt 28:7, 10; Mark 16:6). Or perhaps they were discouraged by Jesus' death and decided to return to their old occupation of fishing. The kingdom had not arrived, and they had to make a living.

3 The leadership of Simon Peter is apparent at this point. Whether he was actuated by the need of earning money for his family or whether he simply wanted some activity to relieve the mental tension after the preceding fortnight in Jerusalem is speculative. The others assented to Peter's proposal; so they embarked in a boat that was available for a night of fishing. The presence of the definite article "the" (*to*) with "boat" (*ploion*) suggests that the boat was Peter's. Their enthusiasm ended in frustration, for no fish were caught.

4 Jesus appeared in the early morning, just as day was breaking. The fishermen no doubt were cold, wet with the dampness and spray of the lake, and discouraged by their lack of success. They failed to recognize Jesus, perhaps because they were preoccupied with their failure, or because they could not see him clearly through the morning mist on the lake.

5 Literally, in the Greek, Jesus was asking the disciples whether they had anything to eat; but in this context it is clear that he was referring to fish, as NIV so renders. The construction of the question implies that he knew they had caught nothing. This was confirmed by their dispirited answer: "No."

6 The command to cast the net on the right side of the ship may be interpreted in two ways. Either Jesus was testing their faith by recommending a procedure the Galilean fishermen never used, or he could discern the presence of a school of fish from the more advantageous viewpoint of the shore. Concrete evidence for the former interpretation is lacking (for a discussion of this, see Morris, NIC, p. 863, n. 17). Whatever the reason for the suggestion, the disciples evidently felt that one more attempt at casting the net could be no more futile than their night-long efforts had been; and it might be worthwhile. The resultant catch was so great that they could not load it into the boat.

Although there are similarities between this episode and that recorded in Luke 5:1–11, there are also important differences; and there is no reason to try to equate the two. In this account the fishermen were still on the lake, not on land; Jesus was not recognized at once, whereas Luke states that Jesus had been talking with them previously and was certainly known; and this event occurred shortly after daybreak whereas Luke says that it was after Jesus had been teaching for a period of time, while the fishermen were mending their nets. A much better explanation is that the similarity of the occasion prompted the recognition of Jesus.

7 "The disciple whom Jesus loved" was the first of the disciples to recognize the mysterious stranger on the shore as none other than the Lord Jesus himself. The repetition of the miracle of the large catch of fish no doubt was a key to John's recognition of Jesus.

Peter's quick reaction revealed his real feeling toward Jesus. Grasping his outer cloak, which he had laid aside to give him more freedom in working, he wrapped it around himself and dived overboard. His eagerness to see Jesus was consistent with his former profession of loyalty, which he had intended to keep and had not. This was probably not the moment of reconciliation, for Luke states that Jesus had met him personally on the first day of the Resurrection (Luke 24:35) as well as at the locked-door episodes (John 20:19–29).

8 A net full of live fish swimming toward the depths rather than toward the shore would be difficult to manage. The disciples in the ship pulled the net into shallow water where they could disembark and then sort out the fish.

9–10 Jesus had breakfast ready for the disciples, but he suggested that they bring some of the fish they had caught. Earlier, in the miraculous feedings of the multitudes with the fish and the loaves (Matt 14:15–21; 15:32–39; Mark 6:30–44; 8:1–10; Luke 9:10–17; John 6:1–14), the Lord had taken what the disciples had provided and had multiplied it and used it to supply the needs of many. Here he showed that he would continue to multiply and bless their efforts. However, they were yet to be told what direction those efforts were to take.

11 Simon Peter returned to the boat and pulled the net to land. If he did this by himself, he must have possessed unusual strength. One hundred and fifty-three fish plus a wet net would probably weigh as much as three hundred pounds, or more. The observation of the exact number of the fish and the fact that the net did not break reflect both an eyewitness account and a fisherman's perspective. John was impressed by the numerical size of the catch and the preservation of the net under the stress. Numerous attempts have been made to establish a symbolic meaning for the number of the fish, but no solid results have been achieved. All attempts are too fanciful to be credible. The soundest conclusion is that the figure represents the count taken as the fish were sorted, perhaps for distribution among the disciples, and that the record is the remembrance of an eyewitness.

12–13 When the catch had been safely brought to land and presumably sorted, Jesus invited the men to eat with him. Their attitude was peculiar. They desired to ask his identity, but they dared not do so because somehow they "knew" he was the Lord. He had appeared in their beloved Galilee and had repeated the same kind of miracle by which they first had been called to him. In spite of an apparent change in his outward appearance, the disciples' spiritual instinct confirmed his identity. His action in serving them with the bread and fish must have recalled the Last Supper, when he offered them bread and wine. There was, however, no sacramental overtone to this occasion.

14 The text states that this was Jesus' "third" appearance to the disciples since his resurrection. However, a close count of the resurrection appearances will show that in actuality this was the seventh appearance. Apparently what John meant by "the third time" is linked to the word "disciples." This was the third time Jesus had appeared to the official group of disciples, who were often designated as the Twelve. The other "two" appearances to the disciples were in the locked room, with and without Thomas (John 20:19–29).

B. *The Reinstatement of Peter*

21:15–23

15When they had finished eating, Jesus said to Simon Peter, "Simon son of John, do you truly love me more than these?"

"Yes, Lord," he said, "you know that I love you."

Jesus said, "Feed my lambs."

16Again Jesus said, "Simon son of John, do you truly love me?"

He answered, "Yes, Lord, you know that I love you."

Jesus said, "Take care of my sheep."

17The third time he said to him, "Simon son of John, do you love me?"

Peter was hurt because Jesus asked him the third time, "Do you love me?" He said, "Lord, you know all things; you know that I love you."

Jesus said, "Feed my sheep. 18I tell you the truth, when you were younger you dressed yourself and went where you wanted; but when you are old you will stretch out your hands, and someone else will dress you and lead you where you do not want to go." 19Jesus said this to indicate the kind of death by which Peter would glorify God. Then he said to him, "Follow me!"

20Peter turned and saw that the disciple whom Jesus loved was following them. (This was the one who had leaned back against Jesus at the supper and had said, "Lord, who is going to betray you?") 21When Peter saw him, he asked, "Lord, what about him?"

22Jesus answered, "If I want him to remain alive until I return, what is that to you? You must follow me." 23Because of this, the rumor spread among the brothers that this disciple would not die. But Jesus did not say that he would not die; he only said, "If I want him to remain alive until I return, what is that to you?"

15–17 The chief reason for the narration of this episode seems to be to let Peter know that the Lord still loved him and had not cast him out (cf. 15:6). The three questions Jesus addressed to Peter stand in contrast to Peter's three denials. The disciples were no doubt aware of Peter's denial of Jesus, and the commission that Jesus renewed with him in their presence would reassure them of Peter's place among them. The wording of the first question, "Do you truly love me more than these?" contains an ambiguity. There are three possible solutions:

1. Do you love me more than these other men do?
2. Do you love me more than you love these men?
3. Do you love me more than these things—the boats, the fish, etc.?

Grammatically, the comparative adverb "more" (*pleon*) is followed by the ablative of comparison "these" (*toutōn*). Whether the ablative represents the first or second alternative is not clear (see BDF, 185.1, p. 99). In view of Peter's boastful promise that whatever the others did he would not fail, the former alternative seems more likely. The third solution seems least probable.

The words translated "love" have also raised considerable debate. Two different terms are used: *agapaō* is used in Jesus' first two questions and *phileō* is used in Jesus' third question and in Peter's three replies. *Agapaō* is the same word "love" that appears in John 3:16. It is used of divine love and usually carries the connotation of will or purpose as well as that of affection. *Phileō* implies affinity, friendship, and fondness. Both words represent a high aspect of love. Since they are used of both God (3:16; 5:20) and men (14:21; 16:27) in this Gospel, they seem to be interchangeable with no great difference in meaning. Morris has a thorough discussion of the synonyms in this passage (NIC, pp. 870–75). He maintains that there is no essential difference in meaning between them. On the other hand, a good case can be made for a difference in Jesus' emphasis. There was less doubt concerning Peter's attachment to Jesus than there was concerning his will to love at all costs; and the change of term in Jesus' third question makes his probing of Peter even deeper. If the latter alternative is adopted, it explains better Peter's distress when questioned a third time, since Jesus would not only be challenging his love but would be implying that it was superficial. NIV brings out the nuance between *agapaō* and *phileō* by translating *agapaō* "truly love" and *phileō* "love."

Peter's affirmative answer to each question is substantially the same. The verb "know" (*oida*) implies the intellectual knowledge of a fact. In his third reply, however, Peter strengthened his statement by using *ginōskō* for "know." This word denotes knowledge gained through experience. While one cannot assert beyond contradiction that the distinctions between these two pairs of synonyms are always uniformly observed, in a context where a definite change is made the difference is worth considering. Peter's protestations are emphatic; and even if the conversation were carried on in Aramaic, which would not use separate words where the Greek employs these synonyms, they may represent accurately the meaning of the dialogue as the writer heard and remembered it.

Jesus' commands to Peter also contain fine distinctions:

1. "Feed (pasture) my lambs" (v.15).
2. "Take care of (shepherd) my sheep" (v.16).
3. "Feed (pasture) my sheep" (v.17).

The first and third imply only taking the sheep to pasture where they are fed; the second implies the total guardianship a shepherd exercises. This threefold injunction does not necessarily give Peter the sole responsibility for the oversight of Christ's followers; all of his spiritually mature disciples were called to be shepherds (cf. 1 Peter 5:2). This challenge to Peter demanded a total renewal of his loyalty and reaffirmed his responsibilities.

18–19 The introduction of v.18 by "I tell you the truth," rendered "verily, verily" in KJV, makes the statement of Jesus solemn and important. The author adds an explanation of Jesus' enigmatic words. They were a prediction of Peter's career: a new responsibility, a new danger, and violent death. Jesus placed Peter in a category with himself—a life spent for God and ultimately sacrificed to glorify God. Similar language was used concerning Jesus earlier in the Gospel (12:27–32; 13:31). The command "Follow me" is a present imperative, which literally means "Keep on following me." Jesus showed Peter that if he were to fulfill his promise of loyalty, he would have to follow him to his own cross.

20–21 Peter's question concerning John reflects curiosity and possibly uneasiness. Peter had been given an important commission, but what would his friend be expected to do? Would he share equally in both the responsibilities and the perils of the same task?

22–23 Jesus' reply indicated that even if he intended that "the disciple whom Jesus loved" should outlive Peter, Peter's main concern should not be a comparison of his lot with that of his friend; rather, Peter's concern was to be the fulfillment of Jesus' purpose. The use of the second person pronoun in Jesus' command makes the statement emphatic: "*You* must follow me" (italics mine). Jesus was urging Peter to take his attention off his colleague and focus it on Jesus himself.

Jesus' reference to his return is one of the few clear allusions to the Second Coming in this Gospel. The use here is hyperbolical, for it marks the utmost point to which the beloved disciple could survive and remain active. This utterance was remembered in the church and formed the basis of the rumor that Jesus had promised John that he would live until Jesus returned. As a matter of fact, Jesus had offered a supposition, not a promise. The author's explanation of Jesus' announcement may be taken as evidence that the disciple was still living at the time this Gospel was written and that he was the source of its content. Obviously, if he had died early, the rumor would have had no credence.

C. The Colophon

21:24-25

24This is the disciple who testifies to these things and who wrote them down. We know that his testimony is true.
25Jesus did many other things as well. If every one of them were written down, I suppose that even the whole world would not have room for the books that would be written.

24 The Epilogue contains a number of parenthetic statements that may have been the author's explanatory notes on the scene at the Sea of Galilee. Peter's removal of his cloak (v.7), the hesitancy of the disciples to ask Jesus to identify himself (v.12), the comment on Jesus' prediction of Peter's death (v.19), the identification of the beloved disciple (v.20), and the correction of the false rumor that the beloved disciple would not die mark the author as one of the participants. At the same time, these leave the impression that the account was written for a second generation of believers who were historically remote from the original events. This impression is corroborated by the last two verses, which are the endorsement of the narrative. Although v.24 is in the first person plural ("we know"), as if it were being certified by the testimony of a group, a different division on one word would make it a first person singular. In that case the author (or scribe) would be saying, "And I for my part know that his testimony is valid."

25 The tremendous content of Jesus' teaching and deeds is acknowledged again by the writer. This Gospel must have been written at a period when Christian literature was beginning to multiply and the church was becoming conscious of it. The letters of Paul were collected and circulated before the turn of the century, and the Gospels or writings like them were already known in the church (cf. Luke 1:1). Though John admits that what he recorded is only a fraction of what Jesus said and did, the content of this Gospel is one of the most valuable assets the church possesses.

Notes

24 The early Gr. uncial MSS of the NT were written in all caps. and without word divisions. Thus OIΔAMEN (*oidamen*, "we know") could be divided into OIΔA MEN (*oida men*, "I surely know"), and both renderings of the text are possible. The suggestion is purely speculative, but in its favor is the fact that a rendering of the verb as a first person singular would be in keeping with the second sentence of v.25. However, there are no MSS that make the division in this manner when divisions are recognized.